The Definitive Guide to Security in Jakarta EE

Securing Java-based Enterprise Applications with Jakarta Security, Authorization, Authentication and More

Arjan Tijms
Teo Bais
Werner Keil

APress®

The Definitive Guide to Security in Jakarta EE: Securing Java-based Enterprise Applications with Jakarta Security, Authorization, Authentication and More

Arjan Tijms
AMSTERDAM, Noord-Holland, The Netherlands

Teo Bais
Utrecht, Utrecht, The Netherlands

Werner Keil
Bad Homburg vdH, Hessen, Germany

ISBN-13 (pbk): 978-1-4842-7944-1
https://doi.org/10.1007/978-1-4842-7945-8

ISBN-13 (electronic): 978-1-4842-7945-8

Managing Director, Apress Media LLC: Welmoed Spahr
Acquisitions Editor: Steve Anglin
Development Editor: Laura Berendson
Coordinating Editor: Mark Powers

Cover designed by eStudioCalamar

Cover image by Vincent Law on Unsplash (www.unsplash.com)

Distributed to the book trade worldwide by Apress Media, LLC, 1 New York Plaza, New York, NY 10004, U.S.A. Phone 1-800-SPRINGER, fax (201) 348-4505, e-mail orders-ny@springer-sbm.com, or visit www.springeronline.com. Apress Media, LLC is a California LLC and the sole member (owner) is Springer Science + Business Media Finance Inc (SSBM Finance Inc). SSBM Finance Inc is a **Delaware** corporation.

For information on translations, please e-mail booktranslations@springernature.com; for reprint, paperback, or audio rights, please e-mail bookpermissions@springernature.com.

Apress titles may be purchased in bulk for academic, corporate, or promotional use. eBook versions and licenses are also available for most titles. For more information, reference our Print and eBook Bulk Sales web page at http://www.apress.com/bulk-sales.

Any source code or other supplementary material referenced by the author in this book is available to readers on GitHub (www.github.com). For more detailed information, please visit http://www.apress.com/source-code.

Printed on acid-free paper

Table of Contents

About the Authors

Arjan Tijms was a JSF (JSR 372) and Security API (JSR 375) EG member and is currently project lead for a number of Jakarta projects including Jakarta Security, Authentication, Authorization, and Faces and Expression Language. He is the cocreator of the popular OmniFaces library for JSF that was a 2015 Duke's Choice Award winner and has coauthored two books: *The Definitive Guide to JSF in Java EE 8* and *Pro CDI 2 in Java EE 8*. Arjan holds an MSc degree in computer science from the University of Leiden, the Netherlands. He has been involved with Jakarta EE Security since around 2010, has created a set of tests that most well-known vendors have used (IBM, Oracle, Red Hat) to improve their offerings, was part of the JSR 375 (EE Security) EG, and has been the main architect of the security API and its initial RI implementation Soteria. Arjan has also written and certified the MicroProfile JWT implementation for Payara. He has been mentored by Sun's (later Oracle's) security expert Ron Monzillo. He has written a large series of blog posts about EE Security that have attracted a lot of views. As such, writing a book about Jakarta EE Security is very natural to him.

Teo Bais is a software development manager, Scrum master, and programmer who contributes to the prosperity of the (software) community in several ways. He is the founder and leader of Utrecht Java User Group, which counts over 2600 members and has hosted over 45 events and amazing speakers (James Gosling, Uncle Bob, and over 20 Java Champions, among others), and is running three programs: Devoxx4kids, Speaker Incubator, and uJCP. Teo served JSR-385 (JSR of the Year 2019) as an EG member and was nominated as JCP Participant of the Year in 2019. Teo Bais enjoys sharing his knowledge as a public speaker to help others achieve their goals in career and life.

Werner Keil is a cloud architect, Eclipse RCP, and Microservices expert for a large bank. He helps Global 500 Enterprises across industries and leading IT vendors. He worked for over 30 years as IT manager, PM, coach, SW architect, and consultant for the finance, mobile, media, transport, and public sectors. Werner develops enterprise systems using Java, Java/Jakarta EE, Oracle, IBM, Spring or Microsoft technologies, JavaScript, Node.js, Angular, and dynamic or functional languages. Werner is Committer at the Apache Foundation and the Eclipse Foundation, Babel Language Champion, UOMo Project Lead, and active member of the Java Community Process in JSRs like 321 (Trusted Java), 344 (JSF 2.2), 354 (Money, also Maintenance Lead), 358/364 (JCP.next), 362 (Portlet 3), 363 (Unit-API 1), 365 (CDI 2), 366 (Java EE 8), 375 (Java EE Security), 380 (Bean Validation 2), and 385 (Unit-API 2, also Spec Lead), and was the longest serving Individual Member of the Executive Committee for nine years in a row till 2017. Werner is currently the community representative in the Jakarta EE Specification Committee. He was among the first five Jakarta EE ambassadors when it was founded as Java EE Guardians and is a member of its Leadership Council.

About the Technical Reviewer

Yogesh Shetty works as a senior software engineer for a European financial institution based in Amsterdam. He is currently involved with designing and developing applications in the payments area. He loves to connect problems in the business domain with technologies in the solution domain – mainly using the Java/JEE suite of technologies.

When not working, he unwinds by cycling through the idyllic Dutch countryside or with a book in hand.

CHAPTER 1

Security History

This chapter describes the history of security in Jakarta EE, starting from its early conception and ending where we are today at the moment of writing. We'll take a look at how the security APIs themselves evolved, how various frameworks were created in response to restrictions and shortcomings in Jakarta EE security APIs, and who some of the people were that were involved in this. Note that we'll be mostly using the term "EE" throughout this chapter, even for those moments in time where it was called "Java 2 Enterprise Edition (J2EE)," or "Java EE." Likewise we'll be using Jakarta Authentication for the moment in time where it was called "JMAC" (Java Message Authentication SPI for Container(s)) or JASPIC (Java Authentication SPI for Containers) and use "Jakarta Authorization" for when it was called JACC (Jakarta Authorization Contract for Containers).

The Beginning

The story of security in Jakarta EE starts with how security in Java SE itself was conceived. Java was originally designed to support embedded usage such as running inside set-top boxes. At the time of its introduction, this shifted to so-called applets, which were small applications embedded in web pages that executed on the computer of the user visiting such web page. In that environment, the applet code is foreign and potentially hostile to the user. The local JVM on the user's computer therefore employs a security model that protects the user and the computer against this downloaded code doing anything harmful. In broad lines, this works by a system of permissions being assigned to downloaded application code, like a *java.io.FilePermission* that gives that code permission to access only certain files instead of permission to read and write all files on the file system. This kind of security is often called "code-based security."

A. Tijms et al., *The Definitive Guide to Security in Jakarta EE*, https://doi.org/10.1007/978-1-4842-7945-8_1

Security in Jakarta EE, and actually Jakarta EE itself, started with the release of the Servlet API in November 1998. At that time, there was no Jakarta EE yet, and Servlet was a stand-alone API. It was based on the work pioneered by early Java servers such as the Kiva Enterprise Server from January 1996, which later became the Netscape Application Server (and even later, eventually, became GlassFish), and more directly by the Java Web Server, which was released in December 1996.

In November 1998, the first version of Servlet backed by a specification, Servlet 2.1, was released. It did not contain much, if any, security provisions. The only thing present that remotely had any association with security was the *HttpServletRequest. getRemoteUser()* method. This originated from the time when there was barely such a thing as a Servlet application, let alone a .war archive. At that time, Servlets were akin to CGI scripts, which were called by a separate HTTP server. This HTTP server would carry out authentication itself if needed (mostly BASIC or DIGEST) and, when succeeded, would set the environment variable REMOTE_USER before calling the CGI script, or in this case, the Servlet. It's this CGI era variable that *HttpServletRequest.getRemoteUser()* corresponds to.

Around April 1999, on the Javasoft website, operated by Sun Microsystems, the first mention of a new security extension library for Java appeared:

> *We welcome comments and suggestions regarding the newly proposed Java™ Authentication and Authorization Service (JAAS) APIs. The JAAS framework augments the Java™ 2 Platform with support for both user-based authentication and user-based access controls.*

During the JavaOne 99 conference held between June 15 and 19, 1999, a software engineer working for Sun Microsystems called Charlie Lai held a presentation about that new security extension library for Java. Four years earlier at Sun, in 1995, Lai had been one of the people defining and developing the Pluggable Authentication Modules (PAM) library for Unix and Unix-like systems. PAM is a general API for authentication services. It allows a system administrator to add new identity stores (such as for the Unix password database, NIS, LDAP, and Radius) by means of installing new PAM modules. Central to PAM is the ability to modify authentication policies by editing configuration files.

The new security extension Lai was presenting about was essentially a Java-based implementation of PAM indeed called Java Authentication and Authorization Service (JAAS). Lai explained that Java 1.0 security was about downloaded code and sandbox restricted access, Java 1.1 adding signing to downloaded code and Java 2 adding a security policy and domains. JAAS adds the concept of users and allows one to add permissions to a user via "running as" in a policy file, in addition to "code location" (where the code was downloaded from) and "code signers" (who signed the code). JAAS also adds "action code" as source next to "downloaded code." Action code here means a segment of code that is passed to a specific method as an (inner) class. To model this new user in code, JAAS introduced a new type: Subject. Its name is taken from the X.509 public key certificate that uses the Subject term for any kind of entity (not just persons). More specifically, a Subject is a bag of Principals and Credentials. At this early date, people asked why Subject had no explicit support for the Role concept. The answer given by Lai was that Roles should be specific types of Principals; to be in a role means having a Principal matching that role in this bag of Principals. Unfortunately, nobody at the time asked how one can determine that a specific Principal is in fact a role Principal. A seemingly trivial thing that would come to haunt Jakarta EE for well over 20 years to come. The identity stores that PAM just called modules are called login modules in JAAS. They came with a somewhat controversial concept at the time called a Callback, which is a very open-ended interface without methods (a marker interface) which the login module can use to communicate with its environment. When asked about this, the JAAS team responded that it allows for extensibility and that this design allows for a less painful evolution going forward.

Around October that year, the JAAS 1.0 Early Access class libraries were made available for download, allowing developers to get an early glimpse of the technology.

Enter Jakarta EE

Two months later, in December 1999, just before the turn of the millennium, the first version of Jakarta EE, EE 1.2, was released, containing Servlet 2.2 with a minimal but functioning security framework that seems to have been inspired by the way the aforementioned CGI servers worked; security is largely configured outside of the application. This is either fully outside the application by means of configuring the server on which the application runs or semi-outside the application by means of a deployment descriptor (xml file) that is stored inside the application archive, the latter often being split in two parts: a standard one such as web.xml and ejb-jar.xml and a nonstandard one such as sun-web.xml.

This type of security was soon after dubbed "container security," as it was the container (server) that was configured, as opposed to the application containing code to set up and check security. With it came two other terms as well: "declarative security" and "programmatic security." In declarative security, one defines in a configuration file (typically an XML file) that a resource such as a URL or a method on an EJB bean is constrained (secured). In programmatic security, the code does explicit checks at certain places using the Jakarta APIs.

This initial version of Jakarta EE has a concept of security roles that are used to declaratively constrain URL patterns in web.xml or EJB bean methods in ejb-jar.xml. For the web layer, it introduces four authentication mechanisms, BASIC, DIGEST, FORM, and CLIENT-CERT, which can be set in the web.xml file. Furthermore, there are four main methods for programmatic security: HttpServletRequest.isUserInRole(), HttpServletRequest.getUserPrincipal(), EJBContext.isCallerInRole(), and EJBContext. getCallerPrincipal (and two variants involving the deprecated java.security. Identity type).

A few things are quite striking in this initial release. For starters, there's no explicit concept of the "identity store" (database of user details and roles). This is implied to be an implementation detail. Furthermore, it's not possible to extend the authentication mechanisms and neither is there any type or interface defined for the authentication mechanisms that are there. Striking is also the mirroring of essentially the same methods in the HttpServletRequest and EJBContext this early on. It is indicative of a fundamental problem in Jakarta EE where Jakarta EE is both a platform as a whole, where users would like to see a single *getUserPrincipal()* for the entire platform, and the desire to use specifically Servlet stand-alone (outside Jakarta EE). In other words, if a platform applicable method is in a class that's not part of Servlet, then a stand-alone container like Jetty would not implement it. However, if it's in Servlet-only class that's not applicable to other contexts, it needs to be duplicated.

That same month Lai together with others from Sun Microsystems and IBM published a paper about JAAS titled "Making Login Services Independent of Authentication Technologies." In it, using JAAS for servers and enterprises is mentioned, though there's no explicit reference to Jakarta EE.

Shortly after the release of EE 1.2, the work for EE 1.3 was started in February 2000. As for security enhancements, the plan states that "[...] 1.2 defines a basic architecture for declarative authentication and authorization. There have been requests to provide more flexible control of these in [...] 1.3."

Around March 1, 2000, JAAS 1.0 was released as a stand-alone companion library alongside JDK 1.2.1 and two months later for JDK 1.3.

Enter Jakarta Authorization

On April 3, 2001, Ron Monzillo, a security expert working for Sun Microsystems, became the spec lead of a new JSR filed by Sun: Java Authorization Contract for Containers (later simply called "Jakarta Authorization"). This JSR started before EE 1.3 was released but, due to the anticipated amount of work, targeted the next version of EE, EE 1.4. Its aim is to provide a much more rigid specification of the authorization aspects in security. Specifically, Jakarta Authorization has the aim to map declarative security constraints (such as *auth-constraint* in web.xml) to *java.security.Permission* instances, store these in a repository, and make these available to an authorization module. Furthermore, existing authorization queries in both Servlet and Enterprise Beans, like "has user access to URL" and "is user in role," can be answered by this authorization module by presenting these queries as checks for permissions.

On September 24, 2001, EE 1.3 came out, including Servlet 2.3 and Enterprise Beans 2.0, and the new Connectors 1.0. Connectors 1.0 has an elaborate security model and API. Specifically, it depends on JAAS, which at the time was still an independent framework. This dependency is, however, quite minimal, as the requirement consists merely of using the *javax.security.auth.Subject* type. Furthermore, Connectors 1.0, recommends (but does not mandate) that an application server uses JAAS modules (instances of javax. security.auth.spi.LoginModule, a.k.a. identity stores, a.k.a. authentication modules) for predominantly outbound security. There's unfortunately no concrete specification of how the JAAS modules should be developed, and the Connectors spec even says they are typically specific to an application server. Likewise, the configuration of a JAAS module is left to be specific to an application server as well. Because of Connectors, EE 1.3 has an official dependency on JAAS, but in practice, there's barely anything specified for it. For Servlet and Enterprise Beans, there's even nothing specified at all.

Among EE users, there's some confusion at the time about this, and this confusion would never really go away. Specifically, it results in the belief that the EE Servlet security elements such as *security-constraint* in web.xml and *HttpServletRequest.isUserInRole()* are part of JAAS, which is of course not the case. Not rarely people would report in, for example, support forums that they're using JAAS to secure their application while in reality only using Servlet security. As an example, the Wikipedia page for JAAS had for many years a section on Servlet's FORM authentication, stating that it was a part of JAAS.

On February 6, 2002, JDK 1.4 was released. The former stand-alone JAAS 1.0 library is now integrated into it, meaning later versions of Jakarta EE that depend on JDK 1.4 or higher would no longer need to have the explicit JAAS 1.0 dependency.

Enter Jakarta Authentication

With the Authorization JSR still in the works, on October 22, 2002, Ron Monzillo started on a JSR called the Java Authentication Service Provider Interface for Containers, later simply Jakarta Authentication. This JSR specifically aims to standardize the authentication mechanism concept, specifically the interface that must be implemented by an authentication mechanism and how to add this to a container. Like Jakarta Authorization, Jakarta Authentication from the onset targets both Servlet and Enterprise Beans. Also working on this JSR is Charlie Lai.

The JSR mentions that the authentication mechanism interface could be used to create, for example, a Liberty SSO authentication mechanism. This causes a little row, and eventually IBM votes against the JSR with the following comment related to this:

1) *Potential for adding the Liberty Bindings/Profiles into J2EE.*

   We do understand that Liberty is only one of many potential input specifications into this JSR. We feel that such a decision may have enormous implications and it is too big to be left to an individual expert group to make. The significance is such that the EC should give some direction, as a subset of major J2EE licensees support the WS-Security approach, and potentially a subset support the Liberty Alliance. One solution could be for the JSR to only deal with defining a provider interface for the establishment (process of authentication i.e validating authentication data like userid/ password, or tokens) of an authenticated identity. Therefore, it would be authentication mechanism agnostic.

But it's not just Liberty that concerns IBM, the scope of the JSR also doesn't sit quite well with them:

2) *Over-broad scope for this JSR.*

   a) *The 1st major bullet has a sub bullet that is out of scope "the binding of received transport specific security credentials to authentication modules" as this should be "the binding of received transport mechanism to authentication modules". We feel that we should not mandate semantics in this JSR.*

b) *The 2nd major bullet opens up the scope:*

- *"validating mechanism specific credentials received from container transport mechanisms":*

* *This is out of scope and should be left up to the modules.*

- *The following bullets also talk about "run-as" and this JSR is performing identity and credential mapping / translation.*

* *This is out of scope for a "Authentication Service Provider Interface" JSR, this should be done in a separate JSR.*

- *"creating transport specific responses as necessary to implement authentication mechanisms"*

* *This is also out of scope as this JSR should not be defining any new transport specific mechanisms.*

A very early Spring user, Isabelle Muszynski, asked in April 2003 whether JAAS, with its pluggable authentication and authorization, would be a viable API to support in Spring. At that point, the Spring mailing list had just been opened a few months ago, and it would be almost a year until Spring 1.0 was released. Rod Johnson, the founder of the Spring framework, agreed it might be interesting. Though Spring at that point didn't have any security infrastructure yet, Johnson already had experience with security from his work on Spring's predecessor, the MVC framework he wrote for the FT group, making him knowledgeable on the subject.

Jürgen Höller in May of that same year took a look at Jakarta Authorization, but it left him somewhat disappointed. The main value that Jakarta Authorization adds, providing a repository of permissions based on, for instance, constraints in web.xml, isn't that much needed according to Höller. What he needs above all is an API for portable authentication. In a conversation with Muszynski and others, he argued that an "identity store" (which he called an "authenticator") is now always vendor specific. (Most servers ship with say a ready to use identity store backed by an XML file containing users and roles, but creating a custom one, especially one that's owned by the application, requires the use of vendor specific APIs.)

Here, Höller essentially very early on drew the conclusion that the J2EE security model is essentially targeted at integrating applications into an intranet situation, where a few user types such as admin and employee are centrally managed and shared by different, typically externally obtained, applications used by an office. The opposite situation, a single rich web application with a tightly integrated application user base, where those users subscribe via the Internet and are fully handled by the application, doesn't fit this model very well. Rod Johnson agrees security in J2EE is not really standardized well.

Foreshadowing Shiro Part I - IL DRBAC

Somewhere later that month, Les Hazlewood, a J2EE enterprise architect working at Transdyn Controls, Inc., was plowing through Google and tons of security books in a quest to find a suitable security framework for an enterprise application he was working on. This particular application has very strict but at the same time very dynamic security requirements. After a long search, he ended up finding very little to his liking. Disappointed, Hazlewood started to think about creating something himself and came up with a system he called "Instance-Level, Dynamic Role-Based Access Control (IL DRBAC)." Although intended to run on J2EE, it totally avoids using its existing security system. In his system, there are users having one or more roles, which are each mapped to java.security.Permissions. Permissions give access to instances of a resource, for instance, a web page. Incidentally, this is exactly what JACC does, though it's not clear whether Hazlewood is aware of it at that moment. Hazlewood's system specifically emphasizes dynamic behavior, in that all these elements can be created and modified during the runtime of an application and are immediately applied, even if users are already logged in.

In August 2003, a discussion took place among Tomcat users and committers. The topic of discussion was the almost mythical "j_security_check", which is the path the FORM authentication mechanism in Jakarta EE listens to. A Tomcat user, Al Sutton, was convinced Servlet filters should be invoked when mapped to paths containing this, but legendary Tomcat committer and Servlet EG member Craig McClanahan wasn't easily convinced. In that discussion, John T. Bell, who was writing the J2EE Open Source Toolkit book at that time, pointed out that the current state of security in Jakarta EE Security is too limited. Bell provided the following examples of limitations to make his point clear:

- Logins that require more than just user id and password.

- Support for optional login or login directly from a home page form

- Logins supporting a "remember me" feature

- Situations that require logging and retrieval or recording of information upon each login

Tomcat committer Remy Maucherat pointed out that Tomcat can be extended to accommodate this using Tomcat APIs such as Realm, Authenticator, and the Valve. Bell didn't buy this, however, and argued that this is hardly a valid way, as they are Tomcat-specific APIs. What was needed according to him was a standard API to do those things. Near the end of that month, Servlet spec lead Yutaka Yoshida provided a clarification:

In regards to this issue, servlet EG had a consensus that Filter must not be applied for j_security_check. We believe the application component should not be involved in the container-managed security. Although we understand why people are using filter to manipulate the authentication mechanism, it doesn't solve all issues related to the security and must be addressed in a larger scope of the portable authentication mechanism, which I expect to have in the next version of the specification.

There are a few interesting things to note here besides just the actual clarification regarding j_security_check. The first is that in 2003, the Servlet EG was firmly believing in the total separation between security code and application code, which would be a recurring issue for years to come. Secondly, we see here that the Servlet EG had a plan to introduce portable authentication mechanisms in the Servlet spec. Eagle-eyed readers of the Servlet could have noticed this on April 17, 2003, in the Proposed Final Draft 3 for the Servlet 2.4 spec, where the following somewhat cryptic change note appeared in the appendix:

HttpSession.logout method was removed. The portable authentication mechanism will be addressed in the next version of this specification and logout will also be discussed in that scope.(12.10)

On November 24, 2003, EE 1.4 was released, which included Servlet 2.4 and Authorization 1.0. There were no major security features added to Servlet, though the work on Authorization, and specifically the work to translate the existing constraints to the new set of permissions, resulted in various clarifications:

- Clarification that the security model is also applied to filter (12.2)

- Change the status code from 401 to 200 when FORM authentication is failed as there is no appropriate error status code in HTTP/1.1 (12.5.3)

- Clarification: "run-as" identity must apply to all calls from a servlet including init() and destroy() (12.7)

- Clarification of security constraints, especially in the case of overlapping constraints (12.8)

- Change the word "auth constraint" to "authorization constraint" (12.8)

- Clarification of "overlapping constraint" (12.8.1, 12.8.2)

- Login/Logout description added (12.10)

Authorization 1.0 itself greatly enriches the security framework in Jakarta EE. Having a permission store available makes for a much more powerful authorization model, and having pluggable authorization modules, which can essentially make any kind of authorization decision transparently to the applications running on a server, is indeed powerful. However, not all is well. The fixation on the concept of container security, where security is strictly separated from the application, has led to a setup where authorization modules can only be plugged in at the server level, or actually, only at the JVM level. Furthermore, the specification mentions system properties and a classpath to place authorization module jars on, but for modular servers, it's not clear at all which location a server considers its classpath (if there even is such a location). More problematic is the fact that authorization modules are an all-or-nothing approach; they completely replace the existing authorization structure and are thus not able to simply add some additional rules. As if these issues aren't problematic enough, there are even more serious issues in practice. Though the specification states that a default authorization module should both be present, as well as actually used in a Jakarta implementation, in practice, implementations ignore this. Some implementations don't have a default authorization module present at all, just seeing it as an extension point to the server, while others have such authorization module but then by default use their own authorization code and have server specific switches to enable Jakarta Authorization.

Jakarta Authorization also suffers from the opposite problem we saw with *HttpServletRequest.getUserPrincipal()*, which was duplicated all over the place. Jakarta Authorization is a single, separate, spec that Servlet containers can use to enrich their security model. Except, they don't.

Painfully missing from the EE 1.4 release is the highly anticipated Jakarta Authentication. In fact, nothing has ever been heard of it. According to the plan, a Community Draft would have to be delivered earlier in the year, followed by a Public Draft and a Proposed Final Draft, but nothing happened.

Enter Spring Security

In the same month that EE 1.4 was released, November 2003, Ben Alex, the managing director of his own company, Acegi Technology, looked at the new, at the time not yet officially released, framework sitting on top of Servlets called Spring. Alex inquired about its security features, but its creators, Ron Johnson and Juergen Hoeller, didn't have the time yet to fully look into it. Alex then started writing his own security code using Spring right away. He proposed it a month later but initially didn't get any response.

The following months, Alex gave his proposal more thoughts and struggled with questions such as whether to use JAAS or not, whether to use the authentication data from the container (the principal and its roles) or let the application populate some object for this, and more.

In February 2004 when people asked again about security and Spring, both Alex and Hazlewood seized the opportunity to pitch their work as a base for a Spring security initiative. Alex was very proactive and sent his work in a zip file to Johnson and Höller, proposing it to be simply called "Spring Security," and made a case for it to be part of Spring. At that time, however, Spring committers were frequently debating about the focus of Spring: Should it remain a small DI container, or should it include higher-level frameworks? For the time being, it was decided to develop "Spring Security" outside Spring as Acegi Security, after Alex's company.

On March 3, 2004, the initial public release of Acegi, Acegi 0.1, was presented to the world. At this early point, source code wasn't available from version control yet.

On March 6, 2004, Alex mentioned on the JBoss forum that for Acegi Security, he needed to write security adapters specifically for JBoss, since there was still no standard API for many security-related things. For instance, in this JBoss adapter, Alex obtained an import security object called the "Subject" in a nonstandard way using a JNDI lookup for "java:comp/env/security/subject" and then iterated over all the principles in this Subject until he found the Acegi one. Scott Stark replied that JBoss now marks the caller principal specifically by putting it in a group called "CallerPrincipal," although this is still JBoss specific and not standardized. More than 16 years later, this issue would still not be solved in what's then called Jakarta EE, and Soteria, a Jakarta Security implementation, would use this exact same server-specific knowledge to obtain the caller principal.

Less than two weeks later, on March 17, 2004, Alex checked the code he had developed offline into version control. Its central class for authentication is AuthenticationManager:

```
/*
 * The Acegi Security System for Spring is published under the terms
 * of the Apache Software License.
 *
 * Visit http://acegisecurity.sourceforge.net for further details.
 */

package net.sf.acegisecurity;

/**
 * Processes an {@link Authentication} request.
 *
 * @author Ben Alex
 * @version $Id$
 */
public interface AuthenticationManager {
    //~ Methods ============================================================

    /**
     * Attempts to authenticate the passed {@link Authentication} object,
     * returning a fully populated <code>Authentication</code> object
     * (including granted authorities) if successful.
     *
     * (exceptions omitted for brevity)
     *
     * @param authentication the authentication request object
     * @return a fully authenticated object including credentials
     * @throws AuthenticationException if authentication fails
     */
    Authentication authenticate(Authentication authentication)
        throws AuthenticationException;
}
```

The *Authentication* class it uses doubles as a credential, and an authentication outcome:

```
/**
 * Represents an authentication request.
 *
 * <p>
 * An <code>Authentication</code> object is not considered
   authenticated until
 * it is processed by an {@link AuthenticationManager}.
 * </p>
 *
 * <p>
 * Stored in a request {@link net.sf.acegisecurity.context.SecureContext}.
 * </p>
 *
 * @author Ben Alex
 * @version $Id$
 */
public interface Authentication {
    //~ Methods =============================================================

    public void setAuthenticated(boolean isAuthenticated);

    /**
     * Indicates whether or not authentication was attempted by the {@link
     * net.sf.acegisecurity.SecurityInterceptor}. Note that  classes should
     * not rely on this value as being valid unless it has been set by a
     * trusted <code>SecurityInterceptor</code>.
     *
     * @return true if authenticated by the <code>SecurityInterceptor</code>
     */
    public boolean isAuthenticated();

    /**
     * Set by an <code>AuthenticationManager</code> to indicate the
       authorities
     * that the principal has been granted. Note that classes should not rely
```

```
 * on this value as being valid unless it has been set by a trusted
 * <code>AuthenticationManager</code>.
 *
 * @return the authorities granted to the principal, or
   <code>null</code>
 * if authentication has not been completed
 */
public GrantedAuthority[] getAuthorities();

  /**
  * The credentials that prove the principal is correct. This is
    usually a
  * password, but could be anything relevant to the
  * <code>AuthenticationManager</code>. Callers are expected to
    populate
  * the credentials.
  *
  * @return the credentials that prove the identity of the
  * <code>Principal</code>
  */
public Object getCredentials();

  /**
  * The identity of the principal being authenticated. This is
    usually a
  * username. Callers are expected to populate the principal.
  *
  * @return the <code>Principal</code> being authenticated
  */
public Object getPrincipal();
}
```

The *AuthenticationManager* delegates to one or more *AuthenticationProvider*
instances, which have the same contract as the *AuthenticationManager*, but with an extra
method for checking whether they support a given *Authentication*. The first provider
to recognize an *Authentication* and successfully authenticate wins. Conceptually, an

AuthenticationProvider is an "identity store," a database of user names, along with their credentials and (typically) roles.

This early version of Acegi shipped with one concrete AuthenticationProvider, which is the *DaoAuthenticationProvider*, which in its turn delegates to an *AuthenticationDao*. Essentially, this *AuthenticationDao* transforms the general Authentication authenticate(Authentication) method to a more specific User loadUserByUsername(String username) method, according to the following credential and result transformation:

```
username = authentication.getPrincipal().toString()
Returned authentication =
    user.getUsername(), user.getPassword(),user.getAuthorities())
```

For *AuthenticationDao*, Acegi 0.3 ships with two concrete and recognizable implementations: a JDBC-based one and an InMemory one.

A remarkable aspect of Acegi is that it ships with native identity store implementations for Tomcat, Jetty, JBoss, and Resin (these are respectively called Realm, UserRealm, LoginModule, and Authenticator, an early testimony of the confusion caused by not agreeing on a standard term).

These all essentially work in the same way: obtain the *AuthenticationManager* via a Spring programmatic bean lookup, and then from the container-specific identity store, delegate to this bean.

A simplified example in pseudocode of this for JBoss looks as follows:

```
public class JbossAcegiLoginModule extends AbstractServerLoginModule {

    public void initialize(Subject subject, CallbackHandler
    callbackHandler,
       Map sharedState, Map options) {

    authenticationManager =
        new ClassPathXmlApplicationContext((String) options
           .get("appContextLocation"))
           .getBeansOfType(AuthenticationManager.class, true, true)
           .get(beanName);
    }
```

```java
    public boolean login() throws LoginException {
        super.loginOk = false;

        String[] info = getUsernameAndPassword();

        Authentication request =
            new UsernamePasswordAuthenticationToken(
                info[0, info[1]);

        Authentication response = null;
        try {
            response = authenticationManager.authenticate(request);
        } catch (AuthenticationException failed) {
            throw new FailedLoginException();
        }

        identity = new PrincipalAcegiUserToken(key,
            response.getPrincipal().toString(),
            response.getCredentials().toString(),
            response.getAuthorities());

        if (getUseFirstPass() == true) {
            sharedState.put("javax.security.auth.login.name", username);
            sharedState.put("javax.security.auth.login.password",
            credential);
        }

        super.loginOk = true;

        return true;
    }

    protected Principal getIdentity() {
        return identity;
    }

    protected Group[] getRoleSets() throws LoginException {
        SimpleGroup roles = new SimpleGroup("Roles");

        Authentication user = (Authentication) identity;
```

```
for (int i = 0; i < user.getAuthorities().length; i++) {
    roles.addMember(
        new SimplePrincipal(
            user.getAuthorities()[i].getAuthority()));
}

Group[] roleSets = {roles};
return roleSets;
    }

}
```

The integration that Alex has architected here thus works as follows.

An existing authentication mechanism (e.g., FORM) from the Servlet spec is used for the application. This mechanism collects the username and password and then invokes the container-configured and container-specific identity store to validate them and obtain the user's roles. On JBoss, this would see *JbossAcegiLoginModule* get invoked, which in its turn would invoke the application-configured *AuthenticationManager,* which would invoke the application-configured *AuthenticationProvider* (e.g., *DaoAuthenticationProvider*), which would invoke the application-configured *AuthenticationDao* (e.g., *InMemoryDaoImpl*).

If authentication is successful in the preceding sequence, JBoss would call the getIdentity() and getRoleSets() methods, which return data based on what ultimately the *InMemoryDaoImpl* in the preceding example returned. This "authentication data" is subsequently used by JBoss internally to check authorization when protected resources (URLs) are accessed, to return the principal from HttpServletRequest.getUserPrincipal(), to check the roles specified by @RolesAllowed on an EJB method, etc. Integration for the other supported containers worked very similarly.

The next day, on March 18, 2004, Alex released the first fully public version of Acegi Security as version 0.3 on SourceForge.

On June 23, 2004, developer Luke Taylor did his first commit to the Acegi project. Taylor would later grow to become one of the most prolific committers and eventually even project lead.

Where is Jakarta Authentication? Enter JAuth

While nothing had been heard about Jakarta Authentication for a long time, when Sun on February 8, 2005, released version 8.1 of its Sun Java System Application Server (the server that would later be open sourced and renamed to GlassFish), it contained a remarkable module, "container authentication," which was later described in GlassFish v2 as "Container Authentication (JSR196-like) Implementation" living in a package named "com.sun.enterprise.security.jauth". The main configuration file of this server, domain.xml, contains a new element "message-security-config", which is described as "optional list of layer-specific lists of configured message security providers."

It contains an interface used for authentication mechanisms, which looks as follows:

```
public interface ServerAuthModule {

    void initialize(AuthPolicy requestPolicy, AuthPolicy responsePolicy,
        CallbackHandler handler, Map options);

    void validateRequest(AuthParam param, Subject subject, Map sharedState)
        throws AuthException;

    void secureResponse(AuthParam param, Subject subject, Map sharedState)
        throws AuthException;

    void disposeSubject(Subject subject, Map sharedState)
        throws AuthException;
}
```

Because of the configuration element in domain.xml, users can plug in their own authentication mechanisms, but in Sun Java System Application Server 8.1, only web services (SOAP) make use of this new container authentication system.

In the summer of 2005, after almost three years of silence, Lai and Monzillo released the first early draft of Jakarta Authentication on July 25, 2005. The draft consisted, out of a general description, of the main authentication mechanism interface and a so-called bridge profile, which in a few paragraphs defines how in Jakarta Authentication a mechanism should call a JAAS identity store (login module). This initial draft of the authentication mechanism interface resembled the JAuth version that Sun released earlier quite a bit:

```
public interface ServerAuthModule {

    // Get a MessageLayer instance that identifies the layer implemented by
    the module MessageLayer getMessageLayer();

    void initialize(MessagePolicy requestPolicy, MessagePolicy responsePolicy,
        CallbackHandler handler, Map options, boolean mustBeTransactional);

    // Authenticate a client request.
    void validateRequest(AuthParam param, Subject source, Subject
    recipient, Map sharedState);

    // Secure the response to the client. Sign and encrypt the response,
    for example.
    void secureResponse(AuthParam param, Subject source, Map sharedState);

    void disposeSubject(Subject subject, Map sharedState);

    // Returns a description of the module.
    String toString();
}
```

What immediately stands out here is the general nature of the interface. It doesn't depend directly on any specific other API/protocol. The early draft mentions the wish to target SOAP, JMS, and HTTPServlet but only specifies the *MessageLayer* for SOAP and HTTPServlet and likewise only specifies the *AuthParam* for those. This latter class contains things like *HttpServletRequest* for the Servlet version, so in this early draft, Jakarta Authentication does have those dependencies to other APIs.

Foreshadowing Shiro Part II - JSecurity

Meanwhile, Hazlewood had not been sitting still either, as a few days earlier, on July 13, 2005, he found the jsecurity project on SourceForge and described it as follows:

> *JSecurity is a comprehensive vendor-agnostic POJO-based security framework for Java. It addresses the needs of dynamic instance-level role-based access control, pluggable authentication modules, integrated session management, and more.*

Two days later, on July 15, 2005, the first commit containing code was done. Among the initial classes were the *Authenticator* and the *AuthorizationContext*:

```
package org.jsecurity.authc;

  import org.jsecurity.authz.AuthorizationContext;

 /**
  * @author Les Hazlewood
  */
 public interface Authenticator {
     AuthorizationContext authenticate(AuthenticationToken token )
         throws AuthenticationException;
 }

package org.jsecurity.authz;

 import java.security.Permission;
 import java.security.Principal;
 import java.util.Set;
 import java.io.Serializable;

 /**
  *
  * @author Les Hazlewood
  */
 public interface AuthorizationContext {
     Principal getPrincipal();
     boolean hasRole(Serializable roleIdentifier);
     boolean hasRoles(Set<Serializable> roleIdentifiers);
     boolean hasPermission(Permission permission);
     boolean hasPermissions(Set<Permission> permissions);
     void checkPermission(Permission permission)
         throws AuthorizationException;
     void checkPermissions(Set<Permission> permissions)
         throws AuthorizationException;
     Object getValue( Object key );
 }
```

Setting JSecurity apart at this early stage is its initial concept of an abstract session. Hazlewood didn't hold back here, and in the org.jsecurity.session package, we find elaborate interfaces for a session, session manager, session event, session listener, and more.

```java
package org.jsecurity.session;

import java.security.Principal;
import java.util.Calendar;
import java.io.Serializable;
import java.net.InetAddress;

/**
 * @author Les Hazlewood
 */
public interface Session {

    /**
     * Returns the unique identifier assigned by the system upon session
       creation.
     *
     * <p>All return values from this method are expected to have a proper
     toString() function
     * such that the system identifier can be easily read by a human.
     Good candiadates for such
     * an identifier are {@link java.util.UUID UUID}s, {@link java.lang.
     Integer Integer}s, and
     * {@link java.lang.String String}s.
     *
     * <p>This method was not called <code>getId()</code> or
     <code>getID()</code> as a convenience
     * to the many systems that may already be using such a method name to
     identify objects
     * internally.  If they exist, these methods most likely return a
     database primary key
     * (such as a UUID or Integer).
     *
```

```
* <p>In these types of systems, it would probably make sense for an
implementation of this
* interface to return that internal identifier.  For example:<br/><br/>
*
* <pre>
* public Serializable getSessionId() {
*     return getId(); //system specific identifier
* }</pre>
*
*
* @return The unique identifier assigned to the session upon creation.
*/
Serializable getSessionId();

// Many other methods omitted for brevity
}
```

Jakarta Authentication - Edging closer

Late November that year, a senior software developer at Red Hat who was about to become Lead JBoss Security Architect, named Anil Saldanha, started thinking on how to integrate Jakarta Authentication into the JBoss application server. Together with another engineer at Red Hat, Scott Stark, a plan was drawn up to make Jakarta Authentication a central element in the JBoss security architecture. Stark remarked that Jakarta Authentication doesn't have something like JAAS's *javax.security.auth.login. Configuration* and its standard configuration file. Over the next days, the two set out to enhance the existing JBoss login-config.xml, where they specifically focused on the bridge profile concept.

On March 17, 2006, Saldanha and Stark discussed things that should be added to Jakarta Authentication. Saldanha agreed that a standard configuration similar to the javax.security.auth.login.AppConfigurationEntry in JAAS configuration should be added to the spec. Furthermore, he stated that the spec should cover Enterprise Beans as well. The two then discussed how to apply Jakarta Authentication to Enterprise Beans interceptors. Later, Stark talked about this at JavaOne 2006 and concluded the only

universal Enterprise Beans profile would be based on CORBA portable interceptors. He
suggested having a JBoss-specific profile as a clean integration API as well.

The next month, having worked hard on it, Hazlewood made the first public release
of JSecurity as version 0.1.0 on April 18, 2006. Though not a JSR spec, Hazlewood cleanly
separated the API and implementation and even called his implementation an RI
(reference implementation). Alex in his turn released his 1.0 version of Acegi Security
soon after, on May 30, 2006.

On that very same day, Saldanha, who was still engaged with Jakarta Authentication,
asked Tomcat committer and fellow JBoss software engineer Rémy Maucherat to
consider a proposal to add the follow method to the famous Tomcat *Realm* interface to
prepare it for Jakarta Authentication:

```
Principal authenticate(
    Request request, Response response,
    LoginConfig loginConfig) throws Exception;
```

At that point (and to this day), this interface only contained methods like

```
Principal authenticate(String username, java.lang.String credentials)
```

These methods are essentially tailor-made for the hard-coded authentication
mechanisms in Servlet and not so much suited for custom authentication mechanisms.
Maucherat, however, responded with "No," and that was the end of it. Saldanha tried
to counter that there will be a push for this when Jakarta Authentication becomes
mandatory in EE 6, but Maucherat didn't respond back to that anymore.

Shing Wai Chan, the technical lead of security in GlassFish and an expert group
member for Jakarta Authentication, published in July 2006 an article about security
annotations in EE, such as @RolesAllowed and @DeclareRoles. He mentioned level
message security, the term used by Jakarta Authentication, as something in GlassFish for
web services only.

In March 2007, the in-development version GlassFish V2 has implemented the
public final draft for Jakarta Authentication. In a blog article, Wai Chan explained
how one can obtain all so-called AuthConfigProviders in a (web) application using
code such as

```
AuthConfigFactory factory = AuthConfigFactory.getFactory();
String[] regisIDs = factory.getRegistrationIDs(null);

for (String regisID : regisIDs) {
    RegistrationContext regContext = factory.getRegistrationContext(regisID);

    String layer = regContext.getMessageLayer();
    String appContext = regContext.getAppContext();
    AuthConfigProvider provider = factory.getConfigProvider(layer,
    appContext, null);
}
```

On the surface, it may not seem like much, but it's an early example of Jakarata Authentication, in contrast to Jakarta Authorization, being much more open to application-level security.

On October 10, 2007, after many long years, Jakarta Authentication 1.0 was finally released. Despite Saldanha's best efforts talking to Monzillo, neither Enterprise Beans support nor a standard configuration made it into the final. Jakarta Messaging support didn't make it in either. The authentication mechanism interface has changed a fair bit from its original draft. It's now split in two parts, with *MessageLayer* removed and replaced by a more generic getSupportedMessageTypes. This is now supposed to return the classes *HttpServletRequest* and *HttpServletResponse*. AuthParam and the shared state Map are replaced by MessageInfo, which now contains two Object instances the code must cast to *HttpServletRequest* and *HttpServletResponse*:

```
public interface ServerAuth {

    // Authenticate a client request.
    AuthStatus validateRequest(MessageInfo messageInfo, Subject
    clientSubject, Subject serviceSubject) throws AuthException;

    // Secure the response to the client. Sign and encrypt the response,
    for example. AuthStatus secureResponse(MessageInfo messageInfo, Subject
    serviceSubject) throws AuthException;

    void cleanSubject(MessageInfo messageInfo, Subject subject)
        throws AuthException;

}
```

```
public interface ServerAuthModule extends ServerAuth {

    Class[] getSupportedMessageTypes();

    void initialize(MessagePolicy requestPolicy, MessagePolicy
        responsePolicy, CallbackHandler handler, Map options)
        throws AuthException;
}
```

At this point, Jakarta Authentication is not a part of EE yet, but it is implemented by GlassFish v2 and available in the default downloads of it.

At the start of the new year, on January 22, 2008, Monzillo published a blog about the still-not-very-widely-known Jakarta Authentication. Monzillo, who is a great fan of abbreviations, has dubbed the authentication mechanism interface *ServerAuthModule*, "SAM," and explains that

- [Jakarta Authentication] defines a subject based contract that allows the SAM to, return more than just a single principal and to do so without reliance on proprietary apis.

- [Jakarta Authentication] also defines callbacks that are made available to the SAM, so that the SAM can enlist services of the container including for the purpose of distinguishing the "user" principal among those in the returned subject, to establish group principals in a form understood by the container authorization system, to validate a username and password at the realm bound to the application, or to gain access to the keystores of the container.

Monzillo also explains that a SAM can be defined globally using the GlassFish-specific domain.xml (and that's a major breakthrough for security in EE), can be defined using the GlassFish-specific sun-web.xml for a single application, and can even be done programmatically. For the programmatic case, however, Monzillo hints at needing to override the classes that configure a SAM as well, as implementations of those are now proprietary for a given server. While in general it is great news for security in EE to be able to configure it from the application, it does make it clear that Saldanha was right about needing a standard configuration file or mechanism. Having to use sun-web. xml instead of the standard web.xml would prove to be a big problem, and having to implement an entire configuration system just to register a SAM per application would later prove to be a big detraction of Jakarta Authentication as well.

A few months later, on April 30, 2008, Monzillo published a follow-up article titled "GlassFish v2 and JSR 196." In it, Monzillo takes the reader through the steps of creating and installing a working SAM in GlassFish. In his example, he uses the *PasswordValidationCallback* to validate a username and password credential. This is a callback that delegates to whatever server proprietary identity store has been installed, provided that such store supports username and password credentials.

On October 15, 2008, executing issue SEC-1009, Luke Taylor removed the container adapters from Spring Security. While this has been deprecated for quite some time, this event marks the definite separation between Spring Security and EE containers. Spring Security from then on is a security framework that fully lives in Spring.

With only several months to go until the EE 6 release, the Servlet team presented their new annotation-based approach to secure Servlet methods on May 4, 2009. Essentially, it goes for the Enterprise Beans approach and adopts the annotations *@DenyAll*, *@PermitAll*, and *@RolesAllowed*:

```
@WebServlet("/someUrl")
@RolesAllowed("architect")
public class TestServlet extends HttpServlet {

    protected void doGet(HttpServletRequest req, HttpServletResponse res)
        throws IOException, ServletException {
    }

    @RolesAllowed("admin")
    protected void doPost(HttpServletRequest req, HttpServletResponse res)
        throws IOException, ServletException {
    }

    @PermitAll
    protected void doTrace(HttpServletRequest req, HttpServletResponse res)
        throws IOException, ServletException {
    }

}
```

In the preceding example, a GET request and all HTTP methods not covered by a Servlet class method shown previously require the role "architect," while a POST request requires the role "admin." Finally, a TRACE request is open to anyone.

Happy to have achieved a consistent programming model, the EG is about to sign off on this design. They didn't count on Monzillo, however, who looks at the design and shakes his head. In it, Monzillo discovers two problems. The existing annotations are defined to apply to class-level methods only, not to those inherited. Servlets unfortunately always inherit from base class HttpServlet. This brings with it another even bigger issue, and that's the dreaded *service()* method in this base class. The existence of this method breaks the strict association between a GET request and the *doGet()* method. Early on in the design of Servlet 3.0, attempts had been made to make Servlets more POJO oriented, but these had ultimately failed. With so little time to go for the EE 6 deadline, reviving the POJO project was certainly not an option. Instead, Monzillo came up with three new annotations:

- ServletSecurity

- HttpConstraint

- HttpMethodConstraint

These annotations are somewhat closer to the existing method of declaratively describing the constraints in web.xml, although they have a different format and they apply to the URL pattern of the servlet to which they are attached. With Monzillo's new proposal, the previously shown example looks as follows:

```
@WebServlet("/someUrl")
@ServletSecurity(
    value = @HttpConstraint(rolesAllowed = "architect"),
    httpMethodConstraints={
        @HttpMethodConstraint(value = "POST", rolesAllowed = "admin"),
        @HttpMethodConstraint("TRACE")})
public class TestServlet extends HttpServlet {

    protected void doGet(HttpServletRequest req, HttpServletResponse res)
        throws IOException, ServletException {
    }

    @RolesAllowed("admin")
    protected void doPost(HttpServletRequest req, HttpServletResponse res)
        throws IOException, ServletException {
    }
```

```
@PermitAll
protected void doTrace(HttpServletRequest req, HttpServletResponse res)
    throws IOException, ServletException {
}
}
```

Jakarta Authentication - Finally in Jakarta EE

On December 10, 2009, EE 6 was released. Arguably much too late, but it finally included an updated version of Jakarta Authentication. EE 6 also included Servlet 3.0, which now contains a section on "Additional Container Authentication Mechanisms" that says

> *To facilitate portable implementation and integration of additional container authentication mechanisms, it is recommended that all Servlet containers implement the Servlet Container Profile of [Jakarta Authentication] (i.e., JSR 196).*

Servlet also contains three important new facilities for programmatic security in the following methods on *HttpServletRequest*:

- authenticate

- login

- logout

The *authenticate*() method lets an application instigate (trigger) authentication of the request caller by the container from within a request context. This means a Filter or Server can call this method, and the container will then invoke whatever authentication mechanism has been configured. Such authentication mechanism can interact with the caller, for instance, displaying a login form, or redirecting to an external login service.

The *login()* method is a high-level method that lets the container call whatever identity store has been configured. If the provided credentials pass validation, the container sets the authenticated identity. The method is, however, limited to username/password, so only identity stores supporting this credential type work. The method is also somewhat light on details, as it doesn't say, for instance, whether the passed-in username must be the name that getUserPrincipal returns, or whether it takes the Principal returned by the identity store.

In a strange failure of coordination between APIs, it's not officially specified how these new methods exactly map to the authentication mechanisms of Jakarta Authentication. It's especially strange as Monzillo had been active for both these APIs.

The @ServletSecurity annotation is present as well, as is a variant to do the same thing programmatically. There is, however, no programmatic variant to set constraints for arbitrary URL patterns. This can still only be done using web.xml, or, theoretically, using Jakarta Authorization.

About two months after the release of EE 6, Ralph Soika, the CTO of a company called Imixs Software Solutions in Germany, created an authentication mechanism using Jakarta Authentication for OpenID and wrote extensively about this in a blog article titled "Glassfish & OpenID - JSR-196 with OpenID4Java." Soika also published his source, making it one of the few actual working examples available.

Roberto Chinnici, the EE 6 overall spec lead, delivered a two-day EE 6 workshop to a crowded San Francisco JUG meetup in August 2010. Chinnici talked extensively about Jakarta REST, Enterprise Beans, CDI, and everything else that was new in EE. Jakarta Authentication, however, was barely mentioned, foreshadowing a kind of information deprivation surrounding it.

On February 16, 2012, Red Hat released JBoss AS 7.1, its first EE 6 full profile certified server. It's not entirely clear what happened to Saldanha's and Stark's plans from six years earlier, but despite Jakarta Authentication being a part of EE 6 and despite passing the TCK (a comprehensive suite of tests to assess compatibility), Jakarta Authentication support is barely present. Saldanha in an interview would later say that he thinks this was due to shifting demands and container security being deemphasized in favor of concerns being shifted to the application. Jakarta Authentication, being perceived as targeted at EE vendors and system integrators, was thought to be less important in this world.

Enter OmniSecurity

A few months later, a software engineer named Arjan Tijms, who's working for the German company zanox, which operates a large EE-based software platform, took a look at Jakarta Authentication. Tijms noticed that there were a lot of vendor-specific steps needed to install an authentication module (SAM) and also that the identity store was not really portable and/or easy to define. In response, he filed on May 27, 2012,

JAVAEE_SPEC-9 ("Simplify and standardize authentication & role mapping"), in which he proposed to introduce a standard way to define an authentication module in web.xml and gave the following example:

```
<server-auth-module>
    <class-name>my.example.HTTPBasicServerAuthModule</class-name>
    <property>
        <name>usersProperties</name>
        <value>somepath/users.properties</value>
    </property>
</server-auth-module>
```

In the same issue, a proposal for an identity store is presented as well:

```
@AppLoginModule
public class MyAuthenticator implements PasswordLoginModule {

    private User user;

    @Inject
    private UserService userService;

    public void authenticate(String name, String password) {
        user = userService.getByNameAndPassword(name, password);
        if (user == null) {
            throw new FailedLoginException();
        }
    }

    public String getUserName() {
        return user.getName();
    }

    public List<String> getApplicationRoles() {
        return user.getRoles();
    }
}
```

Monzillo later replied to the filed issue, stating that at the very least, a common *AuthConfigProvider* should be present, so a SAM can be registered right away without putting the burden of implementing an *AuthConfigProvider* on the user.

At the start of November 2012, Tijms, together with Bauke Scholtz and Jan Beernink, was making plans to cofound a new company together with several other people. They have been working together on EE-based applications for quite some time, and earlier that year, they started the OmniFaces library for Jakarta Faces. As security had often been an issue in their projects, they agree to start with looking at this topic for their new web platform, zeef.com. Scholtz is to look at existing security frameworks, where Tijms is to investigate options in EE itself, specifically to take a better look at Jakarta Authentication.

A week later, on November 7, Tijms started the "javaee6-auth-example" project on Google Code, which contains code to easily install a Jakarta Authentication SAM. A few days after that, he published his findings in an article titled "Implementing container authentication in Java EE with JASPIC." In it, Tijms recognized the problems with vendor-specific security with regard to portability, but also because it adds to the feeling of EE being heavyweight. Tijms saw the potential in Jakarta Authentication but also saw many problems, some small, some big. He recognized smaller problems such as Jakarta Authentication being coded for Java SE 1.4, where for EE 6 Java SE 6 is the default, and that at the time, the names "jmac," "jaspi," and "jaspic" were all in use to refer to it. The biggest problem he saw was the fact that vendors had been slow to adopt Jakarta Authentication and that Jakarta Authentication was only mandated for the full profile. Contrary to, say, a Jakarta Messaging broker, Jakarta Authentication is not so much about adding new functionality but, as Tijms argued, about standardizing something that web profile applications already do as well. Tijms ended his findings with publishing a table comparing various tests between JBoss EAP, GlassFish, WebLogic, Geronimo, and WebSphere. The table made it clear that there are worrying differences between them all.

The next month, on December 14, 2012, Tijms, Beernink, and Scholtz started the Java EE Kickoff App project, which is intended as a template for new Jakarta EE web applications. For the security aspect of it, Beernink added the code that was previously written for the "javaee6-auth-example" project.

At the start of the new year, on January 23, Scholtz published his findings regarding existing frameworks in an article titled "Apache Shiro, is it ready for Java EE 6?" In it, Scholtz praises the rich features available in Shiro but is somewhat disappointed about the lack of integration with EE. After discussion with Beernink and Tijms, the decision is made to go forward with using Jakarta Authentication for zeef.com.

That same month, Tijms and Monzillo got into contact and discussed various issues with Jakarta Authentication. Tijms expressed the wish to have security be fully configurable for a single application without needing a single vendor-specific setting or action, and that especially the identity store should be able to come from the application as well. Even though the world has moved to configuring things from the application, having an application-controlled identity store is still somewhat of a radical idea. Even in 2003, the overarching thinking was still that EE is mostly used for shrink wrapped applications that are deployed to a corporate intranet and have to integrate with the corporate office authentication systems (such as LDAP); both Monzillo and another software engineer who briefly joined the discussion, Markus Eisele, had a somewhat different view still. Eisele even suggested to use Servlet filters instead as they are application-centered approaches (implying Jakarta Authentication is not).

Tijms then mentioned several issues with Jakarta Authentication that should be addressed, such as the authenticate/login/logout methods that were missed in EE 6, as well as a definition of the so-called appContext identifier, which is required by the programmatic API but is nowhere defined. Tijms also asked for new features, such as a portable way to programmatically and declaratively just register a SAM. Monzillo committed to addressing the issues in the soon-to-be-released EE 7 but, given the short amount of time left, said he couldn't address the feature requests at this moment. Later that month, Tijms and Monzillo continued the discussion and talked about the support of forward and include from SAMs, what the phrase "after the service invocation" exactly means, and how to remember an authentication until a user logs out.

Meanwhile, on February 21, 2013, Beernink and Tijms found the OmniSecurity project, moving most of the security code from the Kickoff app to it. The goal is stated as follows:

OmniSecurity provides a basic security (login) facility for simple, self-contained web applications with ease of use abstractions on top of Java EE security APIs like JASPIC and JACC.

The focus is on integrating with the Java EE security model and making the low-level security APIs that Java EE offers easier and more approachable.

Monzillo kept his word, and in early April, Jakarta Authentication 1.1 was ready, in time for the EE 7 release. The *AppContextID* is now fully defined using a new Servlet 3.1 method: *ServletContext#getVirtualServerName*. Also, *authenticate/login/logout* is now defined for Jakarta Authentication, as are forwards and includes from a SAM a clarification of what "after the service invocation" means and a method to (semi) automatically register a session. The latter, however, is a little light on details, and the plan is to clarify it further for EE 8 (which, spoiler, didn't happen).

With the biggest API problems now solved, Tijms focuses on testing the various implementations for compatibility. As it turns out, the TCK for Jakarta Authentication tests something, but by far not enough. Therefore, on August 10, 2013, he created the "jaspic-capabilities-test" project, a suite of junit and Arquillian-based tests that verify various behaviors and can be easily run against multiple servers. Monzillo and Tijms frequently discuss failures that occur, and Tijms files issues with the various vendors of those servers in an attempt to get them resolved, often pointing to a test from the suite as a reproducer.

At the end of that year, on December 10, 2013, the jaspic-capabilities-test project was donated to the Java EE 7 samples project, with further enhancements from then on being done in that project.

Meanwhile, at Oracle, early 2014, a survey was conducted to ask the community what their priorities are for EE 8, which should be starting later that year. Software Evangelist David Delabassee presented the results on February 6, 2014. One of the outcomes is that there's a strong demand for modernized, higher-level, security in EE, especially with a focus on application-managed security and breaking away with the old J2EE mindset of having security strictly separated and delegated to nondeveloper roles (like the traditional "assembler" role in J2EE). Finding someone to lead this effort and who therefore has both knowledge of security and is aware of modern technologies in EE (such as CDI) is, however, a hard find. Tijms was asked for the role, but because of recently having cofounded zeef.com and being active there, he was not available.

Near the end of the year, OmniSecurity had matured to version 0.6 and now included an easy-to-use version of the SAM specifically for HTTP, so no casting was required for the *HttpServletRequest* and *HttpServletResponse*. It also included an identity store that could be obtained via CDI from the application. The HTTP-specific SAM is an abstract base class and is registered the same way as every SAM would be, but for which OmniSecurity contains helper code to make this otherwise daunting task trivial.

On his blog, Tijms discussed on November 16, 2014, how to create a stateless header authentication mechanism using OmniSecurity.

The authentication mechanism (a plain SAM):

```java
public class TokenAuthModule extends HttpServerAuthModule {

    private final static Pattern tokenPattern =
        compile("OmniLogin\\s+auth\\s*=\\s*(.*)");

    @Override
    public AuthStatus validateHttpRequest(
        HttpServletRequest request, HttpServletResponse response,
        HttpMsgContext httpMsgContext) throws AuthException {

        String token = getToken(request);
        if (!isEmpty(token)) {

            // If a token is present, authenticate with it whether
            // this is strictly required or not.

            TokenAuthenticator tokenAuthenticator =
                getReferenceOrNull(TokenAuthenticator.class);
            if (tokenAuthenticator != null) {

                if (tokenAuthenticator.authenticate(token)) {
                    return
                        httpMsgContext.notifyContainerAboutLogin(
                            tokenAuthenticator.getUserName(),
                            tokenAuthenticator.getApplicationRoles());
                }
            }
        }

        if (httpMsgContext.isProtected()) {
            return httpMsgContext.responseNotFound();
        }

        return httpMsgContext.doNothing();
    }
}
```

The identity store (a CDI bean):

```
@RequestScoped
public class APITokenAuthModule implements TokenAuthenticator {

    @Inject
    private UserService userService;

    @Inject
    private CacheManager cacheManager;

    private User user;

    @Override
    public boolean authenticate(String token) {
        try {
            Cache<String, User> usersCache = cacheManager.getDefaultCache();

            User cachedUser = usersCache.get(token);
            if (cachedUser != null) {
                user = cachedUser;
            } else {
                user = userService.getUserByLoginToken(token);
                usersCache.put(token, user);
            }
        } catch (InvalidCredentialsException e) {
            return false;
        }

        return true;
    }

    @Override
    public String getUserName() {
        return user == null ? null : user.getUserName();
    }
}
```

```
@Override
public List<String> getApplicationRoles() {
    return user == null ? emptyList() : user.getRoles();
}

}
```

The *HttpServerAuthModule* in a way can be seen as the fourth iteration of the *ServerAuthModule* that started in the JAuth package all the way back in early 2005.

Enter Jakarta Security

Only days later the Jakarta EE Security JSR started. Spec lead is Oracle engineer Alex Kosowski, who had been preparing for the role since last April. Also, in the expert group are Tijms, Hazlewood, and Java legend Adam Bien.

Many discussions ensue. Kosowski argues for elaborate identity stores with a large amount of methods for adding, updating, and deleting users and groups, as well as using JNDI for lookups. Tijms argues for the absolutely most minimal identity store interface imaginable with only the method for validating credentials and returning groups present, as well as using CDI as the main building block, and especially for the application facing parts. Tijms states that by using CDI, no custom file format and factories to register and retrieve artifacts are needed, as CDI is effectively exactly that.

Other discussions focus around making the new security framework completely stand-alone, like Deltaspike Security. Tijms, however, argues to leverage Jakarta Authentication and Jakarta Authorization so that no wheels have to be reinvented, Jakarta Security itself can stay small, and as an added bonus, all existing security APIs in EE, like *HttpServletRequest.isUserInRole()*, *@RolesAllowed*, and much more, would transparently continue to work. It's a hard sell, as most people in the expert group have little to no knowledge about Jakarta Authentication and Jakarta Authorization, and have only heard it's old and not user-friendly, and the very thing they have to replace.

After a year of discussions and considering proposals, Tijms started on October 19, 2015, with a proof of concept not really aptly called "mechanism-to-store," which shows how an authentication mechanism (a SAM) can call out to an identity store. It's based on how OmniSecurity works and on the terminology that has been discussed in the last year. Its identity store interface looks as follows:

```
package javax.security.identitystore;

import javax.security.identitystore.credential.Credential;

/**
 * <code>IdentityStore</code> is a mechanism for validating a Caller's
 * credentials and accessing a Caller's identity attributes, and
   would be used
 * by an authentication mechanism, such as JASPIC. An
   <code>IdentityStore</code>
 * obtains identity data from a persistence mechanism, such as a file,
   database,
 * or LDAP.
 */
public interface IdentityStore {

    /**
     * Validates the given credential.
     *
     * @param credential
     *              The credential
     * @return The validation result, including associated caller roles and
     *           groups.
     */
    public CredentialValidationResult validate(Credential credential);
}
```

There's an @EmbeddedIdentityStore annotation present, which an example app uses as follows:

```
@EmbeddedIdentityStoreDefinition({
    @Credentials(
        callerName = "reza", password = "secret1", groups = { "foo", "bar" }),
    @Credentials(
        callerName = "alex", password = "secret2", groups = { "foo", "kaz" }),
    @Credentials(
        callerName = "arjan", password = "secret3", groups = { "foo" }) })
```

```
@DeclareRoles({ "foo", "bar", "kaz" })
@WebServlet("/servlet")
public class Servlet extends HttpServlet {}
```

And finally, there's a plain SAM in the example app calling out to this identity store (some code omitted for brevity):

```
public class TestServerAuthModule implements ServerAuthModule {

    @Override
    public AuthStatus validateRequest(MessageInfo messageInfo, Subject
    clientSubject, Subject serviceSubject) throws AuthException {

        HttpServletRequest request = (HttpServletRequest)
            messageInfo.getRequestMessage();

        Callback[] callbacks;

        if (request.getParameter("name") != null &&
            request.getParameter("password") != null) {

            String name = request.getParameter("name");
            Password password = new Password(request.
            getParameter("password"));

            // Obtain a reference to the Identity Store
            IdentityStore identityStore =
                CDI.current().select(IdentityStore.class).get();

            // Delegate the {credentials in -> identity data out}
            function to
            // the Identity Store
            CredentialValidationResult result =
                identityStore.validate(
                    new UsernamePasswordCredential(name, password));

            if (result.getStatus() == VALID) {
                callbacks = new Callback[] {
                    // The name of the authenticated caller
                    new CallerPrincipalCallback(
                        clientSubject, result.getCallerName()),
```

```
            // the groups of the authenticated caller (for test
            // assume non-null, non-empty)
            new GroupPrincipalCallback(clientSubject,
                result.getCallerGroups().toArray(new String[0])) };
        }
      }
    }
}
```

The prototype was gradually extended, as the even worse named "mechanism-to-store-x," and on December 15, 2015, an interface for the *HttpAuthenticationMechanism* was added. It looked as follows:

```
package javax.security.authenticationmechanism.http;

public interface HttpAuthenticationMechanism {

    AuthStatus validateRequest(
        HttpServletRequest request, HttpServletResponse response,
        HttpMsgContext httpMessageContext) throws AuthException;

    default AuthStatus secureResponse(
        HttpServletRequest request, HttpServletResponse response,
        HttpMsgContext httpMessageContext) throws AuthException {
        return SEND_SUCCESS;
    }

    default void cleanSubject(
        HttpServletRequest request, HttpServletResponse response,
        HttpMsgContext httpMessageContext) {
        httpMessageContext.cleanClientSubject();
    }
}
```

This is effectively the fifth iteration of the JAuth interface from 2005. It's strongly influenced by OmniSecurity, but where in OmniSecurity it was a base class implementing the *ServerAuthModule* interface, here, it works differently. It's a completely new interface, but there's a bridge *ServerAuthModule* present, which 1:1 delegates to an instance of this interface obtained via CDI.

The code was further worked on by Tijms in his personal GitHub repository until the preparation for the Early Draft Review (EDR), for which the code was briefly transferred to the javaee-security-proposals on January 28, 2016, after which it finally landed in the javaee/security-soteria repo on GitHub. A little over 400 commits later and a lot of intervening discussions, and even the change of the spec lead to Will Hopkins, it was released as the API Jakarta Security 1.0 and the implementation Soteria 1.0 on August 27, 2017.

The *HttpAuthenticationMechanism* has changed a little in the final version; its *AuthStatus* return type has been replaced by a new enum, which is defined to be exactly mapped to the existing AuthStatus. The package has changed to *javax.security.enterprise. authentication.mechanism.http*. The sixth iteration of the JAuth interface hence looks as follows:

```
package javax.security.enterprise.authentication.mechanism.http;;

public interface HttpAuthenticationMechanism {

    AuthenticationStatus validateRequest(
        HttpServletRequest request, HttpServletResponse response,
        HttpMsgContext httpMessageContext) throws AuthException;

    default AuthenticationStatus secureResponse(
        HttpServletRequest request, HttpServletResponse response,
        HttpMsgContext httpMessageContext) throws AuthException {
        return SEND_SUCCESS;
    }

    default void cleanSubject(
        HttpServletRequest request, HttpServletResponse response,
        HttpMsgContext httpMessageContext) {
        httpMessageContext.cleanClientSubject();
    }
}
```

CHAPTER 2

Jakarta EE Foundations

Quite some history to reach the current state, right? That being said, you might be wondering at this moment "why this much history" or "why is security so fundamental to our applications." Well, we will cover everything related to the rationale of this book in this chapter. Besides, we will have a look at the foundations of enterprise security.

First things first, why does a term like security sound that broad?

We could define as *security* any measure taken to protect us and our data against aspiring intruders, from using passwords in our locks to authenticating users in a web application. The surge of cybersecurity attacks has nowadays created the need for defending our organization on multiple security fronts, be it physical, technological, or policies and procedures. Each one of the aforementioned fronts is equally important to your organization's security. None of them should be undermined toward creating a future-proof and secure organization. That is, having only physical security is not enough. Having only physical and technological security could indeed be somewhat more challenging to cyberhackers, yet if your employees are not well educated to protect their passwords, your organization's not secure overall.

Sidebar: Modern organizations should strive for a holistic approach to security which requires that physical security, technological security, and policies and procedures are all in place.

Physical Security

The rapid development of technology contributed to putting all security efforts into developing measures and policies to protect our applications against cyberhackers, which often results in overlooking the importance of physical security. Suppose your company has spent millions of dollars on decent firewalls to be secure. Unfortunately, even the best firewalls in the world can't help enough if an attacker manages to bypass the building security, gain access to the storage room, and steal your servers. That being said, physical security is equally important as the other types of security as well.

41

© Arjan Tijms, Teo Bais, and Werner Keil 2022
A. Tijms et al., *The Definitive Guide to Security in Jakarta EE*, https://doi.org/10.1007/978-1-4842-7945-8_2

Sidebar: As physical security, we define the protection of property and people against events and actions that could cause serious loss or damage to an organization.

Not having enough physical security policies in place could lead to unforeseen disasters. In the following, you can see a quick overview of various disasters that your institution or organization could potentially suffer from:

- Human attacks: Theft, vandalism

- Natural disasters: Fire, flood, tsunami, hurricane, earthquake

- Accidental damage: Electrical surges, road accidents, spilled coffee or water

- Man-made disasters: Explosions, wars

There are several measures we could take to prevent these kinds of disasters; for example, investing in good locks for the server room is a good start but not enough. Setting up surveillance in the server room by adding a guard and printing passes so that only privileged groups of employees (like group system admins) have access to it adds up to a good security measure. Another way to prevent natural disasters is by insuring your physical assets (hardware, building, etc.). Furthermore, to minimize the human attacks in regard to physical security, a document shredder can always come to the rescue before any document disposal.

Technological Security

Nowadays, the term "security" is often associated with technology, yet it is quite broad. To make things easier, we can divide technological security into three main components:

- Application security

- OS security

- Network security

Application Security

Application security is the software development process by which we make our applications more robust against potential threats (e.g., authentication flaws, unfiltered redirects). It comprises the development, testing, and release of new security features to prevent security vulnerabilities within an application. Such security vulnerabilities often involve vulnerabilities in application dependencies. Hence, not only the code we write but also the code we depend on needs to be checked for vulnerabilities.

OS Security

OS security addresses a variety of different techniques and methods that ensure safety from threats and attacks. For example, when we claim that OS security is in place, we mean that we are running different programs and applications that help us perform the necessary tasks to stop any unauthorized interference.

Network Security

Network security is any activity designed to protect the confidentiality, integrity, and accessibility of computer networks and data by using both software and hardware technologies.

Policies and Procedures

Making sure physical and technological security are in place and followed by heart is a great step toward security, yet it's not enough if we keep ignoring the human factor. For example, building the best firewall is useless if one of your employees falls victim to a social engineering attack that could potentially exploit your organization's security measures and gains them access to your systems.

Note   Social engineering is the technique of psychological manipulation of people into giving up confidential information. A common example of social engineering attempts targeting large organizations by calling the company's HQs to chat with the secretaries for details about their boss so they could help guessing their passwords.

That being said, there is some need for additional measures, practices, and policies so that your employees live and breathe security. In technology, we should never skimp the human factor which may leave too many areas exposed. Thus, employees should be educated frequently so they can eventually become somewhat paranoid and assertive toward contributing to collectively creating a secure organization. For example, ABN Amro Bank where Teo used to work had established a standard policy on training its employees on security and compliance monthly in the form of a quiz: by the end of the month, each employee should have a score of at least 70%; otherwise, their manager gets notified. This is a good way to impose continuous education toward secure organizations.

Key Principles of Security

In this book, we will focus on application security and specifically on how to secure our applications using the Jakarta Security specification. Now that we have got well acquainted with the three different components of security, it is about time to also define security as in *information security*:

Sidebar: Information security is the confidentiality, integrity, and availability of information.

The three aforementioned principles form the cornerstone of any organization's security infrastructure. Hence, we often address them as the *CIA Triad*.

In addition to the *CIA Triad*, there are a few more key concepts in security, so let's have a quick look at them on a one-on-one basis.

Overview of the key principles in security

- Authentication

- Authorization

- Confidentiality

- Integrity

- Availability

- Nonrepudiation

- Auditing

Authentication: Users can prove they are who they say they are; for example, a client can prove to a server that they are acting on behalf of an authorized identity and vice versa.

Authorization: Users have enough permissions to access restricted resources or perform specific operations.

Confidentiality: Information should not be read by unauthorized users.

Integrity: Information should not be able to be falsified unnoticed. For example, a hacker should not be able to seize and modify any data before it's sent to the intended recipient.

Availability: Requires that information is accessible whenever authorized users need it.

Nonrepudiation: A user who performed some action cannot reasonably deny having done so.

Auditing: Tamper-resistant records of security-related events are captured by maintaining a record of transactions on the concerned system.

Caution   Authentication vs. authorization

Authentication and authorization are often confused nowadays, so here's a good way to remember how these two terms are different in the world of identity and access management (IAM). Authentication confirms that users are who they say they are, whereas authorization permits those users to access a resource.

Features of a Security Mechanism

It speaks for itself that security is a tough pill to swallow when it comes down to configuring it properly. To properly implement security within our organizations, we need to have some policies in place, which are called *security mechanisms* in the world of security.

Sidebar: As security mechanisms, we define the means that are used to implement security services such as digital certificates, cryptography, authentication mechanisms, and others that we will examine in the course of this book.

Well-implemented security mechanisms can take away much trouble from the developer both in terms of functionality and in a variety of features. The highlights for both of them are listed here:

Functionality

- Nonrepudiation as in holding system users accountable for operations they perform

- Availability as in protecting a system from service interruptions and other glitches that disturb the quality of service

- Authentication as in preventing unauthorized access to application functions and business or personal data

Features

- They offer transparency to system users.

- They are easy to administer.

- They are interoperable across enterprise boundaries and applications.

We will have a chance to have a closer look at the most important concepts of security by looking at a basic application walkthrough. To begin with, it is important to have a basic understanding of how modern applications are built and deployed.

Distributed Multitiered Applications

Let's now have a look at distributed multitiered applications, how single tier applications evolved to multitiered and, of course, a simple application walkthrough.

Single-Tier vs. Multitiered Applications

A software application comprises several different components with the most common ones being the application itself, the web server where it's hosted, and the database of course. Back in the day, we would host each of the aforementioned components in just one server (known as a *layer*), which is the so-called single-tier architecture. That is, in a single-tier application, all the different layers (presentation layer, business logic layer, and data layer) are hosted on a single machine, something that is unscalable, however, as only one user can access the system at a given time via the local client. Hence, that increases the amount of effort we as developers need to put into creating this application as well as the complexity of the architecture and components.

Thanks to the best practices of software engineering, we nowadays develop our applications based on a *multitier architecture*. A multitiered application is any application developed and distributed in more than one layer; it logically separates the different application-specific operation layers. That must be lighter in terms of complexity, isn't it? Yes, multitier architectures are here to improve our applications' security, scalability, reusability, availability, and integrity and of course to increase distribution.

The Jakarta EE Approach

The Jakarta EE platform is also a multitier adopter. Specifically, it uses a distributed multitiered application model for enterprise applications. The theory of operation of that model is quite simple: it focuses on components and machines. In a nutshell, it is the application logic that is first split into components depending on the functionality of each component; a Jakarta EE application comprises such components. Once application logic is split up into components, those components are installed on various machines depending on the Jakarta EE environment tier they belong to.

Take a look at Figure 2-1 to see how two multitiered Jakarta EE applications could be divided into multiple tiers where each tier has its own components depending on the Jakarta EE environment they belong to. From top to bottom, we can observe that

- Client-tier components run on the client machine

- Web-tier and business-tier components run on the Jakarta EE server

- Enterprise information system-tier software runs on the EIS server

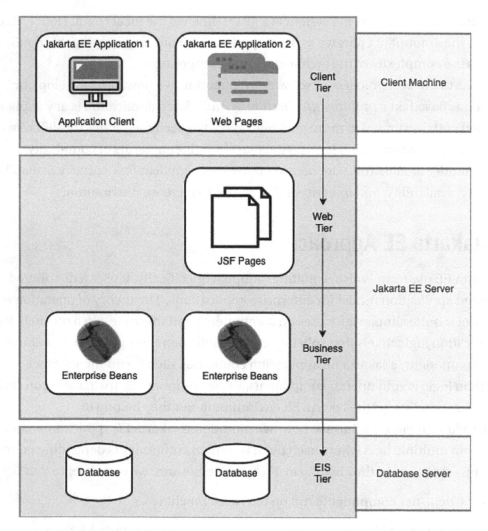

Figure 2-1. *Multitiered applications*

Security in Jakarta EE

Sidebar: New technological trends create new technical challenges.

That is, the arrival of multitiered applications comes with some security risks which we as developers need to minimize. Jakarta EE revolutionizes your security management by

- Allowing you to define security constraints at deployment time

- Enabling portability of applications; the same application works in a wide variety of security environments without changing a single line of code

- Enabling developers to define standard declarative access control rules that are interpreted when the application is deployed on the server

- Enabling developers to save more time by providing standard login mechanisms out of the box

We'll have the chance to delve into each one of the aforementioned characteristics of Jakarta EE Security in the next chapters, which are more technical. For the time being, let's set the ground with some basics; that is, time to have a look at a simple application security walkthrough.

Simple Application Security Walkthrough

What a better way to understand the fundamentals of a Jakarta EE environment than examining what happens in a simple application with a user interface, a web client, and some enterprise bean business logic.

The following example is taken from the Jakarta EE Specification. As we will see, the server here acts as an authentication proxy by asking, collecting, and verifying the login credentials of the client so that it can eventually establish a session where both parties authenticate each other.

Step 1: Initial Request

The web client initiates the transaction between the two entities by requesting the URL of the main application as shown in Figure 2-2.

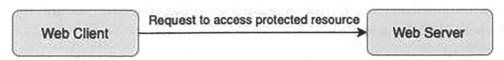

Figure 2-2. *Initial request*

This is the very first interaction between the two entities. The web server first detects that the client has not authenticated itself yet, and second, it invokes the proper authentication mechanism for the requested resource. We will cover authentication mechanisms in more depth later on in this chapter.

Step 2: Initial Authentication

Having invoked the proper authentication mechanism, the web server then returns to the web client a login form so that it can collect the user's login data, such as username and password. The user enters the authentication data, and the web client is then responsible for forwarding them to the web server, where validation takes place as shown in Figure 2-3.

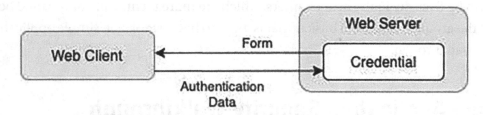

Figure 2-3. *Initial authentication*

There are two different ways to validate data; one is by using a validation mechanism that is local to the server, and the other one is by having the web server leverage the underlying security service. Once the web server can validate the user, it sets a credential for them.

Step 3: URL Authorization

The credential that the server assigns to the user can be used for any future request of the user (web client) to access restricted resources (e.g., the Edit Profile page of their account).

Whenever a web client requests to access a restricted resource, the web server consults the underlying security policy mechanism to determine which security roles may be permitted access to the resource.

Note   Your security policy may be derived either from annotations or from the deployment descriptor.

It is the web container that checks then the user's credentials against each role to determine whether it can map the user to the role. Figure 2-4 depicts this process.

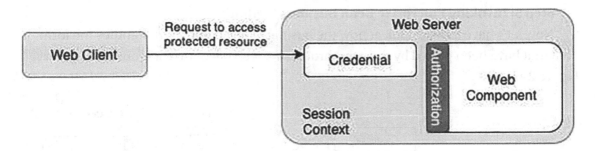

Figure 2-4. *URL authorization*

There are two possible outcomes from a web server's evaluation process:

- *"is authorized"*: The web server was able to map the user to a role.

- *"not authorized"*: The web server was unable to map the user to any of the permitted roles.

Step 4: Fulfilling the Original Request

Upon successful authorization of the user, the web server returns the result of the original URL. Figure 2-5 shows this process.

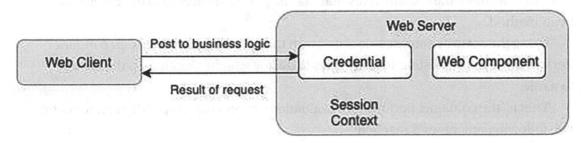

Figure 2-5. *Fulfilling the original request*

As you can see in our example, the web server returns the response URL of a web page, which enables the user to use the returned web page as an interface to interact with the server by posting form data.

Tip   It is the responsibility of the business logic components of a web application to receive data from the client, process it, and send it to the EIS tier for storage. In the next few chapters, you will learn more about securing web applications.

Step 5: Invoking Enterprise Bean Business Methods

Now let's have a closer look at how the business logic component handles the form data that have been posted by the user through the web page. Take a moment to observe Figure 2-6.

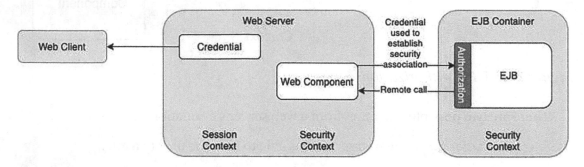

Figure 2-6. *Invoking Bean Business Methods*

To begin with, it is important to mention that managing the access control of enterprise bean methods is the sole responsibility of the enterprise container. To achieve this, an enterprise container consults the security policy associated with the enterprise bean to determine the security roles that may be permitted access to the enterprise bean method.

Using the security context associated with the call, the enterprise bean container iterates through the existing security roles to decide whether it can map the caller to a role.

That is, the container performs an evaluation process that stops when either of the two following outcomes is reached:

- "is authorized"

- "not authorized"

For a quick overview of the explanation of these outcomes and what happens under the hood, consult Table 2-1.

Table 2-1. *Authorization results mapping*

Result	Explanation	Under the hood
is authorized	The container is able to map the caller's credential to a role	The container dispatches control to the enterprise bean method; the result of the bean's execution call is returned to the web page and eventually to the user
not authorized	The container is unable to map the caller to any of the permitted roles	The result causes the container to throw an exception that is propagated back to the caller

Looking Ahead

We had a look at the holistic approach of security, the key principles of security, how Jakarta EE utilizes a distributed multitiered landscape, and a simple application walkthrough, which set the ground for some more in-depth material in the attracting-to-many world of security. See this chapter as your toolbox for the entire book. In the next two sections, we will explore the beautiful world of authentication and authorization, the two backbone principles of security.

Authentication

As *authentication*, we define the process of verifying someone's identity. In order words, authentication is all about proving that you're indeed the person or the system you claim to be. Ok, let's make this rather professional definition a bit easier to understand by pulling our beloved fictitious characters, Alice and Bob. Suppose Alice wants to send a message to Bob. How could Bob be sure that he is indeed texting with Alice and not with someone who claims to be Alice? There are basically three different ways Bob could use to verify Alice's identity: by something she knows, something she has, or something she is.

Sidebar: Authenticating someone's identity may be a result of one or more of three types of methods: *something you know, something you have,* and *something you are.*

Something You Know

We classify information as *something you know* if we store it in our memory and retrieve it when needed. We can identify *something you know* authentication methods in our daily interaction by taking a look at almost any system where we have to authenticate ourselves to interact with: our bank account, our email address, our social media accounts, etc. Yes, you got it right, the most common *something you know* authentication methods are passwords, secret codes, passphrases, and personal identification numbers (PINs).

The *something you know* authentication is the most commonly used authentication method due to its low cost and easy implementation. However, its easy implementation has some side effects, one of which is that it may not be considered strong authentication. Moreover, the *something you know* authentication alone is not enough for applications or systems that require high security.

So how can we make sure strong authentication is in place? Let's have a look at some other authentication methods.

Something You Have

The *something you have* authentication method refers to something that the user has. Did you notice one major drawback the *something you know* method has? It's all about our memory and it's (limited) capacity; that is, passwords can easily be forgotten. The *something you have* method removes that problem, as it's all about some object which must be with you whenever you want to authenticate yourself. Again, here, it's all about possessing some kind of token.

Examples of *something you have* authentication could be a bank card, a USB stick, or an OTP card. Undoubtedly, carrying an authentication object with you entails its risks – they may be stolen, damaged, or lost.

Something You Are

The *something you are* authentication method addresses what the user *is* and mainly refers to biometric authentication methods. Simply put, biometrics are any metrics related to human features that theoretically can be used for identification or verification of identity. There are various biometric data types such as facial recognition, fingerprints, iris and retina recognition, voice recognition, vein recognition, DNA, and digital signatures.

Note   Biometrics can distinguish one person from another.

How does biometrics compare to the other two authentication methods? It's less well understood than the *something you know* and *something you have* methods, yet it can significantly contribute to the strength of authentication when used correctly in addition to the other two methods.

Tip   We consider strong authentication the use of two or more different authentication methods, such as a smart card and a PIN, or a password and a form of biometrics such as a fingerprint or retina scan.

Latest Trends in Authentication Methods

So that's all? We can only use three different authentication methods to secure our systems?

Well, of course not. While hackers are becoming smarter, there is some need for additional (and more complex) authentication methods, such as *somewhere you are* and *something you do.*

Somewhere you are is related to your location and supports two different flavors: *geolocation security checks* where the location of the user is checked against the configured location of their account and *MAC address checks* where, for example, an employee who is trying to access the company network from a different machine will not be granted any access due to a different MAC address.

Something you do is the least popular authentication method. This kind of authentication is all about verifying a user by observing their actions (touches or gestures). An example here could be the *picture password* feature Windows 8 comes with, which allows you to configure touches and gestures on a picture as a way to authenticate yourself. A more common tech-savvy example of *something you do* to authenticate yourself is your smartphone's gesture authentication, where you use your thumb to swipe a gesture pattern on your smartphone's screen so you can unlock it.

Authentication Examples in Practice

In this section, we covered some theoretical ground on the basics of authentication. Aren't you yet as excited as we are to see how that plays out in code? Let's quickly peek through the Jakarta EE door by examining some basic code snippets on authentication.

In Jakarta EE, the component containers are responsible for providing application security. A container provides two types of security: *declarative* and *programmatic*. Declarative security addresses the use of deployment descriptors or annotations to configure a component's security mechanisms, whereas programmatic security is used by security-aware applications to complement their security model.

Note   A deployment descriptor is a configuration file describing an application's security structure. It is external to the application, and you will learn more about configuring it later on.

Authenticating Users Programmatically

Authenticating users programmatically can be done using the *SecurityContext* and *HttpServletRequest* interfaces.

SecurityContext

The Jakarta EE Security API Specification, which you will have the chance to evaluate in the next few chapters, specifies one method to help you trigger an authentication process programmatically:

- *authenticate()* enables an application to notify the container that it should start the authentication process with the caller.

HttpServletRequest

The *HttpServletRequest* interface enables you to authenticate web application users programmatically by specifying three simple methods:

- *authenticate* triggers the specific authentication mechanism that has been configured; for example, if that's a form, a login form will be displayed to the user to collect their username and password, whereas if that's simply a social login like "Login with Google," it will redirect the user to Google.

- *login* validates the provided username and password.

- *logout* resets a request's caller identity.

The following code example shows how to use the authenticate method:

```java
public class FoundationsChapterServlet extends HttpServlet {

    protected void processRequest(HttpServletRequest request,
    HttpServletResponse response) throws ServletException, IOException {
        response.setContentType("text/html;charset=UTF-8");
        try (PrintWriter writer = response.getWriter()) {
            request.authenticate(response);
            writer.println("Successful authentication!");
        }
    }
}
```

The following code example shows how to use the *login* and *logout* methods:

```java
public class SampleLoginLogoutServlet extends HttpServlet {

protected void processRequest(HttpServletRequest request,
HttpServletResponse response) throws ServletException, IOException {
        response.setContentType("text/html;charset=UTF-8");
        try (PrintWriter out = response.getWriter()) {

            out.println("<html>");
            out.println("<body>");
            request.login("Chapter2User", "Chapter2User");

            BigDecimal result =
                converterBean.libresToKilos(new BigDecimal("55.0"));

            out.println("<h1>Servlet SampleLoginLogoutServlet result of
            libresToKilos= " + result + "</h1>");
            out.println("</body>");
            out.println("</html>");
        } catch (Exception e) {
            throw new ServletException(e);
```

```
    } finally {
        request.logout();
    }
  }
}
```

If nothing of the aforementioned makes sense so far, don't worry, we'll dive into the mechanics of authentication, authorization, and security in the next three chapters.

Authorization

Suppose you are a fanatic gamer and wish to upgrade your system so that you're able to play cutting-edge games in your free time. You start surfing the web to find all the necessary parts that could comprise such a geeky system. Once you're done adding everything to your basket, you notice that building such a system would cost you $2000, yet you decide to go for it as if it can give you pleasure; you'll eventually be more proactive in your work-related activities after all. During the checkout process, you fill in your credit card details, but you notice that your transaction has failed with the message "Transaction exceeds the maximum limit of a daily transaction," and you then remember that you've recently set your daily maximum limit of a transaction at $1500.

The aforementioned example is a typical authorization example where a system will not authorize a transaction even if you've successfully authenticated yourself. Moreover, it's also a nice way to distinguish authentication and authorization:

- *Authentication* verifies a user's identity.

- *Authorization* verifies a user's authority.

Having made it thus far, let's try to define authorization.

Sidebar: Authorization is the act of verifying a user's permissions to perform a specific action.

Don't go too far to think of other authorization examples. Just like our previous example with you trying to perform a transaction that exceeds the maximum daily limit, there are tons of other authorization checks taking place in our daily interaction with computers; for example, when you're on Twitter and attempt to delete a tweet that you just posted, the underlying security mechanisms of Twitter will first verify whether you're allowed to do so. Another example could be when you're trying to create a new file at a given directory of your OS; it is then your OS that checks whether you have enough *write* permissions on that directory before allowing you to create the file. Operating systems are quite good at performing this kind of preliminary authorization checks thanks to their so-called access control list (ACL) mechanisms.

Access Control Lists

So what is an access control list and why is it so important to an OS?

Think of an ACL as a table that maps users to system resources and their privileges on them. The operating system then consults that table to decide whether it should allow a user to access a specific resource, based on the user's access rights and the resource's (object's) security attributes. For example, Arjan, Werner, and Teo are book authors. All of them may have access to the *jakartaee-security-book* directory, but Arjan has written a couple more on CDI and JSF, so he should also have access to *cdi2-javaee8-book* and *jsf-javaee8-book* directories. Suppose the three authors' home directory is */home/books*, so their writing engagements could then be modeled by an ACL that could list Arjan as a principal by listing the set of files he's allowed to access as shown in the following table:

User	Resource	Privileges
Arjan	/home/books/*	Read, write, execute
Werner	/home/books/jakartaee-security-book	Read, write, execute
Teo	/home/books/jakartaee-security-book	Read, write, execute

> **Note**   An ACL may optionally include privileges that are associated with resources.

The preceding example works well for small teams or organizations. What happens though in large corporations with thousands of users? Tables listing all existing users are not sustainable, thus the need to introduce more sophisticated schemes where users are mapped to roles, the so-called user-role mapping. Tables 2-2 and 2-3 depict an interpretation of the preceding example to a more modern approach.

Table 2-2. *User-role mapping*

User	Role
Arjan	Admin author, programmer
Werner	Jakarta EE author, programmer
Teo	Jakarta EE author, programmer

Table 2-3. *Role-based ACL*

Role	Resource	Privilege
Admin author	/home/books/*	Read, write, execute
Jakarta EE author	/home/books/jakartaee-security-book	Read, write, execute
Jakarta EE author	/home/books/*	Read

Access Control Models

Access control lists are somewhat abstract as a concept, and they need some formal implementation process so they can be applied to security systems. That's the time when *access control models* can come to the rescue.

As we've seen earlier, when a web client requests a page from a web server, the web server cannot simply return the page unless and until it ensures the right security measures are in place. Specifically, it first needs to check whether the user is authenticated and second if they are authorized to view the requested content. We defined those two processes as *authentication* and *authorization*; however, the broader security policy which they serve is *access control*. Access control dictates who's allowed to access and use company information and resources, and it can be implemented in three different ways, the so-called access control models.

There are three main kinds of access control models:

- The discretionary

- The mandatory

- The role based

Discretionary Access Control (DAC)

From the three aforementioned models, DAC is the most prevalent one. Think of the DAC model as a double-edged sword where the information owner (e.g., the creator of a file) has the mandate to govern access control restrictions on the object at issue (e.g., a file). Why a double-edged sword, though? The main characteristic of the DAC model is the flexibility it comes with; on the one hand, it gives users the power to decide who can access information and what they can do with it (think in terms of permissions like *read*, *write*, *execute*, *delete*, etc.), while on the other hand, being that flexible may result in users making the wrong decisions, by accident or on purpose. For example, providing users with all the freedom to govern access control restrictions could lead to overlooking some details and assign write permissions to the readers of a blog. Similarly, a malicious user could be granted *execute* access on a system file that under their hands could cause a system outage.

Note   The DAC model remains the top choice for the vast majority of operating systems nowadays.

Mandatory Access Control (MAC)

Mandatory access control addresses a stricter access control approach. Specifically, this security policy is centrally controlled by a security policy administrator (such as an operating system) so that users cannot override the policy by any means; for example, granting access to files that would otherwise be restricted is not possible here. MAC-based systems can decide what access control restrictions to enforce by using one or more of the following concepts:

- Data classification levels (such as *public*, *confidential*, *secret*, and *top secret*)

- Security clearance labels that are in line with the data classification levels

- Per-group and/or per-domain division of users

- Security policy set by the system administrator

Supposedly, a document comprising the annual salaries of developers belongs to the management group and has a *secret* label, which means that it may not be accessed by someone belonging to the development group, even if that someone has a higher security clearance level (in this case, *top secret*).

Caution   MAC-based systems may be more secure than systems based on DAC, but on the other hand, they also come with some additional administrative burden that is imposed by the operating system and makes their adoption a tough pill to swallow.

Note   Undoubtedly, a small organization cannot enjoy the direct benefits of a MAC model due to the higher security, complexity, and costs that are involved which may eventually lead to slower processes, something smaller organizations are usually not in favor of. There are, however, some organizations that aim at higher-than-usual security and can tolerate higher costs. These are larger organizations like banks, military, and government.

Role-Based Access Control (RBAC)

In contrast to the other two models, the RBAC model assigns rights and permissions to specific roles instead of individual users. In other words, it's a method for controlling what users can do within a company's IT systems by assigning one or more roles to each user and by providing each role with different permissions.

Tip   The RBAC model adds an extra layer of abstraction that simplifies the access control governance and the underlying administration.

Now, let's see how that plays out in practice with a quick example. Suppose Sally, Mary, and John are engineering managers in your department. That being said, they should be assigned to the role of Engineering Manager, which grants access to management files. Later, when Sally realizes that management isn't for her and decides to pursue a career in marketing and moves from the engineering department, revoking her engineering manager role would be enough.

Note   Applying this approach to an organization with thousands of employees and hundreds of roles can help you see the direct benefits and convenience RBAC can offer.

From DAC to MAC to RBAC, we've come a long way to discover an ACM that fits our challenging security needs in the 21st century. In this section, we made an introduction to the authorization concepts, the way it works in practice (ACL), and the several MAC models that could help you implement it in your organization. Let's now have a closer look at what makes RBAC so unique, why RBAC is important, its benefits, and what does it mean for the greater Jakarta EE ecosystem.

RBAC (Role-Based Access Control)

Role-based access control (RBAC) is a security paradigm whereby users are granted access to resources based on their role in the company.

Benefits of RBAC

An efficient implementation of an RBAC model can be proved beneficial for both your team and the entire organization. The following are a few benefits for both of them.

Benefits for your team:

- Requesting and granting access is a simplified, less error-prone process.

- Time-based access; users are granted access for a specific period.

- Easier and less time-consuming user access recertification process.

- Enhanced ownership in the form of a delegation model.

Benefits for the organization:

- Increased employee productivity.

- Reduced costs, complexity, and customer support.

- "Insider threat" attacks are less likely to happen.

- Increased security.

RBAC – Key Principles

Again, the RBAC model is all about users, groups, and the mapping of users to specific groups so that they can only access the content they are permitted to access.

Tip   In access control models, you will often see the terms *subject* and *object* being used in examples or to better facilitate a concept's explanation. The analogy you can bring to help yourself demystify these two terms is their role in grammar: a *subject* is someone who can act, for example, a user or an application. Similarly, an *object* is something that an action has effect upon, for example, a document or a directory.

RBAC-based systems are characterized by three basic principles (of course, individual organizations may apply some tailor-made adjustments according to their policies and infrastructure, but the main principles are profound):

- Role assignment: A subject cannot utilize any permissions unless it selects a role or is assigned one.

- Role authorization: A subject's active role must be authorized; in other words, you cannot just assign yourself to a role – an authorization process needs to precede that.

- Permission authorization: A subject cannot utilize any permissions unless the specified permission is authorized for its active role.

Caution   Implementing an RBAC model may become a challenging exercise, particularly in large organizations, as it requires you to define all the existing roles in your organization and decide which resources employees having that role should be granted access to.

How to Implement RBAC in Five Simple Steps

1. Define the resources you offer to your users.

2. Map roles to resources.

3. Create security groups for each one of the available roles.

4. Assign users to existing roles.

5. Register groups to access control lists.

RBAC in Jakarta EE

Let's now see how all that plays out in the broader context of Jakarta EE.

As we discussed earlier, a simple application walkthrough mainly comprises the following steps:

1. An application developer writes code so that a web application can prompt for a username and a password. We discussed the various methods of authentication earlier.

2. The application developer configures security for the deployed application using metadata annotations or the deployment descriptor file.

3. The server administrator arranges authorized users and groups in the server of choice.

4. The component responsible for the application deployment maps the application's security roles to users, groups, and principals defined in the server of choice .

Users, Groups, and Roles

Jakarta EE facilitates the RBAC access control model by using users, groups, and roles.

Nowadays, the vast majority of web applications will prompt for a username and a password before granting access to a protected resource. When users enter their username and password, these are passed to the server, which either authenticates the user and returns the protected resource as a response or denies access to the protected resource if the user cannot be authenticated.

In modern applications, authorized users are assigned to roles. In this particular scenario, the role assigned to the application user must be mapped to a principal or group specified in the application server, as shown in Figure 2-7.

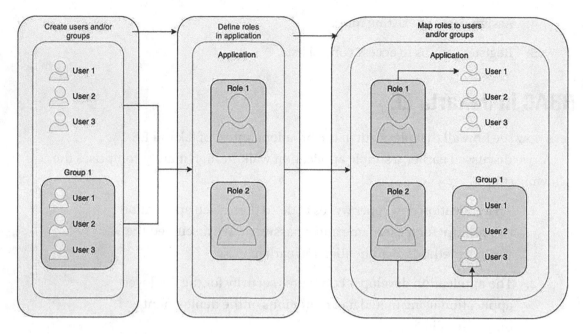

Figure 2-7. *Users, groups, and roles*

So, what's with users, groups, and roles?

What Is a User?

We define as a *user* a physical entity (person) or application program identity that has been defined in a Jakarta EE server (GlassFish, Payara, etc.). A *user* may have been assigned a set of roles that entitle them to access specific resources (protected by those roles) in a given application or system.

A Jakarta EE user does not differ from an OS user, as both types serve physical entities (people like you and me). Nonetheless, these two types should not be confused, as the Jakarta EE server authentication service has no particular knowledge of the username and password it's been provided during the login phase to the operating system – it's independent of the security mechanism of the OS.

What Is a Group?

A *group* is a set of authenticated users classified by common traits (such as job title and subscription package). For example, your organization's developers might belong to the DEVELOPERS groups, with the back enders also belonging to the BACKENDDEV group.

Tip   Classifying users into groups simplifies your governance policy as managing a group's permissions takes less time than an entire organization's employees list.

Caution   A group has a different scope from a role. The former is designated for the entire server (GlassFish, Payara, etc.), whereas the latter is only associated with a specific application of a server.

What Is a Role?

A role is a clearly defined set of abilities or permissions to access a particular set of resources within a corporate system or a web application.

Roles are generic and not tailored to any specific employee within an organization; for example, as a developer, you wouldn't receive permissions set up exclusively for your account. Instead, you would be assigned the "developer" role with all the underlying permissions that come with it, such as the ability to download and install software from the web.

Tip   Think of a role as a key that can open a lock. Dozens of people might have a copy of the key, yet the lock doesn't care about who you are, but only that you have the right key.

Digital Certificates

It is a common belief that technology thrives nowadays. Communication has improved significantly, but as we can remember from Albert Einstein, every technological improvement could be used both for helping and for harming humanity.

Back to our example with Alice and Bob, once Alice and Bob have authenticated themselves and started exchanging messages back and forth, how could they keep being sure their messages are neither eavesdropped nor falsified or tampered with? How could Alice be sure that she's communicating with Bob? Here's where digital certificates can come to the rescue.

What Is a Digital Certificate

Think of a digital certificate as a digital passport for an Internet address. When you show your passport to a higher authority, you actually provide some information about your identity; once the higher authority is able to verify your identity, you then may be granted access to sensitive information. The same goes for your digital certificate: a higher authority (maybe a certificate authority that we'll see later on) will not grant you access to any restricted resources unless it's able to verify your identity.

Note   A digital certificate is also known as a public key certificate. These terms are used interchangeably throughout this book.

Tip   Remember at the beginning of this chapter that we talked about the key principles of security? Digital certificates make sure those principles are held tight during communication between two different entities. Also, remember when we talked about authentication? Digital certificates are the means we use to verify a caller's entity. That is, we use them for authentication purposes.

Introduction to TLS

So how do digital certificates work after all? First of all, it is important to know that to be able to hold up to the Internet communications, we need to have those seven key security principles in place if we want to be safe on the Internet. For our web browser to communicate safely with other browsers or web servers, we need some protocol that allows authentication, encryption, and decryption of data sent over the Internet, such as TLS.

Note   TLS stands for Transport Layer Security, and it's the standard technology for keeping an Internet connection secure by safeguarding any sensitive data that is being sent between two systems, preventing criminals from reading and modifying any information transferred, including personal details. We'll dive into its workings in Chapter 6.

Note   Digital certificates are most commonly used for initializing secure TLS connections between web browsers and web servers.

TLS is based on public-key cryptography and utilizes key pairs. The *key pairs* concept uses two asymmetric keys to establish trust and privacy in transactions: the *public key* and the *private key*. The private key to be kept secret is used to encrypt the hash value of a document, whereas the public key can only be used for decryption and matches only one private key. It can be publicly retrieved and is often sent with the message.

Caution   As a rule of thumb, it is good to mention that no web server can use TLS unless they can provide a valid certificate for each one of the associated external interfaces or IPs that accept secure connections.

Supposedly, a signer wants to send an encrypted document using TLS, as depicted in Figure 2-8. It first computes the hash value of the document (*hash*), which it then encrypts using its private key. The signer has now generated a digitally signed document that can be safely transmitted over the network. Once the digitally signed document reaches its destination, the recipient decrypts its encrypted value using the server's public key (sent with the message). Moreover, it computes its own hash value of the document and then compares it to the decrypted one. If the two values match, the signature is valid, and the recipient (client/verifier) can trust the signature's authenticity.

Note   Browser/server communication uses a slightly different (somewhat inverted) mechanism to ensure encrypted communication, which is probably the most common use case in Jakarta EE as you'll learn in the next few chapters.

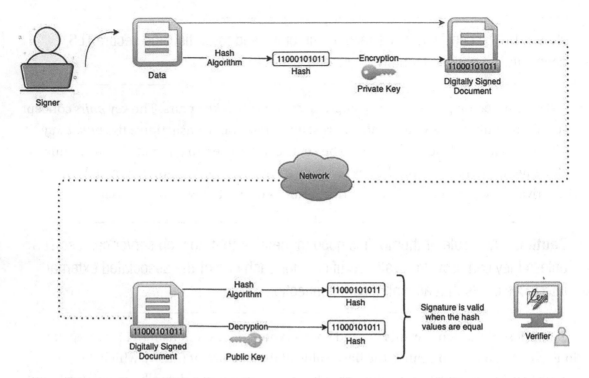

Figure 2-8. *Signing process*

Caution   TLS originates from SSL, which used to be considered a trustworthy protocol for Internet communications for almost two decades until when security researchers published a POODLE attack in 2011 that rendered SSL 2.0 unusable. Many browsers still use SSL, which isn't a best practice anymore. Consult Chapter 6 to see how you can configure TLS in your application.

Tip   Digital certificates are used with HTTPS to authenticate web clients. The HTTPS service of most web servers will not run unless a digital certificate has been installed. In Chapter 6, we'll see how we can create digital certificates.

Who Can Issue Certificates?

Depending on your case, you can decide either to self-sign a certificate or ask a trusted authority to do so.

Self-Signing a Certificate

Sometimes, authentication is not a concern; for example, an administrator might simply want to ensure that data being transmitted and received by the server is private and cannot be snooped on by anyone eavesdropping on the connection. In such cases, you can save the time and expenses involved in obtaining a CA certificate by simply using a self-signed certificate.

Certificate Authority

The vast majority of digital certificates are issued by a *certificate authority* (CA). CAs are trusted third parties that are entitled by the government to issue digital certificates to individuals. Individual entities like you and me can benefit from using digital certificates issued by CAs as these can extend our trustworthiness.

How does a CA issue a certificate? Figure 2-9 shows a simple walkthrough to help you further understand this process.

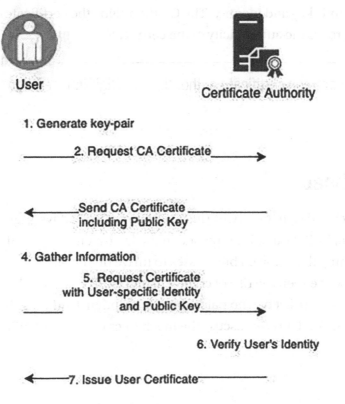

Figure 2-9. *Requesting a certificate from a CA*

- Sally generates her public/private key pair herself or receives one from her organization.

- Sally applies to the CA organization to request a certificate of their server.

- The CA responds to Sally by sending her its Certificate, which contains its public key and its digital signature (signed by them using their private key) and asks Sally for some personal information (e.g., email address, date of birth, full name, or even fingerprints) to verify her identity.

- Sally gathers the necessary information and sends it along with a certificate request that contains CA's public key that Sally earlier has received.

- The CA receives Sally's certificate request, verifies her identity, and generates a certificate for her. This certificate contains, among others, her public key and identity. The CA then signs the certificate, which now proves the authenticity of the certificate.

Note   A few common certificate authorities are DigiSign, VeriSign, DigiCert, and Symantec.

Looking Ahead

In the past, only hand signatures were legally binding. Nowadays, digital signatures are too. For example, in 2000, a law has passed in the UK that made digital signatures legally binding, something that allowed businesses to thrive on the web.

Since then, we've seen the rise of cryptocurrencies like bitcoin. A cryptocurrency is fundamentally a secure list of who paid whom how much. Updating this list depends on digital signatures. We'll further discuss the mechanics of digital certificates in Chapter 6.

Authentication Mechanisms

This section describes the foundations of authentication mechanisms and how Jakarta EE simplifies them. We will have a look at what an authentication mechanism is, how it operates, and which authentication mechanisms are supported by the Jakarta EE platform.

What Is an Authentication Mechanism?

Nowadays, there is a need for safe modern applications more than ever. A web application may consist of several resources, public and restricted. For the former, a caller should be able to access their content without authenticating themselves. For the latter, though, a caller has to prove to the application that they are who they claim they are through an authentication process.

That being said, for the restricted resources, the application prompts the caller to provide some proof of identity (e.g., login credentials) before it can serve the resource. Once the user has provided their proof of identity, the application verifies it, and in case it's valid, it continues with the authorization process where it determines whether the caller has enough permissions to access the requested resources. Authentication mechanisms play an important role in this process, so let's start unveiling their concepts by trying to define them first.

As an *authentication mechanism*, we define the mechanism that helps us implement an authentication process. Taking a close-up in the preceding steps, it is the authentication mechanism that requests from the caller its login credentials, and after collecting them, it passes them on to an identity store, which performs a lookup on its database to match the provided credentials with a known user (identity). Upon a successful match, the authentication mechanism uses the matched identity to construct an authenticated *Subject*. On the contrary, when there is no match found, the authentication mechanism reports a failed authentication, and the caller is not logged in and is not given authorization.

What Does an Authentication Mechanism Specify?

Following the aforementioned definition, a user authentication mechanism specifies three main things:

- How a user gains access to a web resource

- For basic authentication, the specific realm where the user will be authenticated in

- For form-based authentication, any additional attributes

Note   In basic authentication, you will often see the term *realm* being used, so let's briefly define this concept.

You can think of a realm as an informative string that the user passes along in the WWW-Authenticate header. The realm value in conjunction with the canonical root URL of the server being accessed defines the protection space and should not be confused with a named identity store.

Caution   For applications where an authentication mechanism is in place, the very first requirement is that the user is authenticated before granted access to any restricted resource.

Jakarta EE Authentication Mechanisms

The Jakarta EE platform supports the following authentication mechanisms:

- Basic authentication

- Form-based authentication

- Custom form authentication

- Digest authentication

- Client authentication

Note   At this point, it is important to clarify how we came up with these five authentication mechanisms. Everything started with the Servlet specification, which specifies four authentication mechanisms: BASIC, FORM, DIGEST, and CLIENT-CERT. Later on, when the Jakarta Security API was developed, there was a clear need for BASIC and FORM authentication mechanisms to work the same as their BASIC and FORM counterparts in Servlet specification. That said, we can distinguish five authentication mechanisms overall, of which three come from the Jakarta Security API (BASIC, FORM, CUSTOM-FORM) and two from the Servlet Specification (DIGEST, CLIENT).

Now let's have a closer look at the main aspects of each one of the aforementioned authentication mechanisms.

Caution   Before authenticating a user, you have to configure a database of usernames, roles, and passwords on your web or application server.

Basic Authentication
What Is

Basic authentication is the default authentication when you don't specify any authentication mechanism.

How It Works

The web server requests a username and a password from the web client and verifies that both the username and the password are valid by comparing them against a database of authorized users in the specified or default realm.

In the following, you can see the sequence of actions that occur when basic authentication is used:

1. A web client requests access to a protected recourse.

2. The web server returns a dialog box that requests the username and password.

3. The web client submits the username and password to the server.

4. The server authenticates the user in the specified realm and returns the requested resource upon successful authentication.

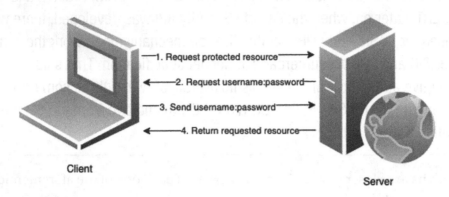

Figure 2-10. *Basic authentication*

How to Configure It

Annotation

```
package jakarta.security.enterprise.authentication.mechanism.http;

@Retention(RUNTIME)
@Target(TYPE)
public @interface BasicAuthenticationMechanismDefinition {

    /**
     * Name of realm that will be sent via the <code>WWW-Authenticate
     * </code> header.
     * <p>
     * Note that this realm name <b>does not</b> couple a named
     * identity store
     * configuration to the authentication mechanism.
     *
     * @return Name of realm
     */
    String realmName() default "";
}
```

Web.xml

```
<login-config>
    <auth-method>BASIC</auth-method>
    <realm-name>eefoundationsbasicrealm</realm-name>
</login-config>
```

Form-Based Authentication

What Is

An authentication mechanism where the user is presented with an editable form to fill in their login credentials to log into some service or system.

How It Works

The developer controls the *look and feel* of the login screens by customizing the login screen and error pages that an HTTP browser presents to the user.

Let's go through the sequence of actions that occur when form-based authentication is used:

1. A web client requests access to a protected resource.

2. If the client is not authenticated yet, the server redirects them to a login page.

3. The client fills in their username and password and submits the login form to the server.

4. The server attempts to authenticate the user.

    a. Upon successful authentication, the authenticated user's principal is checked (section "Java Authentication and Authorization Service (JAAS)" in Chapter 6 explains how) to ensure that it belongs to a role that is authorized to access the resource. If the user is authorized, the server redirects the client to the resource by using the stored URL.

    b. Upon failed authentication, the client is redirected to an error page.

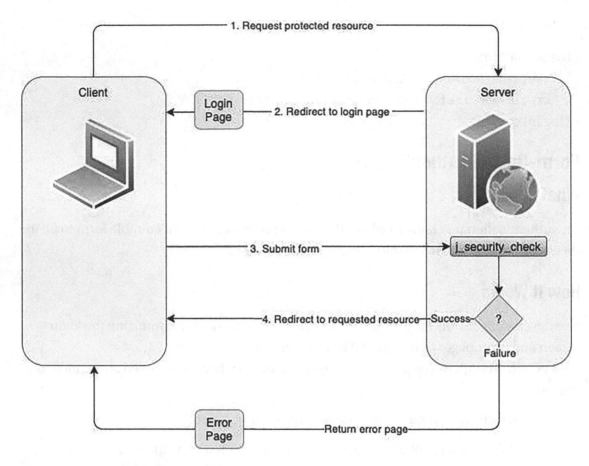

Figure 2-11. *Form-based authentication*

Caution   For a form-based login, be sure to maintain sessions using cookies or TLS session information.

How to Configure It

HTML Form

When working with form-based authentication, be sure to mark your form's action as *j_security_check*. Thus, the login form will work regardless of which resource it is intended for. Moreover, explicitly declaring this action means for the server that it will not have to specify the action field of the outbound form itself. Here's a code snippet that shows how the HTML form should look like:

Code

```
<form method="POST" action="j_security_check">
<input type="text" name="j_username">
<input type="password" name="j_password">
</form>
```

Annotation

```
package jakarta.security.enterprise.authentication.mechanism.http;

@Retention(RUNTIME)
@Target(TYPE)
public @interface FormAuthenticationMechanismDefinition {

    @Nonbinding
    LoginToContinue loginToContinue();
}
```

Web.xml

```
<login-config>
        <auth-method>FORM</auth-method>
        <form-login-config>
        <form-login-page>/login.xhtml</form-login-page>
        <form-error-page>/error.xhtml</form-error-page>
        </form-login-config>
</login-config>
```

Digest Authentication

What Is

An authentication mechanism similar to the basic authentication, which, however, does not send the password in cleartext. This authentication mechanism intends to avoid the most critical flaws of basic authentication.

How It Works

Just like basic authentication, digest authentication authenticates a user based on a username and a password without providing any encryption of the message. It applies a hash function to the username and password before sending them over the network. That is, passwords are not sent over the wire here, yet it requires cleartext password equivalents to be available to the authenticating container so that it can validate received authenticators by calculating the expected digest.

Application walkthrough:

1. A client requests access to a protected resource.

2. The server replies with a nonce and a 401 authentication request.

3. Client sends back a response that contains a checksum (by default, the MD5 checksum) of the username, the password, the realm, the given nonce value, the requested URI, and the HTTP method: *generate_md5_key(nonce, username, realm, URI, password_given_by_user_to_browser))*.

4. The server takes the username, the realm, and the requested *URI*, and it looks up the password for the given username. When found, it generates its own version of let's say *generate_md5_key(nonce, username, realm, URI, HTTP method, password-for-this-user-in-my-db)*.

5. The server then compares the output of *generate_md5()* that it got with the one the client sent, and

   a. If they match, the client sent the correct password.

   b. If they don't match, the password sent was wrong.

How to Configure It

Web.xml

```
<login-config>
        <auth-method>DIGEST</auth-method>
        <realm-name>eefoundationsdigestrealm</realm-name>
</login-config>
```

Client Authentication

What Is

An authentication mechanism where the client is securely granted access to a server by exchanging a digital certificate.

Note   You will often come across the term "public key certificate" instead of "digital certificate." Both terms are equivalent, serve the same purpose, and are used interchangeably throughout this book.

Tip   You can think of a public key certificate as the digital equivalent of a passport.

How It Works

First of all, it is important to stress that *client authentication* is a more secure method of authentication than either *basic* or *form-based authentication*. Its main advantage is that it uses HTTP over SSL (HTTPS), in which the server authenticates the client using the client's public key certificate.

Caution   While *client authentication* may be fine for intranet applications, it may not scale on the Internet because of the challenge of providing client certificates to thousands of users during their registration and revoking them during their de-registration.

Note   SSL technology provides data encryption, server authentication, message integrity, and optional client authentication for a TCP/IP connection.

The certificate is issued by a certificate authority (CA), which is a trusted organization and provides identification to a bearer.

How to Configure It

Web.xml

```
<login-config>
        <auth-method>CLIENT-CERT</auth-method>
</login-config>
```

Custom Form Authentication

What Is

Similar to the form-based authentication with the main difference here being in the continuation of the authentication dialog. So instead of posting back to the predefined *j_security_check* action of the form, the custom form authentication mechanism continues the authentication dialog by invoking *SecurityContext.authenticate()* with the credentials the application collected.

The rest of its concepts are pretty much the same as in form-based authentication, so you can refer back to the latter for the *How it works* and *Simple Application Walkthrough* parts.

How to Define It

```
@Retention(RUNTIME)
@Target(TYPE)
public @interface CustomFormAuthenticationMechanismDefinition {

    @Nonbinding
    LoginToContinue loginToContinue();
}
```

Identity Stores

In this section, you will get introduced to the concepts of identity stores and their importance to security. Also, you will have a brief look at a basic setup of an identity store in Jakarta EE, which will be extended to an in-depth analysis later on in Chapter 5.

What Is an Identity Store?

An *identity store* is a component that stores application-specific identity information for a set of users, such as usernames, groups, roles, group memberships, permissions, and credentials. Occasionally, it may also be used for storing other information such as GUIDs (caller's globally unique identifiers) or other caller attributes.

Tip   To simplify the aforementioned definition, you can think of an identity store as a security-specific DAO (Data Access Object).

What Is the Purpose of an Identity Store?

The purpose of an *identity store* is to validate a caller's identity by accessing a caller's identity attributes. That is, an *identity store* provides access to user information and is required for authentication.

The four most important characteristics of an *identity store* are the following:

1. Provides access to user information

2. Required for authentication

3. Validates credentials

4. Retrieves group membership

Caution   An *identity store* can provide capabilities for authentication, authorization, or both.

Identity Store and Jakarta EE

The broader Jakarta EE ecosystem comprises several APIs to help you govern your web application's authentication (*Jakarta Authentication*, which we will examine in Chapter 3), authorization (*Jakarta Authorization*, which we will examine in Chapter 4), and security standards (*Jakarta Security*, which we will examine in Chapter 5). The Jakarta EE API specifies, among others, the *IdentityStore* interface, which provides an abstraction of an identity store.

Implementing the *IdentityStore* interface enables us as developers to interact with identity stores to authenticate users (i.e., validate their credentials) and to fetch caller groups.

We consider a good *IdentityStore* implementation that one which operates only on context level and is environment agnostic (will run the same way and will provide the same results regardless of the environment that it's ported and run into). That is, a good *IdentityStore* implementation caters a neat *{credentials in, caller data out}* function.

Caution   *IdentityStore* implementations aren't meant to interact with the caller directly nor should they attempt to inspect application state or request context.

IdentityStore – Theory of Operation

Now, let's take a quick look at the complete interface (without default behaviors; signatures only) and try to demystify its methods.

Code

```
public interface IdentityStore {

    enum ValidationType { VALIDATE, PROVIDE_GROUPS }

    CredentialValidationResult validate(Credential credential);

    Set<String> getCallerGroups(CredentialValidationResult
    validationResult);

    int priority();

    Set<ValidationType> validationTypes();
}
```

Note   You can find more about it in the GitHub repository of Jakarta EE Security API: `https://github.com/eclipse-ee4j/security-api`. We will cover the most important topics of it later on as well in Chapter 5.

The two most important methods of the *IdentityStore* interface are

- validate(Credential): Validates a *Credential*

- getCallerGroups(CredentialValidationResult): Fetches caller information

IdentityStore implementations can choose to handle either or both of these methods, depending on their capabilities and configuration. They can hint which of these two methods they handle by utilizing the set of values *validationTypes()* method comes with:

- VALIDATE: Indicates that it handles the *validate()* method

- PROVIDE_GROUPS: Indicates that it handles the *getCallerGroups()* method

- Both VALIDATE and PROVIDE_GROUPS: Indicates that it handles both methods

---

Note   At this point, you might have the feeling that this very setup of declaring capabilities is rather confusing, yet it was a conscious decision to facilitate that an *IdentityStore*'s configuration and implementation are self-governing. That means that an *IdentityStore* could be configured to support one or the other methods during a particular deployment yet it could be written to support both methods.

Validating Credentials

To determine whether a *Credential* is valid or not, you can use the *validate()* method, which, upon successful validation, returns information about the user identified by the *Credential*. An *IdentityStore* may choose not to implement this method as it's an optional one.

Code

```
CredentialValidationResult validate(Credential credential);
```

As you can see from the method's signature, a validation result is returned as a *CredentialValidationResult*, which allows methods to retrieve a validation result's status value and, upon successful validation, the ID of the store that validated the credential, the caller principal, the caller's unique ID in the identity store, and the caller's group memberships (if any).

Note   For a successful validation, only the caller principal is required to be present.

But what's under the hood of *CredentialValidationResult*? The following is the full class's overview containing only the method signatures:

```
public class CredentialValidationResult {

    public enum Status { NOT_VALIDATED, INVALID, VALID }

    public Status getStatus();

    public String getIdentityStoreId();

    public CallerPrincipal getCallerPrincipal();

    public String getCallerDn();

    public String getCallerUniqueId();

    public Set<String> getCallerGroups();
}
```

To begin with, there are three different status values: *NOT_VALIDATED*, *INVALID*, and *VALID*. What do they mean?

- NOT_VALIDATED: Validation was not attempted, because the *IdentityStore* does not handle the supplied *Credential* type.

- INVALID: Validation failed. The supplied *Credential* was invalid or the corresponding user was not found in the user store.

- VALID: Validation succeeded and the user is authenticated. The caller principal and group (if any) are available *only* with this result status.

Moving forward to the rest of *CredentialValidationResult*'s methods, the identity store ID, caller DN, and caller unique ID aim to help you implement an *IdentityStore* by cooperating with the *validate()* and *getCallerGroups()*. They can be used to ensure that the correct caller groups are returned from *getCallerGroups()* even in environments where the caller's principal name alone is insufficient to uniquely identify the correct user account.

Note   The Credential interface is a generic interface that is capable of representing any kind of token or user credential. An *IdentityStore* implementation can support multiple concrete *Credential* types, where concrete *Credential* is an implementation of the *Credential* interface that represents a particular type of credential. That is possible by implementing the *validate(Credential)* method and testing the type of the *Credential* that's passed in.

The *IdentityStore* interface provides a default implementation of the *validate(Credential)* method that delegates to a method that can handle the provided *Credential* type, assuming such a method is implemented by the IdentityStore:

```
default CredentialValidationResult validate(Credential credential) {
    try {
        return CredentialValidationResult.class.cast(
            MethodHandles.lookup()
                .bind(this, "validate",
                    methodType(CredentialValidationResult.class,
                                credential.getClass())))
                .invoke(credential));
    } catch (NoSuchMethodException e) {
        return NOT_VALIDATED_RESULT;
    } catch (Throwable e) {
        throw new IllegalStateException(e);
    }
}
```

That being said, *validate(Credential)* would actually delegate to the following method of ExampleIdentityStore if passed a *UsernamePasswordCredential*:

```
public class ExampleIdentityStore implements IdentityStore {

    public CredentialValidationResult validate(
        UsernamePasswordCredential usernamePasswordCredential) {
        // Implementation ...
        return new CredentialValidationResult(...);
    }
}
```

Retrieving Caller Information

The *getCallerGroups()* method retrieves the set of groups associated with a validated caller. It's an optional method that an *IdentityStore* may choose not to implement.

```
Set<String> getCallerGroups(CredentialValidationResult validationResult);
```

This method supports aggregation of identity stores, where one identity store is used to authenticate users and one or more other stores are used to retrieve additional groups.

Tip   In such cases, querying identity stores without validating the caller's credentials against the stores is vital.

Declaring Capabilities

There are still a few methods of the IdentityStore interface that we didn't discuss, methods that an implementation can use to declare its capabilities and ordinal priority:
    Code

```
enum ValidationType { VALIDATE, PROVIDE_GROUPS }

Set<ValidationType> DEFAULT_VALIDATION_TYPES =
        EnumSet.of(VALIDATE, PROVIDE_GROUPS);
```

```
default int priority() {
    return 100;
}

default Set<ValidationType> validationTypes() {
    return DEFAULT_VALIDATION_TYPES;
}
```

Let's have a closer look at each one of them:

- priority(): Allows an IdentityStore to be configured with an ordinal number indicating the order in which it should be consulted when multiple *IdentityStores* are present. Lower numbers represent higher priority; that is, an *IdentityStore* with a lower priority value is called before an *IdentityStore* with a higher priority value.

- validationTypes(): Returns a set of enum constants of type ValidationType, indicating the purposes for which an IdentityStore should be used:

  - *VALIDATE*, to indicate that it handles *validate()*

  - *PROVIDE_GROUPS*, to indicate that it handles *getCallerGroups()*

  - Both *VALIDATE* and *PROVIDE_GROUPS*, to indicate that it handles both methods

That being said, an *IdentityStore*'s validation types determine three things, whether the store is used for

- Authentication only: Any group data it returns must be ignored

- Providing groups only: Not used for authentication, but only to obtain group data for a caller that was authenticated by a different *IdentityStore*

- Both authentication and any group data it may return

How to Validate a User Credential

As we've seen earlier, we can use an *HttpAuthenticationMechanism* (or other caller) for authenticating a user; however, the former should not interact directly with an *IdentityStore* but instead invoke the *IdentityStoreHandler* to validate credentials. It is the *IdentityStoreHandler* then that invokes on the *IdentityStore*. So what is the

IdentityStoreHandler interface all about? It basically defines a mechanism for invoking on *IdentityStore* to validate a user credential and is considered to be a safer way to authenticate a user.

Note   A default *IdentityStoreHandler* implementation is supplied by the container, but you can also write your own custom implementation

---

Identity stores usually have a 1-to-1 correlation with a data source such as a relational database, LDAP directory, file system, or other similar resource. Hence, implementations of the *IdentityStore* interface use data source-specific APIs to discover authorization data (roles, permissions, etc.), such as JDBC, File IO, Hibernate or JPA, or any other Data Access API.

Looking Ahead

In the first two chapters, you've been introduced to some historical background that led us to Jakarta EE Security and the most important foundations of enterprise security. Time for action, isn't it?! This chapter concludes the introduction of this book, so let's dive into the mechanics of the Jakarta EE Security by starting with a close-up on the Jakarta Authentication API.

CHAPTER 3

Jakarta Authentication

In this chapter, we'll be looking at the Jakarta Authentication API/SPI, which obviously has "authentication" as its central topic. In the previous chapter, we learned authentication is about proving that you are who you say you are. Jakarta Authentication is a lower-level API and as such the underpinning of higher-level APIs in the Jakarta security model. Knowledge of Jakarta Authentication helps one to deepen the understanding of how security works in Jakarta EE, but it's not strictly necessary. The more practical oriented reader may wish to skim this chapter.

What Is Jakarta Authentication?

To answer this question, let's first take a look at the official scope of this API/SPI:

> Jakarta Authentication defines a general low-level SPI for authentication mechanisms, which are controllers that interact with a caller and a container's environment to obtain the caller's credentials, validate these, and pass an authenticated identity (such as name and groups) to the container.

> Jakarta Authentication consists of several profiles, with each profile telling how a specific container (such as Jakarta Servlet) can integrate with- and adapt to this SPI.

Let's digest this scope a little.

First of all, it says Jakarta Authentication is "a general low-level SPI." An SPI, or Service Provider Interface, is a special kind of interface intended to be implemented by the user to extend a framework or application. In this case, to extend the Jakarta Security system. It's roughly analogous to the concept of a plug-in or an extension, which readers may know from systems such as IDEs or web browsers. Jakarta Authentication mostly provides SPIs (interfaces to be implemented) and very few APIs (interfaces intended to be called by an application). The SPIs are also "low level," meaning specifically in the context of Jakarta EE that implementations of them are not beans and are not eligible for

© Arjan Tijms, Teo Bais, and Werner Keil 2022
A. Tijms et al., *The Definitive Guide to Security in Jakarta EE*, https://doi.org/10.1007/978-1-4842-7945-8_3

injection or for decoration. The Jakarta Authentication SPIs are also "general" since they don't refer to any specific Jakarta technology (like Servlet or REST).

The most important part of the scope declaration is that Jakarta Authentication is "for authentication mechanisms." An authentication mechanism is a distinct and primary concept in authentication, even though it's not always directly recognized, or directly recognized by this term. We'll be looking at what an authentication mechanism is in more detail right hereafter, but for now, the scope gives a good initial explanation; they are "controllers that interact with a caller and a container's environment to obtain the caller's credentials, validate these, and pass an authenticated identity (such as name and groups) to the container."

The next part of the scope declaration may need some explanation as well, as it's a recurring source of confusion; "Jakarta Authentication consists of several profiles, with each profile telling how a specific container (such as Jakarta Servlet) can integrate with- and adapt to this SPI."

What this means is that somewhat uniquely within Jakarta EE, Jakarta Authentication describes how other APIs should behave when it comes to authentication. This is different from, say, Jakarta Faces, which merely builds on top of Jakarta Servlet by using its APIs. Jakarta Authentication asks, for instance, Servlet implementations to authenticate in a certain way and use the interfaces provided by Jakarta Authentication at certain moments.

As we discussed previously, the interfaces of Jakarta Authentication itself are technology neutral; they don't contain any references to, for example, Servlet. Instead, the Jakarta Authentication specification contains chapters for several technologies that describe in detail how these technologies should behave. Such a chapter is called a "profile." The profile describing Servlet is called the "Servlet Container Profile."

Next to Servlet, there's a profile for SOAP (Jakarta XML Web Services), aptly called the SOAP Profile. Profiles for Jakarta Messaging and remote enterprise beans (RMI/IIOP) were planned but never came to fruition. With remote enterprise beans, and factually, all of enterprise beans, being deemphasized, it's unlikely we'll ever see an enterprise beans profile. Even more so, with SOAP being deemphasized as well, the Servlet Container Profile is essentially the only profile commonly used. This does beg the question whether it's really necessary to keep Jakarta Authentication around in its current form. It might be better to just merge it into Servlet eventually.

Finally, Jakarta Authentication defines both a server and a client model. The client model is for adding security parameters to a request, for example, adding username and password in a header, while the server model is for validating security for an incoming request, for example, checking that the username and password headers are present and valid.

Although the concept of a request client has been made popular by Jakarta REST and given an extra boost with the Rest Client for MicroProfile, the adoption of Jakarta Authentication for client concerns has been practically zero. Also, though SOAP is still in active use, interest for it is strongly waning. For those reasons, we'll mainly look at the Servlet Container Profile and the server part of Jakarta Authentication.

Jakarta Authentication in Jakarta EE

The concrete security APIs in Jakarta EE are divided into three main APIs:

1. Jakarta Authentication

2. Jakarta Authorization

3. Jakarta Security

These three are largely designed to work together to provide an integrated security solution for Jakarta EE that transparently backs the declarative security model that was discussed in the previous chapters.

In essence, Jakarta Authentication, Authorization, and Security are the standard SPIs and APIs for the functionality that in early Jakarta EE versions was strictly in the vendor's realm.

Jakarta EE supports a hybrid model, where an application or its server/runtime can be configured to either use the standard APIs and associated configuration, or those that are specific to a server or runtime. This is depicted in the following image:

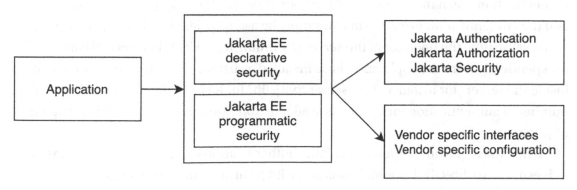

Besides using the standard interfaces or those from the vendor, Jakarta EE implementations typically offer a choice of shipping any custom versions of the various security artifacts (like the aforementioned authentication mechanism) within the application archive, installing them separately on the server, or using a default available one in a way that's transparent to the application. Note that the exact options depend on the specific implementation being used (like GlassFish).

Consider the following diagram:

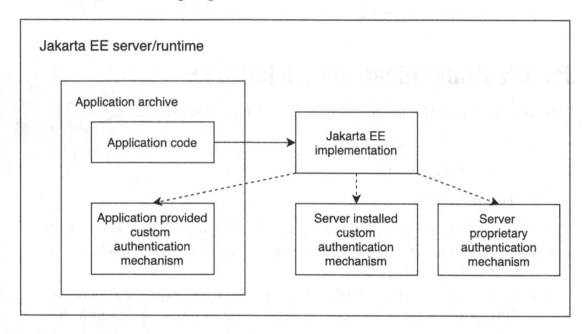

This diagram depicts a typical Jakarta EE scenario, where an application archive (a .war) is deployed to a Jakarta EE server. Such an application archive typically contains normal business code but, in addition to that, can contain, for instance, a custom authentication mechanism. Note that there are no special packaging requirements, and the authentication mechanism can simply be a single class inside any package. At the same time the operator of the server (assuming it's an installed server) can independently from the application have installed a custom authentication mechanism inside the server (for instance, in a [server root]/lib/ folder). Finally, there will be a number of authentication mechanisms available from the server by default (Jakarta EE requires several).

When the application interacts with the authentication mechanism in some way, it doesn't do so directly. Instead, it interacts with Jakarta EE in some way, and then the Jakarta EE implementation in its turn will invoke said authentication mechanism. This allows for a high degree of flexibility; self-sufficient applications can be deployed as is, while at the same time it allows for the integration of third-party applications into, say, an intranet, integrating with its existing security setup.

To put Jakarta Authentication more into perspective, let's expand the previous diagram to show the actual major interfaces and classes from each API, in relation to an implementation. For the implementation, we used Piranha Cloud, a new and, at the moment of writing, not-yet-certified Jakarta EE implementation. With respect to Jakarta EE Security, Piranha Cloud stands out; as one of the few products out there, it provides security by directly leveraging and providing implementations of the Jakarta security APIs. In contrast, many other products either layer the Jakarta security APIs on top of an existing, native, security system, or they provide implementations of it as a parallel option.

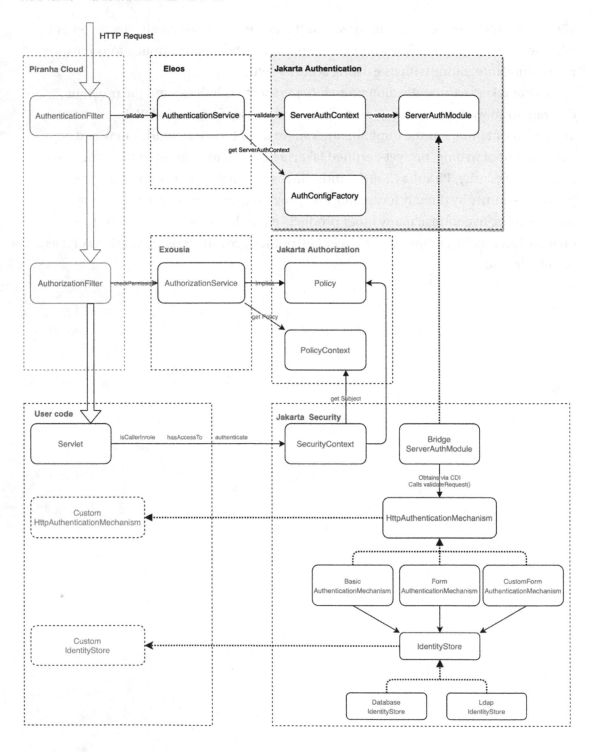

This diagram depicts the handling of an HTTP request by the Servlet container (Piranha Cloud here) and how it invokes the stand-alone Jakarta Authentication implementation called Eleos during that request.

The diagram for now serves only as an overview, and we'll be looking at the various parts in more detail throughout this book.

The Authentication Mechanism

We mentioned the term "authentication mechanism" a couple of times previously and said that it was the most important part of Jakarta Authentication. We'll now take a closer look at what an authentication mechanism exactly is.

An authentication mechanism is somewhat like a controller in the well-known MVC pattern; it's the entity that interacts with the caller (typically a human user, but could be an automated script as well) via some kind of view to collect credentials on the one hand and with the model (business logic) to validate these credentials on the other hand.

In this setup, an authentication mechanism knows about the environment that the caller uses to communicate with the server, which is these days mostly HTTP but could be something else like RMI/IIOP. An authentication mechanism specifically knows, in the case of HTTP, about URLs to redirect or forward to, or about response headers to send to the client. It also knows about the data coming back, such as cookies, request headers, and post data.

On the other hand, an authentication mechanism in this "MVC" setup knows nothing about the specific technology that is used to validate credentials and return attributes associated with a caller. Such technology could include things like a database, a simple file on the file system, an LDAP server, etc.; knowledge about this is encapsulated by the "identity store" (the model).

This is depicted in the following diagram:

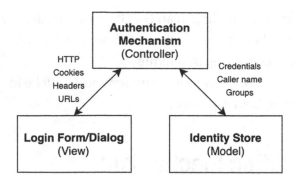

We'll now present a few practical examples of authentication mechanisms.

The Basic Authentication Mechanism

One of the simplest, dare we say, most basic authentication mechanisms is the basic authentication mechanism. This mechanism corresponds to HTTP basic access and is specified by RFC 7617.

In terms of authentication mechanisms as discussed here, this works as follows:

1. The basic authentication mechanism (*the controller*) listens to HTTP requests, roughly like a Servlet filter.

2. When invoked, it checks the request for the "Authorization" HTTP header and checks whether its value starts with "Basic."

3. If that header is not present and if the resource to be accessed is protected, the authentication mechanism

   a. Sets the "WWW-Authenticate" header with value "Basic realm="[x]"", where [x] is an opaque identifier for informational purposes

   b. Sets the response status to 401 (unauthorized)

4. The user agent (e.g., a browser or a command line util like wget or curl) can now display a dialog (*the view*) to the user asking for a username and a password.

5. After the caller provides this data and okays the dialog, step 2 is executed again.

6. With the header now present, the username and password are extracted from it.

7. The authentication mechanism invokes the identity store to validate the username and password (together "the credentials").

8. If the identity store asserts that the credentials are valid, a caller name(*) and zero or more groups are taken from the identity store and returned to the container.

9. The container can now set the caller name and groups as the "authenticated identity"** (also known as "the current user") and continue processing the HTTP request.

* – Typically, the identity store would return the same name here, but it could be a different one. We'll see later that returning a caller name will be essential for credentials such as tokens that don't directly carry a user/caller name.

** – It's not defined where this authenticated identity (name and group information) is exactly stored. This is server/runtime specific. In practice, it's almost always a thread-local though, although in some cases the Subject is used for this as well. The Subject is then passed on in internal invocation calls. Some servers or runtimes essentially do both; the data is stored in the Subject, which is in turn stored in a thread-local.

We've seen here that the authentication mechanism interacts with HTTP by looking at the request headers and setting response headers and a response status code. We didn't see the authentication mechanism interacting with things like LDAP or a database. Instead, it interacted with the abstract concept of the identity store.

One thing that this authentication mechanism does not do is keeping track of whether it has sent out the "WWW-Authenticate" header before. That is, it does not keep track of the state of the interaction with the caller (which we call the "authentication dialog"). A caller can therefore send the "Authorization" without being asked for it and trigger authentication that way. This is called preemptive authentication.

Furthermore, the user agent sends the credentials again with every request, and the authentication mechanism therefore also reauthenticates every request. Specifically, it does not keep any session to store the authenticated identity. For performance reasons, many systems do use some kind of cache.

The Form Authentication Mechanism

Contrary to the basic authentication mechanism, the form authentication mechanism is fairly complex from a technical point of view. It keeps track of the state of the authentication dialog, which is typically done via the HTTP session. It also remembers the authenticated identity, again typically in the HTTP session, and it's capable of redoing (repeating) the original request after authentication has taken place.

The following lists what the form authentication mechanism typically does. We simplify things a little bit by omitting the sequence of actions that happen when a user explicitly clicks on a "login" button and focus on what happens when a user directly accesses a protected URL.

Note that even so the following steps are still fairly detailed. Exact knowledge of these steps is typically not needed but is mostly presented here to illustrate what a more complex authentication mechanism can do.

1. The form authentication mechanism (the controller) listens to HTTP requests, roughly like a Servlet filter.

2. When invoked, it checks whether there's an authenticated identity in the session and if so effectively returns this to the container. The container can then set the caller name and groups as the "authenticated identity" and continue processing the HTTP request (ending this sequence early).

3. The authentication mechanism checks if the request is to an initial protected URL, meaning it checks whether this is the first request in the authentication dialog. It can do this by, for example, checking whether there's an http session and if it contains a "saved request."

4. If we're indeed on an initial request, the mechanism now

    a. Saves the request data to the session, meaning all cookies, all headers, all parameters, etc. (after this step, we now have state)

    b. Forwards or redirects to the URL of a login page

5. Steps 2 and 3 are now executed again, and since we're not on an initial protected URL anymore (there was a saved request), the mechanism checks whether we're handling the login page now; it can do this by, for example, checking whether there's a saved request, but no temporarily saved outcome from an identity store (see step 10.a).

6. If we're indeed handling the login, the mechanism now checks if the login code has requested the authenticated dialog to continue. For the Servlet Form mechanism, it would do this by checking whether the postback URL ends on "j_security_check" and contains request parameters "j_username" and "j_password".

7. As long as no request to continue authentication is received, the authentication mechanism indicates to the container it can continue to process the HTTP request. This would cause the login page (*the view*) to be displayed. Every new request in this state will repeat the previous steps.

8. When the request to continue authentication is received, the authentication mechanism extracts the credentials (in case of servlet, by taking the values from "j_username" and "j_password").

9. The authentication mechanism invokes the identity store to validate the username and password.

10. If the identity store asserts that the credentials are valid, the mechanism now

    a. Temporarily saves the outcome from the identity store

    b. Redirects to the original URL

    c. Takes a shortcut if we're already on the original URL

11. After the redirect, steps until 5 are repeated, but since there's the saved outcome from the identity store now, we don't go into step 6, but skip to the next one.

12. The authentication mechanism checks whether we're on the original URL after authentication has taken place. It can do this by, for example, checking whether we have both a saved request and a saved outcome from the identity store and checking whether the current URL matches the one in the saved request.

13. If we're indeed on this original URL after authentication, the mechanism now

a. Removes all previously saved data

b. Sets the authenticated identity in a place so step 2 can find it

c. Wraps the request to provide all the original request data again, such as the original cookies, headers, and parameters

d. Returns the wrapped request as well as the caller name and the zero or more groups from the identity store outcome to the container

14. The container can now set the caller name and groups as the "authenticated identity" and continue processing the HTTP request using the wrapped request that was provided by the authenticated mechanism (meaning that code, such as Filters or Servlets, doesn't see that there has been a number of redirects to the login page and back).

Jakarta Authentication's ServerAuthModule

The main artifact in Jakarta Authentication is an interface for the authentication mechanism, *jakarta.security.auth.message.module.ServerAuthModule*. It's shown here:

```
public interface ServerAuthModule extends ServerAuth {
  Class[] getSupportedMessageTypes();

  void initialize(
    MessagePolicy requestPolicy,
    MessagePolicy responsePolicy,
    CallbackHandler handler,
    Map options) throws AuthException;
}
```

It inherits from the *jakarta.security.auth.message.ServerAuth* interface, which looks as follows:

```
public interface ServerAuth {
  AuthStatus validateRequest(
    MessageInfo messageInfo,
    Subject clientSubject,
    Subject serviceSubject) throws AuthException;
```

```
  AuthStatus secureResponse(
    MessageInfo messageInfo,
    Subject serviceSubject) throws AuthException;

  void cleanSubject(
    MessageInfo messageInfo,
    Subject subject) throws AuthException;
}
```

We'll briefly discuss the methods next.

getSupportedMessageTypes is used to indicate for which profile of Jakarta Authentication the *ServerAuthModule* is usable. This is needed since, as mentioned before, the Jakarta Authentication interfaces are totally generic and don't themselves refer to any specific technology. There are only two outcomes supported here in the current version:

1. For Servlet:

   jakarta.servlet.http.HttpServletRequest,
   jakarta.servlet.http.HttpServletResponse

2. For SOAP:

   jakarta.xml.soap.SOAPMessage

The *initialize()* method is used to set various configuration options and the all-important *CallbackHandler*. This latter one is the primary means that the *ServerAuthModule* uses to communicate with the container. The *MessagePolicy* parameters, while theoretically SOAP agnostic, are in practice mostly used for SOAP indeed. We'll look at all of these parameters in more detail in the following text.

validateRequest() is the main method of the *ServerAuthModule*. This is the method that is invoked at the start of a request before any Filter or Servlet is called, or for the Servlet Container Profile following a call to *HttpServletRequest.authenticate()* (more details about that later). All the logic to actually authenticate takes place in this method.

secureResponse() is called at the very end of the request after all Servlets and Filters have been called. This method is essentially the opposite of the *validateRequest()* method. For Servlet environments, it's very rare to use this method. For SOAP, however, this is commonly used to encrypt or sign the response.

Finally, *cleanSubject()* is called for the Servlet Container Profile following a call to *HttpServletRequest.logout()*. This can be used to clear out any authentication state beyond that in the current request. For instance, if the authentication mechanism has set a cookie, it can clear out that cookie here.

A ServerAuthModule is called by the container before the first filter in the Servlet invocation chain and again after the last filter. Unlike a Filter or Servlet, a ServerAuthModule is not explicitly mapped to a URL pattern; it's called for every URL, and both for protected (secured) URLs and unprotected (public) ones.

JAKARTA EE 11 LOOKOUT

For Jakarta EE 11 or a later version, it's considered to have multiple ServerAuthModules mapped to different URL patterns.

This is depicted in the following diagram:

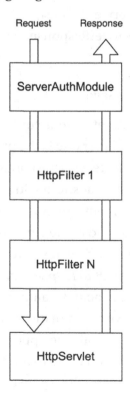

At the start of the request, the (Servlet) container first calls ServerAuthModule#validateRequest. Depending on its return value and whether authentication is mandatory or not, the container calls the HttpFilter#doFilter methods of the filter chain (if any) and eventually the Servlet#service method (again, if any). When the Servlet and/or Filters return from their methods, the container calls ServerAuthModule#secureResponse.

Just like an HttpFilter or an HttpServlet, a ServerAuthModule can interact with the request and response objects in all the usual ways:

- Redirect

- Include

- Set and get request attributes

- Set and read cookies and other headers

- Create and use the HTTP session

- Pass a wrapped request and/or wrapped response forwards in the chain

- And so on

As per the aforementioned, it's clear that a ServerAuthModule functions pretty much like a Filter does. Despite that fact though, there are a few key differences:

- Ability to use the authentication CallBackHandler (discussed later)

- Returning a status code to direct the container what to do next

- Able to be called mid-request, outside the servlet chain

Of these things, the ability to be called mid-request and not as part of the servlet invocation chain is the most distinguishing feature. Such a call happens in response to *HttpServletRequest#authenticate(),* which is said to "trigger the authentication dialog" (i.e., starts the interaction with the remote user):

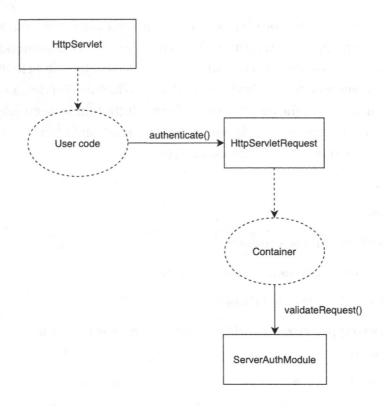

In the preceding diagram, some kind of user code that is ultimately called from a Servlet, perhaps a Faces backing bean, calls the *authenticate()* method on an *HttpServletRequest* object. Following that call, the container in its turn calls the ServerAuthModule.

At that point, this ServerAuthModule can start the interaction with the user, for instance, sending a redirect. Obviously for such kinds of interactions, the response cannot have been committed yet. It's the responsibility of the user code to make sure that the call to *authenticate()* happens at the appropriate time. Of course, if the ServerAuthModule is able to do its work without writing to the response (such as inspecting a header in the current request), it can be called at any time.

Example ServerAuthModule

Let us now take a look at a trivial ServerAuthModule in a trivial web application. Let's start with a ServerAuthModule:

```java
public class TestServerAuthModule
    implements ServerAuthModule {

    private CallbackHandler handler;

    @Override
    public Class<?>[] getSupportedMessageTypes() {
        return new Class[] {
            HttpServletRequest.class,
            HttpServletResponse.class };
    }

    @Override
    public void initialize(
        MessagePolicy requestPolicy,
        MessagePolicy responsePolicy,
        CallbackHandler handler,
        @SuppressWarnings("rawtypes") Map options)
        throws AuthException {
        this.handler = handler;
    }

    @Override
    public AuthStatus validateRequest(
        MessageInfo messageInfo,
        Subject clientSubject,
        Subject serviceSubject)
        throws AuthException {
        try {

            handler.handle(new Callback[] {

                // Name of the authenticated user
                new CallerPrincipalCallback(
                    clientSubject, "jsmith"),

                // Groups of the authenticated user
                new GroupPrincipalCallback(
                    clientSubject,
                    new String[] { "user" }) });
```

```
        } catch (IOException
            | UnsupportedCallbackException e) {
          throw (AuthException)
              new AuthException().initCause(e);
        }

        return SUCCESS;
    }

    @Override
    public AuthStatus secureResponse(
        MessageInfo messageInfo,
        Subject serviceSubject)
        throws AuthException {
        return SEND_SUCCESS;
    }

    @Override
    public void cleanSubject(
        MessageInfo messageInfo, Subject subject)
        throws AuthException {
    }
}
```

Let's take a look at what's happening here. The first thing we do is
return *HttpServletRequest.class* and *HttpServletResponse.class* from the
getSupportedMessageTypes() method as explained earlier. This is a fixed requirement for
all *ServerAuthModules* that are used for the Servlet Container Profile.

In the *initialize()* method, we ignore all data we get except for the *CallbackHandler()*,
which we store.

In the *validateRequest()* method, we don't actually interact with anything, and we
also don't call out to an identity store. Instead, for the sake of the simplest example
possible, we set a fixed user/caller name: "jsmith" who is in one group: "user."

The way Jakarta Authentication interacts with the container is perhaps a little
different from what one is normally used to in Jakarta EE, so we'll provide some more
detailed explanation here. Instead of calling methods with a defined signature on some

context object (such as the ServletContext), Jakarta Authentication works with a general *CallbackHandler* that is provided by the container. The *ServerAuthModule* can use this *CallbackHandler* to obtain data from the container, or to pass data into the container.

Both the *ServerAuthModule* and the *CallbackHandler* should be essentially stateless. The *ServerAuthModule* can store the *CallbackHandler* that it receives, but as mentioned, this *CallbackHandler* should be essentially stateless itself. The other data that is passed in *initialize()* should all be immutable data. The "instance" data of a *ServerAuthModule*, which is the per-request data, is swapped in and out via the *MessageInfo* and *Subject* objects that are passed in (for the Servlet Container Profile, only the serviceSubject is used).

Passing certain data into the container can technically be done by storing that data into the *Subject* (the *serviceSubject* one), which is indeed what most implementations of the CallbackHandler would do. In that case, the Callback that we pass into the CallbackHandler functions essentially as a writer for that data into the *Subject*. We can't write that data directly from a portable *ServerAuthModule* into the *Subject* as the two crucial *Principals*, the caller principal and the group principal, have not been standardized. Every Servlet container implementation writes its own version into the *Subject* using its own method to distinguish it from other principals that may or may not be present.

In the preceding code, we passed two *Callbacks* into the *CallbackHandler*. Alternatively, we can also call the handler for each *CallBack* individually, for instance:

```
handler.handle(new Callback[] {
    new CallerPrincipalCallback(clientSubject, "jsmith")
});
```

What happens here is that we ask the container to accept "jmith" as the caller (user) principal. In a more typical API design, we would probably have something like

```
context.setCallerPrincipal(clientSubject, "jsmith");
```

Or assuming *context* is stateful, just

```
context.setCallerPrincipal("jsmith");
```

After this call, likely, but not necessarily, *clientSubject* will contain some *Principal* implementation with value "jsmith".

Similarly, to set the groups that the caller is in, we use

```
handler.handle(new Callback[] {
    new GroupPrincipalCallback(clientSubject, new String[] { "user" })
});
```

We can read this again as if we would write in a more typical API:

```
context.setGroupPrincipal(clientSubject, "user");
```

Finally, we return the constant *AuthStatus.SUCCESS* from the validateRequest() method, indicating to the container that authentication succeeded.

The next step is to add the *ServerAuthModule* to our application. We generally have three options for this:

1. Programmatic

2. Declarative per archive

3. Declarative per server

Only the programmatic option is standardized, with the declarative options being specific to servers (which also may mean a server doesn't have support for that at all). Unfortunately, the programmatic option doesn't allow us to register a ServerAuthModule directly but requires a series of other types to be registered first. These types are more aimed toward server and framework implementors, which implement said declarative support. For this reason, we'll use a small utility library here first, which is OmniFaces Authentication Utils (we'll take a look at the actual types later). In a Maven project, it can be added via the following dependency:

```
<dependency>
    <groupId>org.omnifaces</groupId>
    <artifactId>authentication-utils</artifactId>
    <version>1.0</version>
</dependency>
```

Registering a *ServerAuthModule* then happens in a *ServletContextListener* as follows:

```
@WebListener
public class RegistrationListener
    implements ServletContextListener {
```

```
    @Override
    public void contextInitialized(
        ServletContextEvent sce) {
        AuthenticationUtils
            .registerServerAuthModule(
                new TestServerAuthModule(),
                sce.getServletContext());
    }
}
```

Finally, let's add a Servlet for our example here:

```
@WebServlet(urlPatterns = "/servlet")
@ServletSecurity(@HttpConstraint(rolesAllowed = "user"))
public class TestServlet extends HttpServlet {

    private static final long serialVersionUID = 1L;

    @Override
    public void doGet(HttpServletRequest request,
        HttpServletResponse response)
        throws ServletException, IOException {

        response.getWriter().write(
            "Caller has name: " +
            (request.getUserPrincipal() != null
                ? request.getUserPrincipal()
                : "<unauthenticated>")
            + "\n" +
            "Caller has role \"user\": " +
            request.isUserInRole("user") +
            "\n");
    }
}
```

Packing this all up and putting it in a .war (call it simple-sam.war for this example) and deploying this to, say, GlassFish 6.1.0 would show the following:

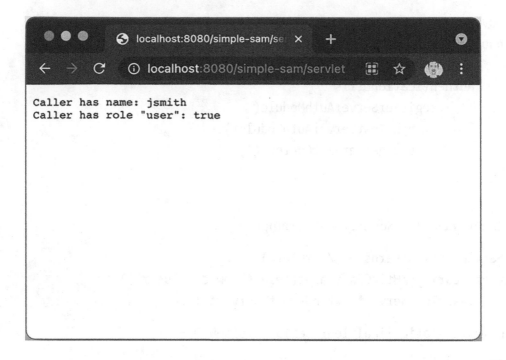

This demonstrates that (a) the *ServerAuthModule* has correctly installed a user with the role "user," so the Servlet could be accessed at all, and (b) *HttpServletRequest* allows us to get the right details.

Example ServerAuthModule – GlassFish

Let's now take a quick look at what a server specific declarative option looks like. We'll be using GlassFish again as an example here.

We'll first create a war file with only the servlet "TestServlet" as shown previously and a *glassfish-web.xml* file in the *WEB-INF* folder to name our application. We'll just call it "simple-sam":

```
<?xml version="1.0" encoding="UTF-8"?>
<!DOCTYPE glassfish-web-app PUBLIC "-//GlassFish.org//DTD GlassFish
Application Server 3.1 Servlet 3.0//EN" "http://glassfish.org/dtds/
glassfish-web-app_3_0-1.dtd">

<glassfish-web-app
  httpservlet-security-provider="simple-sam"
/>
```

Next, we put the same *ServerAuthModule* "TestServerAuthModule" as shown previously in a jar, which we then copy to [glassfish install root]/glassfish/lib. Finally, we edit *[glassfish install root]/glassfish/domains/domain1/config/domain.xml* to insert a new *provider-config* element inside the existing *message-security-config* element with attribute *auth-layer="HttpServlet"*:

```
<message-security-config auth-layer="HttpServlet">
  <provider-config
    provider-type="server"
    provider-id="simple-sam"
    class-name="org.example.TestServerAuthModule"
  />
```

If we now deploy our latest war again and request the same URL as before, we should see the same result. Note that the concept of naming a ServerAuthModule this way and then referencing it by name from an application is effectively the reverse of how it is done in the standard API.

Example ServerAuthModule – Tomcat

In order to deploy to Tomcat, the *WEB-INF/glassfish-web.xml* file is not needed. However, it doesn't hurt if it's there anyway. Tomcat will simply ignore it.

The same jar with the *ServerAuthModule* has to be copied to [tomcat install root]/lib, and we need to edit [tomcat install root]/conf/jaspic-providers.xml to contain the following element inside the root element *jaspic-providers*:

```
<provider name="any"
  className="org.apache.catalina.authenticator.jaspic.
  SimpleAuthConfigProvider"
  layer="HttpServlet"
  appContext="Catalina/localhost /simple-sam"
  description="any">
  <property
    name="org.apache.catalina.authenticator.jaspic.ServerAuthModule.1"
    value="org.example.TestServerAuthModule" />
</provider>
```

We see here that instead of naming the application, the Tomcat configuration file simply refers to the context path on which the application will be deployed, which is "simple-sam" here (by default, that means the war name should then be simple-sam.war).

Tomcat allows us to provide both a full custom *AuthConfigProvider* and just a *ServerAuthModule*. In the latter case, Tomcat cleverly provides a default *AuthConfigProvider* that takes a *ServerAuthModules* as a parameter. Basically, Tomcat uses the same approach here as we saw in the programmatic *AuthenticationUtils* previously, a default convenience *AuthConfigProvider* that just takes a *ServerAuthModule* directly as input.

Example ServerAuthModule – Basic

Having looked at the trivial *ServerAuthModule* that we demonstrated previously, let's now look at a more realistic example; a basic authentication mechanism (a may be a good idea to look back at the general description of this mechanism we gave above).

The full source is given first. We look at some details here:

```
public class BasicServerAuthModule
    implements ServerAuthModule {

    private CallbackHandler handler;

    @Override
    public Class<?>[] getSupportedMessageTypes() {
        return new Class[] {
            HttpServletRequest.class,
            HttpServletResponse.class };
    }

    @Override
    public void initialize(
        MessagePolicy requestPolicy,
        MessagePolicy responsePolicy,
        CallbackHandler handler,
        @SuppressWarnings("rawtypes") Map options)
        throws AuthException {
```

```java
    this.handler = handler;
}

@Override
public AuthStatus validateRequest(
    MessageInfo messageInfo,
    Subject clientSubject,
    Subject serviceSubject)
    throws AuthException {
    try {

        HttpServletRequest request = (HttpServletRequest)
          messageInfo.getRequestMessage();
        HttpServletResponse response = (HttpServletResponse)
          messageInfo.getResponseMessage();

        String[] credentials = getCredentials(request);

        if (credentials != null) {

            // Stand-in for real lookup
            TestIdentityStore identityStore
                = new TestIdentityStore();

            Map<String, ?> validation = identityStore
                .validate(credentials[0],
                    credentials[1]);

            if ((Boolean) validation
                    .get("outcome")) {
                handler
                    .handle(new Callback[] {
                        new CallerPrincipalCallback(
                            clientSubject,
                            (String) validation
                                .get("callerName")),
```

```java
                            new GroupPrincipalCallback(
                                clientSubject,
                                (String[]) validation
                                    .get("groups")) });

                    return SUCCESS;
                }
            }

            if (isProtectedResource(
                messageInfo)) {
                response.setHeader(
                    "WWW-Authenticate",
                    String.format(
                        "Basic realm=\"%s\"",
                        "test"));

                response.sendError(
                    SC_UNAUTHORIZED);

                return SEND_FAILURE;
            }

            handler.handle(new Callback[] {
                new CallerPrincipalCallback(
                    clientSubject,
                    (Principal) null) });
            return SUCCESS;

        } catch (IOException
            | UnsupportedCallbackException e) {
            throw (AuthException) new AuthException()
                .initCause(e);
        }
    }

    @Override
    public AuthStatus secureResponse(
        MessageInfo messageInfo,
```

```java
        Subject serviceSubject)
        throws AuthException {
        return SEND_SUCCESS;
    }

    @Override
    public void cleanSubject(
        MessageInfo messageInfo, Subject subject)
        throws AuthException {
    }

    private String[] getCredentials(
        HttpServletRequest request) {

        String authorizationHeader =
            request.getHeader("Authorization");
        if (authorizationHeader != null &&
            authorizationHeader.startsWith("Basic ")) {
            return new String(
                Base64.getDecoder()
                    .decode(authorizationHeader
                        .substring(6)))
                            .split(":");
        }

        return null;
    }

    public static boolean isProtectedResource(
        MessageInfo messageInfo) {
        return Boolean.valueOf(
            (String) messageInfo.getMap().get(
            "jakarta.security.auth.message.MessagePolicy.isMandatory"
        ));
    }
}
```

The first new thing we see here is the usage of the *MessageInfo* type to obtain the all-important *HttpServletRequest* and *HttpServletResponse* objects:

```
HttpServletRequest request = (HttpServletRequest)
    messageInfo.getRequestMessage();
HttpServletResponse response = (HttpServletResponse)
    messageInfo.getResponseMessage();
```

Remember that the Jakarta Authentication interfaces are technology neutral. Essentially, every technology has some notion of a request and response though, which in the Servlet Container Profile means the "request message" maps to the *HttpServletRequest* and the "response message" to the *HttpServletResponse*.

Following the rules of the basic authentication scheme, the request object is used in this example ServerAuthModule to a username and password from a request header. To mimic an actual authentication mechanism as closely as possible, we're validating these using a test (mock) identity store which we just instantiate in place. In an actual implementation, this would probably use some kind of container-specific lookup mechanism. Remember that Jakarta Authentication has not really standardized the general concept of the identity store, although there's a facility for a specific case that we'll look at shortly.

A mock identity store could look like this:

```
public class TestIdentityStore {

    public Map<String, ?> validate(
        String callerName, String password) {
        return Map.of(
            "outcome", true,
            "callerName", callerName,
            "groups", new String[] { "user" });
    }

}
```

The next important new thing that we see here is how to check for whether authentication is mandatory for the current request. Often, this means that the request is protected (has security constraints defined for it), but not always. If authentication is triggered programmatically in mid-request using, for instance, *HttpServletRequest#*

authenticate, then authentication is also mandatory, yet the current request does not necessarily have to be protected in that case.

JAKARTA EE 10 LOOKOUT

In the version of Jakarta Authentication that's current at the time of writing (2.0), we can't distinguish between authentication being mandatory because of a call to HttpServletRequest#authenticate or because the current request is protected.

Jakarta EE 10 may introduce a boolean to at least check whether it was *authenticate()* that was called or not.

Such check is done by the following code:

```
Boolean.valueOf( (String)
    messageInfo.getMap().get(
        "jakarta.security.auth.message.MessagePolicy.isMandatory"
```

Next to the request and response messages, the *MessageInfo* type also contains a general map, containing *String*-based keys and values. In this case, the key "jakarta. security.auth.message.MessagePolicy.isMandatory" is defined by Jakarta Security, and when authentication is mandatory, the map will contain this string and as value "true." Note that when authentication is NOT mandatory, the key may either be entirely absent, or it may be present with the value "false." That's why *Boolean.valueOf()* must be used to check it, as it will return *true* for the string "true" but *false* for anything else, including *null*.

When authentication did not take place AND authentication is mandatory, the *ServerAuthModule* goes into an authentication dialog with the caller, by doing three things:

1. It sets the "WWW-Authenticate" header.

2. It sets the SC_UNAUTHORIZED (401) HTTP status code.

3. It returns AuthStatus.SEND_FAILURE.

That last status is one we didn't see before; it signals to the container that it should not continue with the filter/servlet chain but instead return the response to the client. This will then result in, for instance, a dialog such as the following to be rendered:

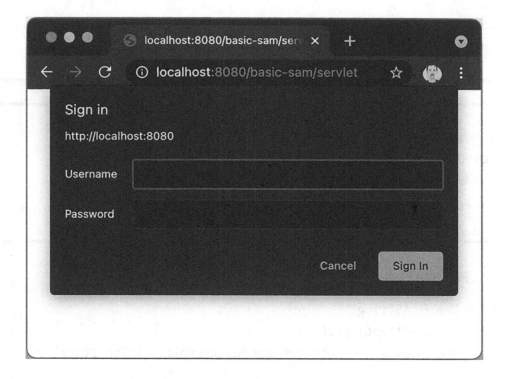

Filling something in here (anything, as the mock identity store doesn't actually test anything) and pressing the "Sign In" button will result in a new request that invokes our *ServerAuthModule* again. This will invoke the *CallerPrincipalCallback* and *GroupPrincipalCallback* again and continue to our Servlet.

The observant reader may notice there's a final fragment of code remaining in our example ServerAuthModule that we didn't discuss yet:

```
handler.handle(new Callback[] {
    new CallerPrincipalCallback(
        clientSubject,
        (Principal) null) });
return SUCCESS;
```

This particular fragment will be executed when we didn't send any credentials, and authentication is not mandatory. It is a specific way to say that the *ServerAuthModule* has "done nothing." This is an approach that we'll see more often in Jakarta Authentication. The designers of the SPI could have chosen to introduce an extra return value for this but instead choose to have the code execute a kind of protocol to indicate this.

Example ServerAuthModule – Basic with Container Identity Store

We mentioned previously that Jakarta Authentication doesn't really standardize the identity store concept. It does, however, provide a facility to interact with the container's native (implementation-specific) default identity store in a limited way. This happens via the *PasswordValidationCallback*. That callback allows us to validate a username and password against such an identity store. The limitation is that only username/password is supported, so if an identity store using any other type of credentials is set as the default, we're out of luck.

Additionally, unlike other standardized or native (implementation-specific) interfaces to identity stores, the *PasswordValidationCallback* does not let us interact with the identity store, and only the identity store. Instead, it automatically provides the following two functions:

1. The expected *{credentials in, caller data out}* function.

2. If the outcome of 1 is successful (credentials validated correctly), set the caller principal and any groups.

This means that when using the *PasswordValidationCallback*, we don't have to handle the *CallerPrincipalCallback* and *GroupPrincipalCallback*. It also means that the *ServerAuthModule* does not get to see the actual caller principal name and the groups that result from the *{credentials in, caller data out}* function and therefore cannot, for instance, add any groups.

In the following, we demonstrate this by giving an updated *validateRequest* method for the *BasicServerAuthModule* that we showed previously:

```
@Override
public AuthStatus validateRequest(
    MessageInfo messageInfo,
    Subject clientSubject,
    Subject serviceSubject)
    throws AuthException {
    try {

        HttpServletRequest request = (HttpServletRequest)
          messageInfo.getRequestMessage();
```

```
HttpServletResponse response = (HttpServletResponse)
    messageInfo.getResponseMessage();

String[] credentials = getCredentials(request);

if (credentials != null) {
    PasswordValidationCallback passwordValidation =
        new PasswordValidationCallback(
            clientSubject, credentials[0],
            credentials[1].toCharArray());

    handler.handle(new Callback[] {passwordValidation} );

    if (passwordValidation
        .getResult()) {
        return SUCCESS;
    }
}

if (isProtectedResource(
    messageInfo)) {
    response.setHeader(
        "WWW-Authenticate",
        String.format(
            "Basic realm=\"%s\"",
            "test"));
    response.sendError(
        SC_UNAUTHORIZED);

    return SEND_FAILURE;
}

handler.handle(new Callback[] {
    new CallerPrincipalCallback(
        clientSubject,
        (Principal) null) });
return SUCCESS;
```

```
    } catch (IOException
        | UnsupportedCallbackException e) {
        throw (AuthException) new AuthException()
            .initCause(e);
    }
}
```

As we see, after validation with the container provided identity store, the only thing our *ServerAuthModule* gets to see is whether validation was successful or not. If it was successful, we can therefore directly return SUCCESS as per the following fragment:

```
if (passwordValidation
    .getResult()) {
    return SUCCESS;
}
```

Note that of course the user and groups have to be added in a server-specific way. For example, in GlassFish, the default identity store is the "file realm," and data can be added via, for instance, its admin console as shown in the following:

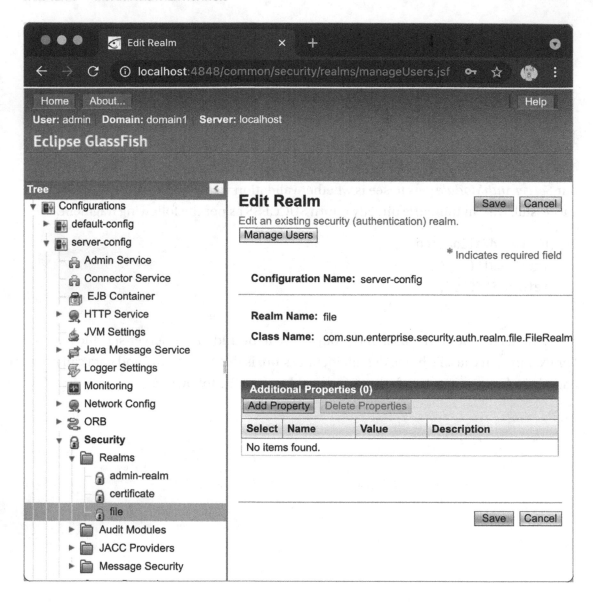

For Tomcat that can be done by editing the *[tomcat install root]/conf/tomcat-users. xml* file, for instance, to look as follows:

```
<tomcat-users version="1.0"
    xmlns="http://tomcat.apache.org/xml"
    xmlns:xsi="http://www.w3.org/2001/XMLSchema-instance"
    xsi:schemaLocation="http://tomcat.apache.org/xml tomcat-users.xsd">
    <role rolename="user"/>
```

```
    <user username="jsmith" password="test" roles="user"/>
</tomcat-users>
```

Obtaining Key Stores and Trust Stores

A number of authentication mechanisms need to make use of some of the cryptographic related facilities of the runtime, such as the keystore with certificates and private keys needed to sign things, or truststores to validate incoming certificates.

Jakarta Authentication has various optional callbacks for this. They are optional in the sense that they do not have to be enabled by default. The Jakarta Authorization specification does say it should be possible to enable them, but such text is typically ignored in practice.

The simplest to use are the *CertStoreCallback* and the *TrustStoreCallback*. The first one, also just called the keystore, contains the credentials of the server itself. For instance, in GlassFish, it would contain a certificate like the following:

```
[
[
  Version: V3
  Subject: CN=localhost-instance, OU=GlassFish, O=Eclipse.org Foundation
  Inc, L=Ottawa, ST=Ontario, C=CA
  Signature Algorithm: SHA256withRSA, OID = 1.2.840.113549.1.1.11

  Key:  Sun RSA public key, 2048 bits
  modulus: 1959608 [...]
  public exponent: 65537
  Validity: [From: Tue Dec 29 14:20:20 CET 2020,
               To: Fri Dec 27 14:20:20 CET 2030]
  Issuer: CN=localhost-instance, OU=GlassFish, O=Eclipse.org Foundation
  Inc, L=Ottawa, ST=Ontario, C=CA
  SerialNumber: [    2d6a826b]

Certificate Extensions: 1
[1]: ObjectId: 2.5.29.14 Criticality=false
SubjectKeyIdentifier [
KeyIdentifier [
```

```
0000: 8D D0 C5 4C DE 41 59 BB    92 F7 9B DC 85 1C 0F E4    ...L.AY.........
0010: 99 E2 B5 3A                                           ...:
]
]
```

The second one, the truststore, holds the certificates that identify others. A truststore has conceptually some overlap with an identity store.

Both these callbacks are simply instances that, when handled by the handler, return the store instances. Note that these are typically a copy and are only usable for reading from. The following shows an example:

```
@Override
public AuthStatus validateRequest(
    MessageInfo messageInfo,
    Subject clientSubject,
    Subject serviceSubject)
    throws AuthException {
    try {
        CertStoreCallback certStoreCallback =
            new CertStoreCallback();
        handler.handle(new Callback[] { certStoreCallback });
        CertStore certStore =
            certStoreCallback.getCertStore();

        TrustStoreCallback trustStoreCallback =
            new TrustStoreCallback();
        handler.handle(new Callback[] { trustStoreCallback });
        KeyStore trustStore =
            trustStoreCallback.getTrustStore();

        // [... rest of code]

    } catch (IOException
        | UnsupportedCallbackException e) {
        throw (AuthException) new AuthException()
            .initCause(e);
    }
}
```

A less commonly used *Callback* is the *SecretKeyCallback*; this is used to obtain essentially named tokens (a.k.a. aliased passwords) that the runtime has stored somewhere safely. This is useful for accessing remote systems without having a token or password immediately in plain text in the code or in a configuration file.

Let's assume our authentication mechanism needs to contact a remote identity provider, and to access, this uses a token with the value "bar." Instead of having "bar" anywhere in either code or a plain text configuration file, we create an alias for it, say, "foo." Creating such an alias is vendor specific; for example, in GlassFish, this can be done using the "create-password-alias" CLI command or by using the graphical admin console:

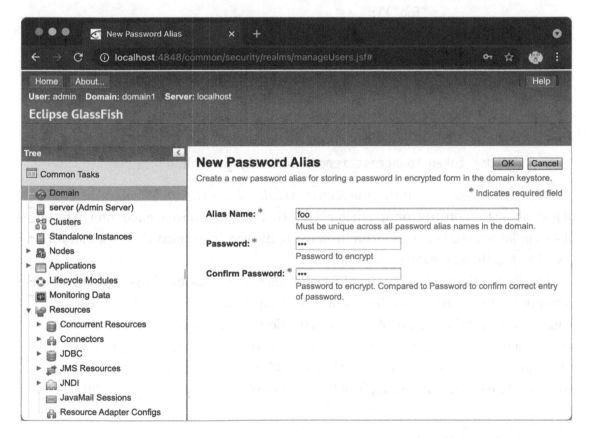

In GlassFish, this would physically be stored encrypted in the *domains/domain1/conf/domain-passwords* file and needs the master password to be decrypted.

We can now access the actual value from a *ServerAuthModule* as shown in the following example code:

```
@Override
public AuthStatus validateRequest(
    MessageInfo messageInfo,
    Subject clientSubject,
    Subject serviceSubject)
    throws AuthException {
    try {
        SecretKeyCallback secretKeyCallback =
            new SecretKeyCallback(
                new SecretKeyCallback.AliasRequest(
                    "foo"));
        handler.handle(new Callback[] {
            secretKeyCallback });

        String token = new String(
            secretKeyCallback.getKey()
                .getEncoded());

        // Use token to access remote identity provider
```

What we also see here is that the *SecretKeyCallback* uses an *AliasRequest* instead of just taking the constructor parameter "foo." This is a pattern we'll encounter at more places in Jakarta Authentication, for instance, right away in the next *Callback* that we'll take a look at there, the *PrivateKeyCallback*.

The *PrivateKeyCallback* is a bit of the odd one out here, as for a large part, it doesn't offer unique functionality, but just a number of ways to fetch a key or certificate chain from the keystore that we can also get with the *CertStoreCallback. PrivateKeyCallback* lets us get this data by means of an alias (key used to store the certificate), the issuer (if any) and serial number, or the subject key identifier (SKID), which is an optional x509 extension (we saw it in the example of the certificate previously as the string "8D D0 C5 4C ...."):

```
SubjectKeyIdentifier [
  KeyIdentifier [
    0000: 8D D0 C5 4C DE 41 59 BB    92 F7 9B DC 85 1C 0F E4   ...L.AY.........
    0010: 99 E2 B5 3A                                          ...:
  ]
]
```

In GlassFish, for instance, we can get the private key associated with the certificate stored under the alias "S1AS" (which is, if anyone wonders, short for Sun One Application Server) using code such as the following:

```
PrivateKeyCallback privateKeyCallback = new PrivateKeyCallback(
    new PrivateKeyCallback.AliasRequest(
        "s1as"));

handler.handle(new Callback[] {
    privateKeyCallback });

PrivateKey privateKey = privateKeyCallback
    .getKey();
```

Alternatively, we can use the subject key identifier as follows:

```
byte[] subjectKeyIdentifier = new BigInteger(
    "36 1D 53 7B AF 4A 8A 19   F2 DD FE EC 63 5E 6D 25   FE 71 AB DF "
    .replace(" ", ""),
    16).toByteArray();
if (subjectKeyIdentifier.length > 20) {
    subjectKeyIdentifier = Arrays.copyOfRange(
        subjectKeyIdentifier, 1,
        subjectKeyIdentifier.length - 1);
}

privateKeyCallback = new PrivateKeyCallback(
    new PrivateKeyCallback.SubjectKeyIDRequest(
        subjectKeyIdentifier));

handler.handle(new Callback[] {
    privateKeyCallback });

privateKey = privateKeyCallback
    .getKey();
```

One specific piece of data that the *PrivateKeyCallback* allows us to get is the *default* private key, which we can obtain by passing in a *null* as the request:

```
PrivateKeyCallback privateKeyCallback = new PrivateKeyCallback(
    null);

PrivateKey privateKey = privateKeyCallback
    .getKey();
```

Semi-auto Register Session

It's perhaps important to reiterate that in Jakarta Authentication, authentication is always per request. That means if a user authenticates (logs in), the authenticated identity is only set for that one request in which the user authenticated. This works transparently for basic authentication, as the user agent will automatically resend the credentials with every next request and the ServerAuthModule then reauthenticates again every request.

For other types of authentication, most specifically form-based authentication, there is no notion of the user agent resending anything automatically. Naturally, we don't want to display a form for the user to log in with every request. One way to handle this situation is by creating a (HTTP) session and storing the authentication details there, so the user stays logged in for the duration of that session. Technically, an HTTP session is realized by setting either a cookie with a JSESSIONID (in Jakarta EE) or appending this same ID to every URL that is rendered (the cookie is typically preferred).

Jakarta Authentication provides some support for this, but it's not fully automatic, hence why it's called "semi-auto register session." In order to use this session mechanism, we have to execute a protocol, which is then recognized by the Jakarta Authentication runtime.

The protocol consists of two steps: indicating that we want to create a session and indicating that we want to opt in to a session.

Creating a Session

Creating an authenticated session is easy enough. We simply put the key "jakarta.servlet. http.registerSession" in the message info map with a value of "true":

```
messageInfo
    .getMap()
    .put(
      "jakarta.servlet.http.registerSession",
      TRUE.toString());
```

Setting that key will tell the container to store the authenticated identity (caller name and zero or more groups) somewhere. The runtime is free to physically store this in whatever location is suitable, which could be but does not necessarily have to be directly the HTTP session.

Continuing a Session

The runtime will, however, not automatically apply the authentication. The *ServerAuthModule* is still called at each next request, and the *ServerAuthModule* still has to reauthenticate, but it can indicate that it wants to retain ("inherit") the authenticated identity that was previously established by executing the following protocol:

```
HttpServletRequest request = (HttpServletRequest)
    messageInfo.getRequestMessage();
Principal callerPrincipal =
    request.getUserPrincipal();

if (callerPrincipal != null) {
    handler.handle(new Callback[] {
        new CallerPrincipalCallback(
            clientSubject,
            callerPrincipal) }
    );

    return SUCCESS;
}
```

What happens here is that the runtime passes in a special wrapper *Principal* that it can recognize later. If we hand exactly this principal back, and nothing else, it's a signal for the runtime to fully restore the previously saved authenticated identity.

A *ServerAuthModule* does not have to execute this protocol and for a single request could decide to do something else, for example, not authenticating at all, or authenticating as another caller principal.

The following shows an example *validateRequest* method to demonstrate this in context (for a complete *ServerAuthModule*, this method can replace any of the ones previously given):

```java
@Override
public AuthStatus validateRequest(
    MessageInfo messageInfo,
    Subject clientSubject,
    Subject serviceSubject)
    throws AuthException {
    try {

        HttpServletRequest request = (HttpServletRequest)
            messageInfo.getRequestMessage();
        Principal callerPrincipal = request
            .getUserPrincipal();

        if (callerPrincipal != null) {
            handler.handle(new Callback[] {
                new CallerPrincipalCallback(
                    clientSubject,
                    callerPrincipal) });

            return SUCCESS;
        }

        handler.handle(new Callback[] {
            new CallerPrincipalCallback(
                clientSubject,
                "jsmith at " + currentTimeMillis()),

            new GroupPrincipalCallback(
                clientSubject,
                new String[] { "user" }) });

            messageInfo
            .getMap()
            .put(
                "jakarta.servlet.http.registerSession",
                TRUE.toString());

        return SUCCESS;
```

```
    } catch (IOException
        | UnsupportedCallbackException e) {
      throw (AuthException)
          new AuthException().initCause(e);
    }
}
```

When this code is initially executed, it will run the branch where it sets "Jsmith at " with the current time as the caller principal. The second request a session would be created, and we shouldn't see the time changing again when we pair this *ServerAuthModule* with the test servlet we used before:

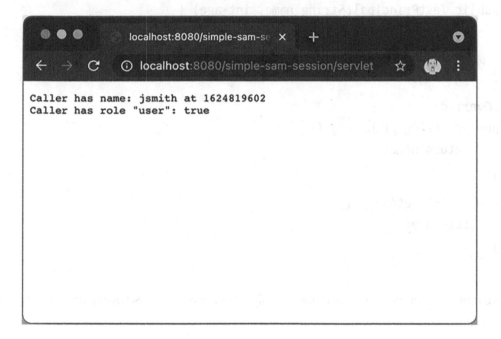

In the example, the name should be displaying 1624819602 when we refresh the page but should display a new number when we fully close the browser here, or when we manually delete the JSESSIONID cookie.

Using a Custom Principal

In all of the previous examples, we set a caller principal simply by passing a *String* representing the caller principal's name into the *CallerPrincipalCallback*. In that case, the actual type of the principal that is returned from, for instance, *HttpServletRequest. getUserPrincipal()* is container specific. Not rarely though we like to associate some extra information with the principal. The default one, however, only allows a simple *String* and nothing else.

For that reason, Jakarta Authentication also allows us to set a principal of our own type, which is referred to here as a "custom principal"; the following shows an example:

```java
public class TestPrincipal implements Principal {

    private final String name;
    private final int age;

    public TestPrincipal(String name, int age) {
        this.name = name;
        this.age = age;
    }

    @Override
    public String getName() {
        return name;
    }

    public int getAge() {
        return age;
    }
}
```

We can set such custom principal simply where we used a *String* before, as per the following:

```java
@Override
public AuthStatus validateRequest(
    MessageInfo messageInfo,
    Subject clientSubject,
    Subject serviceSubject)
    throws AuthException {
    try {
        handler.handle(new Callback[] {
            new CallerPrincipalCallback(
```

```
                clientSubject,
                new TestPrincipal("jsmith", 45)),

            new GroupPrincipalCallback(
                clientSubject,
                new String[] { "user" }) });

        return SUCCESS;

    } catch (IOException
        | UnsupportedCallbackException e) {
        throw (AuthException)
            new AuthException().initCause(e);
    }
}
```

Here, we are setting an instance of our principal TestPrincipal with the usual name "jsmith", but with an extra piece of information, age 45.

In order to demonstrate the usage of this custom principal, let's adjust the servlet we used before to print out the extra information:

```
@WebServlet(urlPatterns = "/servlet")
@ServletSecurity(@HttpConstraint(rolesAllowed = "user"))
public class TestServlet extends HttpServlet {

    private static final long serialVersionUID = 1L;

    @Override
    public void doGet(HttpServletRequest request,
        HttpServletResponse response)
        throws ServletException, IOException {

        response.getWriter()
            .write("Caller has name: " + (request
                .getUserPrincipal()
                    instanceof TestPrincipal principal
                    ? "name "
                        + principal.getName()
                        + " age "
                        + principal.getAge()
```

```
                    : "<unauthenticated>")
            + "\n"
            + "Caller has role \"user\": "
            + request.isUserInRole("user")
            + "\n");

    }
}
```

Notice that we test first if the principal is an instance of type *TestPrincipal* and, when it is, use the pattern variable *principal*. After that, we are able to call the method getName() from the *Principal* type and our own custom method *getAge()* from the *TestPrincipal* type so that our servlet renders the following:

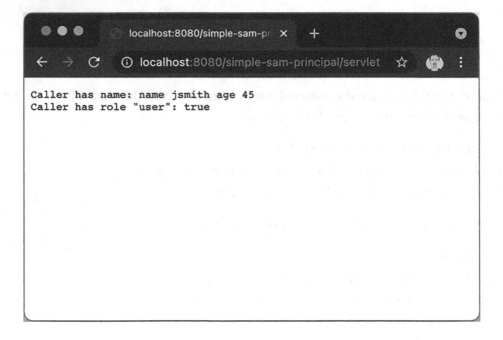

In a typical (web) application, we often have the concept of a "user." There's little consensus on what exactly represents the user in Jakarta EE. Using a custom principal, the principal can be used as a full user, but technically, it just represents a single attribute. A Subject in its turn contains a bag of different principals, but it too does not quite represent a typical "user" domain entity.

Wrapping the Request and Response

In a Servlet filter, we can almost trivially wrap the request and response objects that we received and pass those wrapped versions on to the next filter of servlet. This is trivial, since we explicitly call the chain:

```
protected void doFilter(
    HttpServletRequest request,
    HttpServletResponse response,
    FilterChain chain)
    throws IOException, ServletException {
    chain.doFilter(request, response);
}
```

Earlier we mentioned that a *ServerAuthModule* (for the Servlet Container Profile) can do the same thing, but without a *FilterChain*, how does it do this? The approach that Jakarta Authentication takes is using the same object from which we get the request and response, to also set any wrapped ones; *MessageInfo* has a *setRequestMessage* and a *setResponseMessage* next to the getter ones that we saw before. This can be used to set a wrapped request as follows:

```
messageInfo.setRequestMessage(
    new TestHttpServletRequestWrapper(
        request));
```

The code for setting a wrapped response is similar. We'll give a full example in the following text. First, consider a simple wrapper:

```
public class TestHttpServletRequestWrapper
    extends HttpServletRequestWrapper {

    public TestHttpServletRequestWrapper(
        HttpServletRequest request) {
        super(request);
    }

    @Override
    public Object getAttribute(String name) {
```

```
        if ("isWrapped".equals(name)) {
            return TRUE;
        }

        return super.getAttribute(name);
    }
}
```

A *validateRequest* method applying this wrapper looks as follows:

```
@Override
public AuthStatus validateRequest(
    MessageInfo messageInfo,
    Subject clientSubject,
    Subject serviceSubject)
    throws AuthException {
    try {

        HttpServletRequest request = (HttpServletRequest)
            messageInfo.getRequestMessage();

        handler.handle(new Callback[] {
            new CallerPrincipalCallback(
                clientSubject,
                "jsmith"),

            new GroupPrincipalCallback(
                clientSubject,
                new String[] { "user" }) });

        messageInfo.setRequestMessage(
            new TestHttpServletRequestWrapper(
                request));

        return SUCCESS;
```

```
    } catch (IOException
        | UnsupportedCallbackException e) {
        throw (AuthException) new AuthException()
            .initCause(e);
    }
}
```

Furthermore, let's alter our test Servlet a little to check if the wrapping indeed took place:

```
@WebServlet(urlPatterns = "/servlet")
@ServletSecurity(@HttpConstraint(rolesAllowed = "user"))
public class TestServlet extends HttpServlet {

    private static final long serialVersionUID = 1L;

    @Override
    public void doGet(HttpServletRequest request,
        HttpServletResponse response)
        throws ServletException, IOException {

        response.getWriter().write(
            "Caller has name: " +
            (request.getUserPrincipal() != null
                ? request.getUserPrincipal()
                    .getName()
                : "<unauthenticated>")
            + "\n" +
            "Caller has role \"user\": " +
            request.isUserInRole("user") +
            "\n" +
            "isWrapped " +
            request.getAttribute("isWrapped"));
    }
}
```

In this example, the wrapped specifically listens to the "isWrapped" attribute and returns "true" for that. When we run the application with the preceding classes in it, we'll indeed see that "true" appears on the screen.

The Message Policy

The observant reader might have noticed that the initialization method of a ServerAuthModule contained two *MessagePolicy* parameters that we have ignored until now. This is not for nothing, as the short of it is that in the Servlet Container Profile, those parameters are essentially ignored.

To give a quick overview though, a *MessagePolicy* can have zero or more *TargetPolicies*, and each *TargetPolicy* can have zero or more *Targets* and a single *ProtectionPolicy*, where the latter contains instructions like "#authenticateSender", "#authenticateContent", etc.

This seems to be largely inspired or designed with SOAP/WS-* in mind. There parts of the actual messages can be signed or encrypted in both the request message and the response message. The *Targets* could be used to indicate which part of the message (XML subtree) the policy would apply to, and the *ProtectionPolicy* could indicate encryption or signing.

In web/Servlet security, there's really only one option, and that's to authenticate the "caller," which would be represented here by "#authenticateSender", and the only options would be mandatory or not mandatory. For this information, we, however, already have the "jakarta.security.auth.message.MessagePolicy.isMandatory" key in the *MessageInfo* map.

Furthermore, since this differs per request, and even dynamically based on whether *HttpServletRequest.authenticate()* is called, the fact that MessagePolicy is passed in the initialize method is perhaps somewhat of a mental mismatch. It would only really work if a new *ServerAuthModule* is created for every call to it and then initialized with a *MessagePolicy* based on the current value of the "jakarta.security.auth.message. MessagePolicy.isMandatory". To illustrate the concept, that MessagePolicy would look a little like the one created here:

```
public static MessagePolicy getMessagePolicy(
    boolean mandatory) {
```

```
List<TargetPolicy> targetPolicies =
    new ArrayList<>();

targetPolicies.add(new TargetPolicy(
    null, // No Target
    new ProtectionPolicy() {
        public String getID() {
            return ProtectionPolicy
                .AUTHENTICATE_SENDER;
        }
    }));

return new MessagePolicy(
    targetPolicies.toArray(
        new TargetPolicy[
            targetPolicies
                .size()]),
    mandatory);
}
```

The AuthConfigProvider

Previously in this chapter, we encountered the *AuthConfigProvider* a couple of times; when registering a *ServerAuthModule* programmatically, we avoided this type and used a utility method. We saw the same thing when we declaratively registered a *ServerAuthModule* for Tomcat: Tomcat provided an *AuthConfigProvider* for us, but we could have used our own one.

In practice, we rarely have to write our own *AuthConfigProvider* as they are provided by servers/runtimes like Tomcat, GlassFish, Piranha Cloud, etc., but if we happen to be writing one of these, or when we have special selection needs for our *ServerAuthModule*, it might come in handy to know this exists.

The *AuthConfigProvider* itself is just a factory for an *AuthConfig where * is either the server or the client version. As stated in the beginning of this chapter, we'll ignore the client. It's rare for this factory to do anything else than just return a new instance of, in this case, the *ServerAuthConfig*. This is demonstrated in the following code:

```java
public class TestAuthConfigProvider
    implements AuthConfigProvider {

    private ServerAuthModule serverAuthModule;

    public TestAuthConfigProvider(
        ServerAuthModule serverAuthModule) {
        this.serverAuthModule = serverAuthModule;
    }

    @Override
    public ServerAuthConfig getServerAuthConfig(
        String layer, String appContext,
        CallbackHandler handler)
        throws AuthException, SecurityException {
        return new TestServerAuthConfig(
            layer,
            appContext,
            handler,
            serverAuthModule);
    }

    @Override
    public ClientAuthConfig getClientAuthConfig(
        String layer, String appContext,
        CallbackHandler handler)
        throws AuthException, SecurityException {
        return null;
    }

    @Override
    public void refresh() {
    }

}
```

JAKARTA EE 10 LOOKOUT

For Jakarta EE 10, it's considered to make use of default methods so that we don't need to implement those methods that we don't need.

The *ServerAuthConfig* is the type where most of the work of selecting a *ServerAuthModule* should be done.

Here, we could, for example, have parsed some XML configuration file that is used to configure *ServerAuthModules* declaratively, such as the one we showed for GlassFish previously. The *ServerAuthConfig* receives from its factory in some way the all-important *CallbackHandler* (we used a constructor here), as well as the "layer" and the "appContext".

The "layer" is a well-defined string referring to the technology for which a ServerAuthModule is needed. For Servlet, this is "HttpServlet", and for SOAP, this is "SOAP". The "appContext" is a unique identifier for an application (it should actually be called "appContextId").

For the Servlet Container profile, an AppContextId is specified to be what the following method returns:

```
String getAppContextId(ServletContext context)
 return
    context.getVirtualServerName() +
    " " +
    context.getContextPath();
}
```

JAKARTA EE 11 LOOKOUT

For Jakarta EE 11, it's considered to add this getAppContextId() directly to the ServletContext.

The only method of real importance in the *ServerAuthConfig* is the *getAuthContext* method. As the *ServerAuthConfig* is already obtained for a specific layer (e.g., servlet) and AppContextId (e.g., for /my-app), it's not needed to specify those selection criteria in this method. The two parameters that are passed in, "authContextId" and "serviceSubject", are unused and reserved for future profiles and/or for future use of the existing profiles.

So in our simple example here, there's little else the *getAuthContext* method has to do but to conceptually return the one and only *ServerAuthModule*. There's one twist though, and the name of the method kinda gave it away, and that's that the *ServerAuthModule* has to be wrapped by a *ServerAuthContext*. We'll look at this type further in the following text.

For now, consider the following example implementation of the *ServerAuthConfig*:

```
public class TestServerAuthConfig
    implements ServerAuthConfig {

    private CallbackHandler handler;
    private ServerAuthModule serverAuthModule;

    private String layer;
    private String appContext;

    public TestServerAuthConfig(String layer,
        String appContext,
        CallbackHandler handler,
        ServerAuthModule serverAuthModule) {
        this.handler = handler;
        this.serverAuthModule = serverAuthModule;

        this.layer = layer;
        this.appContext = appContext;
    }

    @Override
    public ServerAuthContext getAuthContext(
        String authContextId,
        Subject serviceSubject,
        Map properties)
        throws AuthException {
```

```
        return new TestServerAuthContext(
            handler,
            serverAuthModule);
    }

    @Override
    public String getMessageLayer() {
        return layer;
    }

    @Override
    public String getAuthContextID(
        MessageInfo messageInfo) {
        return appContext;
    }

    @Override
    public String getAppContext() {
        return appContext;
    }

    @Override
    public void refresh() {
    }

    @Override
    public boolean isProtected() {
        return false;
    }

}
```

The *ServerAuthContext* is a type that is intended to wrap one or more
ServerAuthModules, essentially with the purpose of stacking them (meaning calling
multiple ones until, for instance, one succeeds). Such stacking algorithm, however,
has never been standardized for Jakarta Authentication, so this potential feature
is essentially unused. A *ServerAuthContext* has the same methods as a *ServerAuth*
which we showed all the way in the beginning of this chapter as the base interface of a
ServerAuthModule.

For our example here (and for most practical purposes), we just delegate to our own and only *ServerAuthModule*:

```java
public class TestServerAuthContext
    implements ServerAuthContext {

    private final ServerAuthModule serverAuthModule;

    public TestServerAuthContext(
        CallbackHandler handler,
        ServerAuthModule serverAuthModule)
        throws AuthException {
        this.serverAuthModule = serverAuthModule;

        serverAuthModule.initialize(
            null, null,
            handler,
            Collections.<String, String>emptyMap());
    }

    @Override
    public AuthStatus validateRequest(
        MessageInfo messageInfo,
        Subject clientSubject,
        Subject serviceSubject)
        throws AuthException {

        return serverAuthModule.validateRequest(
            messageInfo,
            clientSubject,
            serviceSubject);
    }

    @Override
    public AuthStatus secureResponse(
        MessageInfo messageInfo,
        Subject serviceSubject)
        throws AuthException {
```

```
    return serverAuthModule.secureResponse(
        messageInfo,
        serviceSubject);
}

@Override
public void cleanSubject(
    MessageInfo messageInfo,
    Subject subject)
    throws AuthException {

    serverAuthModule.cleanSubject(
        messageInfo,
        subject);
}
}
```

The preceding code is surely not difficult in any way, but it has been tedious enough to generally decrease the usage of the API. It's in that sense a "good" example how a seemingly small design choice in the overall scheme of things can greatly influence the perception of a technology even when, as said, we don't often have to write this code.

Case Study – Implementation-Specific Identity Stores

In this section, we provide a case study where we look at a number of native (implementation-specific) solutions for the identity store. Obviously, this information is not required to understand or use Jakarta Authentication and/or Jakarta Security. It's presented here to give some idea how Servlet Containers work with identity stores.

Identity stores are somewhat shrouded in mystery and not without reason. Jakarta Authentication has not standardized any identity store, nor has it really standardized any API or interface for them. There is a bridge profile for JAAS LoginModules, which are arguably the closest thing to a standard interface, but JAAS LoginModules cannot be used in a portable way in Jakarta Authentication or generally in Jakarta EE since essential elements of them are not standardized.

Therefore, almost every Servlet container provides a native (implementation-specific) interface and lookup method for identity stores. Nearly all of them ship with a couple of default implementations for common storage systems that the developer can choose to use. The most common ones are the following:

- In-memory (properties file/xml file based)

- Database (JDBC/DataSource based)

- LDAP

As a direct result of not being standardized, not only do Servlet containers provide their own implementations, they also each came up with their own names. Up till now, no less than 16(!) terms were discovered for essentially the same thing:

1. Authenticator

2. Authentication provider

3. Authentication repository

4. Authentication realm

5. Authentication store

6. Identity manager

7. Identity provider

8. Identity store

9. Login module

10. Login service

11. Realm

12. Relying party

13. Security policy domain

14. Security domain

15. Service provider

16. User registry

To give an impression of how a variety of servlet containers have each implemented the identity store concept, we analyzed a couple of them. For each one, we list the main interface one has to implement for a custom identity store and if possible an overview of how the container actually uses this interface in their native (implementation-specific) authentication mechanism interface (which is the counterpart to the Jakarta Authentication *ServerAuthModule*).

The servlet containers and application servers containing such containers that we've looked at are given in the following list. Each one is described in greater detail later.

- Tomcat

- Jetty

- Undertow

- JBoss EAP/WildFly

- Resin

- GlassFish

- Open Liberty

- WebLogic

Tomcat

Tomcat calls its identity store "Realm." It's represented by the interface shown here:

```
public interface Realm {

    Principal authenticate(
        String username);
    Principal authenticate(
        String username, String credentials);
    Principal authenticate(
        String username, String digest, String nonce,
        String nc, String cnonce, String qop,
        String realm, String md5a2);
    Principal authenticate(
        GSSContext gssContext, boolean storeCreds);
```

```
    Principal authenticate(
        X509Certificate certs[]);

    void backgroundProcess();
    SecurityConstraint [] findSecurityConstraints(
        Request request, Context context);
    boolean hasResourcePermission(
        Request request, Response response,
        SecurityConstraint[] constraint,
        Context context) throws IOException;
    boolean hasRole(
        Wrapper wrapper, Principal principal,
        String role);
    boolean hasUserDataPermission(
        Request request, Response response,
        SecurityConstraint[] constraint) throws IOException;

    void addPropertyChangeListener(
        PropertyChangeListener listener);
    void removePropertyChangeListener(
        PropertyChangeListener listener);

    Container getContainer();
    void setContainer(
        Container container);
    CredentialHandler getCredentialHandler();
    void setCredentialHandler(
        CredentialHandler credentialHandler);
}
```

According to the documentation, "A Realm [identity store] is a "database" of usernames and passwords that identify valid users of a web application (or set of web applications), plus an enumeration of the list of roles associated with each valid user."

Tomcat's bare identity store interface is rather big as can be seen. In practice though, implementations inherit from RealmBase, which is a base class (as its name implies). Somewhat confusingly its JavaDoc says that it's a realm "that reads an XML file to configure the valid users, passwords, and roles."

The only methods that most of Tomcat's identity stores implement are authenticate(String username, String credentials) for the actual authentication, String getName() to return the identity store's name (this would perhaps have been an annotation if this was designed today), and startInternal() to do initialization (would likely be done via an @PostConstruct annotation today).

Tomcat's authentication mechanism interface is based on the general Tomcat Valve (a kind of filter) and is a subclass of the *AuthenticatorBase* class. This has as the most important method the abstract authenticate method:

```
public abstract boolean authenticate(
    HttpRequest request,
    HttpResponse response,
    LoginConfig config)
```

Example of Usage

The following code shows an example of how Tomcat actually uses its identity store. The following shortened fragment is taken from the implementation of the Servlet FORM authentication mechanism in Tomcat called *FormAuthenticator*:

```
// Obtain reference to identity store
Realm realm = context.getRealm();

if (characterEncoding != null) {
    request.setCharacterEncoding(characterEncoding);
}
String username = request.getParameter(FORM_USERNAME);
String password = request.getParameter(FORM_PASSWORD);

// Delegating of authentication mechanism to identity store
principal = realm.authenticate(username, password);

if (principal == null) {
    forwardToErrorPage(request, response, config);
    return false;
}

if (session == null) {
    session = request.getSessionInternal(false);
}
```

```
// Save the authenticated Principal in our session
session.setNote(FORM_PRINCIPAL_NOTE, principal);
```

What sets Tomcat aside from most other systems is that the authenticate() call in most cases directly goes to the custom identity store implementation instead of through many levels of wrappers, bridges, delegators, and what have you. This is even true when the provided base class *RealmBase* is used.

Jetty

Jetty calls its identity store *LoginService*. It's represented by the interface shown here:

```
public interface LoginService {
    String getName();
    UserIdentity login(
        String username,
        Object credentials,
        ServletRequest request);
    boolean validate(
        UserIdentity user);

    IdentityService getIdentityService();
    void setIdentityService(
        IdentityService service);

    void logout(
        UserIdentity user);
}
```

According to its JavaDoc, a "Login service [identity store] provides an abstract mechanism for an [authentication mechanism] to check credentials and to create a UserIdentity using the set [injected] IdentityService."

There are a few things to remark here. The getName() method names the identity store. This would likely be done via an annotation had this interface been designed today.

The essential method of the Jetty identity store is *login()*. It is username/credentials based, where the credentials are an opaque *Object*. The *ServletRequest* is not often used, but a JAAS bridge uses it to provide a *RequestParameterCallback* to Jetty-specific JAAS *LoginModules*.

validate() is essentially a kind of shortcut method for login() != null, albeit without using the credentials.

A distinguishing aspect of Jetty is that its identity stores get injected with an IdentityService, which the store has to use to create user identities (users) based on a Subject, (caller) Principal, and a set of roles. It's not 100% clear what this was intended to accomplish, since the only implementation of this service just returns new *DefaultUserIdentity(subject, userPrincipal, roles)*, where *DefaultUserIdentity* is mostly just a simple POJO that encapsulates those three data items.

Another remarkable method is *logout()*. This is remarkable since the identity store typically just returns authentication data and doesn't hold state per user. It's the authentication mechanism that knows about the environment in which this authentication data is used (e.g., knows about the HTTP request and session). Indeed, almost no identity stores make use of this. The only one that does is the special identity store that bridges to JAAS LoginModules. This one isn't stateful but provides an operation on the passed-in user identity. As it appears, the principal returned by this bridge identity store encapsulates the JAAS *LoginContext*, on which the *logout()* method is called at this point.

Example of Usage

The following code shows an example of how Jetty uses its identity store. The following shortened and "unfolded" fragment is taken from the implementation of the Servlet FORM authentication mechanism in Jetty.

```
if (isJSecurityCheck(uri)) {
    String username =
        request.getParameter(__J_USERNAME);
    String password =
        request.getParameter(__J_PASSWORD);

    // Delegating of authentication mechanism
    //to identity store
    UserIdentity user =
        _loginService.login(
            username, password, request);
```

```
    if (user != null) {
        renewSession(
            request,
            (request instanceof Request?
                ((Request)request).getResponse() :
                    null));

        HttpSession session =
            request.getSession(true);
        session.setAttribute(
            __J_AUTHENTICATED,
            new SessionAuthentication(
                getAuthMethod(),
                user, password));

        // ...

        base_response.sendRedirect(
            redirectCode,
            response.encodeRedirectURL(nuri));

        return form_auth;
    }
    // ...
}
```

In Jetty, a call to the identity store's *login()* method will in most cases directly call the installed identity store and will not go through many layers of delegation, bridges, etc. There is a convenience base class that identity store implementations can use, but this is not required.

If the base class is used, two abstract methods have to be implemented: *UserIdentity loadUser(String username)* and *void loadUsers()*, where typically only the former really does something. When this base class is indeed used, the preceding call to *login()* goes to the implementation in the base class. This first checks a cache and if the user is not there calls the subclass via the mentioned *loadUser()* class.

```
public UserIdentity login(
    String username,
    Object credentials,
    ServletRequest request) {

    UserIdentity user = _users.get(username);

    if (user == null)
        user = loadUser(username);

    if (user != null) {
        UserPrincipal principal =
            (UserPrincipal) user.getUserPrincipal();
        if (principal.authenticate(credentials))
            return user;
    }

    return null;
}
```

The user returned from the subclass has a feature that's a little different from most other servers; it contains a Jetty-specific principal that knows how to process the opaque credentials. It delegates this, however, to a *Credential* implementation as shown in the following:

```
public boolean authenticate(
    Object credentials) {
    return credential != null &&
    credential.check(credentials);
}
```

The credential used here is put into the user instance and represents the – expected – credential and can be of a multitude of types, for example, Crypt, MD5, or Password. MD5 means the expected password is MD5 hashed, while just Password means the expected password is plain text. The check for the latter looks as follows:

```
public boolean check(Object credentials) {
    if (this == credentials)
        return true;
```

```
    if (credentials instanceof Password)
        return credentials.equals(_pw);
    if (credentials instanceof String)
        return credentials.equals(_pw);
    if (credentials instanceof char[])
        return
            Arrays.equals(
                _pw.toCharArray(),
                (char[]) credentials);
    if (credentials instanceof Credential)
        return
            ((Credential) credentials).check(_pw);

    return false;
}
```

Undertow

Undertow is a Servlet container created by Red Hat. A long time ago it replaced Tomcat (JBossWeb) in JBoss EAP and was introduced with WildFly 8. Undertow can also be used stand-alone.

The native identity store interface of Undertow is the *IdentityManager,* which is shown here:

```
public interface IdentityManager {
    Account verify(
        Credential credential);
    Account verify(
        String id, Credential credential);
    Account verify(
        Account account);
}
```

Peculiar enough there are no direct implementations for actual identity stores shipped with Undertow.

Example of Usage

The following code shows an example of how Undertow actually uses its identity store. The following shortened fragment is taken from the implementation of the Servlet FORM authentication mechanism in Undertow.

```
FormData data = parser.parseBlocking();
FormData.FormValue jUsername =
    data.getFirst("j_username");
FormData.FormValue jPassword =
    data.getFirst("j_password");
if (jUsername == null || jPassword == null) {
    return NOT_AUTHENTICATED;
}

String userName = jUsername.getValue();
String password = jPassword.getValue();
AuthenticationMechanismOutcome outcome = null;
PasswordCredential credential =
    new PasswordCredential(
        password.toCharArray());

// Obtain reference to identity store
IdentityManager identityManager =
    securityContext.getIdentityManager();

// Delegating of authentication mechanism
// to identity store
Account account =
    identityManager.verify(
        userName, credential);

if (account != null) {
    securityContext
        .authenticationComplete(
            account, name, true);
    outcome = AUTHENTICATED;
```

```
} else {
    securityContext
        .authenticationFailed(
            MESSAGES.authenticationFailed(
                userName),
            name);
}

if (outcome == AUTHENTICATED) {
    handleRedirectBack(exchange);
    exchange.endExchange();
}

return
    outcome != null ?
        outcome :
        NOT_AUTHENTICATED;
```

JBoss EAP/WildFly

JBoss identity stores are based on the JAAS LoginModule, which is shown here:

```
public interface LoginModule {
    void initialize(
        Subject subject,
        CallbackHandler callbackHandler,
        Map<String,?> sharedState,
        Map<String,?> options);
    boolean login() throws LoginException;
    boolean commit() throws LoginException;
    boolean abort() throws LoginException;
    boolean logout() throws LoginException;
}
```

As with most application servers, the JAAS LoginModule interface is used in a highly application server-specific way.

It's a big question why this interface is used at all, since you can't just implement that interface. Instead, you have to inherit from a credential-specific base class. Therefore, the *LoginModule* interface is practically an internal implementation detail here, not something the user actually uses. Despite that, it's not uncommon for users to think "plain" JAAS is being used and that JAAS login modules are universal and portable, but they are anything but.

For the username/password credential, the base class to inherit from is *UsernamePasswordLoginModule*. As per the JavaDoc of this class, there are two methods that need to be implemented: *getUsersPassword()* and *getRoleSets()*.

getUsersPassword() has to return the actual password for the provided username, so the base code can compare it against the provided password. If those passwords match, *getRoleSets()* is called to retrieve the roles associated with the username. Note that JBoss typically does not map groups to roles, so it returns roles here which are then later on passed into APIs that normally would expect groups. In both methods, the username is available via a call to *getUsername()*.

The "real" contract as *hypothetical* interface could be thought of to look as follows:

```
public interface JBossIdentityStore {
    String getUsersPassword(
        String username);
    Group[] getRoleSets(
        String username)
        throws LoginException;
}
```

Example of Usage

There's no direct usage of the LoginModule in JBoss. JBoss EAP and WildFly directly use Undertow as their Servlet container, which means the authentication mechanisms shipped with that use the *IdentityManager* interface exactly as shown previously in the "Undertow" section.

For usage in JBoss, there's a bridge implementation of the *IdentityManager* to the JBoss-specific JAAS LoginModule available.

The ")" call shown previously ends up at *JAASIdentityManagerImpl#verify*. This first wraps the username but extracts the password from *PasswordCredential*. Abbreviated, it looks as follows:

```java
public Account verify(
    String id,
    Credential credential) {

    if (credential
        instanceof DigestCredential) {
        // ..
    } else if(credential
                instanceof PasswordCredential) {
        return verifyCredential(
            new AccountImpl(id),
            copyOf(
                ((PasswordCredential) credential)
                    .getPassword())

        );
    }
    return
        verifyCredential(
            new AccountImpl(id), credential);
}
```

The next method called in the "password chain" is somewhat troublesome, as it doesn't just return the account details but as an unavoidable side effect also puts the result of authentication in TLS. It takes a credential as an *Object* and delegates further to an *isValid()* method. This one uses a *Subject* as an output parameter (meaning it doesn't return the authentication data but puts it inside the *Subject* that's passed in). The calling method then extracts this authentication data from the subject and puts it into its own type instead.

Abbreviated again, this looks as follows:

```java
private Account verifyCredential(
    AccountImpl account,
    Object credential)
```

```
    Subject subject = new Subject();
    boolean isValid =
        securityDomainContext
            .getAuthenticationManager()
            .isValid(
                account.getOriginalPrincipal(),
                credential, subject);

    if (isValid) {

        // Stores details in TLS
        getSecurityContext()
            .getUtil()
            .createSubjectInfo(
                account.getOriginalPrincipal(),
                credential, subject);

        return new AccountImpl(
            getPrincipal(subject),
            getRoles(subject),
            credential,
            account.getOriginalPrincipal()
        );
    }

    return null;
}
```

The next method being called is *isValid()* on a type called *AuthenticationManager.*
Via two intermediate methods, this ends up calling *proceedWithJaasLogin.*

This method obtains a *LoginContext,* which wraps a *Subject,* which wraps the
Principal and roles shown previously (yes, there's a lot of wrapping going on).
Abbreviated, the method looks as follows:

```
private boolean proceedWithJaasLogin(
    Principal principal,
    Object credential,
    Subject theSubject) {
```

```
try {
    copySubject(
        defaultLogin(
            principal, credential).getSubject(),
        theSubject);
    return true;
} catch (LoginException e) {
    return false;
}
}
```

The *defaultLogin()* method finally just calls plain Java SE JAAS code, although just before doing that, it uses reflection to call a *setSecurityInfo()* method on the *CallbackHandler*. It's remarkable that even though this method seems to be required and known in advance, there's no interface used for this. The handler being used here is often of the type *JBossCallbackHandler*.

Brought back to its essence, the method looks like this:

```
private LoginContext defaultLogin(
    Principal principal,
    Object credential)
    throws LoginException {

    CallbackHandler theHandler =
        (CallbackHandler)
        handler.getClass().newInstance();
    setSecurityInfo.invoke(
        theHandler,
        new Object[] {principal, credential});

    LoginContext lc =
        new LoginContext(
            securityDomain, subject, handler);
    lc.login();

    return lc;
}
```

Via some reflective magic, the JAAS code shown here will locate, instantiate, and at long last will call our custom LoginModule's initialize(), login(), and commit() methods, which in their turn will call the two methods that we needed to implement in our subclass.

Resin

Resin calls its identity store "Authenticator". It's represented by a single interface shown here:

```
public interface Authenticator {
    String getAlgorithm(
        Principal uid);
    Principal authenticate(
        Principal user,
        Credentials credentials,
        Object details);
    boolean isUserInRole(
        Principal user, String role);
    void logout(
        Principal user);
}
```

There are a few things to remark here. The *logout()* method doesn't seem to make much sense, since it's the authentication mechanism that keeps track of the login state in the overarching server. Indeed, the method does not seem to be called by Resin, and there are no identity stores implementing it except for the *AbstractAuthenticator* that does nothing there.

isUserInRole() is somewhat remarkable as well. This method is not intended to check for the roles of any given user, such as you could, for instance, use in an admin UI. Instead, it's intended to be used by the *HttpServletRequest#isUserInRole* call and therefore only for the *current* user. This is indeed how it's used by Resin. This is remarkable, since most other systems keep the roles in memory. Retrieving it from the identity store every time can be rather heavyweight. To combat this, Resin uses a *CachingPrincipal*, but an identity store implementation has to opt in to actually use this.

Example of Usage

The following code shows an example of how Resin actually uses its identity store. The following shortened fragment is taken from the implementation of the Servlet FORM authentication mechanism in Resin.

```
// Obtain reference to identity store
Authenticator auth = getAuthenticator();

// ..

String userName =
    request.getParameter("j_username");
String passwordString =
    request.getParameter("j_password");

if (userName == null ||
    passwordString == null)
    return null;

char[] password =
    passwordString.toCharArray();
BasicPrincipal basicUser =
    new BasicPrincipal(userName);
Credentials credentials =
    new PasswordCredentials(password);

// Delegating of authentication mechanism
// to identity store
user =
    auth.authenticate(
        basicUser, credentials, request);

return user;
```

A nice touch here is that Resin obtains the identity store via CDI injection. A somewhat unknown fact is that Resin has its own CDI implementation, CanDI, and uses it internally for a lot of things. Unlike some other servers, the call to *authenticate()* here goes straight to the identity store. There are no layers of lookup or bridge code in between.

That said, Resin does encourage (but not require) the usage of an abstract base class it provides: *AbstractAuthenticator*. IFF this base class is indeed used (again, this is not required), then there are a few levels of indirection the flow goes through before reaching one's own code. In that case, the authenticate() call shown previously will start with delegating to one of three methods for known credential types. This is shown here:

```
public Principal authenticate(
    Principal user,
    Credentials credentials,
    Object details) {

    if (credentials instanceof PasswordCredentials)
        return authenticate(
            user,
            (PasswordCredentials) credentials,
            details);
    if (credentials instanceof HttpDigestCredentials)
        return authenticate(
            user,
            (HttpDigestCredentials) credentials,
            details);
    if (credentials instanceof DigestCredentials)
        return authenticate(
            user,
            (DigestCredentials) credentials,
            details);

    return null;
}
```

Following the password trail, the next level will merely extract the password string:

```
protected Principal authenticate(
    Principal principal,
    PasswordCredentials cred,
    Object details) {
    return authenticate(
        principal, cred.getPassword());
}
```

The next authenticate method will call into a more specialized method that only obtains a User instance from the store. This instance has the expected password embedded, which is then verified against the provided password. Abbreviated, it looks as follows:

```
protected Principal authenticate(
    Principal principal,
    char[] password) {

    PasswordUser user =
        getPasswordUser(principal);

    if (user == null ||
        user.isDisabled() ||
        (!isMatch(
            principal,
            password,
            user.getPassword()) &&
          !user.isAnonymous()))
        return null;

    return user.getPrincipal();
}
```

The getPasswordUser() method goes through one more level of convenience, where it extracts the caller name that was wrapped by the Principal:

```
protected PasswordUser getPasswordUser(
    Principal principal) {
    return getPasswordUser(
        principal.getName());
}
```

This last call to *getPasswordUser(String)* is what typically ends up in our own custom identity store.

Finally, it's interesting to see what data PasswordUser contains. Abbreviated again, this is shown here:

```
public class PasswordUser {
  Principal principal;
  char[] password;

  boolean disabled;
  boolean anonymous;
  String[] roles;
}
```

GlassFish

GlassFish identity stores are based on the JAAS LoginModule, which is shown here:

```
public interface LoginModule {
    void initialize(
        Subject subject,
        CallbackHandler callbackHandler,
        Map<String,?> sharedState,
        Map<String,?> options);
    boolean login() throws LoginException;
    boolean commit() throws LoginException;
    boolean abort() throws LoginException;
    boolean logout() throws LoginException;
}
```

Just as we saw with JBoss previously, the *LoginModule* interface is again used in a very application server–specific way. In practice, you don't just implement a *LoginModule* but inherit from *com.sun.enterprise.security.BasePasswordLoginModule* or its empty subclass *com.sun.appserv.security.AppservPasswordLoginModule* for password-based logins, or *com.sun.appserv.security.AppservCertificateLoginModule/ com.sun.enterprise.security.BaseCertificateLoginModule* for certificate ones.

As per the JavaDoc of those classes, the only method that needs to be implemented is *authenticateUser()*. Inside that method, the username is available via the protected variable(!) "_username", while the password can be obtained via *getPasswordChar()*. When a custom identity store is done with its work, *commitUserAuthentication()* has to be called with an array of groups when authentication succeeded and a *LoginException* thrown when it failed. So essentially that's the "real" contract for a custom login module. The fact that the other functionality is in the same class is more a case of using inheritance where aggregation might have made more sense. As we saw with JBoss, the *LoginModule* interface itself seems more like an implementation detail instead of something a client can really take advantage of.

The "real" contract as *hypothetical* interface looks as follows:

```java
public interface GlassFishIdentityStore {
    String[] authenticateUser(
        String username,
        char[] password)
        throws LoginException;
}
```

Even though a *LoginModule* is specific for a type of identity store (e.g., File, JDBC/ database, LDAP, etc.), *LoginModules* in GlassFish are mandated to be paired with another construct called a *Realm*. While having the same name as the Tomcat equivalent and even a nearly identical description, the type is completely different. In GlassFish, it's actually a kind of DAO, albeit one with a rather heavyweight contract.

Most of the methods of this DAO are not actually called by the runtime for authentication, nor are they used by the application themselves. They're likely intended to be used by the GlassFish admin console, so a GlassFish administrator can add and delete users. However, very few actual realms support this and with good reason. It just doesn't make much sense for many realms really. For example, LDAP and Solaris have their own management UI already, and JDBC/database is typically intended to be application specific so there the application already has its own DAOs and services to manage users and exposes its own UI as well.

A custom *LoginModule* is not forced to use this *Realm*, but the base class code will try to instantiate one and grab its name, so one must still be paired to the *LoginModule*.

The following lists the public and protected methods of this *Realm* class. Note that the body is left out for the non-abstract methods and modifiers have been omitted.

```java
public abstract class Realm implements Comparable {

    Realm getDefaultInstance();
    String getDefaultRealm();
    Enumeration getRealmNames();
    void getRealmStatsProvier();
    Realm  getInstance(String);
```

```
    Realm instantiate(String, File);
    Realm instantiate(String, String, Properties);
    void setDefaultRealm(String);
    void unloadInstance(String);
    isValidRealm(String);
    void updateInstance(Realm, String);

    void addUser(String, String, String[]);
    User getUser(String);
    void updateUser(String, String, String, String[]);
    void removeUser(String);

    Enumeration getUserNames();
    Enumeration getGroupNames();
    Enumeration getGroupNames(String);

    void persist();
    void refresh();

    AuthenticationHandler getAuthenticationHandler();
    boolean supportsUserManagement();
    String getAuthType();

    int compareTo(Object);
    String FinalgetName();
    String getJAASContext();
    String getProperty(String);
    void setProperty(String, String);

    void init(Properties);
    ArrayList<String> getMappedGroupNames(String);
    String[] addAssignGroups(String[]);
    void setName(String);
    Properties getProperties();
}
```

Example of Usage

To make matters a bit more complicated, there's no direct usage of the *LoginModule* in GlassFish either. GlassFish's Servlet container is internally based on Tomcat, and therefore, the implementation of the FORM authentication mechanism is a Tomcat class (which strongly resembles the class in Tomcat itself but has small differences here and there). Confusingly, this uses a class named *Realm* again, but it's a totally different *Realm* than the one shown previously. This is shown here:

```
// Obtain reference to identity store
Realm realm = context.getRealm();

String username =
    hreq.getParameter(FORM_USERNAME);
String pwd =
    hreq.getParameter(FORM_PASSWORD);
char[] password =
    ((pwd != null)? pwd.toCharArray() : null);

// Delegating of authentication mechanism
// to identity store
principal =
    realm.authenticate(username, password);

if (principal == null) {
    forwardToErrorPage(
        request, response, config);
    return (false);
}

if (session == null)
    session =
        getSession(request, true);

session.setNote(
    FORM_PRINCIPAL_NOTE, principal);
```

This code is largely identical to the Tomcat version shown previously. The Tomcat Realm in this case is not the identity store directly, but an adapter called *RealmAdapter*. It first calls the following slightly abbreviated method for the password credential:

```
public Principal authenticate(
    String username,
    char[] password) {
```

```
    if (authenticate(
        username, password, null)) {
        return
            new WebPrincipal(
                username,
                password,
                SecurityContext.getCurrent());
    }

    return null;
}
```

which in its turn calls the following abbreviated method that handles two supported types of credentials:

```
protected boolean authenticate(
    String username,
    char[] password,
    X509Certificate[] certs) {
    try {
        if (certs != null) {
            // ... create subject
            LoginContextDriver
                .doX500Login(
                    subject, moduleID);
        } else {
            LoginContextDriver
                .login(
                    username,
                    password,
                    _realmName);
        }

        return true;
    } catch (Exception le) {}

    return false;
}
```

Again (strongly) abbreviated, the login method called looks as follows:

```
public static void login(
    String username,
    char[] password,
    String realmName){
    Subject subject = new Subject();
    subject.getPrivateCredentials()
        .add(new PasswordCredential(
        username, password, realmName));

    LoginContextDriver
        .login(subject, PasswordCredential.class);
}
```

This new login method checks for several credential types, which abbreviated looks as follows:

```
public static void login(Subject subject, Class cls) throws
LoginException {
    if (cls.equals(PasswordCredential.class))
        doPasswordLogin(subject);
    else if (cls.equals(X509CertificateCredential.class))
        doCertificateLogin(subject);
    else if (cls.equals(AnonCredential.class)) {
        doAnonLogin();
    else if (cls.equals(GSSUPName.class)) {
        doGSSUPLogin(subject);
    else if (cls.equals(X500Name.class)) {
        doX500Login(subject, null);
    else
        throw new LoginException(
            "Unknown credential type, cannot login.");
}
```

As we're following the password trail, we're going to look at the doPasswordLogin() method here, which strongly abbreviated looks as follows:

```
private static void doPasswordLogin(
    Subject subject)
    throws LoginException
    try {
        new LoginContext(
            Realm.getInstance(
                getPrivateCredentials(
                    subject,
                    PasswordCredential.class)
                .getRealm()
            ).getJAASContext(),
            subject,
            dummyCallback
        ).login();
    } catch (Exception e) {
        throw new
            LoginException(
                "Login failed: " +
                e.getMessage()).initCause(e);
    }
}
```

We're now five levels deep, and we're about to see our custom login module being called.

At this point, it's down to plain Java SE JAAS code. First, the name of the realm that was stuffed into a *PasswordCredential* which was stuffed into a Subject is used to obtain a Realm instance of the type that was shown way above, the GlassFish DAO-like type. Via this instance, the realm name is mapped to another name, the "JAAS context." This JAAS context name is the name under which our *LoginModule* has to be registered. The *LoginContext* does some magic to obtain this *LoginModule* from a configuration file and initializes it with the *Subject* among others. The *login()*, *commit()*, and *logout()* methods can then make use of this *Subject* later on.

At long last, the *login()* method call (via two further private helper methods, not shown here) will at seven levels deep cause the *login()* method of our *LoginModule* to be called. This happens via reflective code, which looks as follows:

```
// methodName == "login" here

// find the requested method in the LoginModule
for (mIndex = 0; mIndex < methods.length; mIndex++) {
    if (methods[mIndex].getName().equals(methodName))
        break;
}

// set up the arguments to be passed to the LoginModule method
Object[] args = { };

// invoke the LoginModule method
boolean status =
    ((Boolean) methods[mIndex].invoke(
        moduleStack[i].module, args)).booleanValue();
```

But remember that in GlassFish we didn't directly implemented LoginModule#login() but the abstract authenticateUser() method of the BasePasswordLoginModule, so we still have one more level to go. The final call at level 8 that causes our very own custom method to be called can be seen here:

```
final public boolean login() throws LoginException {

    // Extract the username, password and
    // realm name from the Subject
    extractCredentials();

    // Delegate the actual authentication to
    // subclass (finally!)
    authenticateUser();

    return true;
}
```

Open Liberty

Open Liberty calls its identity stores "user registry". It's shown here:

```java
public interface UserRegistry {
    void initialize(
        Properties props)
        throws CustomRegistryException,
        RemoteException;

    String checkPassword(
        String userSecurityName,
        String password)
        throws PasswordCheckFailedException,
        CustomRegistryException, RemoteException;
    String mapCertificate(
        X509Certificate[] certs)
        throws CertificateMapNotSupportedException,
        CertificateMapFailedException,
        CustomRegistryException,
        RemoteException;
    String getRealm()
        throws CustomRegistryException,
        RemoteException;

    Result getUsers(String pattern, int limit)
        throws CustomRegistryException,
        RemoteException;
    String getUserDisplayName(
        String userSecurityName)
        throws EntryNotFoundException,
        CustomRegistryException, RemoteException;
    String getUniqueUserId(String userSecurityName)
        throws EntryNotFoundException,
        CustomRegistryException, RemoteException;
    String getUserSecurityName(String uniqueUserId)
        throws EntryNotFoundException,
        CustomRegistryException, RemoteException;
```

```
boolean isValidUser(
    String userSecurityName)
    throws CustomRegistryException,
    RemoteException;

Result getGroups(
    String pattern, int limit)
    throws CustomRegistryException,
    RemoteException;
String getGroupDisplayName(
    String groupSecurityName)
    throws EntryNotFoundException,
    CustomRegistryException, RemoteException;
String getUniqueGroupId(String groupSecurityName)
    throws EntryNotFoundException,
    CustomRegistryException, RemoteException;
List getUniqueGroupIds(
    String uniqueUserId)
    throws EntryNotFoundException,
    CustomRegistryException, RemoteException;
String getGroupSecurityName(
    String uniqueGroupId)
    throws EntryNotFoundException,
    CustomRegistryException, RemoteException;
boolean isValidGroup(
    String groupSecurityName)
    throws CustomRegistryException,
    RemoteException;

List getGroupsForUser(
    String groupSecurityName)
    throws EntryNotFoundException,
    CustomRegistryException, RemoteException;
WSCredential createCredential(
    String userSecurityName)
    throws NotImplementedException,
    EntryNotFoundException,
```

```
    CustomRegistryException,
    RemoteException;

}
```

As can be seen, it's clearly one of the most heavyweight interfaces for an identity store that we've seen till this far.

As can be seen though, it has methods to list all users and groups that the identity store manages (*getUsers()*, *getGroups()*) as well as methods to get what IBM calls a "display name," "unique ID," and "security name" that are apparently associated with both user and role names. According to the published JavaDoc, display names are optional. It's perhaps worth asking the question if the richness that these name mappings potentially allow for is worth the extra complexity that's seen here.

createCredential() stands out as the JavaDoc mentions it's never been called for at least the 8.5.5 release of Liberty.

The main method that does the actual authentication is *checkPassword()*. It's clearly username/password based. Failure has to be indicated by throwing an exception; success returns the passed-in username again (or optionally any other valid name, which is a bit unlike what most other systems do). There's support for certificates via a separate method, *mapCertificate()*, which seemingly has to be called first, and then the resulting username passed into *checkPassword()* again.

WebLogic

It's not entirely clear what an identity store in WebLogic is really called. There are many moving parts. The overall term seems to be "security provider," but these are subdivided in authentication providers, identity assertion providers, principal validation providers, authorization providers, adjudication providers, and many more providers.

One of the entry points seems to be an "Authentication Provider V2," which is given here:

```
public interface AuthenticationProviderV2
    extends SecurityProvider {

    AppConfigurationEntry getAssertionModuleConfiguration();
    IdentityAsserterV2 getIdentityAsserter();
    AppConfigurationEntry getLoginModuleConfiguration();
    PrincipalValidator getPrincipalValidator();
}
```

Here, it looks like the getLoginModuleConfiguration() has to return an AppConfigurationEntry that holds the fully qualified class name of a JAAS LoginModule, which is given here:

```
public interface LoginModule {
    void initialize(
        Subject subject,
        CallbackHandler callbackHandler,
        Map<String,?> sharedState,
        Map<String,?> options);
    boolean login() throws LoginException;
    boolean commit() throws LoginException;
    boolean abort() throws LoginException;
    boolean logout() throws LoginException;
}
```

It seems WebLogic's usage of the *LoginModule* is not as highly specific to the application server as we saw was the case for JBoss and GlassFish. The user can implement the interface directly but has to put WebLogic-specific principals in the Subject as these are not standardized.

CHAPTER 4

Jakarta Authorization

In the previous chapter, we looked at Jakarta Authentication, which was about proving you are who you say you are. We also learned that authorization is about granting permissions to (mostly) someone who is authenticated. Authorization is handled in Jakarta EE by Jakarta Authorization. Like Jakarta Authentication, Jakarta Authorization is a lower-level API and as such the underpinning of higher-level APIs in the Jakarta security model. Knowledge of Jakarta Authorization helps one to deepen the understanding of how security works in Jakarta EE, but it's not strictly necessary. The more practical oriented reader may wish to skim this chapter again.

What Is Jakarta Authorization?

Let's take a look at the official scope:

> *Jakarta Authorization defines a low-level SPI for authorization modules, which are repositories of permissions facilitating subject based security by determining whether a given subject has a given permission, and algorithms to transform security constraints for specific containers (such as Jakarta Servlet or Jakarta Enterprise Beans) into these permissions.*

For starters, consider "Jakarta Authorization defines a low-level SPI." This is important to realize. Low-level here means that Jakarta Authorization is mainly targeted at library writers and system integrators and not so much at developers building actual, "normal," applications. Being an SPI, or Service Provider Interface, means that Jakarta Authorization mainly consists of interfaces to be implemented, which will then be called by the system. There's very few elements in Jakarta Authorization that would qualify as API, or Application Programming Interface, which are the types and methods an application would call.

© Arjan Tijms, Teo Bais, and Werner Keil 2022
A. Tijms et al., *The Definitive Guide to Security in Jakarta EE*, https://doi.org/10.1007/978-1-4842-7945-8_4

The most important bit here is that Jakarta Security is "for authorization modules." An authorization module is a module that is generally capable of deciding whether a permission is granted or not in a certain context.

This brings us to the next important part of the scope description: "facilitating subject based security." As was explained before in this book, Java's security model started as a code-based model, meaning permissions are granted or rejected based on the currently executing code. This made sense in the applet period, since applets were essentially foreign, untrusted pieces of code downloaded from somewhere and executed on the user's machine. In that scenario, the user is always local and the same, while the code depends on essentially which web page the user visits. For server security, it's the other way around; the code is always the same and local (to the server), while the users are different and remote. Subject-based security, in contrast to code-based security, means that the security applies to those different remote users. Jakarta Authorization therefore deals with authorizing users (callers) and not with authorizing code. Note that as of Java 17, authorizing code (via the venerable security manager) has been deprecated for removal.

Another key aspect of Jakarta Authorization is captured by the following part from the scope definition: "algorithms to transform security constraints for specific containers (such as Jakarta Servlet or Jakarta Enterprise Beans) into these permissions."

This is a crucial feature of Jakarta Authorization; as we explained before, the authorization module deals with *permissions*. Jakarta EE, most clearly Jakarta Servlet, however, deals with *constraints*. Therefore, we need a well-defined way to transform collections of constraints into collections of permissions. We'll take a deeper look at the difference between constraints and permissions and how they map to each other later in this chapter.

Jakarta Authorization in Jakarta EE

Recall from the previous chapter that the concrete security APIs in Jakarta EE are divided into three main APIs:

1. Jakarta Authentication

2. Jakarta Authorization

3. Jakarta Security

These three are largely designed to work together to provide an integrated security solution for Jakarta EE that transparently backs the declarative security model that was discussed in the previous chapters.

In essence, Jakarta Authentication, Authorization, and Security are the standard SPIs and APIs for the functionality that in early Jakarta EE versions was strictly in the vendor's realm.

Jakarta EE supports a hybrid model, where an application or its server/runtime can be configured to either use the standard APIs and associated configuration, or those that are specific to a server or runtime. This is depicted in the following image:

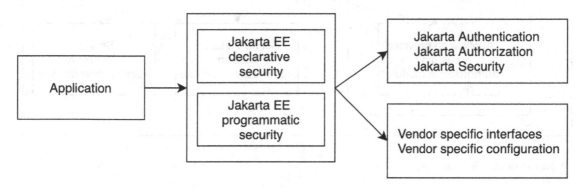

Besides using the standard interfaces or those from the vendor, Jakarta EE implementations typically offer a choice of shipping any custom versions of the various security artifacts (like the aforementioned authorization module) within the application archive, installing them separately on the server, or using a default available one in a way that's transparent to the application. Note that the exact options depend on the specific implementation being used (like GlassFish). Unlike Jakarta Authentication, Jakarta Authorization has not standardized how to ship its main artifact (the authorization module) within the application archive. Only a few servers, such as Payara, offer this as a proprietary feature.

JAKARTA EE 10 LOOKOUT

For Jakarta EE 10 or a later version, it's considered to standardize shipping authorization modules from within an application archive.

Consider the following diagram:

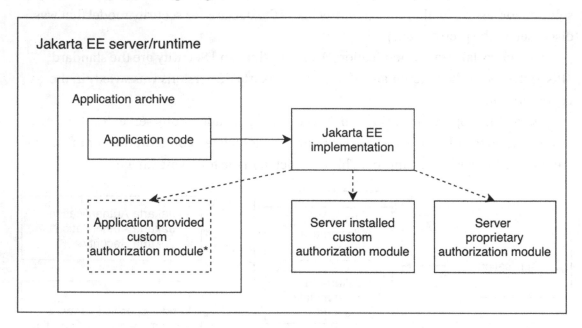

* This is relatively rare

Application code interacts with the authorization modules indirectly and does so via the programmatic APIs or via declarative security. A prime example of the programmatic API would be Jakarta Servlet's *HttpServletContext.isUserInRole* method, or Jakarta Security's *SecurityContext.isCallerInRole* method (we'll look at Jakarta Security in the next chapter). A prime example of the declarative security is the *@ServletSecurity* annotation or the *security-constraint* tag for usage in web.xml.

In response to the API call or when encountering the declarations mentioned before, the Jakarta EE implementation should consult a default Jakarta authorization module. Every compliant implementation officially has to use such a module by default. In practice, however, this doesn't always happen, and various vendors use a proprietary alternative. For the application code, this is typically transparent, and it shouldn't notice any difference.

To put Jakarta Authorization more into perspective, let's recall the diagram we showed in this chapter and highlight Jakarta Authorization this time. As an example implementation, we used Exousia here. Exousia is used by GlassFish and Piranha, which both only use Jakarta Authorization for their authorization needs and don't have any native authorization system running in parallel or underneath Jakarta Authorization.

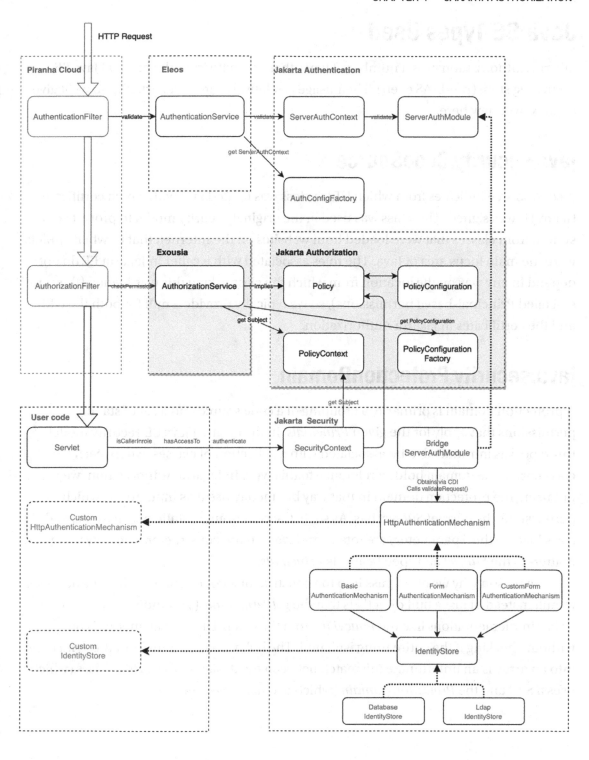

Java SE Types Used

Jakarta Authorization uses a number of types that originate from the original Java SE security system (pre-JAAS even). Their usage is relatively rare in Jakarta EE, so we'll give a quick overview here.

java.security.CodeSource

A code source indicates from which URL a class was loaded and with which certificates (if any) it was signed. This class was used in the original security model to protect your system from classes that were loaded from websites on the Internet, that is, when applets were the main focus area of Java. The roles associated with a caller in Jakarta EE do not depend in any way on the location from which the class asking this was loaded (they are so-called Principal-based permissions), so we typically provide a null for both the URL and the certificates in Jakarta Authorization.

java.security.ProtectionDomain

A protection domain is primarily a grouping of a code source and a set of static permissions that apply for the given *Principals*. In the original Java SE security model, this type was introduced to be associated with a collection of classes, where each class part of the domain holds a reference to this type. In Jakarta Authorization, we're not using the protection domain in that way but merely use it as input to ask which permissions the current *Subject* has. As such, the code source, static permissions, and class loader (third parameter) are totally irrelevant in the constructor. The only thing that matters is the *Subject* and specifically its *Principals*.

The reason why we often pass into the constructor a code source with all its fields set to null instead of just a null directly is that the *getPermissions*() method of well-known *Policy* implementations like the *PolicyFile* from the OpenJDK will call methods on it without checking if the entire thing isn't null. The bulky code to transform the *Principals* into an array is an unfortunate mismatch between the design of the *Subject* class (which uses a Set) and the *ProtectionDomain* (which uses a native array).

java.security.Policy

A policy is the main mechanism in Java SE that originally encapsulated the mapping between code sources and a global set of permissions that were given to that code source. Via its *implies()* method, it can be used to test if a given protection domain has a given permission, and via its *getPermissions()*, all permissions associated with a protection domain can be obtained.

java.security.PermissionCollection

At first glance, a *PermissionCollection* is exactly what its name implies: a collection of permissions. So why does the JDK have a special type for this and doesn't it just use a *Collection<Permission>* or a *List<Permission>*? Maybe part of the answer is that *PermissionCollection* was created before the Collection Framework in Java was introduced.

But this may be only part of the answer. A *PermissionCollection* and its most important subclass *Permissions* make a distinction between homogenous and heterogenous *Permissions*. Adding an arbitrary *Permission* to a *Permissions* class is supposed to not just add it randomly in sequence but to add it internally to a special "bucket." This bucket is another *PermissionCollection* that stores permissions of the same type. It's typically implemented as a Class to *PermissionCollection* Map. This somewhat complex mechanism is used to optimize checking for a permission; iterating over every individual permission would not be ideal. We at least should be able to go right away to the right type of permission. For example, when checking for permission to access a file, it's useless to ask every socket permission whether we have access to that.

The Authorization Module

Let's now take a closer look at what we called the "authorization module" previously. In practice, there's no single entity called that, but in fact, this logical concept is comprised of three separate entities:

1. PolicyConfigurationFactory

2. PolicyConfiguration

3. Policy

We'll look at these individually in the following text.

PolicyConfigurationFactory

The *PolicyConfigurationFactory* is a factory that provides an object that collects permissions. This is the entity that one typically registers with a Jakarta EE implementation, and that is used by that implementation to obtain the *PolicyConfiguration* which we will discuss below.

A *PolicyConfigurationFactory* does not just provide (new) instances of the *PolicyConfiguration* but is also required to keep a reference to these instances and provide the same instance again for any so-called context id. This context id is an important concept in Jakarta Authorization, and it corresponds to the application in case of an application that consists of a single web module (.war) with no Jakarta Enterprise Beans. In case of an enterprise archive (.ear) with potentially multiple web modules and separate enterprise beans modules, there's a context id for each such module.

Obtaining a *PolicyConfiguration* from the *PolicyConfigurationFactory* has a mandatory side effect that it shifts the *PolicyConfiguration* to the "open state" (we'll look at the various states down below).

JAKARTA EE 10 LOOKOUT

For Jakarta EE 10 or a later version, it's considered to add a method to the *PolicyConfigurationFactory* that returns just the (existing) PolicyConfiguration, without any transition requirements.

Furthermore, the PolicyConfigurationFactory contains a method to let us check whether a given context id is associated with an active *PolicyConfiguration*.

A typical implementation of a PolicyConfigurationFactory looks as follows:

```
public class DefaultPolicyConfigurationFactory
    extends PolicyConfigurationFactory {

    private static final
    ConcurrentMap<String, DefaultPolicyConfigurationStateMachine>
        configurators = new ConcurrentHashMap<>();
```

```java
@Override
public PolicyConfiguration getPolicyConfiguration(
    String contextID,
    boolean remove)
    throws PolicyContextException {

    DefaultPolicyConfigurationStateMachine
        defaultPolicyConfigurationStateMachine =
        configurators.computeIfAbsent(contextID,
            contextId -> new DefaultPolicyConfigurationStateMachine(
                new DefaultPolicyConfiguration(
                    contextID)));

    if (remove) {
        defaultPolicyConfigurationStateMachine
            .delete();
    }

    defaultPolicyConfigurationStateMachine
        .open();

    return
        defaultPolicyConfigurationStateMachine;
}

@Override
public boolean inService(
    String contextID)
    throws PolicyContextException {
    DefaultPolicyConfigurationStateMachine
        defaultPolicyConfigurationStateMachine =
        configurators.get(contextID);

    if (defaultPolicyConfigurationStateMachine == null) {
        return false;
    }
```

```
        return defaultPolicyConfigurationStateMachine
            .inService();
    }
}
```

In practice, we'd often add a method such as the following:

```
public static DefaultPolicyConfiguration
getCurrentPolicyConfiguration(String contextId) {
    return (DefaultPolicyConfiguration) configurators
            .get(contextId)
            .getPolicyConfiguration();
}
```

PolicyConfiguration

The PolicyConfiguration is conceptually simple; it just stores permissions. This essentially makes it what is also called a "permission store." However, there are various requirements for this artifact that make it less than trivial to implement. We'll first list these requirements and will then look at each of them individually.

- Collecting and managing permissions

- A state machine that controls the life cycle of this permission collector

- Linking permissions of multiple modules and utilities

- Processing permissions after collecting

Collecting and Managing Permissions

The prime requirement of the *PolicyConfiguration* is collecting permissions. Since we're talking about an SPI here, it means the *PolicyConfiguration* gets these permissions handed over to it by the Jakarta EE runtime. It does not actively have to find and load permissions itself.

To fulfill this part of the requirements, we have to maintain three collections:

1. Excluded permissions

2. Unchecked permissions

3. Per-role permissions

Excluded permissions are permissions that exclude access to a resource. It means nobody is allowed to access such a resource. In practical terms, this can be used to quickly remove access to some part of, say, a website, or to make sure some web resources that for some reason can't be in the WEB-INF folder of a web archive are not accessible to any external caller. Such excluded resources are still accessible via includes or internal forwards, as these aren't subject to the standard access controls.

In order to demonstrate the code required, we'll provide individual subclasses for each requirement. A typical example implementation for the collection part looks as follows:

```java
public abstract class DefaultPolicyConfigurationPermissions
    extends
    DefaultPolicyConfigurationBase {

    private Permissions excludedPermissions =
        new Permissions();
    private Permissions uncheckedPermissions =
        new Permissions();
    private Map<String, Permissions> perRolePermissions =
        new HashMap<>();

    public DefaultPolicyConfigurationPermissions(
        String contextID) {
        super(contextID);
    }

    @Override
    public void addToExcludedPolicy(
        Permission permission)
        throws PolicyContextException {
        excludedPermissions
            .add(permission);
    }

    @Override
    public void addToUncheckedPolicy(
        Permission permission)
        throws PolicyContextException {
```

```java
        uncheckedPermissions
            .add(permission);
    }

    @Override
    public void addToRole(
        String roleName,
        Permission permission)
        throws PolicyContextException {
        Permissions permissions = perRolePermissions
            .get(roleName);
        if (permissions == null) {
            permissions = new Permissions();
            perRolePermissions.put(
                roleName, permissions);
        }

        permissions.add(permission);
    }

    @Override
    public void removeExcludedPolicy()
        throws PolicyContextException {
        excludedPermissions = new Permissions();
    }

    @Override
    public void removeUncheckedPolicy()
        throws PolicyContextException {
        uncheckedPermissions = new Permissions();
    }

    @Override
    public void removeRole(
        String roleName)
        throws PolicyContextException {
        if (perRolePermissions
            .containsKey(roleName)) {
```

```
        perRolePermissions
            .remove(roleName);
    } else if ("*"
        .equals(roleName)) {
        perRolePermissions.clear();
    }
}

@Override
public void delete()
    throws PolicyContextException {
    removeExcludedPolicy();
    removeUncheckedPolicy();
    perRolePermissions.clear();
}
}
```

As can be seen, the implementation is relatively straightforward. It keeps three collections, one for each type of permission. There are methods to add permissions to each of those collections and to remove all elements from each of them. The role removal method stands out, as it requires a "*" to be passed in to remove all permissions from this collection. Because the "*" role was added later in Jakarta Authorization's life, there are a lot of rules in the SPI to deal with old implementations of a *PolicyConfiguration* that used "*" as a regular role name. We see an example of that here.

While there are methods to add and remove permissions, there aren't methods to get permissions. In practice, implementations may add methods like these:

```
public Permissions getExcludedPermissions() {
    return excludedPermissions;
}

public Permissions getUncheckedPermissions() {
    return uncheckedPermissions;
}

public Map<String, Permissions> getPerRolePermissions() {
    return perRolePermissions;
}
```

JAKARTA EE 10 LOOKOUT

For Jakarta EE 10 or a later version, it's considered to add the missing getter methods to the PolicyConfiguration.

A State Machine That Controls the Life Cycle of This Permission Collector

Jakarta Authorization defines that a *PolicyConfiguration* exists in one of several states: *open, inService,* and *deleted.* When *open,* permissions can be added to it; when *inService,* it's actively used; and when deleted, it's effectively destroyed and can't be used anymore (i.e., until reopened).

Jakarta Authorization defines the following state transitions when various methods of the *PolicyConfiguration* are called for each state it is in:

| Method | Current State to Next State | | |
	deleted	open	inService
addToExcludedPolicy	Unsupported Operation	open	Unsupported Operation
addToRole	Unsupported Operation	open	Unsupported Operation
addToUncheckedPolicy	Unsupported Operation	open	Unsupported Operation
commit	Unsupported Operation	inService	inService
delete	deleted	deleted	deleted
getContextID	deleted	open	inService
inService	deleted	open	inService
linkConfiguration	Unsupported Operation	open	Unsupported Operation
removeExcludedPolicy	Unsupported Operation	open	Unsupported Operation
removeRole	Unsupported Operation	open	Unsupported Operation
removeUncheckedPolicy	Unsupported Operation	open	Unsupported Operation

Jakarta Authorization puts the burden of implementing a state machine for this requirement on the author of the authorization module.

JAKARTA EE 10 LOOKOUT

For Jakarta EE 10 or a later version, it's considered to provide a default implementation of the *PolicyConfiguration* state machine so custom implementations don't have to implement this from scratch.

While the requirement could be implemented with an actual state machine, the transitions are simple enough for implementations to satisfy this requirement with just a number of checks.

The following provides a typical implementation:

```java
public class DefaultPolicyConfigurationStateMachine
    implements PolicyConfiguration {

    public static enum State {
        OPEN, INSERVICE, DELETED
    };

    private State state = OPEN;
    private PolicyConfiguration policyConfiguration;

    public DefaultPolicyConfigurationStateMachine(
        PolicyConfiguration policyConfiguration) {
        this.policyConfiguration = policyConfiguration;
    }

    public PolicyConfiguration getPolicyConfiguration() {
        return policyConfiguration;
    }

    // ### Methods that can be called in any state
    // and don't change state
```

```java
@Override
public String getContextID()
    throws PolicyContextException {
    return policyConfiguration
        .getContextID();
}

@Override
public boolean inService()
    throws PolicyContextException {
    return state == INSERVICE;
}

// ### Methods where state should be OPEN
// and don't change state

@Override
public void addToExcludedPolicy(
    Permission permission)
    throws PolicyContextException {
    checkStateIs(OPEN);
    policyConfiguration
        .addToExcludedPolicy(
            permission);
}

@Override
public void addToUncheckedPolicy(
    Permission permission)
    throws PolicyContextException {
    checkStateIs(OPEN);
    policyConfiguration
        .addToUncheckedPolicy(
            permission);
}

@Override
public void addToRole(
```

```java
    String roleName,
    Permission permission)
    throws PolicyContextException {
    checkStateIs(OPEN);
    policyConfiguration.addToRole(
        roleName, permission);
}

@Override
public void addToExcludedPolicy(
    PermissionCollection permissions)
    throws PolicyContextException {
    checkStateIs(OPEN);
    policyConfiguration
        .addToExcludedPolicy(
            permissions);
}

@Override
public void addToUncheckedPolicy(
    PermissionCollection permissions)
    throws PolicyContextException {
    checkStateIs(OPEN);
    policyConfiguration
        .addToUncheckedPolicy(
            permissions);
}

@Override
public void addToRole(
    String roleName,
    PermissionCollection permissions)
    throws PolicyContextException {
    checkStateIs(OPEN);
    policyConfiguration.addToRole(
        roleName, permissions);
}
```

```java
@Override
public void linkConfiguration(
    PolicyConfiguration link)
    throws PolicyContextException {
    checkStateIs(OPEN);
    policyConfiguration
        .linkConfiguration(link);
}

@Override
public void removeExcludedPolicy()
    throws PolicyContextException {
    checkStateIs(OPEN);
    policyConfiguration
        .removeExcludedPolicy();

}

@Override
public void removeRole(
    String roleName)
    throws PolicyContextException {
    checkStateIs(OPEN);
    policyConfiguration
        .removeRole(roleName);
}

@Override
public void removeUncheckedPolicy()
    throws PolicyContextException {
    checkStateIs(OPEN);
    policyConfiguration
        .removeUncheckedPolicy();
}

// Methods that change the state
//
```

```java
// commit() can only be called when
// the state is OPEN or INSERVICE
// and next state is always INSERVICE
//
// delete() can always be called and
// target state will always be DELETED
//
// open() can always be called and
// target state will always be OPEN

@Override
public void commit()
    throws PolicyContextException {
    checkStateIsNot(DELETED);

    if (state == OPEN) {
        policyConfiguration
            .commit();
        state = INSERVICE;
    }
}

@Override
public void delete()
    throws PolicyContextException {
    policyConfiguration.delete();
    state = DELETED;
}

// ### Private methods

private void checkStateIs(
    State requiredState) {
    if (state != requiredState) {
        throw new IllegalStateException(
            "Required status is "
                + requiredState
                + " but actual state is "
```

```
                        + state);
        }
    }

    private void checkStateIsNot(
        State undesiredState) {
        if (state == undesiredState) {
            throw new IllegalStateException(
                "State could not be "
                    + undesiredState
                    + " but actual state is");
        }
    }
}
```

The (simplified) "state machine" here is provided as a wrapper around any *PolicyConfiguration* and can thus be universally applied.

Missing from the official *PolicyConfiguration* interface is a method that's needed by the *PolicyConfigurationFactory*, namely, a method to transition to open. This can be easily provided as follows:

```
/**
 * Transition back to open.
 */
public void open() {
    state = OPEN;
}
```

JAKARTA EE 10 LOOKOUT

For Jakarta EE 10 or a later version, it's considered to add this *open* method to the *PolicyConfiguration* interface.

Linking Permissions of Multiple Modules and Utilities

Jakarta Authorization provides facilities to link together *PolicyConfigurations* belonging to different contexts in the same logical applications (such as different web or enterprise bean modules in an ear archive). This can be used to make sure all of these contexts have the same "role mapper" (explained later in this chapter) applied. Since these types of modules are deemphasized in modern Jakarta EE, we won't elaborate on this much.

The *PolicyConfiguration* interface requires a context id to be kept and has some convenience methods to set multiple permissions. In practice, these multiple permission convenience methods aren't often, if at all, called by Jakarta EE implementations, but they still need to be there.

JAKARTA EE 10 LOOKOUT

For Jakarta EE 10 or a later version, it's considered to provide default methods for some of the convenience methods, so it's not mandatory to implement these.

The following shows a typical implementation of these:

```
public abstract class DefaultPolicyConfigurationBase
    implements PolicyConfiguration {

    private final String contextID;
    private final Set<String> linkedContextIds =
        new HashSet<>();

    public DefaultPolicyConfigurationBase(
        String contextID) {
        this.contextID = contextID;
    }

    @Override
    public String getContextID()
        throws PolicyContextException {
        return contextID;
```

```
    }

    @Override
    public void addToExcludedPolicy(
        PermissionCollection permissions)
        throws PolicyContextException {
        for (Permission permission : list(
            permissions.elements())) {
            addToExcludedPolicy(
                permission);
        }
    }

    @Override
    public void addToUncheckedPolicy(
        PermissionCollection permissions)
        throws PolicyContextException {
        for (Permission permission : list(
            permissions.elements())) {
            addToUncheckedPolicy(
                permission);
        }
    }

    @Override
    public void addToRole(
        String roleName,
        PermissionCollection permissions)
        throws PolicyContextException {
        for (Permission permission : list(
            permissions.elements())) {
            addToRole(roleName,
                permission);
        }
    }

    @Override
```

```
public void linkConfiguration(
    PolicyConfiguration link)
    throws PolicyContextException {
    linkedContextIds
        .add(link.getContextID());
}

@Override
public boolean inService()
    throws PolicyContextException {
    // Not used, taken care of by
    // PolicyConfigurationStateMachine
    return true;
}

}
```

Processing Permissions After Collecting

The final part of the *PolicyConfiguration* concerns a kind of life cycle method again, namely, a method that the Jakarta EE implementation calls to indicate all permissions have been handed over to the *PolicyConfiguration*. In a higher-level SPI or API, this might have been an @PostConstruct annotated method.

Contrary to most methods of the *PolicyConfiguration* that we've seen until now, what happens here is pretty specific to the custom policy provider. Some implementations do a lot of work here and generate a .policy file in the standard Java SE format and write that to disk. This file is then intended to be read back by a standard Java SE Policy implementation.

Other implementations use this moment to optimize the collected permissions by transforming them into their own internal data structure.

We'll show here what the default implementation of Exousia does, which is essentially just instantiating a role mapper using the set of roles that are associated with permissions:

```
public class DefaultPolicyConfiguration
    extends
    DefaultPolicyConfigurationPermissions {
```

```java
    public DefaultPolicyConfiguration(
        String contextID) {
        super(contextID);
    }

    private PrincipalMapper roleMapper;

    @Override
    public void commit()
        throws PolicyContextException {

        roleMapper = (PrincipalMapper) PolicyContext
            .getContext(
                PRINCIPAL_MAPPER);
        if (roleMapper == null) {
            roleMapper = new DefaultRoleMapper(
                getContextID(),
                getPerRolePermissions()
                    .keySet());
        }
    }

    public PrincipalMapper getRoleMapper() {
        return roleMapper;
    }
}
```

Policy

The *Policy* is responsible for determining whether a subject (the caller) has permission to perform a security-sensitive operation as expressed by a permission. Jakarta Authorization reuses this type from Java SE, where it has mostly been used to do code-based security checks. Mixing code-based and subject-based security is not always ideal, and this somewhat shows in the code that needs to be implemented here. Note that code-based security at the moment of writing is being deprecated for Java SE 17 (via JEP 411).

Jakarta Authorization implementations should all provide a *Policy* that implements the default authorization algorithm originally defined by Jakarta Servlet and Jakarta Enterprise Beans, which does the following checks in order:

1. Is permission excluded? (nobody can access those)

2. Is permission unchecked? (everyone can access those)

3. Is permission granted to every authenticated user?

4. Is permission granted to any of the roles the current caller is in?

5. Is permission granted by the previous (if any) policy?

While a default *Policy* has to be provided, this default *Policy* is not made available for extension by developers. Specifically, this means that if a customization is needed to the default algorithm, then this full default algorithm has to be reimplemented.

The following gives an example of an implementation:

```
public class DefaultPolicy
    extends Policy {

    private final static Logger logger = Logger
        .getLogger(DefaultPolicy.class
            .getName());

    private Policy defaultPolicy = getDefaultPolicy();

    @Override
    public boolean implies(
        ProtectionDomain domain,
        Permission permission) {

        String contextId = PolicyContext.getContextID();

        DefaultPolicyConfiguration policyConfiguration =
            getPolicyConfiguration(contextId);
        PrincipalMapper roleMapper = policyConfiguration
            .getRoleMapper();

        if (isExcluded(
            policyConfiguration
                .getExcludedPermissions(),
```

```
        permission)) {
        // Excluded permissions cannot be accessed
        // by anyone
        return false;
    }

    if (isUnchecked(
        policyConfiguration
            .getUncheckedPermissions(),
        permission)) {
        // Unchecked permissions are free to
        // be accessed by everyone
        return true;
    }

    List<Principal> currentUserPrincipals = asList(
        domain.getPrincipals());

    if (!roleMapper
        .isAnyAuthenticatedUserRoleMapped()
        && !currentUserPrincipals
            .isEmpty()) {
        // The "any authenticated user" role is not
        // mapped, so available to anyone and the current
        // user is assumed to be authenticated (we assume
        // that an unauthenticated user doesn't have any
        // principals whatever they are)
        if (hasAccessViaRole(
            policyConfiguration
                .getPerRolePermissions(),
            "**", permission)) {
            // Access is granted purely based
            // on the user being authenticated
            // (the actual roles, if any, the user
            // has it not important)
            return true;
        }
```

```
    }

    Subject subject;
    try {
        subject = (Subject) PolicyContext
            .getContext(
                "javax.security.auth.Subject.container");
    } catch (PolicyContextException ex) {
        throw new RuntimeException(
            ex);
    }

    if (hasAccessViaRoles(
        policyConfiguration
            .getPerRolePermissions(),
        roleMapper.getMappedRoles(
            currentUserPrincipals,
            subject),
        permission)) {
        // Access is granted via role. Note that if
        // this returns false
        // it doesn't mean the permission is not
        // granted. A role can only grant, not take
        // away permissions.
        return true;
    }

    if (defaultPolicy != null) {
        return defaultPolicy
            .implies(domain,
                permission);
    }

    return false;
}

@Override
public PermissionCollection getPermissions(
```

```
ProtectionDomain domain) {

Permissions permissions = new Permissions();

DefaultPolicyConfiguration policyConfiguration =
    getCurrentPolicyConfiguration();
PrincipalMapper roleMapper = policyConfiguration
    .getRoleMapper();

Permissions excludedPermissions = policyConfiguration
    .getExcludedPermissions();

// First get all permissions from the previous (original)
// policy
if (defaultPolicy != null) {
    collectPermissions(
        defaultPolicy
            .getPermissions(
                domain),
        permissions,
        excludedPermissions);
}

// If there are any static permissions, add those next
if (domain
    .getPermissions() != null) {
    collectPermissions(
        domain.getPermissions(),
        permissions,
        excludedPermissions);
}

// Thirdly, get all unchecked permissions
collectPermissions(
    policyConfiguration
        .getUncheckedPermissions(),
    permissions,
    excludedPermissions);
```

```java
        Subject subject;
        try {
            subject = (Subject) PolicyContext
                .getContext(
                    "javax.security.auth.Subject.container");
        } catch (PolicyContextException ex) {
            throw new RuntimeException(
                ex);
        }

        // Finally get the permissions for each role
        // *that the current user has*
        //
        Map<String, Permissions> perRolePermissions =
            policyConfiguration.getPerRolePermissions();

        for (String role : roleMapper
            .getMappedRoles(
                domain.getPrincipals(),
                subject)) {
            if (perRolePermissions
                .containsKey(role)) {
                collectPermissions(
                    perRolePermissions
                        .get(role),
                    permissions,
                    excludedPermissions);
            }
        }

        return permissions;
    }

    @Override
    public PermissionCollection getPermissions(
        CodeSource codesource) {

        Permissions permissions = new Permissions();
```

```
    DefaultPolicyConfigurationPermissions policyConfiguration =
        getCurrentPolicyConfiguration();
    Permissions excludedPermissions = policyConfiguration
        .getExcludedPermissions();

    // First get all permissions from the previous
    // (original) policy
    if (defaultPolicy != null) {
        collectPermissions(
            defaultPolicy
                .getPermissions(
                    codesource),
            permissions,
            excludedPermissions);
    }

    // Secondly get the static permissions.
    // Note that there are only two sources
    // possible here, without knowing the roles
    // of the current user we can't check the per
    // role permissions.
    collectPermissions(
        policyConfiguration
            .getUncheckedPermissions(),
        permissions,
        excludedPermissions);

    return permissions;
}

// ### Private methods

private Policy getDefaultPolicy() {
    Policy policy = Policy
        .getPolicy();
    if (policy instanceof DefaultPolicy) {
        logger.warning(
            "Cannot obtain default / previous policy.");
```

```java
            return null;
        }

        return policy;
    }

    private boolean isExcluded(
        Permissions excludedPermissions,
        Permission permission) {
        if (excludedPermissions
            .implies(permission)) {
            return true;
        }

        for (Permission excludedPermission : list(
            excludedPermissions
                .elements())) {
            if (permission.implies(
                excludedPermission)) {
                return true;
            }
        }

        return false;
    }

    private boolean isUnchecked(
        Permissions uncheckedPermissions,
        Permission permission) {
        return uncheckedPermissions
            .implies(permission);
    }

    private boolean hasAccessViaRoles(
        Map<String, Permissions> perRolePermissions,
        List<String> roles,
        Permission permission) {
        for (String role : roles) {
```

```
            if (hasAccessViaRole(
                perRolePermissions,
                role, permission)) {
                return true;
            }
        }

        return false;
    }

    private boolean hasAccessViaRole(
        Map<String, Permissions> perRolePermissions,
        String role,
        Permission permission) {
        return perRolePermissions
            .containsKey(role)
            && perRolePermissions
                .get(role)
                .implies(permission);
    }

    /**
     * Copies permissions from a source into a target
     * skipping any permission that's excluded.
     *
     * @param sourcePermissions
     * @param targetPermissions
     * @param excludedPermissions
     */
    private void collectPermissions(
        PermissionCollection sourcePermissions,
        PermissionCollection targetPermissions,
        Permissions excludedPermissions) {

        boolean hasExcludedPermissions = excludedPermissions
            .elements()
            .hasMoreElements();
```

```
for (Permission permission : list(
    sourcePermissions
        .elements())) {
    if (!hasExcludedPermissions
        || !isExcluded(
            excludedPermissions,
            permission)) {
        targetPermissions
            .add(permission);
    }
  }
}

}
```

There's quite a lot going on in the preceding code, so let's briefly highlight some elements. The two main methods here are *implies()* and *getPermissions(ProtectionDomain)*. The *implies* method is most typically used to check specific permissions, while the *getPermissions* one is only occasionally used for some custom queries (we'll give some examples of these in the following text).

The *implies* method first needs to obtain the current context id, which is set by the calling Jakarta EE implementation, and can be obtained via the PolicyContext class. The context id in its turn can be used to obtain the *PolicyConfiguration* and its role mapper:

```
String contextId = PolicyContext.getContextID();

DefaultPolicyConfiguration policyConfiguration =
    getPolicyConfiguration(contextId);
PrincipalMapper roleMapper = policyConfiguration
    .getRoleMapper();
```

Here, we see that the *Policy* needs to have knowledge of the specific *PolicyConfiguration* it's being paired with, as it needs to call its own *getPolicyConfiguration* method.

Subsequently, the method checks whether the permission to be checked is either excluded or unchecked. For these checks, we don't need any details of the current caller. When it comes time to check for role-based permissions, we do need those details.

Here's where things get a little complicated. Jakarta EE never standardized which *Principals* represent the caller principal and the role principals (or, in fact, whether roles are actually represented by principals at all).

Via the *ProtectionDomain*, we can obtain a list of *Principals*:

```
List<Principal> currentUserPrincipals = asList(
    domain.getPrincipals());
```

We also need the *Subject* as some Jakarta EE implementations don't represent roles as principals but instead store them as private credentials. The Subject is obtained via the *PolicyContext*, just as the context id was:

```
Subject subject;
try {
    subject = (Subject) PolicyContext
        .getContext(
            "javax.security.auth.Subject.container");
} catch (PolicyContextException ex) {
    throw new RuntimeException(
        ex);
}
```

The verbose style with casting and checked exceptions is a reminder to the age of Jakarta Authorization, which was originally conceived in a time when these things were very popular.

Finally, to actually get the list of roles, which are, when all is said and done, just opaque identifiers, we use the role mapper that we obtained before. Note that the role mapper is a required but not standardized artifact. In case of Exousia, on which we based the examples, the role mapper it provides has built-in knowledge of a large number of existing Jakarta EE implementations.

The code to do so looks as follows:

```
for (String role : roleMapper
        .getMappedRoles(
            domain.getPrincipals(),
            subject)) {
}
```

```
┌─────────────────────────────────────────────────────────────────┐
│                    JAKARTA EE 10 LOOKOUT                         │
└─────────────────────────────────────────────────────────────────┘
```

For Jakarta EE 10 or a later version, it's considered to standardize the role mapper.

Transforming Security Constraints to Permissions

Remember from the scope statement that Jakarta Authorization next to the authorization module SPI provides an algorithm to

transform security constraints for specific containers (such as Jakarta Servlet or Jakarta Enterprise Beans) into these permissions

Contrary to the authorization module and its constituent parts, we don't have to write or customize this algorithm ourselves; it's provided by the Jakarta Authorization implementation. As a user of Jakarta Authorization, it's normally not necessary to be fully aware of all the intricate details of this algorithm, but it's good to have some idea of what is going on. We'll demonstrate this using an example.

Consider the following constraints in a web.xml file:

```
<security-constraint>
    <web-resource-collection>
        <web-resource-name>Forbidden Pattern</web-resource-name>
        <url-pattern>/forbidden/*</url-pattern>
    </web-resource-collection>
    <auth-constraint/>
</security-constraint>

<security-constraint>
    <web-resource-collection>
        <web-resource-name>Protected Pattern</web-resource-name>
        <url-pattern>/protected/*</url-pattern>
    </web-resource-collection>
    <auth-constraint>
```

```
        <role-name>architect</role-name>
        <role-name>administrator</role-name>
    </auth-constraint>
</security-constraint>

<security-constraint>
    <web-resource-collection>
        <web-resource-name>Protected Exact</web-resource-name>
        <url-pattern>/adminservlet</url-pattern>
    </web-resource-collection>
    <auth-constraint>
        <role-name>administrator</role-name>
    </auth-constraint>
</security-constraint>

<security-role>
    <role-name>architect</role-name>
</security-role>
<security-role>
    <role-name>administrator</role-name>
</security-role>
```

The preceding constraints express that nobody is allowed to access "/forbidden/*", while for "/protected/*", the caller needs to have either the "architect" role or the "administrator" role. Finally, for "/adminservlet", only the admin role is allowed.

Jakarta Authorization will generate three types of *Permission* instances when translating constraints expressed in web.xml:

1. WebRoleRefPermission

2. WebUserDataPermission

3. WebResourcePermission

We'll briefly discuss these here.

WebRoleRefPermission

A web role ref permission is about mapping Servlet local roles to application roles. Especially with MVC frameworks like Jakarta Faces and Jakarta MVC, the use for this is perhaps questionable, as there's only one Servlet in that case that serves many different views.

WebUserDataPermission

A web user data permission is about the transport level guarantees for accessing resources (practically, this almost always means HTTP vs HTTPS). This can be specified using the *<user-data-constraint>* element in web.xml, which we have omitted here.

WebResourcePermission

The web resource permission is about the actual access to a resource. This can be specified using the *<web-resource-collection>* element in web.xml, which we have used in the preceding example.

Given the previously shown constraints in web.xml, the following *WebResourcePermission* instances will be generated in three collections as shown in the following. For brevity, only *WebResourcePermission* is shown. The other types are omitted.

Excluded

- WebResourcePermission "/forbidden/*"

Unchecked

- WebResourcePermission "/:/adminservlet:/protected/*:/forbidden/*"

Per Role

- Architect

  - WebResourcePermission "/protected/*"

- Administrator

  - WebResourcePermission "/protected/*"

  - WebResourcePermission "/adminservlet"

So let's take a look at what's going on here.

Our first web.xml constraint shown previously defined so-called excluded access, which, as explained before, means that nobody can access the resources defined by that pattern. In XML, this is accomplished by simply omitting the *auth-constraint* element. This was translated to Java code by means of putting a *WebResourcePermission* with the pattern "/forbidden/*" in the "Excluded" collection. Although there are some differences, this is a reasonably direct translation from the XML form.

The permission shown previously for the "Unchecked" collection concerns the so-called unchecked access, which means that everyone can access those resources.

This one wasn't explicitly defined in XML, although XML does have syntax for explicitly defining unchecked access. The permission shown here concerns the Servlet default mapping (a fallback for everything that doesn't match any other declared Servlet pattern).

The pattern used here may need some further explanation. In the pattern, the colon (:) is a separator of a list of patterns. The first pattern is the one we grant access to, while the rest of the patterns are the exceptions to that. So unchecked access for "/:/ adminservlet:/protected/*:/forbidden/*" means access to everything (e.g., /foo/readme. text) is granted to everyone, with the exception of "/adminservlet" and paths that start with either "/protected" or "/forbidden". In this case, the translation from the XML form to Java is not as direct.

The next two constraints that we showed in web.xml concerned "role-based access," which means that only callers who are in the associated roles can access resources defined by those patterns. In XML, this is accomplished by putting one or more patterns together with one or more roles in a security constraint. This is translated to Java by generating {role, permission} pairs for each unique combination that appears in the XML file. It's typically most convenient then to put these entries in a map, with role the key and permission the value, as was done before, but this is not strictly necessary. Here, we see that the translation doesn't directly reflect the XML structure, but the link to the XML version can surely be seen in the translation.

Authorization Queries

Jakarta Authorization provides an API and a means to ask the container several authorization-related things. This API is used by the Jakarta EE implementation but can be used by user code as well.

Just like Jakarta Authentication, Jakarta Authorization provides an API here that's rather abstract and which seems to be infinitely flexible. Unfortunately, this also means it's initially difficult for users to find out how to perform certain common tasks. So while Jakarta Authorization enables us to ask things like "What roles does the current caller have?" and "Will this caller have access to this URL?" there aren't any convenience methods in Jakarta Authorization such as "List<String> getAllUserRoles();" or "boolean hasAccess(String url);". In the following, we'll show how these things are being done in Jakarta Authorization. Note that some things have convenience methods in Jakarta Security, which we will discuss in a next chapter.

Get All Users Roles

We'll start with obtaining the Subject instance corresponding to the current caller. For simplicity, we assume the caller is indeed authenticated (logged in) here.

```
Subject subject = (Subject) PolicyContext.getContext("javax.security.auth.
Subject.container");
```

After that, we'll get the so-called permission collection from the container that corresponds to this Subject:

```
PermissionCollection permissionCollection = Policy.getPolicy().
getPermissions(
    new ProtectionDomain(
        new CodeSource(null, (Certificate[]) null),
        null, null,
        subject.getPrincipals().toArray(new Principal[subject.
        getPrincipals().size()])
    )
);
```

After this, we call the implies() method on the collection:

```
permissionCollection.implies(new WebRoleRefPermission("", "nothing"));
```

This is a small trick, hack if you will, to get rid of a special type of permission that might be in the collection; the *UnresolvedPermission*. This is a special type of permission that may be used when permissions are read from a file. Such a file then typically contains the fully qualified name of a class that represents a specific permission. If this class hasn't been loaded yet or has been loaded by another class loader than the one from which the file is read, an *UnresolvedPermission* will be created that just contains this fully qualified class name as a String. The *implies*() method checks if the given permission is implied by the collection and therefore forces the actual loading of at least the *WebRoleRefPermission* class. This class is the standard permission type that corresponds to the nonstandard representation of the group/roles inside the collection of principals that we're after.

Finally, we iterate over the permission collection and collect all role names from the *WebRoleRefPermission*:

```
Set<String> roles = new HashSet<>();
for (Permission permission : list(permissionCollection.elements())) {
    if (permission instanceof WebRoleRefPermission) {
        String role = permission.getActions();

        if (!roles.contains(role) && request.isUserInRole(role)) {
            roles.add(role);
        }
    }
}
```

A thing to note here is that there's no such thing as a *WebRolePermission*, but only a *WebRoleRefPermission*. In the Servlet spec, a role ref is the thing that you use when inside a specific Servlet a role name is used that's different from the role names in the rest of your application. In theory, this could be handy for secured Servlets from a library that you include in your application. Role refs are fully optional, and when you don't use them, you can simply use the application wide role names directly.

In Jakarta Authorization, however, there are only role refs. When a role ref is not explicitly defined, then they are simply defaulted to the application role names. Since a role ref is per servlet, the number of *WebRoleRefPermission* instances that will be created is *at least* the number of roles in the application plus one (for the '**' role), times the number of servlets in the application (typically plus three for the default and JSP servlet and an extra one for the so-called unmapped context). So given an application with two roles, "foo" and "bar", and two Servlets named "servlet1" and "servlet2", the WebRoleRefPermission instances that will be created is as follows:

- servlet1 - foo
- servlet1 - bar
- servlet1 - **
- servlet2 - foo
- servlet2 - bar
- servlet2 - **
- default - foo

- default - bar

- default - **

- jsp - foo

- jsp - bar

- jsp - **

- "" - foo

- "" - bar

- "" - **

In order to filter out the duplicates, the preceding code uses a *Set* and not, for example, a *List*. Additionally, to filter out any role refs other than those for the current Servlet from which we are calling the code, we additionally do the *request. isUserInRole(role)* check. Alternatively, we could have checked the name attribute of each *WebRoleRefPermission* as that one corresponds to the name of the current Servlet, which can be obtained via *GenericServlet#getServletName*. If we're sure that there aren't any role references being used in the application, or if we explicitly want all global roles, the following code can be used instead of the last fragment given previously:

```
Set<String> roles = new HashSet<>();
for (Permission permission : list(permissionCollection.elements())) {
    if (permission instanceof WebRoleRefPermission && permission.getName().
    isEmpty()) {
        roles.add(permission.getActions());
    }
}
```

Typically, Jakarta Authorization implementations will create the total list of *WebRoleRefPermission* instances when an application is deployed and then return a subselection based on the *Principals* that we (indirectly) passed in our call to *Policy#getPermission*s. This, however, requires that all roles are statically and upfront declared. But a Jakarta Authentication *ServerAuthModule* can dynamically return any amount of roles to the container, and via *HttpServletRequest#isUserInRole()*, an application can dynamically query for any such role without anything needing to be declared. Unfortunately, such dynamic role usage typically doesn't work well together with Jakarta Authorization.

Has Access

Asking whether a user has permission to access a given resource (e.g., a Servlet) is luckily a bit smaller:

```
Subject subject = (Subject) PolicyContext.getContext("javax.security.auth.
Subject.container");

boolean hasAccess = Policy.getPolicy().implies(
    new ProtectionDomain(
        new CodeSource(null, (Certificate[]) null),
        null, null,
        subject.getPrincipals().toArray(new Principal[subject.
        getPrincipals().size()])
    ),
    new WebResourcePermission("/protected/Servlet", "GET"));
```

We first get the *Subject* and create a *ProtectionDomain* in the same way as we did before. This time around, we don't need to get the permission collection but can make use of a small shortcut in the API. Calling *implies()* on the Policy instance effectively invokes it on the permission collection that this instance maintains. Besides being ever so slightly shorter in code, it's presumably more efficient as well.

The second parameter that we pass in is the actual query; via a *WebResourcePermission* instance, we can ask whether the resource "/protected/Servlet" can be accessed via a GET request. Both parameters support patterns and wildcards (see the JavaDoc). It's important to note that a *WebResourcePermission* only checks permission for the resource name and the HTTP method. There's a third aspect for checking access to a resource, and that boils down to the URI scheme that's used (http vs. https) and which corresponds to the *<transport-guarantee>* in a *<user-data-constraint>* element in web.xml. In Jakarta Authorization, this information is NOT included in the *WebResourcePermission*, but a separate permission has been created for that, the *WebUserDataPermission*, which can be individually queried.

Role Mapping

"Role mapping," or fully, "Group to Role mapping," is a concept we briefly touched upon in the previous sections. It's a concept that's implicitly part of Jakarta EE, though not explicitly defined. Remember from the previous chapter that Jakarta Authentication returns "groups," yet here for Jakarta Authorization, we talk about "roles." This is not just a terminology confusion such as with "caller" and "user." They are actually different things or rather can be different things.

The basic idea behind "groups" is that these are the opaque identifiers that are native to an identity store that's used for multiple applications. A prime example would be an office-wide LDAP server that holds data for office workers. Here, someone might have the office role "adm." With several office applications in use, one application could use the term "admin," while another may use "administrator" or something else entirely. Role mapping can then be used to map "adm" at the office level to "administrator" at the application level.

Essentially, role mapping could be done right away by the *ServerAuthModule* in Jakarta Authentication, but the convention is to do this in the authorization module, so by Jakarta Authorization.

When roles are not being actually mapped, that is, if the group name and role name are both, say, "adm," we speak about 1:1 role mapping. In Jakarta EE, 1:1 role mapping is the default. Even when there's 1:1 role mapping taking place, a role mapper may still be needed for determining how a given Jakarta EE implementation represents its roles. Since this has never been standardized, a role mapper with knowledge of a specific representation is needed. For example, in GlassFish (Exousia), the role mapper knows how to extract the roles from a list of principals in GlassFish. Recall that we briefly demonstrated this in the preceding *Policy* example:

```
PrincipalMapper roleMapper = policyConfiguration
        .getRoleMapper();

for (String role : roleMapper
        .getMappedRoles(
            domain.getPrincipals(),
            subject)) {
}
```

There are essentially three main ways to design an authorization module with respect to the role mapper:

1. Fetch roles externally (and don't map).

2. Knowledge of Jakarta EE implementation and/or auth module.

3. Use a universal role mapper (and in future, standardized role mapper).

For the first option, the idea is that a custom authorization module is coupled with a (custom) authentication mechanism that only provides a caller principal (which contains the user/caller name). That authorization module then contacts an (external) authorization system to fetch authorization data based on this single caller principal. This authorization data can then be a collection of roles or anything that the authorization module can either locally map to roles, or something to which it can map the permissions that a *PolicyConfiguration* initially collects. For this option, it's not necessary to have portable access to groups or a role to groups mapper.

Additionally, when a custom caller principal is used, an authorization module that knows about the Jakarta Authentication ServerAuthModule that sets that principal can unambiguously pick out that caller principal from the set of principals in a subject.

To illustrate the basic process for a custom authorization module according to this first option:

Authentication mechanism ——*provides*——▶ Caller Principal (name = "someuser")

Authorization module ——*contacts—with—*"someuser"——▶ **Authorization System**

Authorization System ——*returns*——▶ roles ["admin", "architect"]

Authorization module ——*indexes—with—*"admin"——▶ rolesToPermissions
Authorization module ——*indexes with—*"architect"——▶ rolesToPermissions

For the default implementation of a proprietary authorization module that ships with a Jakarta EE implementation, the basic process is a little bit different as shown next:

Role	Groups
"admin"	["admin-group"]
"architect"	["architect-group"]
"expert"	["expert-group"]

Authorization module ——*calls*—*with*—["admin", "architect", "expert"] ——▶ **Role Mapper**

Role mapper ——*returns*——▶ ["admin-group", "architect-group", "expert-group"]

Authentication mechanism ——*provides*——▶ Caller Principal (name = "someuser")

Authentication mechanism ——*provides*——▶ Group Principal (name = "admin-group", name = "architect-group")

Authorization module maps "admin-group" to "admin"

Authorization module maps "architect-group " to "architect"

Authorization module ——*indexes*—*with*—"admin"——▶ rolesToPermissions

Authorization module ——*indexes*—*with*—"architect"——▶ rolesToPermissions

In the second option, the role mapper and possibly knowledge of which principals represent groups are needed, but since this authorization module is the one that ships with a Jakarta EE implementation, it's arguably "allowed" to use proprietary techniques.

Do note that the mapping technique shown maps a subject's groups to roles and uses that to check permissions. While this may conceptually be the most straightforward approach, it's not the only way, as we discuss in the next section.

Alternative Mappings

Groups to Permission Mapping

An alternative approach is to remap the roles-to-permission collection to a groups-to-permission collection using the information from the role mapper.

The following is an illustration of this process. Suppose we have a role to permissions map as shown in the following table:

Role	Permission
"admin"	[WebResourcePermission ("/protected/*" GET)]

This means a user that's in the logical application role "admin" is allowed to do a GET request for resources in the /protected folder. Now suppose the role mapper gave us the following role to group mapping:

Role	Groups
"admin"	["admin-group", "adm"]

This means the logical application role "admin" is mapped to the groups "admin-group" and "adm". What we can now do is first reverse the last mapping into a group-to-roles map as shown in the following table:

Group	Roles
"admin-group"	["admin"]
"adm"	["admin"]

Subsequently, we can then iterate over this new map and look up the permissions associated with each role in the existing role to permissions map to create our target group to permissions map. This is shown in the following table:

Group	Permissions
"admin-group"	[WebResourcePermission ("/protected/*" GET)]
"adm"	[WebResourcePermission ("/protected/*" GET)]

Finally, consider a current subject with principals as shown in the next table:

Type	Name
com.somevendor. CallerPrincipalImpl	"someuser"
com.somevendor. GroupPrincipalImpl	"admin-group"
com.somevendor. GroupPrincipalImpl	"architect-group"

Given the preceding group to permissions map and subject's principals, an authorization module can now iterate over the group principals that belong to this subject and via the map check each such group against the permissions for that group. Note that the authorization module does have to know that *com.somevendor. GroupPrincipalImpl* is the principal type that represents groups.

Principal to Permission Mapping

Yet another alternative approach is to remap the roles-to-permission collection to a principals-to-permission collection, again using the information from the role mapper.

Principal to permission mapping basically works like group to permission mapping, except that the authorization module doesn't need to have knowledge of the principals involved. For the authorization module, those principals are pretty much opaque then, and it doesn't matter if they represent groups, callers, or something else entirely. All the authorization module does is compare (using equals() or implies()) principals in the map against those in the subject.

The following code fragment taken from Geronimo 3.0.1 demonstrates the mapping algorithm:

```
for (Map.Entry<Principal, Set<String>> principalEntry :
    principalRoleMapping.entrySet()) {

    Principal principal =
        principalEntry.getKey();
    Permissions principalPermissions =
        principalPermissionsMap.get(principal);
```

```
    if (principalPermissions == null) {
        principalPermissions = new Permissions();
        principalPermissionsMap.put(
            principal, principalPermissions);
    }

    Set<String> roleSet = principalEntry.getValue();
    for (String role : roleSet) {
        Permissions permissions =
            rolePermissionsMap.get(role);
        if (permissions == null) {
            continue;
        }
        for (
            Enumeration<Permission> rolePermissions =
                permissions.elements();
            rolePermissions.hasMoreElements();) {
            principalPermissions.add(
                rolePermissions.nextElement());
        }
    }
}
```

In the preceding code fragment, *rolePermissions* is the map the authorization module created before the mapping, *principalRoleMapping* is the mapping from the role mapper, and *principalPermissions* is the final map that's used for access decisions.

CHAPTER 5

Jakarta Security

The previous two chapters dealt with Jakarta Authentication and Jakarta Authorization, which are the low-level APIs and SPIs on which the higher-level security functionality is built. In this chapter, we'll take a look at Jakarta Security, which is the regular application developer facing part of security in Jakarta EE. Practically oriented readers can focus on this chapter and take a peek if needed for some of the underlying concepts that are explained in the previous two chapters.

What Is Jakarta Security?

Let's take a look at the official scope again:

> *Jakarta Security provides a set of required security functionalities including authentication, authorization, data integrity, and transport security.*

Here, contrary to Jakarta Authentication and Jakarta Authorization, the scope is perhaps a little too generic. It essentially explains what "security" is.

So let's take a look at the description of Jakarta Security by its main author (and also author of this book) instead:

> *[Jakarta Security] aims to bridge some of the gaps that have traditionally been left unspecified and for which vendor specific (proprietary) solutions were required. By bridging those gaps it should be possible to enable security in applications without requiring any kind of vendor specific configuration.*

As was mentioned in the history chapter, Jakarta EE initially adopted "container security," where applications were totally or largely unaware of the security mechanisms in place. In that setup, security indeed had to be configured using these "vendor-specific (proprietary) solutions."

227

© Arjan Tijms, Teo Bais, and Werner Keil 2022
A. Tijms et al., *The Definitive Guide to Security in Jakarta EE*, https://doi.org/10.1007/978-1-4842-7945-8_5

Jakarta Security represented the definite move away from a strictly container-managed model and standardized what pretty much all Jakarta EE servers were already doing, although by using modern and easy-to-use CDI-based artifacts and giving much attention to defaults in order to minimize configuration.

An important design consideration of the Jakarta Security API is that it does not replace any of the existing security machinery but provides alternative ways to define or configure things such as identity stores and authentication mechanisms. Existing declarative security as expressed by constraints in *web.xml* or annotations like *@RolesAllowed* keep working as they have always worked.

Switching between an in-app custom identity store and a traditional vendor-specific (proprietary) identity store equivalent is as simple as not defining that in-app custom identity store and instead defining the vendor-specific one using the traditional vendor-specific mechanism (e.g., using a security domain in standalone.xml for JBoss/WildFly). Likewise, some of the functionality like the security context or the security interceptors functions identical when either Jakarta Security or traditional authentication mechanisms and identity stores are used.

Jakarta Security in Jakarta EE

Jakarta Security primarily provides easy-to-install and easy-to-use versions of the authentication mechanism and the identity store. Recall from the explanation in previous chapters that an authentication mechanism is the artifact that deals with the interaction of a caller (a user) and the server in some environment (e.g., HTTP), while the identity store deals with verifying a credential (such as username and password) and optionally returning data associated with that credential (such as potentially a different username and groups that the caller is in).

To put Jakarta Security into perspective, let's take a look again at the diagram we showed in Chapter 3 and in Chapter 4 and highlight Jakarta Security this time:

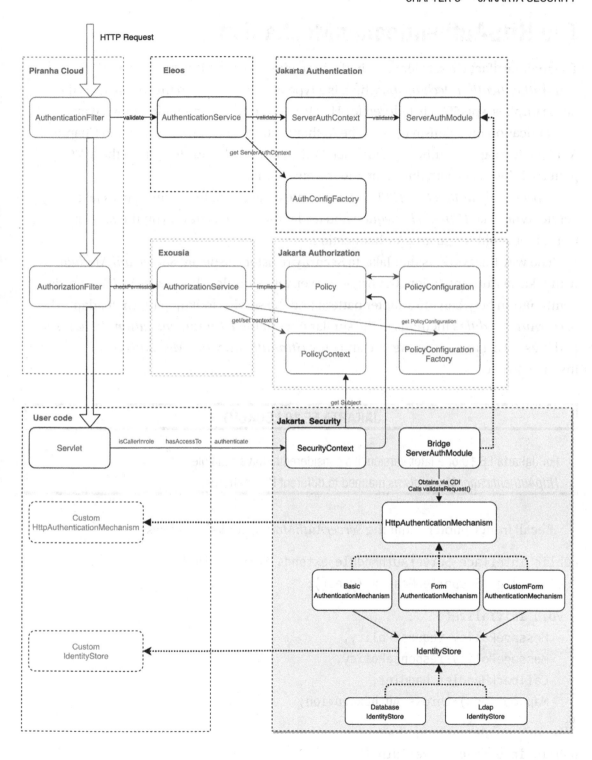

The HttpAuthenticationMechanism

The main artifact we see depicted in the preceding diagram is the *HttpAuthenticationMechanism,* which is a type of authentication mechanism, as the name implies, specifically tailored for HTTP. For a general explanation of what an authentication mechanism is, see "The Authentication Mechanism" section in Chapter 3. As a quick recap, an authentication mechanism is like a "controller" from the MVC pattern. It interacts with the caller and the environment.

`Specifically tailored for HTTP` in the context of Jakarta EE means it uses Jakarta Servlet types like *HttpServletRequest* and under the covers, it layers on the Servlet Container Profile of Jakarta Authentication.

The way this works is that Jakarta Security registers a special *ServerAuthModule* with Jakarta Authentication, the BridgeServerAuthModule. This *ServerAuthModule* is a combination between the adapter pattern and the service lookup pattern. It adapts the *ServerAuthModule's* methods to the similar ones of the *HttpAuthenticationMechanism,* and it uses CDI to look up the one and only *HttpAuthenticationMechanism* instance to use.

JAKARTA EE 10 LOOKOUT

For Jakarta EE 10 or a later version, it's considered to have multiple *HttpAuthenticationMechanisms* mapped to different URL patterns.

Recall from Chapter 3 that the *ServerAuthModule* looks as follows:

```
public interface ServerAuthModule extends ServerAuth {
  Class[] getSupportedMessageTypes();

  void initialize(
    MessagePolicy requestPolicy,
    MessagePolicy responsePolicy,
    CallbackHandler handler,
    Map options) throws AuthException;
}

public interface ServerAuth {
```

```
  AuthStatus validateRequest(
    MessageInfo messageInfo,
    Subject clientSubject,
    Subject serviceSubject) throws AuthException;

  AuthStatus secureResponse(
    MessageInfo messageInfo,
    Subject serviceSubject) throws AuthException;

  void cleanSubject(
    MessageInfo messageInfo,
    Subject subject) throws AuthException;
}
```

By contrast, the *HttpAuthenticationMechanism* has the following definition:

```
public interface HttpAuthenticationMechanism {

  AuthenticationStatus validateRequest(
    HttpServletRequest request,
    HttpServletResponse response,
    HttpMessageContext httpMessageContext) throws AuthenticationException;

  default AuthenticationStatus secureResponse(

    HttpServletRequest request,
    HttpServletResponse response,
    HttpMessageContext httpMessageContext) throws AuthenticationException {
        return SUCCESS;
  }

  default void cleanSubject(
    HttpServletRequest request,
    HttpServletResponse response,
    HttpMessageContext httpMessageContext) {
        httpMessageContext.cleanClientSubject();
    }
}
```

An implementation of the adapter/service lookup pattern that Jakarta Security could use internally may look something like the following fragment of code:

```
@Override
public AuthStatus validateRequest(
    MessageInfo messageInfo,
    Subject clientSubject,
    Subject serviceSubject) throws AuthException {

    HttpMessageContext msgContext =
      new HttpMessageContextImpl(
        handler, messageInfo, clientSubject);

    // Service lookup pattern
    HttpAuthenticationMechanism mechanism =
      Cdi.lookup(HttpAuthenticationMechanism.class)

    // Adapter pattern
    mechanism.validateRequest(
            msgContext.getRequest(),
            msgContext.getResponse(),
            msgContext);
    // ...
}
```

This is also depicted in the following diagram:

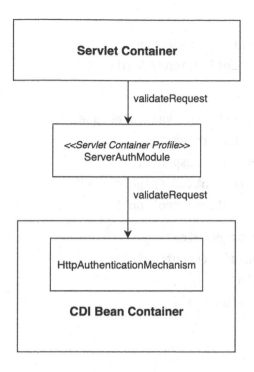

Because of this relationship chain, a built-in Servlet authentication mechanism (such as FORM), a *ServerAuthModule*, and an *HttpAuthenticationMechanism* are all functionally identical. Specifically, this means that a Principal and groups returned by any of them are treated in the same way. This is why an *HttpAuthenticationMechanism* is compatible with most existing Servlet security rules and APIs and with any other container the *Principal* and groups propagate to (such as Jakarta Enterprise Beans); an *HttpAuthenticationMechanism* is not a replacement for existing artifacts but an extension of those.

It also means no new rules apply regarding the order in which Servlet filters and the authentication mechanism are called; recall from Chapter 3 that the *ServerAuthModule* is always called before any Servlet filters. This therefore automatically holds for the *HttpAuthenticationMechanism*, as we saw in the example code and diagram before that the *HttpAuthenticationMechanism* is always called from the *ServerAuthModule*.

Example HttpAuthenticationMechanism

Let us now take a look at a trivial *HttpAuthenticationMechanism* in a trivial web application. Let's start with an *HttpAuthenticationMechanism*:

```
@ApplicationScoped
public class TestAuthenticationMechanism
    implements HttpAuthenticationMechanism {

    @Override
    public AuthenticationStatus validateRequest(
        HttpServletRequest request,
        HttpServletResponse response,
        HttpMessageContext httpMessageContext)
        throws AuthenticationException {

        return httpMessageContext
            .notifyContainerAboutLogin(
                "jsmith",
                Set.of("user"));
    }

}
```

Note that this example mirrors the one we have in Chapter 3 showing a simple *ServerAuthModule*. Let's take a look again at what's happening here.

First of all, our *HttpAuthenticationMechanism* is a CDI bean and should be given an appropriate scope. Often, we don't keep state in an authentication mechanism itself, so application scoped is a good scope to use. We can of course choose to use a request scope, session scope, or whatever other scope when that is appropriate for a given interaction between the caller and the system. Jakarta Security doesn't care about the scope, but it does care that there is a scope. When the scope is omitted, a bean is given the pseudoscope "dependent," which means it is destroyed when the bean in which it is injected is destroyed. Since in this case there is no injection, and Jakarta Security doesn't expect a dependent scoped bean, a bean without a scope will not be destroyed. Hence, we need to give it a scope.

Our bean needs to implement the *HttpAuthenticationMechanism* interface, but only the *validateRequest* method needs to be implemented. The other methods are optional.

The *validateRequest* method gets request and response objects passed in, via which it can interact with the caller over HTTP. In this simple example, we don't do any interaction but directly set the caller name and a group using the *HttpMessageContext* instance. This instance is the third parameter passed in to the *validateRequest* method shown previously. The *notifyContainerAboutLogin* method that we use for this does two things. It sends the caller name and groups to the container (typically the Servlet container here), and as a convenience, it returns a status indicating *SUCCESS*.

How the caller name and groups are initially stored (when we first call *notifyContainerAboutLogin*) and where it's exactly stored after the container has processed the *SUCCESS* return value from *validateRequest* are implementation dependent. That implementation, however, will know where to retrieve it from when user code calls things such as *HttpServletRequest.getUserPrincipal()*. We'll look at a practical example of this in the following text.

The exact *Principal* type that will be returned by that aforementioned call will be implementation specific as well. Instead of passing in a *String* for the caller name, we can pass in our own *Principal* implementation as well. Jakarta Security provides a simple default implementation called *CallerPrincipal* for this.

Just as the *ServerAuthModule* in Jakarta Authentication, the *HttpAuthenticationMechanism* is called every request, and when *SUCCESS* is returned, the caller name and groups only take effect for the request in which authentication took place. We'll look at various ways in which such "authenticated identity" can be remembered beyond a single request later in this chapter.

We can now combine the preceding example with a test servlet:

```
@WebServlet(urlPatterns = "/servlet")
@ServletSecurity(@HttpConstraint(rolesAllowed = "user"))
public class TestServlet extends HttpServlet {

    private static final long serialVersionUID = 1L;

    @Override
    public void doGet(HttpServletRequest request,
        HttpServletResponse response)
        throws ServletException, IOException {

        response.getWriter().write(
            "Caller has name: " +
            (request.getUserPrincipal() != null
                ? request.getUserPrincipal()
                        .getName()
                : "<unauthenticated>")
```

```
          + "\n" +
          "Caller has role \"user\": " +
          request.isUserInRole("user") +
          "\n");

   }

}
```

For Jakarta Security, that's all that is needed. There is no explicit programmatic registration or utility code required as we saw was the case for the *ServerAuthModule*. Somewhat like the Servlet, the *HttpAuthenticationMechanism* is automatically detected and used.

Packaging the preceding two classes in a war called, for example, *simple.war* and deploying it to a Jakarta EE server like GlassFish will yield the following result when we request its URL:

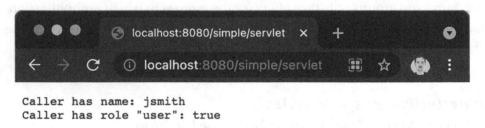

This demonstrates that (a) the *HttpAuthenticationMechanism* has correctly installed a user with the role "user," so the Servlet could be accessed at all, and (b) *HttpServletRequest* allows us to get the right details.

Of course, directly setting the authenticated identity is not that interesting for anything other than demonstrating Jakarta Security. Let's therefore take a look at an example with some more interaction:

```java
@ApplicationScoped
public class TestAuthenticationMechanism
    implements HttpAuthenticationMechanism {

    @Override
    public AuthenticationStatus validateRequest(
        HttpServletRequest request,
        HttpServletResponse response,
        HttpMessageContext httpMessageContext)
        throws AuthenticationException {

        String name = request
            .getParameter("name");
        String password = request
            .getParameter("password");

        if (name != null && password != null) {
            if (name.equals("john")
                && password.equals("password")) {
                return httpMessageContext
                    .notifyContainerAboutLogin(
                        "jsmith", Set.of("user"));
            }

            return httpMessageContext
                .responseUnauthorized();
        }

        return httpMessageContext.doNothing();
    }

}
```

In this version, we demonstrate a more typical scenario, where one provides a name and password via a URL, which the authentication mechanism then verifies. If it's correct, the authenticated identity is set as before; if not, an HTTP status code 401 (unauthorized) is returned to the caller. If there are no credentials provided at all, we tell the container to "do nothing," which means it just invokes the next Filter of Servlet as if the mechanism was never called.

If we now combine this with a Servlet without the security constraint, we can specifically test the "do nothing" scenario.

```
@WebServlet(urlPatterns = "/servlet")
public class TestServlet extends HttpServlet {

    private static final long serialVersionUID = 1L;

    @Override
    public void doGet(HttpServletRequest request,
        HttpServletResponse response)
        throws ServletException, IOException {

        response.getWriter().write(
            "Caller has name: " +
            (request.getUserPrincipal() != null
                ? request.getUserPrincipal()
                        .getName()
                : "<unauthenticated>")
            + "\n" +
            "Caller has role \"user\": " +
            request.isUserInRole("user") +
            "\n");

    }

}
```

Requesting the Servlet URL without request parameters from a browser will yield a result like the following:

```
Caller has name: <unauthenticated>
Caller has role "user": false
```

Providing the wrong credentials, however, will on GlassFish look somewhat like the following screen. This particular screen is server specific, and on other servers such as WildFly and Tomcat, the screen will look different.

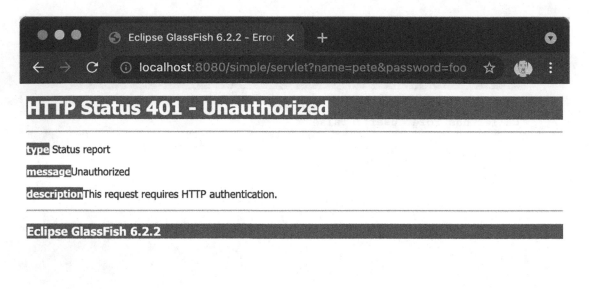

Warning   Note that passing a name and password using request parameters in a URL is terribly insecure, as browsers will remember the URL without protection, proxy servers may cache the URL, etc. It's here only used for a simple example but thus should absolutely not be done this way in practice.

Example IdentityStore

While the authentication mechanism is absolutely allowed to handle the verification of credentials itself, in practice, we often want to delegate this task to a dedicated component: the identity store.

The identity store is responsible for providing access to a storage system where caller data and credentials are stored. For example, when being given a valid caller name and password as input, it returns a (possibly different) caller name and zero or more groups associated with the caller. As such, it's roughly equivalent to a model in the MVC architecture; the identity store knows nothing about its environment and does not interact with the caller. It only performs the *{credentials in, caller data out}* function.

Identity stores are a well-known concept in Jakarta EE, although confusingly almost every other server internally uses a different name for this type of artifact. The following gives a partial overview of the names that have been used or are currently still used:

- Authenticator

- Login module

- Authentication provider

- Login service

- Authentication repository

- Realm

- Authentication realm

- Relying party

- Authentication store

- Security policy domain

- Identity manager

- Security domain

- Identity provider

- Service provider

- Identity store

- User registry

Conceptually, the identity store interface looks as follows:

```
public interface IdentityStore {
    CredentialValidationResult validate(Credential credential);
}
```

The interface was originally designed to be as minimal as possible, only capturing the *{credentials in, caller data out}* requirement. A *Credential* will in practice be some subtype, like *UsernamePasswordCredential*. The return type, *CredentialValidationResult*, contains a status code the caller can use to see if authentication succeeded, the (new) caller name, and optionally a list of groups the caller is in.

The actual identity store interface looks a bit more complex in code, although since default methods are used for the extra complexity, we don't often have to worry about these:

```
public interface IdentityStore {

    Set<ValidationType> DEFAULT_VALIDATION_TYPES = EnumSet
        .of(VALIDATE, PROVIDE_GROUPS);

    default CredentialValidationResult validate(
        Credential credential) {
        try {
            return CredentialValidationResult.class
                .cast(MethodHandles.lookup().bind(
                    this, "validate",
                    methodType(
                        CredentialValidationResult.class,
                        credential.getClass()))
                    .invoke(credential));
        } catch (NoSuchMethodException e) {
            return NOT_VALIDATED_RESULT;
        } catch (Throwable e) {
            throw new IllegalStateException(e);
        }
    }

    default Set<String> getCallerGroups(
        CredentialValidationResult validationResult) {
        return emptySet();
    }

    default int priority() {
        return 100;
    }

    default Set<ValidationType> validationTypes() {
        return DEFAULT_VALIDATION_TYPES;
    }
```

```
enum ValidationType {
    VALIDATE,
    PROVIDE_GROUPS
}
}
```

We'll look at some of the extra methods in the following text. For now, we'll only consider the *validate* method.

Similarly to an authentication mechanism, an application can install an identity store by simply having an implementation of this interface on the class path. The following shows an example with a single hard-coded user mimicking what the authentication mechanism we showed before did:

```
@ApplicationScoped
public class TestIdentityStore
    implements IdentityStore {

    public CredentialValidationResult validate(
        UsernamePasswordCredential usernamePasswordCredential) {
        if (usernamePasswordCredential
            .compareTo("john", "password")) {
            return new CredentialValidationResult(
                "john", Set.of("user"));
        }

        return INVALID_RESULT;
    }
}
```

It should be noted that the identity store does not have any global effect on the authentication state. It's merely a data store (data repository/database) to retrieve authentication data from. After calling the *validate* method, the result of the validation only exists in the *CredentialValidationResult* object and still has to be applied by the container to be actually visible in things like *HttpServletRequest.getUserPrincipal()*.

An authentication mechanism rarely, if ever, uses an identity store directly but instead does so via the identity store handler. This allows the container to try multiple identity stores, which we will discuss further in the following text.

The identity store handler has the following interface:

```
public interface IdentityStoreHandler {
    CredentialValidationResult validate(Credential credential);
}
```

Note that this interface is essentially identical to that of the conceptual identity store interface, which is no coincidence.

To make use of the *TestIdentityStore* identity store that we defined before, we need to inject the identity store handler (or programmatically obtain it via CDI). This is shown in the following modified authentication mechanism:

```
@ApplicationScoped
public class TestAuthenticationMechanism
    implements HttpAuthenticationMechanism {

    @Inject
    private IdentityStoreHandler identityStoreHandler;

    @Override
    public AuthenticationStatus validateRequest(
        HttpServletRequest request,
        HttpServletResponse response,
        HttpMessageContext httpMessageContext)
        throws AuthenticationException {

        String name = request
            .getParameter("name");
        String password = request
            .getParameter("password");

        if (name != null && password != null) {

            CredentialValidationResult result =
                identityStoreHandler.validate(
                    new UsernamePasswordCredential(
                        name, password));

            if (result.getStatus() == VALID) {
                return httpMessageContext
```

```
            .notifyContainerAboutLogin(
                result.getCallerPrincipal(),
                result.getCallerGroups());
        }

        return httpMessageContext
            .responseUnauthorized();
    }

    return httpMessageContext.doNothing();
    }

}
```

As can be seen, we @Inject the *IdentityStoreHandler* type, and whatever instance we get from CDI is used in the *validate()* method. In this case, we construct a *UsernamePasswordCredential* that will function as a holder for our username and password that we pass into the *validate()* method of the handler. The handler in its turn will invoke the *TestIdentityStore*.

The most important status that we're interested in at this point is simply the *VALID* status, which means the credentials validated and the result should be passed on. If the credentials did not validate, it typically depends on the authentication mechanism what should be done. For example, redirect the caller to an error page, return a special header in the response, etc.

Security Flow

With all major security components now broadly discussed, let's take a look at what happens during a request to a protected servlet. We'll illustrate this using the diagram "Jakarta Security in Jakarta EE," where we are using Piranha Cloud as the server, with Eleos as implementation of Jakarta Authentication, Exousia as implementation of Jakarta Authorization, and Soteria as implementation of Jakarta Security.

GlassFish (which is also using Exousia and Soteria) and other servers such as WildFly and Open Liberty would have somewhat similar flows.

We'll look at an http request, http://localhost:8080/servlet?name=john&password=password, to the application we just showed previously deployed to Piranha Cloud Micro.

As far as security goes, the request first lands in the *AuthorizationPreFilter*. Because the check for http/https is technically an authorization check, this check happens before any authentication takes place:

```
protected void doFilter(
    HttpServletRequest request,
    HttpServletResponse response,
    FilterChain chain) throws IOException, ServletException {
        WebApplication context = (WebApplication)
            request.getServletContext();
        PolicyContext.setContextID(
            context.getServletContextId());

        if (!securityManager.isRequestSecurityAsRequired(
                request, response)) {
            response.setStatus(SC_FORBIDDEN);
            return;
        }

    chain.doFilter(request, response);
}
```

We see two things happening here; the context id is being set in thread local storage (effectively taken hold for the remainder of the request). This context id is used by the security specs to identify the application for which things like security constraints apply. Obviously, this only really matters for those types of servers that run multiple applications and not for runtimes that run a single war or other archive directly from, for example, the command line.

The *securityManager.isRequestSecurityAsRequired()* is a razor-thin Piranha-specific abstraction over the Exousia *AuthorizationManager.checkWebUserDataPermission()* call.

```
@Override
public boolean isRequestSecurityAsRequired(HttpServletRequest request …
    return getAuthorizationService(request).checkWebUserDataPermission
    (request);
}
```

This call fairly directly checks whether the Jakarta Authorization policy (authorization module) grants a *WebUserDataPermission(request)*. It's therefore only a small abstraction over the lower-level Jakarta Authorization APIs.

Note that a data constraint of this type would be expressed in code via, for example, the *transportGuarantee* attribute as follows:

```
@ServletSecurity(@HttpConstraint(
    rolesAllowed = "user",
    transportGuarantee = CONFIDENTIAL))
```

In our example, there's no such constraint to require https (CONFIDENTIAL), so our http request is granted and our request arrives at the following location in the *AuthenticationFilter*:

```
protected void doFilter(
    HttpServletRequest request,
    HttpServletResponse response,
    FilterChain chain) throws IOException, ServletException {
        if (securityManager.authenticate(
            request, response, PRE_REQUEST_CONTAINER)) {
            chain.doFilter(
                securityManager.getAuthenticatedRequest(
                    request, response),
                securityManager.getAuthenticatedResponse(
                    request, response));

            securityManager.postRequestProcess(request, response);

            return;
        }

        if ((response.getStatus() < 400 ||
            response.getStatus() > 599) &&
            !response.isCommitted()) {
            // Authentication Mechanism did not set an error status.
            //Set the default 403 here.
            response.setStatus(SC_FORBIDDEN);
```

```
        response.getWriter().println("Forbidden");
    }
  }
```

The most important bit here is the call to *securityManager.authenticate()*. This contains somewhat more code as the thin wrapper for the authorization call that we saw previously. Among others, it contains a call to the *AuthenticationManager* from Eleos:

```
Caller caller = authenticationService.validateRequest(
            request,
            response,
            source == MID_REQUEST_USER,
            source == MID_REQUEST_USER?
                true :
                !isRequestedResourcePublic(request));
```

Here, we see that the Piranha runtime code adds information about when/where the call to validateRequest is being made. This is something that Jakarta Authentication and Jakarta Security use; a call to validateRequest can be made in the middle of the request by user code, or it can be called right at the start of the request by the container, and those behave slightly differently. In this case, the call is at the start by the container, which we see previously by the Eleos-specific *PRE_REQUEST_CONTAINER* constant being passed in.

The *isRequestedResourcePublic()* call here is to determine whether authentication is mandatory or not. The implementation of this method is a thin wrapper again around asking the authorization API whether a *WebResourcePermission(requestUri, uriMethod)* is granted or not. In this case, that requestUri would be "/servlet", and the method would be GET. The result would be false, meaning that resource is not public (or in other terms, it's "secured" or "constrained").

```
    public Caller validateRequest(
        HttpServletRequest servletRequest,
        HttpServletResponse servletResponse,
        boolean calledFromAuthenticate,
        boolean isMandatory) throws IOException {

        Subject subject = new Subject();
        MessageInfo messageInfo = getMessageInfo(
            servletRequest, servletResponse);
```

```
    try {
        if (isMandatory
            || calledFromAuthenticate) {
            setMandatory(messageInfo);
        }

        if (!SUCCESS.equals(
            getServerAuthContext(messageInfo)
                .validateRequest(messageInfo,
                    subject, null))) {
            return null;
        }

        return Caller.fromSubject(subject);

    } catch (AuthException
        | RuntimeException e) {
        throw new IllegalStateException(e);
    }
}
```

Here, we see that the implementation obtains the *MessageInfo* structure, which is used to correlate calls to the authentication module within a single request, and the information regarding at which point the validateRequest method is called and whether the resource to be accessed is public or not is used here to set in the *MessageInfo* whether authentication is mandatory.

The most important bit here is obtaining the *ServerAuthContext*, which, though not shown here, largely involves standard Jakarta Authentication code involving the *AuthConfigFactory*, and calling the *validateRequest()* method on it.

With obtaining the *ServerAuthContext* and calling validateRequest() on it, we move into Soteria, which is the Jakarta Security implementation used in this example. Soteria installs ServerAuthContext and ServerAuthModule, where its validateRequest method looks approximately as follows:

```
public AuthStatus validateRequest(
    MessageInfo messageInfo,
    Subject clientSubject,
    Subject serviceSubject)
```

```
        throws AuthException {

        HttpMessageContext msgContext = new HttpMessageContextImpl(
            handler, messageInfo, clientSubject);

        AuthenticationStatus status = NOT_DONE;
        setLastAuthenticationStatus(
            msgContext.getRequest(), status);

        try {
            status = CdiUtils.getBeanReference(
                HttpAuthenticationMechanism.class)
                .validateRequest(
                    msgContext.getRequest(),
                    msgContext.getResponse(),
                    msgContext);
        } catch (AuthenticationException e) {
            setLastAuthenticationStatus(
                msgContext.getRequest(),
                SEND_FAILURE);
            throw (AuthException) new AuthException(
                "Authentication failure")
                    .initCause(e);
        }

        setLastAuthenticationStatus(
            msgContext.getRequest(),
            status);

        return fromAuthenticationStatus(status);
    }
```

Here, we see that Soteria's role in this particular call is not that big: it essentially just obtains from CDI a bean that implements the *HttpAuthenticationMechanism* interface and delegates the *validateRequest* call to it. As we can see here, the *HttpMessageContext* wraps the callback handler, message info, and subject artifacts. It does this to provide a higher-level HTTP specific abstraction over the lower-level Jakarta Authentication artifacts and API.

The request will now reach our own HttpAuthenticationMechanism, the one that we displayed before. We'll take a somewhat closer look at the handler invocation. Recall that the relevant code here looked as follows:

```
@Inject
private IdentityStoreHandler identityStoreHandler;

@Override
public AuthenticationStatus validateRequest(
  [..]

  CredentialValidationResult result =
      identityStoreHandler.validate(
          new UsernamePasswordCredential(
              name, password));
```

The *validate()* method here will invoke Soteria's *DefaultIdentityStoreHandler,* with part of the code looking as follows:

```
    @Override
    public CredentialValidationResult validate(
        Credential credential) {

        CredentialValidationResult validationResult = null;
        IdentityStore identityStore = null;
        boolean isGotAnInvalidResult = false;

        // Check stores to authenticate until
        // one succeeds.
        for (IdentityStore authenticationIdentityStore :
          authenticationIdentityStores) {
            validationResult = authenticationIdentityStore
                .validate(credential);
            if (validationResult
                .getStatus() == VALID) {
                identityStore = authenticationIdentityStore;
                break;
            } else if (validationResult
                .getStatus() == INVALID) {
```

```
                isGotAnInvalidResult = true;
            }
        }

        if (validationResult == null
            || validationResult
                .getStatus() != VALID) {
            // Didn't get a VALID result. If we
            // got an INVALID result at any point,
            // return INVALID_RESULT. Otherwise,
            // return NOT_VALIDATED_RESULT.
            if (isGotAnInvalidResult) {
                return INVALID_RESULT;
            } else {
                return NOT_VALIDATED_RESULT;
            }
        }

        [...]
    }
```

Without going too deep into the details here, what we see here is that the default identity store handler checks a collection of identity stores until one of them succeeds. There's a little bit more going on, but for now, that's the important part to take away here.

If there's only one identity store, such as in our example application here, this will call that store right away, and we'll end up in the *validate()* identity store that we provided:

```
public CredentialValidationResult validate(
    UsernamePasswordCredential usernamePasswordCredential) {
    if (usernamePasswordCredential
        .compareTo("john", "password")) {
        return new CredentialValidationResult(
            "john", Set.of("user"));
    }

    return INVALID_RESULT;
}
```

In the identity store, we're returning a result with the caller name "john" in group "user."

This propagates back to our authentication mechanism, where we hand it to the runtime (Soteria in this example):

```
@ApplicationScoped
public class TestAuthenticationMechanism
    implements HttpAuthenticationMechanism {

 [...]


            if (result.getStatus() == VALID) {
                return httpMessageContext
                    .notifyContainerAboutLogin(
                        result.getCallerPrincipal(),
                        result.getCallerGroups());
            }
[...]

}
```

Under the covers, this uses the Jakarta Authentication API as discussed in Chapter 3. Just for illustration of what Jakarta Security shields us from, the most important part of that code looks like this:

```
    public static void notifyContainerAboutLogin(
        Subject clientSubject,
        CallbackHandler handler,
        String callerPrincipalName,
        Set<String> groups) {
        handleCallbacks(clientSubject, handler,
            new CallerPrincipalCallback(
                clientSubject,
                callerPrincipalName),
            groups);
    }
```

```java
    private static void handleCallbacks(
        Subject clientSubject,
        CallbackHandler handler,
        CallerPrincipalCallback callerPrincipalCallback,
        Set<String> groups) {
        if (clientSubject == null) {
            throw new IllegalArgumentException(
                "Null clientSubject!");
        }
        if (handler == null) {
            throw new IllegalArgumentException(
                "Null callback handler!");
        }
        try {
            if (groups == null || isEmpty(groups)
                || (callerPrincipalCallback
                    .getPrincipal() == null
                    && callerPrincipalCallback
                        .getName() == null)) {
                // don't handle groups if
                // null/empty or if caller is null
                handler.handle(new Callback[] {
                    callerPrincipalCallback });
            } else {
                handler.handle(new Callback[] {
                    callerPrincipalCallback,
                    new GroupPrincipalCallback(
                        clientSubject,
                        groups.toArray(
                            new String[groups
                                .size()])) });
            }
        } catch (IOException
            | UnsupportedCallbackException e) {
```

```
        throw new IllegalStateException(e);
    }
}
```

This now again propagates back to the Eleos AuthenticationService shown before, specifically to this part of that code:

```
return Caller.fromSubject(subject);
```

It may not be immediately clear how these things connect. What happens here is that a new *Subject* instance was created and passed into the validateRequest method, which eventually passed it into the CallbackHandler shown in the *handleCallbacks* method before.

What this *CallbackHandler* does is storing the caller name and groups inside the *Subject* instance in an implementation specific way. Jakarta Authentication works this way, since it's a low-level SPI/API that can be used this way for many different things.

There is no standard way in Jakarta Authentication to read back something that has been written into the *Subject,* but within Eleos, Eleos knows which *CallbackHandler* was used as it supplied this itself. It therefore also knows how it can read this data in the Eleos-specific format (the *Caller* type).

The *Caller* instance now propagates back to the calling Piranha code, which we had shown before and will repeat here for convenience with the segment added which will actually set the authenticated identity for the current request:

```
Caller caller = authenticationService.validateRequest(
            request,
            response,
            source == MID_REQUEST_USER,
            source == MID_REQUEST_USER?
                true :
                !isRequestedResourcePublic(request));
[...]

if (caller != null &&
    caller.getCallerPrincipal() != null) {
    setIdentityForCurrentRequest(
        request,
```

```
        caller.getCallerPrincipal(),
        caller.getGroups(), "authenticate");
}
```

The *setIdentityForCurrentRequest* is a Piranha-specific method, which stores the identity details in a Piranha-specific way (which will be in a thread-local storage variable and as an optimization directly in the current *HttpServletRequest* instance as well). Though the exact details will differ as mentioned between Jakarta EE implementations, other ones like GlassFish will use a very similar approach.

Jakarta EE implementations like Piranha now internally need to make sure when integrating components that need access to this data that these components will be able to find these identity details. This is typically done by implementing SPIs of such components. For instance, the CDI implementation Weld requires implementers to implement the *org.jboss.weld.security.spi.SecurityServices* interface for this.

Developers of implementations that run on Jakarta EE obviously don't need to worry about this integration, as this is what Jakarta EE does for them internally.

Now authenticated, the request arrives in Piranha's *AuthorizationFilter*:

```
protected void doFilter(
    HttpServletRequest request,
    HttpServletResponse response,
    FilterChain chain)
    throws IOException, ServletException {

    if (!securityManager
            .isCallerAuthorizedForResource(
                request)) {
        response.setStatus(SC_FORBIDDEN);
        return;
    }

    chain.doFilter(request, response);
}
```

Here, the runtime/container (Piranha in this case) does the check corresponding to the role constraint for a resource, for example, the one we expressed with the *rolesAllowed* attribute here:

```
@ServletSecurity(@HttpConstraint(rolesAllowed = "user"))
```

The *isCallerAuthorizedForResource* method is a thin abstraction again over the Exousia *AuthorizationManager*, which checks for a permission.

This time, however, the permission check is done with the help of the current *Subject*:

```
public boolean checkWebResourcePermission(
    HttpServletRequest request) {

    Subject subject = (Subject)
        PolicyContext.getContext(SUBJECT);

    return checkWebResourcePermission(request,
        subject == null ?
            null :
            subject.getPrincipals());
}
```

The *PolicyContext* here is an example of Piranha providing details about where to get this current subject to Exousia and thus to Jakarta Authorization. The Exousia AuthorizationManager in Piranha is created via code like the following:

```
AuthorizationService authorizationService =
    new AuthorizationService(
        factoryClass, policyClass,
        context.getServletContextId(),
        DefaultAuthenticatedIdentity::getCurrentSubject,
        new PiranhaPrincipalMapper());
```

As the one but last parameter, we see a method reference to the Piranha-specific way to get the *Subject* which we mentioned before. Jakarta Authorization, contrary to, for example, CDI, has a standard API for setting this, as the following fragment shows:

```
public void AuthorizationService(
    PolicyConfigurationFactory factory,
    Policy policy, String contextId,
    Supplier<Subject> subjectSupplier,
    PrincipalMapper principalMapper) {
```

```
    policyConfiguration =
        factory
            .getPolicyConfiguration(contextId, false);
        policy = Policy.getPolicy();

        PolicyContext.setContextID(contextId);

        PolicyContext.registerHandler(SUBJECT,
            new DefaultPolicyContextHandler(
                SUBJECT, subjectSupplier),
            true);

    [...]

}
```

Back to the preceding method, the *checkWebResourcePermission* creates one of the standard Jakarta Authorization permissions, namely, a *WebResourcePermission*, where the constrained URI is "/servlet" as per our request and the method GET. This permission is then checked with Jakarta Authorization:

```
public boolean checkWebResourcePermission(
    HttpServletRequest request,
    Set<Principal> principals) {

    return checkPermission(
        new WebResourcePermission(
            getConstrainedURI(request),
            request.getMethod()),
        principals);
}
```

The checkPermission method finally is only a small wrapper around the *Policy* call:

```
boolean checkPermission(
    Permission permissionToBeChecked,
    Set<Principal> principals) {
```

```
    return policy.implies(
        newProtectionDomain(principals),
        permissionToBeChecked);
}
```

JAKARTA EE FUTURE LOOKOUT

As the *Policy* class is deprecated for removal in JDK 17, Jakarta EE 10 will deprecate it as well. This means Jakarta Authorization will almost certainly replace the usage of *Policy* as shown previously with a replacement type of its own.

After the authorization check (the check for the *WebResourcePermission*) is okay, the runtime will finally call our Servlet.

The following diagram shows a graphical representation of the flow we explained previously:

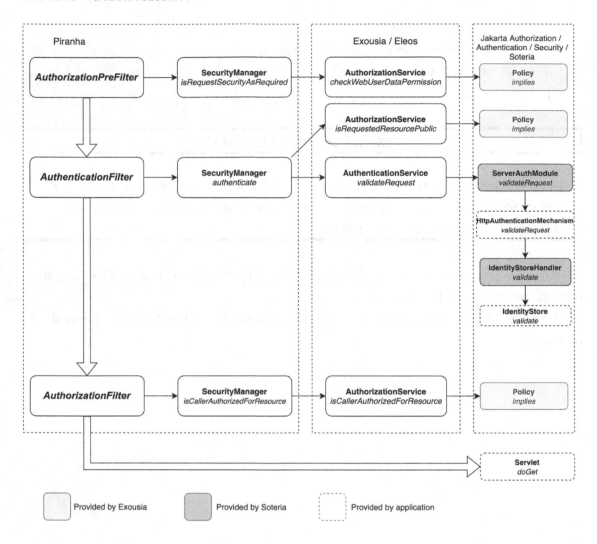

Note that in this example, the Policy implementation is a default one provided by Exousia, and the IdentityStoreHandler is a default one provided by Soteria. Both are pluggable according to the specifications and can be replaced by user-provided ones in a standard way.

Default Authentication Mechanisms

The Servlet spec already defines four standard authentication mechanisms:

1. Basic

2. Digest (encouraged to be supported, not required)

3. Client-cert

4. Form

However, just based on the Servlet spec, these currently cannot delegate to a Jakarta Security identity store, nor are they CDI beans, and therefore, no CDI decorators can be applied to them. At the moment, they are in practice also not based on the Jakarta Authentication interfaces.

Therefore, Jakarta Security redefines the two most frequently used ones: Basic and Form as Jakarta Security authentication mechanisms. They are mandated by the specification to be compatible with their Servlet counterparts. Servers that implement both Servlet and Jakarta Security are explicitly allowed to only implement these authentication mechanisms based on the Jakarta EE interfaces and requirements and internally delegate the Servlet functionality to these. Piranha Micro is one of the servers that indeed does this.

Jakarta EE defines the following authentication mechanisms:

1. Basic

2. Form

3. Custom Form

JAKARTA EE FUTURE LOOKOUT

Jakarta EE 10 may contain an additional authentication mechanism for OpenID Connect. This mechanism will likely be based on the one for Jakarta Security that Payara ships with their server.

OpenID itself is a decentralized authentication protocol from the OpenID Foundation.

All of the authentication mechanisms provided by Jakarta Security are installed and configured via its own *AuthenticationMechanismDefinition* annotation. This annotation tells the container which type of authentication mechanism to install and with which configuration. The annotation can be placed on pretty much every class on the classpath.

Do recall that the current version of Jakarta Security only allows one authentication mechanism to be active at the same time, independent whether we use an *AuthenticationMechanismDefinition* annotation or provide our own implementation.

Technically, what happens when the container encounters a *AuthenticationMechanismDefinition* annotation is that it programmatically adds an enabled CDI bean to the system of type *HttpAuthenticationMechanism*. This is important to know, since its being a regular CDI bean means we can inject it, decorate it, intercept it, and basically do everything with it that we can normally do with CDI beans. It also means that after the container adds such a bean, it sits at the same level as our own implementations of the *HttpAuthenticationMechanism* interface that we used earlier in this chapter.

The Basic Authentication Mechanism

The basic authentication mechanism allows callers to authenticate via the well-known HTTP basic access authentication. It's selected and configured via the @ *BasicAuthenticationMechanismDefinition* annotation.

The Soteria-specific implementation, for instance, is done by *org.glassfish.soteria. mechanisms.BasicAuthenticationMechanism*.

The following shows an example:

```
@BasicAuthenticationMechanismDefinition(
    realmName="test realm"
)
```

By contrast, the similar Servlet authentication mechanism is selected and configured in web.xml as follows:

```
<login-config>
    <auth-constraint>BASIC</auth-constraint>
    <realm-name>test realm</realm-name>
</login-config>
```

One difference with the Servlet version is that the realmName is strictly informational in the Jakarta Security version, while for the Servlet implementations, it depends. For some servers, it's indeed informational; for others, like GlassFish, it can be a key that links to a named server specific identity store.

As mentioned before, a specific implementation is allowed to treat the web.xml login-config and the annotation the same and internally configure the same Jakarta Security authentication mechanism for this. This is, however, not mandated by the specifications, so user code cannot depend on this being done.

To demonstrate, we take the same example as used earlier but now add the @ *BasicAuthenticationMechanismDefinition* annotation as follows:

```
@WebServlet(
    urlPatterns = "/servlet")
@ServletSecurity(@HttpConstraint(
    rolesAllowed = "user"))
@BasicAuthenticationMechanismDefinition(
    realmName="test")
public class TestServlet extends HttpServlet {

    private static final long serialVersionUID = 1L;

    @Override
    public void doGet(HttpServletRequest request,
        HttpServletResponse response)
        throws ServletException, IOException {

        response.getWriter().write(
            "Caller has name: " +
            (request.getUserPrincipal() != null
                ? request.getUserPrincipal()
                        .getName()
                : "<unauthenticated>")
            + "\n" +
            "Caller has role \"user\": " +
            request.isUserInRole("user") +
            "\n");

    }

}
```

The identity store can remain the same:

```
@ApplicationScoped
public class TestIdentityStore
    implements IdentityStore {

    public CredentialValidationResult validate(
        UsernamePasswordCredential usernamePasswordCredential) {
        if (usernamePasswordCredential
            .compareTo("john", "password")) {
            return new CredentialValidationResult(
                "john", Set.of("user"));
        }

        return INVALID_RESULT;
    }

}
```

Compiling this application consisting of just two classes, deploying it to a server, and requesting the /servlet URL using a web browser should now pop up a dialog from the browser asking for the name and password.

The Form Authentication Mechanism

The Form authentication mechanism mirrors, by definition, the Servlet version exactly. It's selected and configured via the *@FormAuthenticationMechanismDefinition* annotation.

The Soteria-specific implementation, for instance, is done by *org.glassfish.soteria. mechanisms.FormAuthenticationMechanism*.

The following shows an example:

```
@FormAuthenticationMechanismDefinition(
    loginToContinue = @LoginToContinue(
        loginPage="/login-servlet",
        errorPage="/error-servlet"
    )
)
```

By contrast, the similar Servlet authentication mechanism is selected and configured in web.xml as follows:

```
<login-config>
    <auth-method>FORM</auth-method>
    <form-login-config>
        <form-login-page>/login-servlet</form-login-page>
        <form-error-page>/error-servlet</form-error-page>
    </form-login-config>
</login-config>
```

Note that we sometimes see the following, even in official documentation:

```
<login-config>
    <auth-method>FORM</auth-method>
    <realm-name>file</realm-name>
    <form-login-config>
        <form-login-page>/login-servlet</form-login-page>
        <form-error-page>/error-servlet</form-error-page>
    </form-login-config>
</login-config>
```

The *<realm-name>* being used here is not officially supported but happens to be allowed since the somewhat overly general XML schema allows it there. Some implementations like GlassFish use *realm-name* as a proprietary interpretation of that tag to configure a proprietary named identity store. Since this is a proprietary (ab)use of this tag, there is no 1:1 equivalent for this in the annotation. Of course, configuring a standard identity store is easy in Jakarta Security (see further text for more details on that).

The following shows an example of this. In the main Servlet, we now put the @ *FormAuthenticationMechanismDefinition* as follows:

```
@WebServlet(
    urlPatterns = "/servlet")
@ServletSecurity(@HttpConstraint(
    rolesAllowed = "user"))
@FormAuthenticationMechanismDefinition(
    loginToContinue = @LoginToContinue(
```

```
        loginPage="/login-servlet",
        errorPage="/error-servlet"))
public class TestServlet extends HttpServlet {

    private static final long serialVersionUID = 1L;

    @Override
    public void doGet(HttpServletRequest request,
        HttpServletResponse response)
        throws ServletException, IOException {

        response.getWriter().write(
            "Caller has name: " +
            (request.getUserPrincipal() != null
                ? request.getUserPrincipal()
                            .getName()
                : "<unauthenticated>")
            + "\n" +
            "Caller has role \"user\": " +
            request.isUserInRole("user") +
            "\n");

    }
}
```

We're referencing here two other Servlets that we define as follows:

```
@WebServlet({ "/login-servlet" })
public class LoginServlet extends HttpServlet {

    private static final long serialVersionUID = 1L;

    @Override
    public void doGet(HttpServletRequest request,
        HttpServletResponse response)
        throws ServletException, IOException {
        response.getWriter().write(
            """

            <html><body>
```

```
            Login to continue

            <form method="POST" action="j_security_check">
                <p><strong>Username </strong>
                <input type="text" name="j_username">

                <p><strong>Password </strong>
                <input type="password" name="j_password">

                <p>
                <input type="submit" value="Submit">
            </form>
        </body></html>
        """);
    }
}
```

and

```
@WebServlet({ "/error-servlet" })
public class ErrorServlet extends HttpServlet {

    private static final long serialVersionUID = 1L;

    @Override
    public void doGet(HttpServletRequest request,
        HttpServletResponse response)
        throws ServletException, IOException {
        response.getWriter().write(
            """

            <html><body>
                Login failed!
                <a href="login-servlet">Try again</a>
            </body></html>
            """);
    }

}
```

Deploying these three Servlets together with the identity store used in the previous example and requesting /servlet will now yield the login form as shown in the following:

The Custom Form Authentication Mechanism

The custom form authentication mechanism is a variant of the regular form authentication mechanism but where the authentication dialog can be continued programmatically. This is suitable for those environments where custom code needs to execute between the postback of the form and the authentication mechanism validating its return values.

Form and Custom Form are both suitable for interactive web applications, such as the ones we would build primarily with a view framework such as Jakarta Faces. We'll be using this particular framework for the following examples but realize not everyone will use Jakarta Faces or even a server-side rendering (SSR) framework. The information in the following sections should apply roughly to other server-side rendering frameworks as well. Users of client-side frameworks such as Angular may wish to skim over it.

Contrary to, say, BASIC, the FORM authentication mechanisms call back into the application and let it render the form that asks the caller for credentials, hence the name of these mechanisms.

The difference between the two is mainly in how the mechanism requires the application to continue the aforementioned authentication dialog after it has rendered the form. In Form, this is done by letting the caller post the filled-out form to the virtual URL *j_security_check*, while in Custom Form, this is done programmatically via a call to an injected *SecurityContext*.

This small difference makes all the difference for Jakarta Faces though. In Jakarta Faces, a form view by default submits to the same URL it was requested from, so posting back to a single mechanism mandated URL is not at all natural. In addition to that, in Jakarta Faces, we often need to have server-side code running after a postback; just think about converters and validators and the ability to emit a Faces message. We can't really do any of this if we have to post back to the virtual nonfaces *j_security_check* URL, but it's quite doable when we can continue the authentication dialog programmatically from the backing bean's action method.

We'll first show you how to configure a web application to use the Custom FORM authentication mechanism. Later on, we'll explain how to actually use Jakarta Faces to fulfill the requirements this mechanism imposes on the application.

Custom Form is selected and configured via the @ *CustomFormAuthenticationMechanismDefinition* annotation.

The Soteria-specific implementation, for instance, is done by *org.glassfish.soteria. mechanisms.CustomFormAuthenticationMechanism*.

In a Jakarta Faces application, we normally don't configure a Servlet directly, so contrary to the previous examples, we won't put the annotation on a Servlet now. However, it logically fits in quite well with the *@FacesConfig* annotation. The following shows an example:

```
@CustomFormAuthenticationMechanismDefinition(
    loginToContinue = @LoginToContinue(
        loginPage = "/login.xhtml",
        errorPage = ""
    )
)
```

```
@FacesConfig @ApplicationScoped
public class ApplicationConfig {
    // ...
}
```

A perhaps somewhat unfortunate requirement here is that the *errorPage* attribute has to be specified and set to the empty string. This is needed since the @ *LoginToContinue* element has a default value for an actual error page. In Jakarta Faces, we rarely use an explicit error page to display errors but instead redisplay the original page with the error messages rendered on it via Faces messages.

The *loginToContinue* attribute is used to configure the view that the container forwards to whenever the caller tries to access a protected view. This is called "container-initiated authentication"; the container starts the authentication dialog as opposed to the application.

The default is to forward to the login page, meaning that if the caller tries to access `https://example.com/foo.xhtml` and /foo.xhtml is protected, the caller will still see / foo.xhtml in the address bar and not /login.xhtml. However, the postback is to /login. xhtml, so after entering credentials, the caller would get to see this in the address bar. Alternatively, we can configure the *loginToContinue* attribute to use a redirect instead.

```
@CustomFormAuthenticationMechanismDefinition(
    loginToContinue = @LoginToContinue(
        loginPage = "/login.xhtml",
        useForwardToLogin = false,
        errorPage = ""
    )
)
@FacesConfig @ApplicationScoped
public class ApplicationConfig {
    // ...
}
```

An additional consequence of not having an explicit Servlet in a Jakarta Faces application is that we need to define the constraints using XML in web.xml, for example, as follows:

```
<security-constraint>
    <web-resource-collection>
        <web-resource-name>User pages</web-resource-name>
```

```
            <url-pattern>/user/*</url-pattern>
        </web-resource-collection>
        <auth-constraint>
            <role-name>VIEW_USER_PAGES</role-name>
        </auth-constraint>
    </security-constraint>
    <security-constraint>
        <web-resource-collection>
            <web-resource-name>Admin pages</web-resource-name>
            <url-pattern>/admin/*</url-pattern>
        </web-resource-collection>
        <auth-constraint>
            <role-name>VIEW_ADMIN_PAGES</role-name>
        </auth-constraint>
    </security-constraint>
    <security-role>
        <role-name>VIEW_USER_PAGES</role-name>
    </security-role>
    <security-role>
        <role-name>VIEW_ADMIN_PAGES</role-name>
    </security-role>
```

In the preceding fragment, we define two security constraints – one for the /user/* pattern, for which the caller needs to have the role "VIEW_USER_PAGES", and one for the /admin/* pattern, for which the caller needs the role "VIEW_ADMIN_PAGES". With the preceding constraints in place, a caller accessing, say, /user/account.xhtml has to be authenticated and has to have the mentioned role.

An auth-constraint can contain multiple roles, for which OR semantics are applied. This means the authenticated caller only needs to have one of the roles in that constraint in order to be granted access. Constraints can additionally be restricted to a specific HTTP method (such as GET or POST). This does come with a caveat, since by default all methods that are not specified will be unchecked (public). This can be countered by using the top-level <deny-uncovered-http-methods/> tag. The following gives an example of this:

```
<deny-uncovered-http-methods />
<security-constraint>
    <web-resource-collection>
        <web-resource-name>User pages</web-resource-name>
        <url-pattern>/user/*</url-pattern>
        <http-method>GET</http-method>
        <http-method>POST</http-method>
    </web-resource-collection>
    <auth-constraint>
        <role-name>VIEW_USER_PAGES</role-name>
    </auth-constraint>
</security-constraint>
```

Providing Our Custom Jakarta Faces Code

In the preceding sections, we first defined our security constraints (which views are protected), and then we set up the authentication mechanism (how do our callers interact with our application in order to authenticate).

It's now time to plug our own custom code into the authentication process. This primarily happens by providing the view that the authentication mechanism directs to when it needs to collect the caller's credentials (email and password in this case).

The login page can be kept relatively simple – a standard form page, with two inputs bound to our backing bean, and a button to submit.

```
<!DOCTYPE html>
<html lang="en"
    xmlns:h="jakarta.faces.html"
>
    <h:head>
        <title>Log In</title>
    </h:head>
    <h:body>
        <h1>Log In</h1>
        <h:form>
            <h:outputLabel for="email" value="Email" />
            <h:inputText id="email" value="#{login.email}" />
            <br />
```

```
        <h:outputLabel for="password" value="Password" />
        <h:inputSecret id="password" value="#{login.password}" />
        <br />
        <h:commandButton value="Login" action="#{login.submit}" />
        <h:messages />
    </h:form>
  </h:body>
</html>
```

The preceding page is a totally normal Jakarta Faces view. This specifically means that contrary to classical HTML *<form method="post" action="j_security_check">* of Form authentication, the authentication mechanism does not monitor the postback URL in any way, and therefore, there aren't any constraints being placed on the input elements that collect the credentials.

Instead, the Jakarta Faces backing bean has to collect these credentials and then programmatically pass these along and signal the authentication mechanism to continue the dialog.

Before passing the credentials along, Jakarta Faces is free to do its own validation and engage in its own dialog with the caller without the authentication mechanism having to be involved with this. Note that the command button explicitly doesn't use Ajax to submit. You can do so, but then the average web browser won't suggest the end user to remember the login credentials on its behalf.

The following shows a full example of the backing bean handling the login call. We'll discuss the parts individually in the following text.

```
@Named @RequestScoped
public class Login {

    @NotNull
    @Email
    private String email;

    @NotNull
    @Size(min = 8, message = "Password must be at least 8 characters")
    private String password;

    @Inject
    private SecurityContext securityContext;
```

```java
@Inject
private ExternalContext externalContext;

@Inject
private FacesContext facesContext;

public void submit() {
    switch (continueAuthentication()) {
        case SEND_CONTINUE:
            facesContext.responseComplete();
            break;
        case SEND_FAILURE:
            facesContext.addMessage(null, new FacesMessage(
                FacesMessage.SEVERITY_ERROR, "Login failed", null));
            break;
        case SUCCESS:
            facesContext.addMessage(null, new FacesMessage(
                FacesMessage.SEVERITY_INFO, "Login succeed", null));
            break;
        case NOT_DONE:
            // Doesn't happen here
    }
}

private AuthenticationStatus continueAuthentication() {
    return securityContext.authenticate(
        (HttpServletRequest) externalContext.getRequest(),
        (HttpServletResponse) externalContext.getResponse(),
        AuthenticationParameters.withParams().credential(
            new UsernamePasswordCredential(email, password))
    );
}

public String getEmail() {
    return email;
}

public void setEmail(String email) {
```

```
        this.email = email;
    }

    public String getPassword() {
        return password;
    }

    public void setPassword(String password) {
        this.password = password;
    }
}
```

We start the backing bean with two instance variables corresponding with the credentials we collect.

```
@NotNull
@Email
private String email;.
```

```
@NotNull
@Size(min = 8, message = "Password must be at least 8 characters")
private String password;
```

This clearly shows the advantage over the Form authentication mechanism in that we can easily prevalidate the user's input using bean validation. Because of Jakarta Faces built-in integration with bean validation, a standard faces message will be made available for rendering should the input not pass validation.

Next, we defined injecting the contextual objects it needs. These are

```
@Inject
private SecurityContext securityContext;
```

```
@Inject
private ExternalContext externalContext;
```

```
@Inject
private FacesContext facesContext;
```

The observant reader will recognize *ExternalContext* and *FacesContext* as being two well-known native Jakarta Faces classes, with the *SecurityContext* being the odd one out.

This class is from Jakarta Security, and we'll use that here to communicate with the authentication mechanism.

Continuing the dialog happens in the continueAuthentication() method as follows:

```
private AuthenticationStatus continueAuthentication() {
    return securityContext.authenticate(
        (HttpServletRequest) externalContext.getRequest(),
        (HttpServletResponse) externalContext.getResponse(),

        AuthenticationParameters
            .withParams()
            .credential(
                new UsernamePasswordCredential(
                    email, password))
    );
}
```

The call to *SecurityContext#authenticate()* will trigger the authentication mechanism again. Since that mechanism will be a state where it waits for credentials to be passed, it will indeed look for the credentials we pass in and use those to continue. As we'll later see, we can also request that any potentially existing state is discarded and a new dialog is started. Note that we have to cast the request and response objects to HttpServletRequest and HttpServletResponse. Unfortunately, this is needed since *ExternalContext* abstracts over Servlet and Portlet requests and only returns *Object* for those two.

The *SecurityContext#authenticate()* method returns a status that indicates in broad lines what the authentication mechanism did. The action method of our Jakarta Faces backing bean has to handle the following:

```
switch (continueAuthentication()) {
    case SEND_CONTINUE:
        facesContext.responseComplete();
        break;
    case SEND_FAILURE:
        facesContext.addMessage(null, new FacesMessage(
            FacesMessage.SEVERITY_ERROR, "Login failed", null));
        break;
```

```
case SUCCESS:
    facesContext.addMessage(null, new FacesMessage(
        FacesMessage.SEVERITY_INFO, "Login succeed", null));
    break;
case NOT_DONE:
    // Doesn't happen here
}
```

As can be seen, there are four possible outcomes.

The first one is SEND_CONTINUE, which basically means "authentication in progress." The authentication mechanism returned that status when it took over the dialog again (e.g., by rendering its own response or, more likely, by redirecting the caller to a new location). A Jakarta Faces backing bean should make sure the Jakarta Faces life cycle is ended by calling *FacesContext#responseComplete()* and furthermore refrain from interacting with the response itself in any way.

The second one is SEND_FAILURE, which basically means "authentication failed." This status is returned when the authentication mechanism wasn't able to validate the credentials that were provided. In most cases, this is when the caller provided the wrong credentials. A Jakarta Faces backing bean can respond to this by setting a Faces message and redisplay the login form.

The third status is SUCCESS, which means "authentication succeeded." This is returned when the authentication mechanism successfully validates the credentials provided. It's only after this status is returned that *HttpServletRequest#getUserPrinc ipal()*, *SecurityContext#getCallerPrincipal()*, etc., return non-null values to indicate the current caller is authenticated. A Jakarta Faces backing bean can respond to this in various ways (e.g., by setting a faces message and continuing to render the view, or issuing a redirect of itself).

The fourth and final status is NOT_DONE, which is returned when the authentication mechanism chooses to not authenticate at all. This happens, for instance, when the authentication mechanism is preemptively called but authentication appears not to be necessary. Typically, a Jakarta Faces backing bean would not need to take any special action here.

Caller-Initiated Authentication

The previous code discussed the situation where an unauthenticated caller tries to access a protected resource (URL/page) and the authentication dialog is automatically started. Since this authentication dialog is started by the container, we call this "container-initiated authentication."

Another case is where a caller explicitly starts the authentication dialog (e.g., by clicking on a "login" button). Because the caller starts this dialog, we call it "caller-initiated authentication."

In case of caller-initiated authentication, the core authentication mechanism is effectively directly invoked, and the platform-provided login-to-continue functionality is skipped. This means that if an authentication mechanism depends on login-to-continue to redirect to a login page and after authentication to redirect back to the protected resource, neither of these two actions will happen when the application programmatically triggers authentication.

The *CustomFormAuthenticationMechanism* that we defined earlier via an annotation is indeed a mechanism that uses the platform's login-to-continue service, so we'll start the authentication dialog by directing to the same login view we used before. To indicate this is a new login, an extra request parameter is provided. The view from which we start looks as follows:

```
<!DOCTYPE html>
<html lang="en"
    xmlns:f="jakarta.faces.core"
    xmlns:h="jakarta.faces.html"
    xmlns:c="jakarta.tags.core"
>
    <h:head>
        <title>Welcome</title>
    <h:head>
    <h:body>
        <c:if test="#{not empty request.userPrincipal}">
            <p>Logged-in as #{request.userPrincipal}</p>
        </c:if>
        <c:if test="#{empty request.userPrincipal}">
            <h:form>
```

```
        <h:button value="Login" outcome="/login">
            <f:param name="new" value="true" />
        </h:button>
    </h:form>
</c:if>
    </h:body>
</html>
```

In the backing bean, we'll inject two additional objects: an instance to obtain and store the mentioned request parameter and a reference to the Flash, which we'll use later.

```
@Inject
private Flash flash;

@Inject @ManagedProperty("#{param.new}")
private boolean isNew;
```

The managed bean's scope needs to be changed to *@ViewScoped*, so we can retain the value of the isNew instance variable after the login form's postback.

An important addition is to the *SecurityContext#authenticate()* method where we'll now provide an extra parameter: *newAuthentication.* The authentication mechanism does not strictly need this though, and it's just smart enough to distinguish between an initial new authentication and continuing an authentication dialog that's in progress. However, things get more difficult when a caller is in the midst of an authentication dialog and then navigates away, only to explicitly click a login button later. If the state associated with said dialog hasn't expired at that point, the authentication mechanism doesn't know a new authentication is required and will likely continue the aborted but still valid dialog.

To prevent this, we can force a new authentication by setting *newAuthentication* to true. This will discard all existing states. The modified *continueAuthentication()* method looks as follows:

```
private AuthenticationStatus continueAuthentication() {
    return securityContext.authenticate(
        (HttpServletRequest) externalContext.getRequest(),
        (HttpServletResponse) externalContext.getResponse(),
```

```
        AuthenticationParameters
            .withParams()
            .newAuthentication(isNew)
            .credential(
                new UsernamePasswordCredential(
                    email, password))
    );
}
```

Note that this version can be used for the case where we continue the dialog as well as to start a new one. When we continue the dialog, isNew will simply be false, which also happens to be the default when the parameter is not specified at all.

When using the *CustomFormAuthenticationMechanism*, we know there will not be any redirects or other writes to the response after we provide the credentials in caller-initiated authentication, so that gives us a convenient location to handle the redirect to a landing page after the caller authenticates: the SUCCESS case.

```
case SUCCESS:
    flash.setKeepMessages(true);
    facesContext.addMessage(null, new FacesMessage(
        FacesMessage.SEVERITY_INFO, "Login succeed", null));
    externalContext.redirect(
        externalContext.getRequestContextPath() + "/index.xhtml");
    break;
```

We're redirecting the caller here to the *index.xhtml* landing page. Note that this is also the view where the caller initiated the authentication dialog, but that's just a coincidence in this example. In general, the view or even URL where we redirect the caller to is completely free for the application developer to choose. Typically, a landing page of some sort is chosen, which could be the index of the application or a dashboard corresponding to the main role the caller is in. As we mentioned before, when SUCCESS is returned, the caller is fully authenticated. This means we can query the caller's roles and use these in our decision where to redirect to.

JAKARTA EE FUTURE LOOKOUT

A future version of Jakarta EE Security may introduce a hybrid option where caller-initiated authentication can still start with the same redirect as container-initiated authentication and allows for the redirect-back URL to be provided by the application.

Default Identity Stores

Until now, we have used our own implementations for the identity store. But just as for authentication mechanisms, Jakarta Security provides two implementations of these out of the box:

1. Database

2. LDAP (Lightweight Directory Access Protocol)

Soteria, the Eclipse implementation of Jakarta EE that we talked about before, additionally ships with an embedded identity store. Most application servers provide additional ones of their own, which are often configured outside the application (e.g., via an admin console, CLI, or XML configuration file that's stored inside the server).

The following table gives an overview for several well-known servers:

Store	JBoss	GlassFish	Liberty	WebLogic	Tomcat	Resin	Jetty
LDAP	V	V	V	V	V	V	V (via JAAS bridge)
JDBC/ Database	V	V	X	V	V	V	V
File	V (.properties)	V (.csv)	X	X	V (.xml)	V	V (.properties)
Embedded	V single user only	X	V	X	V	X	X
X.509	V	V	X	V	X	X	X
JAAS bridge	X	X	X	X	V	V	V
SPNEGO	X	X	X	V	X	X	V
SAML	X	X	X	V	X	X	X

As can be seen, LDAP support is pretty universal, closely followed by some kind of database support (via a data source stored in JNDI and/or directly via a JDBC driver). Some kind of file support is pretty universal as well. Although file formats differ, it's almost always {name, (hashed) password, zero or more groups} in some form.

Embedded is supported by less than half of the servers shown here. Embedded means that whatever location is used to say what identity store is being used has the caller data at that same location, typically as nested XML tags.

X.509 is a somewhat more special type of store. In all cases, this one is backed by a keystore that is only able to check whether the presented client certificate has been issued by a trusted CA. Contrary to almost all other stores, it's not capable of returning a new caller name and optionally groups. In order to get these groups, this store either has to be combined with another store, or the server's proprietary principal to role mapping has to be used (meaning that you have to hard-code all possible callers (users) in some XML file, which is often a downright impossible requirement).

Setting and configuring the Jakarta Security provided identity stores and the one provided by Soteria happens in a similar fashion as the authentication mechanisms: via an *IdentityStoreAnnotation*. Just like the authentication mechanism version, this will cause the container to add an enabled CDI bean to the system, this time one implementing the IdentityStore interface.

The following shows an example together with our earlier definition of the custom form authentication mechanism:

```
@CustomFormAuthenticationMechanismDefinition(
    loginToContinue = @LoginToContinue(
        loginPage = "/login.xhtml",
        useForwardToLogin = false,
        errorPage = ""
    )
)
@EmbeddedIdentityStoreDefinition({
    @Credentials(
        callerName = "admin@example.com",
        password = "secret1",
        groups = { "VIEW_USER_PAGES", "VIEW_ADMIN_PAGES" }
    ),
```

```
@Credentials(
    callerName = "user@example.com",
    password = "secret2",
    groups = { "VIEW_USER_PAGES" })
)
})
@FacesConfig @ApplicationScoped
public class ApplicationConfig {
    // ...
}
```

The aforementioned causes an embedded (in-memory) store to be created, with two callers (users): the first one being in the groups "VIEW_USER_PAGES" and "VIEW_ADMIN_PAGES" and the second one only in the group "VIEW_USER_PAGES".

The Database Identity Store

Let's now take a look at one of the identity stores that's provided by the Jakarta Security API – the database identity store. This store is activated and configured using the *@DatabaseIdentityStoreDefinition* annotation. The three most important attributes to configure are the data source (which represents the SQL database), the SQL query to obtain the (hashed!) password given a caller name, and the SQL query to identify which groups a caller is in given the caller name. The following gives an example:

```
@CustomFormAuthenticationMechanismDefinition(
    loginToContinue = @LoginToContinue(
        loginPage = "/login.xhtml",
        errorPage = ""
    )
)
@DatabaseIdentityStoreDefinition(
    dataSourceLookup = "java:app/MyDataSource",
    callerQuery = "SELECT password FROM caller WHERE name = ?",
    groupsQuery = "SELECT name FROM groups WHERE caller_name = ?"
)
```

```
@DataSourceDefinition(
    name = "java:app/MyDataSource",
    className = "org.h2.jdbcx.JdbcDataSource",
    url="jdbc:h2:~/test;DB_CLOSE_ON_EXIT=FALSE"
)
@FacesConfig @ApplicationScoped
public class ApplicationConfig {
    // ...
}
```

In this example, a data source is defined for the H2 database using the *org.h2.jdbcx. JdbcDataSource* driver. Naturally, this can be done in a similar way for any other database that has a JDBC driver. Alternatively, the data source can be defined externally to the application. The caller query that we used is "select password from caller where name = ?", which means we assume a table with at least two columns: one holding the caller name and the other the hashed password. Such table could be created by, for example, the following SQL statement:

```
CREATE TABLE caller(
    name VARCHAR(32) PRIMARY KEY,
    password VARCHAR(255)
)
```

The query that we used for the groups is "select name from groups where caller_ name = ?", which assumes a table with at least two columns: the caller name and the group name, with one row for each group the caller is in. Such a table could be created by, for example, the following SQL statement:

```
CREATE TABLE caller_groups(
    caller_name VARCHAR(32),
    name VARCHAR(32)
)
```

When populating the caller table, it must be noted that a default hash algorithm is assumed for the password column, namely, *PBKDF2WithHmacSHA256*. This algorithm can (should) be customized by setting the number of iterations, the key size, and the salt size.

The LDAP Identity Store

The LDAP identity store allows authentication data to be stored in an external LDAP server. It's selected and configured via the @LdapIdentityStoreDefinition annotation.

The Soteria implementation is done by org.glassfish.soteria.identitystores. LdapIdentityStore.

There's a very wide variety of ways to model users and groups in LDAP.

The following shows a minimal example relying on the defaults for most attributes:

```
@LdapIdentityStoreDefinition(
    url = "ldap://localhost:33389/",
    callerBaseDn = "ou=caller,dc=jsr375,dc=net",
    groupBaseDn  = "ou=group,dc=jsr375,dc=net"
)
```

Identity Stores Using Application Services

The custom identity stores that we have looked at before were merely trivial example stores. Let's now take a look at something a wee bit more realistic. A common use case is using the application's own services to load the application-specific user data.

The following shows an example of an identity store using such services:

```
@ApplicationScoped
public class UserServiceIdentityStore implements IdentityStore {

    @Inject
    private UserService userService;

    @Override
    public CredentialValidationResult validate(Credential credential) {
        UsernamePasswordCredential login =
            (UserNamePasswordCredential) credential;
        String email = login.getCaller();
        String password = login.getPasswordAsString();
        Optional<User> optionalUser =
            userService.findByEmailAndPassword(email, password);

        if (optionalUser.isPresent()) {
```

```
        User user = optionalUser.get();

        return new CredentialValidationResult(
            user.getEmail(),
            user.getRolesAsStrings()
        );
    }

    return CredentialValidationResult.INVALID_RESULT;
    }
}
```

The *UserServiceIdentityStore* as given previously delegates most of the work to a *UserService*, which would be responsible for handling *User* entities in the application. Fully discussing such service is outside the scope of this book, but we can imagine it could use, for example, Jakarta Persistence to persist and load *User* entities. Our custom identity store uses the service to try to find a *User* based on the username and the password that's being passed in via the credentials. If a *User* instance is returned, it means the name referred to an existing user, and the password was the correct one. In that case, the identity store in turn returns a *CredentialValidationResult*, which does two things: it indicates that authentication was successful, and it provides the container with the data that will eventually be used to set the authenticated identity for the current request. If the service couldn't find the user, then either the name or the password was wrong. In that case, the store returns *INVALID_RESULT* to indicate that authentication was not successful.

Authentication Mechanism Interceptors

Jakarta Security provides several interceptors that can be applied to HTTP authentication mechanisms to add common services.

Auto Apply Session

The authenticated identity set by an authentication mechanism is by default only applied to the current request. This means the mechanism will be called for every request, even when authentication already took place earlier within the same HTTP session. It's the authentication mechanism's responsibility to reauthenticate at the start of each request.

While at first sight this may not seem logical, it's what makes the authentication mechanism naturally suitable for stateless architectures and makes preemptive authentication effortless.

In order to couple authentication to an HTTP session, a typical approach would be to store the authenticated identity manually in the HTTP session or in an instance field of an *@SessionScoped* bean implementing *HttpAuthenticationMechanism*. Then as the first order of business, the *validateRequest* method checks if the authenticated identity is available at one of those locations and if so applies it. If not, it proceeds with the regular logic.

While not particularly difficult, it's a somewhat tedious pattern to implement, and Jakarta Security therefore provides an annotation to automate this: *@AutoApplySession*

This is a CDI interceptor that intercepts calls to the *validateRequest* method. All that's needed for the application developer is to annotate the authentication mechanism bean with this annotation.

The following shows an example of this:

```
@RequestScoped
@AutoApplySession
public class TestAuthenticationMechanism
    implements HttpAuthenticationMechanism {

    @Inject
    private IdentityStore identityStore;

    @Override
    public AuthStatus validateRequest(
        HttpServletRequest request,
        HttpServletResponse response,
        HttpMessageContext httpMessageContext) throws AuthException {

        if (isAnyNull(
                request.getParameter("name"),
                request.getParameter("password")) {
            return httpMessageContext.doNothing();
        }

        String name = request.getParameter("name");
        Password password =
```

```
            new Password(request.getParameter("password"));

        CredentialValidationResult result = identityStore.validate(
            new UsernamePasswordCredential(name, password));

        if (result.getStatus() != VALID) {
            throw new AuthException("Login failed");
        }

        return httpMessageContext.notifyContainerAboutLogin(
            result.getCallerPrincipal(),
            result.getCallerGroups());
    }
}
```

Remember Me

Once a caller has been authenticated for a Jakarta Faces (web) application, we naturally don't want to ask the caller to reauthenticate with every request. To prevent this, the result of a successful authentication is typically coupled in some way to the caller's HTTP session. In fact, the *CustomFormAuthenticationMechanism* internally uses the Jakarta EE Security's provided "auto-apply-session" service to do just this. This service stores the data associated with said successful authentication (at least the caller name plus any groups the caller is in). Although implementation ultimately depends on where this data exactly lives and with what lifetime, in practice, it's typically in a special section of the server's memory associated with the HTTP session. This section is special in the way that it's typically session scoped, but the data is not accessible via *HttpSession#getAttribute()*.

In order to not exhaust the server's memory, an HTTP session expires after a certain amount of time. Typical expiration times are between ten minutes and an hour. If the caller accesses the application after this time, authentication is required to be performed again.

Often though, reauthenticating after a period of inactivity as long as an hour is undesirable. But extending the HTTP session to a longer period is undoable for the aforementioned reasons of server resource exhaustion.

Here's where "Remember Me" (remember-me) comes in. Remember-me is a somewhat playful term for a process where the caller's credentials are exchanged for a token and where this token is typically stored in a cookie that's distinct from the HTTP session cookie and has a longer time to live.

A remember-me token effectively functions as a new credential for the caller, without exposing the caller's original password. A remember-me token can basically be vended multiple times, for instance, once per device or IP (Internet protocol) that the caller uses to connect to the application. Care must be taken that while the token does not expose the caller's original credentials, it still functions as the key to a caller's account and therefore should be treated with the same precautions as one would apply to any other type of credential. Specifically, cookies containing the remember-me token should be sent over HTTPS/SSL only, and applications should not store the actual token verbatim but a strong hash of it.

As the primary reason for having remember-me is to not exhaust server memory and to be long-lived, the remember-me token is almost always stored in stable storage (e.g., a database). As such, a lookup from such storage is costlier than a lookup from the server's memory, and this could seriously affect performance when required to be done for every request, especially when many Ajax requests are being done all the time.

For this reason, remember-me is almost always used in combination with some kind of cache. The modular nature of the services that the *CustomFormAuthenticationMechanism* uses makes it possible for remember-me to be inserted between the auto-apply-session service mentioned previously and the actual authentication mechanism. That way, we effectively get a kind of memory hierarchy; the authentication data is first attempted to be found in the HTTP session storage; if it's not there, the remember-me service is attempted, and if that one doesn't contain the data, then finally the authentication mechanism is tried.

To make use of remember-me, two things have to be done.

1. Activating the remember-me service for the installed authentication mechanism

2. Providing a special identity store that's capable of vending and validating the remember-me token

Activating Remember-Me Service

The remember-me service in Jakarta EE Security is represented by an interceptor. Via the interceptor binding annotation *@RememberMe*, the remember-me service is easily applied to our own custom authentication mechanism, one for which we have the source code. Unfortunately, it isn't as easy when these have to be applied to a bean for which we don't have the source code and in fact for which we don't even know the exact implementation type.

As the *CustomFormAuthenticationMechanism* that we've been using for the earlier examples is indeed of the latter type, there's a bit more work to do. Essentially, we need to obtain a reference of the actual *CustomFormAuthenticationMechanism* implementation that the container makes available and then use the CDI 2.0 InterceptionFactory to programmatically add the *@RememberMe annotation*. The result is then to be returned from an alternative producer method.

This is demonstrated in the following code via the new method *produceAuthenticationMechanism()* in the *ApplicationConfig* bean which we showed before:

```
@CustomFormAuthenticationMechanismDefinition(
    loginToContinue = @LoginToContinue(
        loginPage = "/login.xhtml",
        useForwardToLogin = false,
        errorPage = ""
    )
)
@FacesConfig @ApplicationScoped
@Alternative @Priority(500)
public class ApplicationConfig {
    @Produces
    public HttpAuthenticationMechanism produceAuthenticationMechanism(
        InterceptionFactory<HttpAuthenticationMechanismWrapper>
        interceptionFactory, BeanManager beanManager
    ) {
        @RememberMe
        class RememberMeClass {};

        interceptionFactory.configure().add(
            RememberMeClass.class.getAnnotation(RememberMe.class));

        return interceptionFactory.createInterceptedInstance(
            new HttpAuthenticationMechanismWrapper(
                (HttpAuthenticationMechanism) beanManager
                .getReference(beanManager
                .resolve(beanManager
                .getBeans((HttpAuthenticationMechanism.class).stream()
```

```
        .filter(b -> b.getBeanClass() != ApplicationConfig.class)
        .collect(Collectors.toSet())),
            HttpAuthenticationMechanism.class,
            beanManager.createCreationalContext(null))));
    }
}
```

The *ApplicationConfig* bean is annotated with the *@Alternative* and *@Priority* annotations. *@Alternative* is used here to indicate that the producer is not just any regular producer but one that should be called instead of any existing producer or bean. That is, the bean we are producing here is an alternative for the bean with the same type that would otherwise be selected by CDI for injection. *@Priority* is used to enable (activate) our alternative producer. Without this annotation, the producer is present but not enabled, meaning that CDI won't call it. Another way of enabling an alternative is using *beans.xml*. The number 500 here is used to select between various alternatives if multiple alternatives are enabled. In that case, the one with the highest number is selected.

The code shown previously uses the somewhat well-known CDI pattern *BeanManager#getBeans()/resolve()/getReference()* to obtain the *CustomFormAuthenticationMechanism* that the container makes available. This pattern is more verbose than the simpler *CDI.current().select(…)* variant, but it allows us to filter out the *Bean<T>* that represents the producer method. Getting a reference from that *Bean<T>* from within the producer method would invoke that same producer method again and thus would cause a recursive series of calls eventually leading to a stack overflow. It goes without saying this is unwanted, hence the reason we filter that particular *Bean<T>* out.

The bean instance that is returned from the *BeanManager#getReference()* is almost certainly a proxy; *CustomFormAuthenticationMechanism* is specified to be application scoped, and it implicitly makes use of an interceptor. Due to the technical difficulty of proxying an existing proxy (think of generated proxies often being final and proxy caches being used), CDI 2.0 imposes a limitation on what types of objects it can create an intercepted instance from. To work around this limitation, we have little choice but to insert an extra manually created "pass-through wrapper" *HttpAuthenticationMechanismWrapper* instance as shown in the preceding code. The code of this wrapper is as follows:

```java
public class HttpAuthenticationMechanismWrapper
    implements HttpAuthenticationMechanism {
    private HttpAuthenticationMechanism wrapped;

    public HttpAuthenticationMechanismWrapper() {
        //
    }

    public HttpAuthenticationMechanismWrapper
        (HttpAuthenticationMechanism httpAuthenticationMechanism) {
        this.wrapped = httpAuthenticationMechanism;
    }

    public HttpAuthenticationMechanism getWrapped() {
        return wrapped;
    }

    @Override
    public AuthenticationStatus validateRequest(
        HttpServletRequest request,
        HttpServletResponse response,
        HttpMessageContext context) throws AuthenticationException {
        return getWrapped().validateRequest(request, response, context);
    }

    @Override
    public AuthenticationStatus secureResponse(
        HttpServletRequest request,
        HttpServletResponse response,
        HttpMessageContext context) throws AuthenticationException {
        return getWrapped().secureResponse(request, response, context);
    }

    @Override
    public void cleanSubject(
        HttpServletRequest request,
        HttpServletResponse response,
        HttpMessageContext context) {
```

```
        getWrapped().cleanSubject(request, response, context);
    }
}
```

The remember-me functionality can be combined with the auto apply session feature. In that case, the runtime will first check for the authentication data in the session; if it doesn't find it there, it will check for the remember-me token, and if present, it will try the remember-me identity store, and if that doesn't work, it will finally try the main identity store. The following shows a brief example of this:

```
@RequestScoped
@AutoApplySession
@RememberMe
public class TestAuthenticationMechanism
    implements HttpAuthenticationMechanism {
    // ...
}
```

JAKARTA EE 10 LOOKOUT

For Jakarta EE 10 or a later version, it's considered to add the HttpAuthenticationMechanismWrapper shown previously to the API of Jakarta Security, as well as have annotation literals in annotations such as @RememberMe.

Additionally, it is considered to add a convenience method or mechanism to CDI, further simplifying the preceding task.

Logging Out

Regardless of which method to log in has been used, at some point, the caller may wish to explicitly log out. A normal login (authentication) in Jakarta EE is always primarily valid per request only, but various authentication mechanisms or the services they're using (such as *AutoApplySession* and *RememberMe*) may keep the state beyond a single request and automatically reauthenticate the caller at every next request.

This state may be kept at various places: in cookies, in the HTTP session, in client storage, etc. In order to log out, we have to make sure all this state is cleared. In Jakarta Faces, we can do this simply by calling the *HttpServletRequest#logout()* method. This will immediately remove the authenticated identity from the current request and call the *cleanSubject()* method of the authentication mechanism, which in turn will remove any session data, cookies, etc., that it used.

The following gives an example:

```
@Named @RequestScoped
public class Logout {

    @Inject
    private HttpServletRequest request;

    public void submit() throws ServletException {
        request.logout();
        request.getSession().invalidate();
    }
}
```

Note that for a full logout, it's typically good practice to invalidate the session as well. The call to *HttpServletRequest#logout()* should only remove the session state used by the authentication mechanism (if any), while after a full logout, we often don't want any other session state lingering around either. Depending on the application design, it's typical to redirect the caller to the home page of the application after a logout as well.

Custom Principals

The default principal that we can obtain from the security context contains very little other than just the name or, more exactly, the caller principal name (also known as the user principal name). This is typically a unique name and often, but not necessarily, the name the caller used to authenticate with.

In practice, a web application almost always needs more information than just this name, and a richer application-specific model object representing the user is often desired. The lifetime of this model object does need to be very tightly coupled to that of the principal. For example, if the caller is logged out mid-request, the associated model object must disappear right away, and if the caller is logged in again right after (possibly still in the same request), a new model object must become available.

There are various patterns to realize this, some of them including Servlet filters and others containing CDI producers. The pattern we're going to show here, though, involves a custom principal.

A custom principal means that a specific Principal type is returned from the identity store, instead of just providing a String and letting the container decide the type. This specific Principal type can then either contain our model object (aggregation) or be the model object (inheritance). We'll give an example of the aggregation approach here.

First, consider the following custom Principal:

```
public class UserPrincipal extends CallerPrincipal {

    private final User user;

    public UserPrincipal(User user) {
        super(user.getEmail());
        this.user = user;
    }

    public User getUser() {
        return user;
    }
}
```

This *Principal* extends from *jakarta.security.enterprise.CallerPrincipal*, which is the Jakarta Security–specific caller principal representation.

With this *Principal* implementation, we can now adjust the identity store that we presented earlier to return our custom principal instead.

```
@ApplicationScoped
public class UserServiceIdentityStore implements IdentityStore {

    @Inject
    private UserService userService;

    @Override
    public CredentialValidationResult validate(Credential credential) {
```

295

```
        UsernamePasswordCredential login =
            (UserNamePasswordCredential) credential;
        String email = login.getCaller();
        String password = login.getPasswordAsString();
        Optional<User> optionalUser =
            userService.findByEmailAndPassword(email, password);

        if (optionalUser.isPresent()) {
            User user = optionalUser.get();

            return new CredentialValidationResult(
                new UserPrincipal(user), // Principal instead of String.
                user.getRolesAsStrings()
            );
        }

        return CredentialValidationResult.INVALID_RESULT;

    }
}
```

Subsequently, we can access our model object again from an injected security context.

```
@Inject
private SecurityContext securityContext;

[...]

Optional<User> OptionalUser =
    securityContext.getPrincipalsByType(
        UserPrincipal.class)
            .stream()
            .map(e -> e.getUser())
            .findAny();
```

Conditionally Rendering Based on Access

In web applications, one often wants to render parts of a view differently based on whether a caller is authenticated or not and if so based on what roles this caller is in.

296

Jakarta Faces component tags don't really need special attributes for this, as the existing implicit objects combined with expression language are powerful enough to do most of the checks needed for this.

One of the most common checks is determining whether the user is authenticated. This was briefly shown in the preceding index.xhtml view:

```
<c:if test="#{not empty request.userPrincipal}">
    <p>Logged-in as #{request.userPrincipal}</p>
</c:if>
```

Note that we're using the implicit object #{request} here instead of the more general *SecurityContext*. This is because in Jakarta EE 9, there's no implicit EL object available corresponding to this *SecurityContext*. In Jakarta Security, as well as in the Jakarta Servlet API (from which the request, which is of type *HttpServletRequest*, originates), it's defined that a null return from *getUserPrincipal()* means the user is not authenticated.

JAKARTA EE 10 LOOKOUT

For Jakarta EE 10 or a later version, a better alignment between Jakarta Security and Expression Language is considered.

Another common check as mentioned is to test for the caller being in a specific role. Here too we can use the implicit object #{request}, as shown in the following:

```
<c:if test="#{request.isUserInRole('foo')}">
    <!-- foo specific things here -->
</c:if>
```

It's good to remember that as explained before, the role "foo" doesn't have to be something that we would call a role in our normal usage of the word. That is, it doesn't have to be something like "admin," or "manager." In fact, for such very local usage as in a fragment on a view, it's often preferred to use a finer-grained name (e.g., "CAN_UPDATE_SALARY"). A common technique is to map fine-grained roles to more coarse-grained roles, such as, indeed, "ADMIN." Via this technique, a user is given these more coarse-grained roles, and the data store that stores the authentication data then only contains these coarse-grained roles as well. When an identity store such as we saw previously retrieves this authentication data for a certain caller and sees "ADMIN," it would return a collection of roles to which "ADMIN" is mapped (e.g., {"CAN_UPDATE_SALARY", "CAN_ADJUST_MARGINS", ...}).

A special role that we can test for is the "**" role, which is an alternative for the #*{not empty request.userPrincipal}* check. This role is implicitly assigned to any authenticated caller, but with the caveat that the application has not declared this in any way. If it has done so, "**" loses its special meaning and is just another opaque string for which the security system explicitly tests. Using the "**" check, the first fragment that we showed in this section looks as follows:

```
<c:if test="#{request.isUserInRole('**')}">
    <p>Logged-in as #{request.userPrincipal}</p>
</c:if>
```

In the standard Jakarta EE programmatic APIs, there are no methods available to test whether the caller is in any of two or more roles, or in all of two or more roles. If this is required, utility methods such as shown in the following code can be used:

```
public static boolean isInAnyRole
    (HttpServletRequest request, String... roles) {
    for (String roles : roles) {
        if (request.isUserInRole(role)) {
            return true;
        }
    }

    return false;
}

public static boolean isInAllRoles
    (HttpServletRequest request, String... roles) {
    for (String roles : roles) {
        if (!request.isUserInRole(role)) {
            return false;
        }
```

```
    }

    return true;
}
```

Sometimes, it's necessary not only to render content on a view differently, depending on what roles a caller is in, but also to take into account what other views (web resources) a caller is allowed to access. This comes into play, for instance, when rendering navigation menus (omitting the entries for views a caller does not have access to), or rendering links or buttons that navigate to views to which the caller does not have access in a special way (e.g., in red or with a lock icon next to it).

A traditional way to implement this is to test for the roles that the programmer knows give access to the given view. While this may seem to work well, it's often brittle in practice as it lets the code work under the assumption of a specific role/view relationship without any strong guarantees that this relationship actually holds.

A more stable way to test whether a caller has access to a given view is quite simply to test directly for exactly that; does the caller have access to this view (web resource). The *SecurityContext* has a method that can be used for almost exactly this: *SecurityContext#hasAccessToWebResource()*. Since the *SecurityContext* is not a named bean or implicit object, we have to create a small helper bean in order to use this in EL. This is shown as follows:

```
@Named @ApplicationScoped
public class Security {

    @Inject
    private SecurityContext securityContext;

    public boolean hasAccessToWebResource(String resource) {
        return securityContext.hasAccessToWebResource(resource, "GET");
    }
}
```

There are two things to be aware of here.

First, the *hasAccessToWebResource()* method takes a web resource pattern, which is the same pattern as used for the *url-pattern* in the *web.xml* fragment we looked at earlier. This is close to, but not exactly the same as, the Jakarta Faces view. The Jakarta Faces view is often specified in a mapping independent way (e.g., /foo instead of /faces/ foo or /foo.xhtml). The web resource pattern, however, has to be the URL itself, with the mapping included.

Second, *hasAccessToWebResource()* requires us to specify the HTTP method for which we test the access. This is required since in Jakarta EE Security, constraints actually apply per URL and per HTTP method. For instance, a caller can have access to POST to /foo.xhtml but not to GET /foo.xhtml. As we're going to use our utility method for navigation tests, GET is typically the right HTTP method to use, but we should be aware that sometimes we may need to test for another HTTP method.

With the helper bean in place, we can now easily check for access to a target resource on a view and alter the rendering based on that. To demonstrate this, we'll first define three new web resource constraints in web.xml.

```xml
<security-constraint>
    <web-resource-collection>
        <web-resource-name>Bar</web-resource-name>
        <url-pattern>/bar.xhtml</url-pattern>
    </web-resource-collection>
    <auth-constraint>
        <role-name>bar</role-name>
    </auth-constraint>
</security-constraint>
<security-constraint>
    <web-resource-collection>
        <web-resource-name>Foo</web-resource-name>
        <url-pattern>/foo.xhtml</url-pattern>
    </web-resource-collection>
    <auth-constraint>
        <role-name>foo</role-name>
    </auth-constraint>
</security-constraint>
<security-constraint>
    <web-resource-collection>
        <web-resource-name>Baz</web-resource-name>
        <url-pattern>/baz.xhtml</url-pattern>
    </web-resource-collection>
    <auth-constraint>
```

```
    <role-name>baz</role-name>
  </auth-constraint>
</security-constraint>
```

After these constraints have been defined, we can render links to them with access checks on the enabled attribute.

```
<h:link value="Go to Bar" outcome="/bar"
    disabled="#{not security.hasAccessToWebResource('/bar.xhtml')}" />
<h:link value="Go to Foo" outcome="/foo"
    disabled="#{not security.hasAccessToWebResource('/foo.xhtml')}" />
<h:link value="Go to Baz" outcome="/baz"
    disabled="#{not security.hasAccessToWebResource('/baz.xhtml')}" />
```

Authenticating with a caller having, for instance, the roles "bar" and "foo," but not "baz," will result in the link to /baz being rendered as disabled.

Jakarta Security and Tomcat

One of the compatible implementations of Jakarta Security that we mentioned before is Soteria. Soteria has been designed as a stand-alone library that can be integrated with multiple servers. It depends on CDI and the lower-level SPIs Jakarta Authentication and Jakarta Authorization.

Another issue was that Tomcat implements the servlet container profile of Jakarta Authentication, but not Jakarta Authorization. There are essentially two options to overcome that here:

1. Add Jakarta Authorization support to Tomcat.

2. Implement an SPI for Soteria to use native Tomcat Authorization code.

The Exousia project that we mentioned before is an implementation of Jakarta Authorization and is able to function stand-alone. It contains integration support specifically for Tomcat so that we only need to add that as a dependency. To use Jakarta Security in Tomcat, we can create a Maven project with the following dependencies:

```
<dependency>
    <groupId>jakarta.platform</groupId>
```

```
    <artifactId>jakarta.jakartaee-api</artifactId>
    <version>9.0.0</version>
    <scope>provided</scope>
</dependency>

<dependency>
    <groupId>org.glassfish.soteria</groupId>
    <artifactId>jakarta.security.enterprise</artifactId>
    <version>2.0.1</version>
</dependency>

<dependency>
    <groupId>org.glassfish.exousia</groupId>
    <artifactId>exousia.spi.tomcat</artifactId>
    <version>1.0.0</version>
</dependency>

<dependency>
    <groupId>org.jboss.weld.servlet</groupId>
    <artifactId>weld-servlet-shaded</artifactId>
    <version>4.0.2.Final</version>
</dependency>
```

Additionally, since Tomcat has a read-only JNDI, a file in [war root]/META-INF/ context.xml is needed with the following content to make the BeanManager available:

```
<?xml version='1.0' encoding='utf-8'?>
<Context>
    <Resource
        name="BeanManager"
        auth="Container"
        type="javax.enterprise.inject.spi.BeanManager"
        factory="org.jboss.weld.resources.ManagerObjectFactory"
    />
</Context>
```

To test if everything works, put an empty beans.xml file in WEB-INF and a web.xml file with the following content:

```
<web-app
    xmlns="http://xmlns.jcp.org/xml/ns/javaee"
    xmlns:xsi="http://www.w3.org/2001/XMLSchema-instance"
    xsi:schemaLocation="https://jakarta.ee/xml/ns/jakartaee https://
    jakarta.ee/xml/ns/jakartaee/web-app_5_0.xsd"
    version="5.0">
    <security-constraint>
        <web-resource-collection>
            <url-pattern>/foo/*</url-pattern>
            <http-method>GET</http-method>
        </web-resource-collection>
        <auth-constraint>
            <role-name>g1</role-name>
        </auth-constraint>
    </security-constraint>

    <security-constraint>
        <web-resource-collection>
            <url-pattern>/foox/*</url-pattern>
            <http-method>GET</http-method>
        </web-resource-collection>
        <auth-constraint>
            <role-name>g2</role-name>
        </auth-constraint>
    </security-constraint>
</web-app>
```

Then add two classes:

```
@BasicAuthenticationMechanismDefinition(
    realmName = "realm")
@ServletSecurity(
    value = @HttpConstraint(rolesAllowed = "g1"))
@WebServlet(
    urlPatterns = "/SecureServlet")
public class SecureServlet extends HttpServlet {
```

```
    private static final long serialVersionUID = 1L;

    @Inject
    SecurityContext securityContext;

    @Override
    protected void doGet(
        HttpServletRequest request,
        HttpServletResponse response)
    throws ServletException, IOException {
        response.getWriter().println(
            "Has access to /foo/bar " +
            securityContext.hasAccessToWebResource("/foo/bar", "GET"));
        response.getWriter().println(
            "Has access to /foox/bar " +
            securityContext.hasAccessToWebResource("/foox/bar", "GET"));
    }

}


@ApplicationScoped
public class MyIdentityStore implements IdentityStore {
    public CredentialValidationResult validate(
        UsernamePasswordCredential usernamePasswordCredential) {
        if (usernamePasswordCredential.compareTo("u1", "p1")) {
            return new CredentialValidationResult(
                "u1", new HashSet<>(asList("g1")));
        }

        return INVALID_RESULT;
    }
}
```

Naming the app "security-test", deploying this to a default installed Tomcat 10, and requesting "http://localhost:8080/security-test/SecureServlet" via a web browser will show the basic authentication dialog from that browser. If we then authenticate with username "u1" and password "p1", we'll get to see the following result:

```
Has access to /foo/bar true
Has access to /foox/bar false
```

So what happened here?

Behind the scenes, quite a lot. Soteria installed a *ServerAuthModule* with Tomcat, which uses Weld to find and call the CDI bean installed by @ *BasicAuthenticationMechanismDefinition*. This bean calls the *IdentityStore MyIdentityStore*, which is the one we defined in our small application and that validates the credentials we submit.

Furthermore, Exousia copied the security constraints that Tomcat collected to a Jakarta Authorization module, which is a store of permissions (a.k.a. Permission Store) that among others can be queried by Jakarta Authorization. The default implementation in Soteria of *SecurityContext#hasAccessToWebResource* indeed results in such a query. In our web.xml file, we defined two constraints on URL patterns: /foo/* needing role g1 and /foox/* needing role g2. At the point of making that call, we're in role g1, so asking if we can access /foo/bar results in a true, while asking for access to /foox/bar results in a false. This shows that Jakarta Authentication (Exousia) works correctly on Tomcat and works correctly with Soteria.

There's a small caveat here. Exousia at the moment of writing now copies the security constraints from Tomcat, but Tomcat keeps using its own internal repository for authorization decisions. The assumption here is that both Tomcat and Exousia perform the exact same algorithm, but there can of course be small subtle differences. A next step would be to integrate Exousia further in Tomcat by wrapping the Tomcat-specific *Realm* and delegating methods like *hasUserDataPermission*, *hasResourcePermission*, and *hasRole*.

Simplified Custom Authorization Rules

In Chapter 4, we looked at implementing a Jakarta EE authorization module using the Jakarta Authorization specification. This module implemented the default authorization rules as specified by the Jakarta Authorization, Servlet, and EJB specifications. We now go beyond that default algorithm and take a look at providing our own custom authorization rules.

JAKARTA EE 10 LOOKOUT

For Jakarta EE 10 or a later version, the simplified authorization rules as explained here are proposed to become a part of the API by default.

In order to implement custom rules, one would traditionally ship an entire Jakarta Authorization provider with factory, configuration, and policy. Not only is this a lot of code (Jakarta Authorization doesn't have any code that can be reused; for the smallest change, everything needs to be implemented from scratch), it's also problematic that a Jakarta Authorization provider is global for the entire application server, while authorization rules are almost always specific for an individual application. Even when you adhere to the best practice of using one application per server, it's still quite a hassle to reinstall the Jakarta Authorization provider after every little change separately from the application.

For this section, we're therefore going to employ a different approach; use CDI to delegate from a single Jakarta Authorization provider that's installed once to an application specific CDI bean. As explained previously in this chapter, this is largely the same thing Jakarta Security is doing for authentication mechanisms, with the key difference that the Jakarta Authentication SPI does allow authentication modules to be installed per application.

Consider the following question:

Is it possible to determine group membership of a user on demand instead of when logging in via a ServerAuthModule (JASPIC)?

As it appears, the answer to this question is yes.

In order to come to a solution for the previously stated problem, take the Jakarta Authorization provider from the previous chapter and refactor it a little. The permissions that were previously put in the intermediate base class *TestPolicyConfigurationPermissions* can be factored out to a separate struct like class:

```
public class SecurityConstraints {

    private Permissions excludedPermissions = new Permissions();
    private Permissions uncheckedPermissions = new Permissions();
    private Map<String, Permissions> perRolePermissions = new
    HashMap<String, Permissions>();

    // + getters/setters
```

Furthermore, a new class can be introduced that holds the caller (name) principal, the (mapped) roles, and the raw set of unmapped principals (which are often server specific):

```
public class Caller {

    private Principal callerPrincipal;
    private List<String> roles;
    private List<Principal> unmappedPrincipals;

    // + getters/setters
```

Next, define an interface for the application to implement. Our Jakarta Authorization provider will call this at certain points during the authorization process:

```
public interface AuthorizationMechanism {

    default Boolean preAuthenticatePreAuthorize(
        Permission requestedPermission,
        SecurityConstraints securityConstraints) {
        return null;
    }

    default Boolean preAuthenticatePreAuthorizeByRole(
        Permission requestedPermission,
        SecurityConstraints securityConstraints) {
        return null;
    }

    default Boolean postAuthenticatePreAuthorize(
        Permission requestedPermission,
        Caller caller,
        SecurityConstraints securityConstraints) {
        return null;
    }

    default Boolean postAuthenticatePreAuthorizeByRole(
        Permission requestedPermission,
        Caller caller,
```

```
        SecurityConstraints securityConstraints) {
        return null;
    }
}
```

As can be seen, we distinguish for authorization decisions before authentication has taken place and thereafter and for those at the start of an authorization decision and right before it comes time to check for role-based permissions. The difference between those last two moments is that for the latter, the tests for excluded permissions (those granted to no one) and unchecked permissions (permissions granted to everyone) have already been performed. (Note that methods have been used for now, but perhaps events are the better solution here.)

With these artifacts in place, we can now modify the Jakarta Authorization Policy class to request a bean via CDI that implements the *AuthorizationMechanism* interface, and if it exists, we call one of the appropriate methods. The following shows an excerpt of this:

```
boolean postAuthenticate = domain.getPrincipals().length > 0;

AuthorizationMechanism mechanism = getBeanReferenceExtra(AuthorizationMecha
nism.class);
Caller caller = null;

if (postAuthenticate) {
    caller = new Caller(
        roleMapper.getCallerPrincipalFromPrincipals(currentUserPrincipals),
        roleMapper.getMappedRolesFromPrincipals(currentUserPrincipals),
        currentUserPrincipals);
}

if (mechanism != null) {
    Boolean authorizationOutcome = postAuthenticate?
        mechanism.postAuthenticatePreAuthorize(requestedPermission, caller,
        securityConstraints) :
        mechanism.preAuthenticatePreAuthorize(requestedPermission,
        securityConstraints);

    if (authorizationOutcome != null) {
```

```
            return authorizationOutcome;
        }
    }
}
```

In the preceding code, *getBeanReferenceExtra* uses CDI to fetch a bean of type *AuthorizationMechanism*. If the mechanism is not null, then depending on whether authentication has already happened or not, either the *postAuthenticatePreAuthorize* or the *preAuthenticatePreAuthorize* is called.

The Jakarta Authorization Policy doesn't tell us explicitly if the call is before or after authentication, but we can deduct this by looking at the passed-in principals. The assumption is that before authentication, there are no principals at all, and after authentication, there's at least one (if there was no actual authentication being done, the so-called unauthenticated caller principal is added).

With the Jakarta Authorization provider in place, we can now create a Jakarta EE web application that takes advantage of it. We'll start with a custom *IdentityStore* that only authenticates a single user named "test" and doesn't return any groups:

```
@RequestScoped
public class CustomIdentityStore
    implements IdentityStore {

    public CredentialValidationResult validate(
        UsernamePasswordCredential usernamePasswordCredential) {

        if (usernamePasswordCredential.getCaller().equals("test") &&
            usernamePasswordCredential.getPassword().
            compareTo("secret1")) {

            return new CredentialValidationResult(
                new CallerPrincipal("test"),
                // no static groups, dynamically handled
                // via authorization mechanism
                null            );
        }

        return INVALID_RESULT;
    }

}
```

We also add a custom *HttpAuthenticationMechanism,* one that's just used for testing purposes:

```java
@RequestScoped
public class CustomAuthenticationMechanism
    implements HttpAuthenticationMechanism {

    @Inject
    private IdentityStore identityStore;

    @Override
    public AuthStatus validateRequest(
        HttpServletRequest request,
        HttpServletResponse response,
        HttpMessageContext httpMessageContext)
        throws AuthException {

        if (request.getParameter("name") != null &&
            request.getParameter("password") != null) {

            CredentialValidationResult result =
                identityStore.validate(
                    new UsernamePasswordCredential(
                        request.getParameter("name"),
                        request.getParameter("password")));

            if (result.getStatus() == VALID) {
                return httpMessageContext
                    .notifyContainerAboutLogin(
                        result.getCallerPrincipal(),
                        result.getCallerGroups());
            } else {
                throw new AuthException("Login failed");
            }
        }

        return httpMessageContext.doNothing();
    }

}
```

Note that we could have omitted both the custom identity store and custom authentication mechanism and instead configured the default embedded store and the default BASIC authentication mechanism, but now we more clearly see what's exactly happening in the authentication process.

Let's now finally look at our custom authorization rule, which basically looks as follows:

```
@ApplicationScoped
public class CustomAuthorizationMechanism
    implements AuthorizationMechanism {

    @Override
    public Boolean postAuthenticatePreAuthorizeByRole(
        Permission requestedPermission,
        Caller caller,
        SecurityConstraints securityConstraints) {

        return
            getRequiredRoles(
                securityConstraints.getPerRolePermissions(),
                requestedPermission)
                  .stream()
                  .anyMatch(role ->
                    isInRole(
                      caller.getCallerPrincipal().getName(),
                      role));
    }
}
```

What's happening here is that our custom code is being asked to authorize the caller for some requested permission. Such permission can, for example, be a *WebResourcePermission* for a given protected path like /foo/bar.

In order to do an on-demand membership check, we start with using the *getRequiredRoles* method and the collected *SecurityConstraints* to obtain a list of roles that are required for the requested permission. We then look if the current caller is in any of those roles using the *isInRole* method. This method can do whatever back-end lookup is needed, but for an example application, we'll mock it using a simple map where we put caller "test" in roles "foo", "bar", and "kaz".

For completeness, the getRequiredRoles method gets the roles that are required for a requested permission as follows:

```
return perRolePermissions
        .entrySet().stream()
        .filter(entry -> entry.getValue().implies(requestedPermission))
        .map(e -> e.getKey())
        .collect(toList());
```

In order to test if the authorization rule works, we add a protected Servlet as follows:

```
@DeclareRoles({ "foo", "bar", "kaz" })
@WebServlet("/protected/servlet")
@ServletSecurity(@HttpConstraint(rolesAllowed = "foo"))
public class ProtectedServlet extends HttpServlet {

    private static final long serialVersionUID = 1L;

    @Override
    public void doGet(
        HttpServletRequest request,
        HttpServletResponse response)
        throws ServletException, IOException {

        response.getWriter().write(
            "This is a protected servlet \n");

        String webName = null;
        if (request.getUserPrincipal() != null) {
            webName = request.getUserPrincipal().getName();
        }

        response.getWriter().write(
            "web username: " + webName + "\n");

        response.getWriter().write(
            "web user has role \"foo\": " +
            request.isUserInRole("foo") + "\n");
        response.getWriter().write(
            "web user has role \"bar\": " +
```

```
            request.isUserInRole("bar") + "\n");
        response.getWriter().write(
            "web user has role \"kaz\": " +
            request.isUserInRole("kaz") + "\n");
    }

}
```

The Servlet shown here is protected by the role "foo", so with the previously given IdentityStore that doesn't return any groups/roles for our caller "test", we would normally not be able to access this Servlet. Yet with the custom authorization rule in place, we're able to access this Servlet just fine when authenticating as user "test".

Next, add a *preAuthenticatePreAuthorize* method to the authorization mechanism with some logging and also add logging to the existing *postAuthenticatePreAuthorizeByRole* method.

Deploy the application as "custom-authorization" and request http://localhost:8080/custom-authorization/protected/servlet?name=test&password=secret1.

This should result in log entries like the following:

```
preAuthenticatePreAuthorize called. Requested permission: ("jakarta.
security.jacc.WebUserDataPermission" "/protected/servlet" "GET")
preAuthenticatePreAuthorize called. Requested permission: ("jakarta.
security.jacc.WebResourcePermission" "/protected/servlet" "GET")

validateRequest called. Authentication mandatory: true

postAuthenticatePreAuthorizeByRole called. Requested permission: ("jakarta.
security.jacc.WebResourcePermission" "/protected/servlet" "GET")

postAuthenticatePreAuthorizeByRole called. Requested permission: ("jakarta.
security.jacc.WebRoleRefPermission" "org.omnifaces.authorization.
ProtectedServlet" "foo")
postAuthenticatePreAuthorizeByRole called. Requested permission: ("jakarta.
security.jacc.WebRoleRefPermission" "org.omnifaces.authorization.
ProtectedServlet" "bar")
postAuthenticatePreAuthorizeByRole called. Requested permission:
("javjakartaax.security.jacc.WebRoleRefPermission" "org.omnifaces.
authorization.ProtectedServlet" "kaz")
```

What we see happening here is that our authorization mechanism is initially called twice before authentication: first, to see if the request can be aborted early by checking if the protocol (http/https) is allowed and, second, to see if the resource is allowed to be accessed publicly. If the resource is allowed to be accessed publicly, authentication is still being asked for, but it's not mandatory then.

For the request to "/protected/servlet", authentication is mandatory as shown previously. Since authentication is thus mandatory, our authorization mechanism is called again after authentication for the same requested WebResourcePermission permission, but this time the caller data corresponding to the authenticated identity is also available. Our method will return "true" here, since ("jakarta.security.jacc. WebResourcePermission" "/protected/servlet" "GET") will turn out to require the role "foo", and our mock "isInRole" method will return "true" for caller "test" and role "foo".

We therefore continue to our requested resource, which means the servlet will be invoked.

Interesting to note here is that *HttpServletRequest#isUserInRole* is not implemented internally by checking a simple list of roles, but by calling our authorization module with a requested permission ("jakarta.security.jacc.WebRoleRefPermission" "org. omnifaces.authorization.ProtectedServlet" "[role name]"). The three *isUserInRole* calls that the servlet shown previously does therefore show up in the log as three calls to our authorization mechanism, each for a different role.

Also interesting to note is that our authorization mechanism handles a requested permission to access "/protected/servlet" and a requested permission for isUserInRole("foo") completely identical. If necessary, the authorization mechanism can of course inspect the requested permission, but for this use case, that wasn't necessary.

To contrast the call to the protected servlet, let's also take a quick look at the log entries resulting from a call to a public servlet that's otherwise identical to the protected one:

```
preAuthenticatePreAuthorize called. Requested permission: ("jakarta.
security.jacc.WebUserDataPermission" "/public/servlet" "GET")
preAuthenticatePreAuthorize called. Requested permission: ("jakarta.
security.jacc.WebResourcePermission" "/public/servlet" "GET")

validateRequest called. Authentication mandatory: false

postAuthenticatePreAuthorizeByRole called. Requested permission: ("jakarta.
security.jacc.WebRoleRefPermission" "org.omnifaces.authorization.
PublicServlet" "foo")
```

```
postAuthenticatePreAuthorizeByRole called. Requested permission: ("jakarta.
security.jacc.WebRoleRefPermission" "org.omnifaces.authorization.
PublicServlet" "bar")
postAuthenticatePreAuthorizeByRole called. Requested permission: ("jakarta.
security.jacc.WebRoleRefPermission" "org.omnifaces.authorization.
PublicServlet" "kaz")
```

What we see here is that our authorization mechanism is initially called twice again, but since the default authorization algorithm will grant access to the anonymous caller, the subsequent authentication is not mandatory, and our authorization mechanism will also not be called a second time for the same resource permission.

Dynamically Adding an Interceptor to a Built-in CDI Bean

In Jakarta EE's CDI, beans can be augmented via two artifacts: decorators and interceptors.

- **Decorators** are typically owned by the application code and can decorate a bean that's shipped by the container (built-in beans) or a library.

- **Interceptors** are typically shipped by a library and can be applied (bound) to a bean that's owned by the application.

So how do you bind a library shipped interceptor to a library shipped/built-in bean? In CDI 1.2 and before, this wasn't really possible, but in CDI 2.0, we can take advantage of the *InterceptionFactory* to do just this. It's not entirely trivial yet, but it's doable. In this section, we'll demonstrate how to apply the *@RememberMe* interceptor binding to a built-in bean of type *HttpAuthenticationMechanism*.

First, we configure our authentication mechanism by means of the following annotation:

```
@BasicAuthenticationMechanismDefinition(
    realmName="foo"
)
```

This will cause the container to enable a built-in bean with interface type *HttpAuthenticationMechanism*, but having an unknown (vendor-specific) implementation.

Next, we'll define an alternative for this bean via a CDI producer:

```
@Alternative
@Priority(500)
@ApplicationScoped
public class ApplicationInit {

    @Produces
    public HttpAuthenticationMechanism produce(
        InterceptionFactory<HttpAuthenticationMechanismWrapper>
            interceptionFactory,
        BeanManager beanManager) {
        return ...
    }
}
```

Note that perhaps somewhat counterintuitively the @Alternative annotation is put on the bean hosting the producer method, not on the producer method itself.

A small challenge here is to obtain the bean with type *HttpAuthenticationMechanism* that would have been chosen by the CDI runtime had our producer not been there. For a decorator, this is easy as CDI makes that exact bean injectable via the @Decorated qualifier. Here, we'll have to do this manually. One way is to get all the beans of type *HttpAuthenticationMechanism* from the bean manager (this will include both alternatives and non-alternatives), filter ourselves from that set, and then let the bean manager resolve the set to the one that would be chosen for injection. We then create a reference for that chosen bean.

The following shows this in code:

```
HttpAuthenticationMechanism mechanism =
    createRef(
        beanManager.resolve(
            beanManager.getBeans(HttpAuthenticationMechanism.class)
                    .stream()
                    .filter(e -> !e.getBeanClass().
                    equals(ApplicationInit.class))
```

```
            .collect(toSet()))),
        beanManager);
```

with createRef being defined as

```
HttpAuthenticationMechanism createRef(Bean<?> bean, BeanManager
beanManager) {
    return (HttpAuthenticationMechanism)
        beanManager.getReference(
            bean,
            HttpAuthenticationMechanism.class,
            beanManager.createCreationalContext(bean));
}
```

We now have an instance to the bean to which we like to apply the interceptor binding. Unfortunately, there's a somewhat peculiar and very nasty note in the CDI spec regarding the method that creates a proxy with the required interceptor attached.

If the provided instance is an internal container construct (such as client proxy), nonportable behavior results.

Since the *HttpAuthenticationMechanism* is a client proxy (it's application scoped by spec definition), we have no choice but to introduce some extra ceremony here, and that's by providing a wrapper ourselves. The interceptor will be applied to the wrapper then, and the wrapper will delegate to the actual *HttpAuthenticationMechanism* instance:

```
HttpAuthenticationMechanismWrapper wrapper =
    new HttpAuthenticationMechanismWrapper(mechanism);
```

Having our *HttpAuthenticationMechanism* instance ready, we can now dynamically configure an annotation instance. Such instance can be created via CDI's provided AnnotationLiteral helper type:

```
interceptionFactory.configure().add(
    new RememberMeAnnotationLiteral(
        86400, "",        // cookieMaxAgeSeconds
        false, "",        // cookieSecureOnly
        true, "",         // cookieHttpOnly
        "JREMEMBERMEID", // cookieName
```

```
        true, ""              // isRememberMe
    )
);
```

Finally, we create the aforementioned new proxy with the configured interceptor binding applied to it using the interception factory's *createInterceptedInstance* method and return this from our producer method:

```
return interceptionFactory.createInterceptedInstance(
    new HttpAuthenticationMechanismWrapper(wrapper));
```

CHAPTER 6

Java SE Underpinnings

So far, you have had the chance to learn about the fundamental concepts of security and how these are applied in the Jakarta EE world. Moreover, you have had the chance to learn about the importance of the main APIs that comprise the Jakarta EE Security framework (Jakarta Authentication, Jakarta Authorization, and Jakarta Security).

In this chapter, we have a little gift for you before diving into a couple of specific Jakarta EE implementations. We thought it would be nice to give you an idea of other security-related trends that may not be directly related to Jakarta EE yet are profound in the Java ecosystem.

In this chapter, we will investigate the so-called underpinnings of the Standard Edition of Java. That is, this chapter is about security features and mechanisms Java SE supports out of the box.

Note   The code examples of this chapter are organized according to the section they belong to. The main module is *chapter6-javase-underpinnings/*, and then you will find a couple of more child modules in it, depending on the topic each section investigates (such as *jaas*, *digital-signatures*, *jce-providers*, *pki*, and *tls*).

Java Authentication and Authorization Service (JAAS)

Remember when in Chapter 2 we said security can be programmatic or declarative? JAAS provides a programmatic approach to enhancing your application's security, as it's a Java SE low-level security framework that augments the security model from code-based security to user-based security.

© Arjan Tijms, Teo Bais, and Werner Keil 2022
A. Tijms et al., *The Definitive Guide to Security in Jakarta EE*, https://doi.org/10.1007/978-1-4842-7945-8_6

The Java Authentication and Authorization Service (JAAS) facilitates a smooth authentication and authorization process for Jakarta EE applications. That is, we can use JAAS for two purposes:

- Authentication: Identify who is running the code.

- Authorization: Ensure the authenticated users have the necessary permissions to execute sensitive code.

JAAS (pronounced "Jazz") is a Java programming language version of the standard Pluggable Authentication Module (PAM) framework, which extends the Java platform security architecture to support user-based authorization. As you've seen in the History chapter, PAM was introduced as an extension library to Java 1.3 and was integrated with version 1.4.

In this section, we will discuss and demonstrate the main workings of JAAS: common classes that are used throughout a transaction, authentication classes, and authorization classes.

Note   The code snippets we will use throughout this section are part of the *chapter6-javase-underpinnings/jaas* module of our GitHub repository.

Common Classes

JAAS defines two main components: JAAS Authentication and JAAS Authorization. These two components share a few classes that are defined as *common classes* in JAAS terminology.

Subject

Applications grant access rights to resources once they're able to authenticate an incoming request. JAAS facilitates such incoming requests using the *javax.security.auth. Subject* class. A Subject may refer to a physical entity (person) or service, and once it's authenticated, a *javax.security.auth.Subject* is populated with any associated identities (or Principals in JAAS terminology, which we'll investigate in the "Principals" section).

Key Features

The following are the key features of a Subject class:

- May have multiple identities
- May own security-related attributes such as credentials
- Can retrieve principals associated with it
- Governs the accessibility of credentials (private, public)
- Uses static methods to perform an action as a particular Subject

Retrieving a Subject

As we'll see in the "LoginContext" section, we as developers do not need to instantiate a Subject but only perform any necessary actions to retrieve it upon successful authentication. To retrieve a Subject and assign it to the caller, you can use the following method of *LoginContext*:

```
public Subject getSubject();
```

Once a Subject is authenticated, it may be associated with an access control context to perform authorized actions using the *doAs* and *doAsPrivileged* static methods. You will learn about these concepts in the "JAAS Authentication" section.

Principals

A Subject may have many Principals, thereby distinguishing it from other Subjects. For example, Werner is a subject that may have a name Principal ("Werner Keil") and an SSN Principal ("012-34-5678").

To facilitate a Principal class in JAAS, you need to implement the *java.security. Principal* and *java.io.Serializable* interfaces. Again, following the lead of Subject, a Principal may also represent any entity (physical or not), like a person, an organization, or a smart card login id.

As a developer, you might often need to retrieve the associated name of a Principal (e.g. audit purposes, etc.), something that can happen using the *Principal#getName()* method.

Retrieving Principals Associated with a Subject

There are two methods that you can use to retrieve principals associated with a Subject:

```
public Set getPrincipals(); // return all Principals contained in
the Subject
public Set getPrincipals(Class c); // return Principals that are an
instance of Class c
```

You may also modify principals or credentials associated with a Subject (for instance, upon successful authentication). The following example demonstrates how that can be done:

```
Subject subject;
Principal principal;
Object credential;
. . .

// adding a Principal with its credentials to a Subject
subject.getPrincipals().add(principal);
subject.getPublicCredentials().add(credential);
```

Credentials

Besides Principals, a Subject may also define credentials either to facilitate a subject's authentication to new services or perform certain cryptographic operations. That is, a credential may be a password, a public key certificate, or even a cryptographic key. Table 6-1 demonstrates how credential types are mapped to storage types.

Table 6-1. *Mapping Credential types to storage types*

Type of credential	Type of storage	Example
Sensitive	Private credential Set	Cryptographic keys
Intended to be shared	Public credential Set	Public key certificates

JAAS Authentication

JAAS Authentication works in a plug-n-play fashion, which allows us as developers to integrate any new authentication components or technologies seamlessly. It is the runtime then that determines which particular implementation of the available authentication technologies to use. An authentication technology's implementation is specified in the so-called login configuration file, which we'll further investigate in the "Configuration" section.

Take a moment to analyze Figure 6-1, which demonstrates the pluggable components, and let's try to demystify any gray areas together.

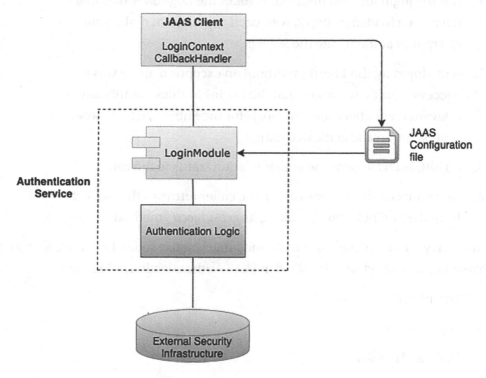

Figure 6-1. *JAAS Authentication architecture diagram*

As we've seen in Chapter 2, authentication is the process whereby a Subject is verified. As developers, we need to make sure a secure authentication is in place so that no intruder can gain access to our systems. The Subject often plays an important role in the authentication process with most of the time being required to provide some form of identity evidence belonging to either of the *something you know, something you have,* or *something you are* category.

The following is a step-by-step overview for a Subject's authentication:[1]

1. A caller uses a web interface (application or service) to instantiate a *LoginContext*.

2. The *LoginContext* loads the *LoginModules* configured for the specified application. To do so, it consults a *Configuration* that provides an overview of the *LoginModules*.

3. Upon successful instantiation of a *LoginContext*, the caller invokes *LoginContext#login()* method to authenticate a *Subject*.

4. It is the login method then that invokes the LoginModules that have been loaded in step 2, with each one of them making an attempt to authenticate the Subject.

5. If the login method returns without an exception, there was a successful authentication, and the LoginModules identify any relevant credentials and Principals for the Subject, which now represents an authenticated entity.

6. *LoginContext* returns the authentication status to the caller.

7. Upon successful authentication, the caller retrieves the *Subject* from the *LoginContext* by calling its *getSubject()* method.

Don't worry if none of the aforementioned made sense so far. Let's have a quick look at each one of the main classes involved in JAAS Authentication, which are

- LoginContext

- LoginModule

- CallbackHandler

- Configuration

LoginContext

LoginContext provides the brains for authentication, as it defines all the necessary methods to authenticate Subjects. Let's see what its key features are.

Key Features

- Reads a configuration file to determine the *LoginModule*s that apply to the caller.

- Supports *pluggable authentication*: Its agnostic construction enables you to plug in any kind of *LoginModule* (older version, different system, etc.) without having to configure the application accordingly.

- Supports *stacked authentication,* which enables the developer to configure an application so that it can use more than one *LoginModule*.

Theory of Operation

The *LoginContext* class is used to authenticate a caller and comes with four constructors:

```
public LoginContext(String name) throws LoginException;
```

```
public LoginContext(String name, CallbackHandler callbackHandler)
        throws LoginException;
```

```
public LoginContext(String name, Subject subject) throws LoginException;
```

```
public LoginContext(String name, Subject subject,CallbackHandler
callbackHandler)throws LoginException;
```

Caution   Null input is disallowed for all constructors.

As you can see, all constructors require you to pass at least a *name* argument, which is used by the *LoginContext* as the index into the *Configuration* (explained further in the "Configuration" section) to determine first the modules to be used and second the ones that must succeed to achieve a successful authentication. The most commonly used *LoginContext* constructor is the third one in the preceding list, which takes a name and a *CallbackHandler*. For the constructors that do not take a *Subject* argument, *LoginContext#login()* method instantiates a new empty *Subject* (which represents the user or service being authenticated).

Caution   To instantiate a *LoginContext*, a caller needs to define an *AuthPermission* in their policy file. You will learn more about the *AuthPermission* class in the "JAAS Authorization" section, which covers JAAS Authorization.

Parameters Explained

- name: Used as an index for loading only the necessary *LoginModule*(s) as configured in the Configuration file

- subject: A user or service that wants to authenticate themselves

- callbackHandler: Passes user credentials from the application to the *LoginModule*

A LoginContext identifies three methods:

- login(): Invokes all the LoginModules that have been configured in the specified Configuration so that it can perform the authentication

- getSubject(): Retrieves the Subject (which may now hold Principals, public credentials, and private credentials) upon successful authentication

- logout(): Logs out the Subject and discards any authenticated credentials and Principals associated with it

The following is a quick example demonstrating how to utilize a *LoginContext*'s methods for the entire workflow of an authentication process:

```
// initialize a LoginContext
LoginContext loginContext = new LoginContext("SimpleJaasApp", new
SimpleCallbackHandler());

// authenticate the user
loginContext.login();
System.out.println("authentication successful"); // the login() method
creates a new instance of our LoginModule and calls its login()
method, and, upon successful authentication, we may retrieve the
authenticated Subject
```

```
// retrieve the authenticated Subject
Subject subject = loginContext.getSubject();

...
// all finished - logout
loginContext.logout();
...
```

LoginModule

As developers, we can exploit JAAS's pluggable authentication capabilities by utilizing the LoginModule class to facilitate the different kinds of authentication technologies we wish to implement in our application (e.g., username/password-based forms, smart cards, biometric devices, etc.).

Key Features

- They can be initialized with a *Subject* and a *CallbackHandler*.

- The *Subject* represents the Subject currently being authenticated, and it updates it with relevant credentials upon successful authentication.

- They use *CallbackHandler* to communicate with users (gather input such as password or smart card pin from users or prompt for a username/pass via a GUI, or supply information such as status info to users) by passing an array of appropriate callbacks to the *CallbackHandler's* *handle()* method (i.e., *NameCallBack* for a username or *PasswordCallback* for a password).

- The *LoginModule*-specific options can be defined in the Configuration file and represent behavior-specific options; for instance, it could be that a *LoginModule* defines options to support testing or debugging activities.

How to Implement a LoginModule

For demonstration purposes, we'll provide an implementation that stores hard-coded users.

```
public class SimpleLoginModule implements LoginModule {

    private static final String USERNAME = "admin";
    private static final String PASSWORD = "test";

    private Subject subject;
    private CallbackHandler callbackHandler;
    private boolean loginSucceeded = false;
    private SimpleUserPrincipal userPrincipal;// a custom user principal
    //...
}
```

Let's now investigate the role the most important methods play in the life cycle management of a *LoginModule* component.

initialize()

Once the requested *LoginModule* has been loaded, this method can be called to initialize the same with a *Subject* and a *CallbackHandler*. Optionally, *LoginModule*s may decide to specify two additional *Map*s: one to facilitate a smooth data exchange among themselves and another one to store private configuration data:

```
public void initialize(
  Subject subject, CallbackHandler callbackHandler, Map<String, ?>
  sharedState, Map<String, ?> options) {
    this.subject = subject;
    this.callbackHandler = callbackHandler;
}
```

login()

It facilitates a login process between a client and a server; for instance, that could be a web form that prompts the client to enter their username and password. To pass the username a client has entered to the server, you can use *NameCallback*. The same goes for a client's password and *PasswordCallback*. Once our callbacks are filled in with client data, we can invoke the *CallbackHandler#handle()* method to pass them on to the server for verification. Here's a code snippet that demonstrates what we've discussed so far:

```java
@Override
public boolean login() throws LoginException {
    NameCallback nameCallback = new NameCallback("Username: ");
    PasswordCallback passwordCallback = new PasswordCallback("Password: ",
    false);
    try {
        callbackHandler.handle(new Callback[]{nameCallback, passwordCallback});
        String username = nameCallback.getName();
        String password = new String(passwordCallback.getPassword());
        if (USERNAME.equals(username) && PASSWORD.equals(password)) {
            loginSucceeded = true;
        }
        if (!loginSucceeded) throw new FailedLoginException
        ("Authentication failure...");

    } catch (IOException | UnsupportedCallbackException e) {
        //...
    }
    return loginSucceeded;
}
```

As you might have already noticed, the *login()* method returns a boolean. Hence, you should return a *true* value upon successful verification and *false* otherwise.

commit()

It updates the Subject with an additional Principal (which belongs to the credential that has just been authenticated) upon a successful login:

```java
@Override
public boolean commit() throws LoginException {
    if (!loginSucceeded) {
        return false;
    }
    subject.getPrincipals().add(userPrincipal);
    return true;
}
```

Otherwise, the *abort()* method is called to abort the authentication and perform the logout procedures. To logout a subject, you can call the logout method that cleans up the subject by removing any associated principals or credentials to the subject.

CallBackHandler

A *LoginModule* uses a *CallbackHandler* to interact with users (e.g., gathering user credentials, providing users with application-specific information, etc.). Specifically, the *LoginModule* calls the *CallbackHandler#handle()* method passing it an array of callbacks (e.g., *NameCallback*, *PasswordCallback*, etc.) with the *CallbackHandler* and then implementing some logic to set the appropriate values in the different callbacks and eventually return the result to the user.

CallbackHandler is an interface that has one method, *handle()*, that accepts an array of *Callback*s:

```
void handle(Callback[] callbacks)throws java.io.IOException,
UnsupportedCallbackException;
```

That being said, applications wishing to employ a CallbackHander to facilitate a smooth user interaction need to implement the CallbackHandler interface and pass its instance to a LoginContext, which in turn will forward it directly to the respective LoginModules.

JAAS already provides many Callback implementations, so let's take NameCallback and PasswordCallback as an example. These are used for obtaining the username and password, respectively.

```
public class ConsoleCallbackHandler implements CallbackHandler {

    @Override
    public void handle(Callback[] callbacks) throws
    UnsupportedCallbackException {
        Console console = System.console();
        for (Callback callback : callbacks) {
            if (callback instanceof NameCallback) {
                NameCallback nameCallback = (NameCallback) callback;
                nameCallback.setName(console.readLine(nameCallback.
                getPrompt()));
```

```
        } else if (callback instanceof PasswordCallback) {
            PasswordCallback passwordCallback = (PasswordCallback)
            callback;
passwordCallback.setPassword(console.readPassword(passwordCallback.
getPrompt()));
        } else {
            throw new UnsupportedCallbackException(callback);
        }
    }
}
}
```

Let's take a moment to zoom into the two *Callback*s. We use a NameCallback instance to set the username by using the built-in Console to prompt the user to enter their username:

```
NameCallback nameCallback = (NameCallback) callback;
nameCallback.setName(console.readLine(nameCallback.getPrompt()));
```

The same goes for prompting for and obtaining the password:

```
PasswordCallback passwordCallback = (PasswordCallback) callback;
passwordCallback.setPassword(console.readPassword(passwordCallback.getPrompt()));
```

Configuration

JAAS uses a *Configuration* service provider to load *LoginModule*s at runtime and to specify the order in which the *LoginModule*s should be invoked. By default, JAAS provides and uses the ConfigFile class (which extends from Configuration)[2] where LoginModules are configured through a login file that may have the name of your preference and could be similar to *jaas.config*.

Here's the default syntax for your configuration file:

```
Name {
        LoginModule    Flag    ModuleOptions;
        LoginModule    Flag    ModuleOptions;
        LoginModule    Flag    ModuleOptions;
    };
```

Parameters Explained

- Name: The name of the login configuration entry

- LoginModule: The fully qualified class name of the *LoginModule* to be used

- Flag: Specifies whether the success of the module is required with available values being REQUIRED, REQUISITE, SUFFICIENT, and OPTIONAL

- ModuleOptions: Defines the behavior of a *LoginModule* (as discussed in the "LoginModule" section, such behavior could involve testing, debugging, or other capabilities)

For example, to define that our configuration entry with the name *SimpleJaas* will use the *SimpleLogin* module with enabled debugging, we could configure our configuration file like this:

```
SimpleJAASApp {
    com.apress.chapter6.jaas.SimpleLoginModule required debug=true;
};
```

Note   *SimpleJAASApp* is just a name we chose for this example; as a developer, you're free to choose your configuration entry's name as long as it is properly reflected in your policy file as well.

We can specify the config file to be used using the *java.security.auth.login.config* system property:

```
java -Djava.security.auth.login.config=src/main/resources/jaas/jaas.
login.config
```

How to Run the JAAS Authentication Example

In the README.md file of our GitHub repository, you will find instructions about packaging and running the JAAS Authentication example we investigated so far. Let's now see how a successful run looks like:

```
> chapter6-javase-underpinnings/jaas$ java -Djava.security.auth.login.
config=src/main/resources/jaas.config -classpath target/jaas-1.0.0-
SNAPSHOT.jar com.apress.chapter6.jaas.SimpleJaasAuthentication
Username: admin
Password:
Authentication succeeded!
MyUserPrincipal: admin successfully logged in and has 0 Public
Credential(s) and 0 Private Credential(s)
```

If the login is not successful (say, wrong username or password), a *FailedLoginException* will be thrown as indicated in the *login()* method of the SimpleLoginModule.

```
Username: admin1
Password:
Exception in thread "main" javax.security.auth.login.FailedLoginException:
Authentication failure...
```

JAAS Authorization

JAAS Authorization grants an authenticated user the right permissions to perform security-sensitive operations. To do so, it associates the authenticated Subject with the current access control context (type of *AccessControlContext* class).

Note An *AccessControlContext* is used to make system resource access decisions based on the context it encapsulates. We will dive into it in the section "Performing Restricted Actions As an Authenticated Subject."

As a rule of thumb, subjects may perform security-sensitive operations based on the permissions their associated Principals are granted with. You can specify which permissions (access rights) you wish to grant to a specific Principal in your policy file (typically named *jaas.policy*). For example, your policy file could include a statement like this:

```
grant codebase "file:./target/SimpleJaas.jar" {
    permission javax.security.auth.AuthPermission "createLoginContext.
    SimpleJAASApp";
};
```

This grants the code in the *SimpleJaas.jar* file, located in the current directory, the permission to instantiate the *LoginContext* referred to as *SimpleJAASApp* in your configuration file (*jaas.config* for our example).

That is, for a caller to instantiate a LoginContenxt, they need to define an AuthPermission with a target value set to "createLoginContext.<name>" in their policy file. As we have discussed in the "Configuration" section, the name parameter refers to the name of the login configuration entry.

JAAS Authorization in Three Steps

To trigger JAAS Authorization, you need to meet the following conditions:

- The caller is authenticated.

- Principal-based entries are configured in the security policy file.

- The authenticated Subject is associated with the current access control context.

The Policy File

Using the Java security policy, we can grant one or more access control rights to Principals. The policy file can be configured during the runtime (see the "Runtime Configuration" section), and it looks like this:

```
grant <signer(s) field>, <codeBase URL> <Principal field(s)> {
    permission perm_class_name "target_name", "action";
    ....
    permission perm_class_name "target_name", "action";
};
```

The fields *signer*, *codeBase*, and *Principal* are optional, while their order doesn't matter. Moreover, the *code base* parameter refers to the jar file of your application.

A Principal field looks like the following:

```
Principal Principal_class "principal_name"
```

For example, Principal com.apress.chapter6.jaas.SimpleUserPrincipal "admin" refers to the admin principal defined in the SimpleUserPrincipal class.

Now, the permission entries define the type of permission a principal of a code base is granted, and it can be of many types as Table 6-2 depicts.

Table 6-2. *Permission types sample*

Permission type	Class	Permission example
Runtime	java.lang.RuntimePermission	readFileDescriptor
File	java.io.FilePermission	"foo.txt", read
AuthPermission	java.security.auth.AuthPermission	doAsPrivileged
Property Permission	java.util.PropertyPermission	java.home

Here's the code snippet to grant the "admin" principal of SimpleUserPrincipal read access rights to the JAVA_HOME environment variable and the foo.txt file:

```
grant Principal com.apress.chapter6.jaas.SimpleUserPrincipal "admin" {
    permission java.util.PropertyPermission "java.home", "read";
    permission java.io.FilePermission "foo.txt", "read";
};
```

Caution   A *grant* statement may address more than one *Principal* if only the Subject associated with the current access control context contains all of those Principals.

To grant the same set of permissions to different Principals, you need multiple *grant* entries with each one of them addressing a different Principal.

Runtime Configuration

The principle behind configuring a file instead of a class follows the same way of having our configuration in properties files like in other frameworks such as Spring. The main class here is *java.security.Policy*, which is an abstract class for representing the system-wide access control policy. During the runtime, the abstract class will look for a parameter *java.security.policy*. Here's an example of how to pass that while invoking the execution of an application.

```
java -Djava.security.manager -Djava.security.policy=someURL SomeApp
```

Note   The *-Djava.security.manager* notifies your runtime that the application is subject to policy checks. It is not required if the application *SomeApp* installs a security manager or uses the default one.

Using a custom security policy file that limits `SocketPermission` and only grants it in a few places like its networking library, loading data or remote code is not possible from the logging library inside products like Elasticsearch, so these products are not affected by a major security flaw in the commonly used Log4J library (CVE-2021-45105[3]) unlike many others.

Caution   JEP 411[4] (April 5, 2021) deprecated the Security Manager for removal in a future Java release.

Performing Restricted Actions As an Authenticated Subject

For a Subject to access restricted resources (or in other words, perform privileged actions), it first needs to be authorized. To authorize a Subject to perform privileged actions, you first need to associate a Subject with an access control context.

An access control context encloses information about the code executed since the Subject was instantiated. That information may be the location of the code or the permissions the code is granted by the policy.

Associating a Subject with the current access control context involves the following steps:

- Authenticate the caller:

  ```
  LoginContext loginContext = new LoginContext("SimpleJAASApp",
  new SimpleCallbackHandler());
  loginContext.login();

  // return the authenticated Subject
  return loginContext.getSubject();
  ```

- Call the *Subject#doAs()* method by passing it an authenticated Subject and a *PrivilegedAction* or a *PrivilegedExceptionAction*. Alternatively, you can call *Subject#doAsPrivileged()*, which behaves the same but takes an extra argument – the one of the *AccessControlContext*:

```
PrivilegedAction privilegedAction = new ReadEnvVariablesAction();
Subject.doAsPrivileged(subject, privilegedAction, null);
```

The *doAs()* method associates the provided Subject with the current access control context and then invokes your custom action's *run()* method.

- Define the security-sensitive action that you want to be performed in your custom action's class *run()* method:

```
public class ReadEnvVariablesAction implements PrivilegedAction {

    public Object run() {
        System.out.println("\nYour JAVA.HOME environment
        variable is: "
                    + System.getProperty("java.home"));

        return null;
    }
}
```

The action thus executes as the specified Subject.

Caution   Again, nothing of these will succeed unless our policy file is in place and has the permissions expected from the application and the application points to the right location of it. Continue reading to see a happy flow scenario and what happens when we miss something in the policy file.

JAAS Authorization is based on two main classes: *java.security.Policy*, which we covered already, and *javax.security.auth.AuthPermission*, which encapsulates the basic permissions required for JAAS. While the signature of permission statements looks like this:

```
permission permission_class_name "target_name", "action";
```

that one of *AuthPermission* only contains a name but no action list:

```
permission auth_permission_class_name "target_name";
```

Note   Consult Appendix 1 for an overview of the most commonly used permissions.

Just like we did for authentication, we'll run a simple application for the authorization where, in addition to the *LoginModule*, we provide a permissions configuration file:

```
$ mvn clean package
$ chapter6-javase-underpinnings/jaas$ java -Djava.security.manager -Djava.
security.policy=src/main/resources/jaas.policy       -Djava.security.
auth.login.config=src/main/resources/jaas.config       -classpath target/
jaas-1.0.0-SNAPSHOT.jar com.apress.chapter6.jaas.SimpleJaasAuthorization
Username: admin
Password:
Authentication succeeded!

Your JAVA.HOME environment variable is: /Library/Java/JavaVirtualMachines/
jdk-15.jdk/Contents/Home

Your USER.HOME environment variable is: /Users/apress
```

What would have happened if our *PrivilegedAction* class (in this case, *ReadEnvVariablesAction*) tried to read the *java.home* variable but the policy file didn't specify any *grant* permissions to it? For demonstration purposes, let's try to remove that line from our policy file and run the code:

```
Username: admin
Password:
Authentication succeeded!
Exception in thread "main" java.security.AccessControlException: access
denied ("java.util.PropertyPermission" "java.home" "read")
        at ...
```

That is, there is an exception thrown since the permission to read that variable is not mentioned in the policy file anymore. Try to experiment with the code examples of our repository to see for yourself how different actions cause different behaviors.

Note   Permission management involves three steps: defining, granting, and verifying a permission. Granting can only happen through your policy file. However, defining and verifying permissions can also happen programmatically. Feel free to have a look at the *CustomResourceAction* and *CustomResourcePermission* files of the *consolemenu* example of the repository.

Again, we here demonstrated the most important APIs and classes involved in JAAS authentication. Important to note here is that we deliberately omitted specific documentation like method signatures of specific classes or methods, etc. – otherwise, we would be out of scope for this book. If you wish to dive into the workings of it, feel free to have a closer look at the official JAAS Reference Guide.[5]

Introduction to Cryptography

In the next few sections of this chapter, we will examine fundamental encryption concepts like digital signatures, Public Key Infrastructure (PKI), and the TLS protocol, which require some basic understanding of their profound concepts like key pairs and symmetric and asymmetric encryption. Let's quickly introduce these concepts.

Sidebar: New digital trends create new technical challenges

The rise of the Internet increased our knowledge in data transmission and network communications which eventually made hackers smarter and exposed the vulnerabilities of traditional transmission mechanisms. Hence, the need for secure data transmission is bigger than ever. We can achieve secure data transmission by using cryptography.

Cryptography is a method that uses advanced mathematical principles to store and transmit data in a particular form so that only the intended recipients can read and process it.

Key Concepts in Cryptography

- Encryption: The process of encoding a message in such a format that eavesdroppers are not able to read or understand it. An encrypted message is referred to as *ciphertext*.

- Decryption: The process of converting an encrypted message (ciphertext) back to a readable format (plain text) using cryptographic techniques.

- Key: A secret piece of information used for encryption and decryption. There are two main types of keys depending on the cryptographic technique at hand: symmetric and asymmetric keys.

Two Basic Encryption Methods

Nowadays, we have two main encryption methods: symmetric and asymmetric encryption.

Symmetric Encryption

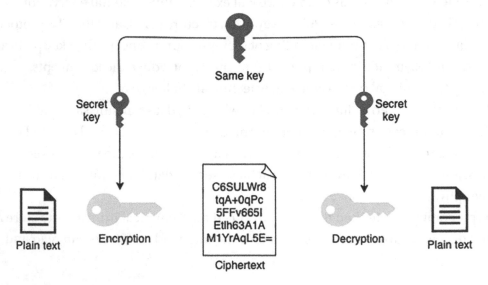

Figure 6-2. *Symmetric encryption*

Symmetric encryption is an old and best-known kind of encryption that requires one secret key to securely encrypt and decrypt a message. The secret key may contain any combination of alphanumeric characters (only numbers, only words, string of random letters) and is blended with the message to change its content so that is not understandable by eavesdroppers or intruders. Symmetric encryption is fast, but less secure, given that both sender and receiver need to know the secret key – the more the people that have access to a secret, the more vulnerable it becomes.

Key Characteristics

- Efficient in terms of computation, but more vulnerable due to the requirement for both sender and receiver to know the key.

- Key length size: 128 bits, but preferably 256 bits; anything less than 80 bits is considered insecure.

- Example methods: Blowfish, AES, RC4, DES, RC5, and RC6.

- Older algorithms that are either not used anymore or soon to be discontinued: DES, 3DES.

- Prevalent algorithms: AES-128, AES-192, and AES-256.

Asymmetric Encryption

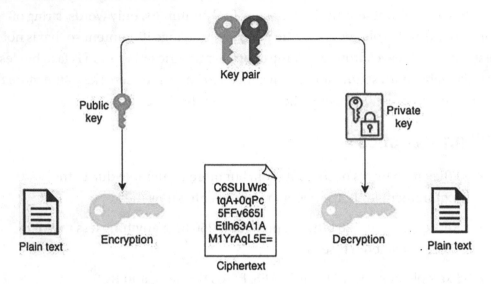

Figure 6-3. *Asymmetric encryption*

Asymmetric encryption is a relatively new method (compared to symmetric encryption) and is based on the *key pairs* concept which we briefly touched upon in Chapter 2, whereby two keys are used to establish trust and privacy in transactions: the *public key* and the *private key*.

When digitally signing documents, the private key to be kept secret is used to encrypt the hash value of a document, whereas the public key can only be used for decryption and matches only one private key. It can be publicly retrieved and is often sent with the message.

On the other hand, in public key encryption (Figure 6-3), the sender encrypts a message using the recipient's public certificate, whereas the recipient decrypts a message using the associated private key.

Key Characteristics

- Mostly used in day-to-day Internet communications.

- Stronger in ensuring the security of information transmitted during a transaction.

- Recommended key length size is 1024 bits, with 2048 bits preferred (but computationally intensive, which makes this method slower).

- Popular asymmetric key encryption algorithms are Diffie-Hellman, ECC, and PKCS.

Symmetric vs. Asymmetric Encryption

Let's now have a look at a head-to-head comparison between the two encryption methods:

- Symmetric encryption requires at least two people that possess the secret key. The more people that know a secret, the more vulnerable it is. On the contrary, the use of two keys by asymmetric encryption boosts security.

- Asymmetric encryption is a more modern approach to cryptography.

- Asymmetric encryption is more expensive in terms of time.

- Symmetric encryption is faster but more vulnerable.

As you can see, no solution is a silver bullet when it comes to encryption. The best solution always depends on what is right for the task at hand. For example, TLS, which we will examine in the "TLS in Java and TLS 1.3" section, is based on a hybrid model that uses both symmetric and asymmetric encryption.

All in all, new algorithms are being developed in a bid to secure information from eavesdroppers and enhance confidentiality, yet the biggest challenge still is to find a solution that offers the perfect compromise between performance and security.

X.509 Digital Certificates

Encryption alone is enough to set up a secure connection, but there's no guarantee that you're talking to the server that you think you're talking to. Hence, there is a need for integrity in your secure communications. That's when digital certificates come into play. Remember when we talked about digital certificates in Chapter 2? Yes, it was there that we promised to further discuss their mechanics in this chapter. In order not to break that promise, it is important to quickly recap on what a digital certificate is and why all this fuss about the rather cryptic X.509s.

A digital certificate is an electronic document that provides information about the identity of an entity.

In practice, it's an electronic document that verifies the ownership of a public key.

To perform these kinds of validations, we need some standards to describe the format of digital certificates. X.509 is one of those standards and the most prevalent one in information technology.

In this section, we'll examine the key features of X.509 certificates, how to generate them, and what the role of certificate chains is.

Note   The code snippets we will use throughout this section are part of the *chapter6-javase-underpinnings/digital-certificates* module of our GitHub repository.

Key Features of an X.509 Certificate

An X.509 certificate consists of a public key and other identity-related information of the owner, such as hostname, organization name, and even individual name. Certificates are considered valid when they are digitally signed. There are two ways to digitally sign a certificate: using the help of a Certificate Authority (CA) or sign it yourself (self-signed certificates).

A CA is a trustworthy service that issues certificates. That is, holding a certificate signed by a CA means you can rely on its validity and use it to establish secure communications or validate digital signatures associated with its private key. You'll get to know more about CAs and self-signed certificates later on in this section.

Other key features of X.509 certificates may address their validity, such as certificate chains or certificate revocation lists. The former refers to an X.509 certificate's validation process that involves the intermediate signing authorities (consult the "Certificate Chains" section for more details on certificate chains). The latter facilitates an overview of digital certificates that have been revoked by the issuing CA before their scheduled expiration date and should therefore no longer be trusted.

Let's now see a few common applications of X.509 certificates.

Common Applications of X.509

The initial intent of X.509 protocol was to improve some gaps of its predecessor X.500 before the Internet was a thing; however, its latest version X.509v3 is widely used in web browsers nowadays to establish secure communications using TLS protocol, which we examine in depth in the "TLS in Java and TLS 1.3" section.

Other technologies that rely on X.509 digital certificates:

- HTTPS

- SSL/TLS

- Offline applications, like electronic signatures

- Code signing (Java ARchives, Microsoft Authenticode)

- Secure email standards like S/MIME and PEM

- Digital IDs issued by the government

Key Pairs and Signatures

A digital signature is the encoded hash of a document that has been encrypted with a private key. That is, digital signatures are based on public key cryptography. As we've seen in the "Introduction to Cryptography" section, public key cryptography is based on key pairs. A key pair encloses a private and a public key.

An X.509 certificate includes a public key, a digital signature, and some information concerning the entity associated with the certificate and its issuing certificate authority (CA) (if any).

The key pair each X.509 certificate is constructed with has the following characteristics:

- Allows the owner of the private key to digitally sign documents; these signatures can be verified by anyone with the associated public key.

- Enables third parties to send encrypted messages with the public key that corresponds to the intended recipient of the message; the recipient then decrypts using the associated private key.

Certificate File Name Extensions

X.509 digital certificate files may come in several file name extensions such as *.crt*, *.cer*, *.pem*, and *.der*. However, the file name extension doesn't necessarily describe the kind of file at hand; for instance, there are scenarios where the .pem extension could be used for a public key file.

As a rule of thumb, you can remember that for X.509 certificates and keys, we mainly use *.pem* (Base64 ASCII) and *.der* (binary format) extensions. Moreover, as we'll see in the "JCE Providers" section, two of the most common algorithms to create key pairs are RSA and DSA, which may be stored using several formats. Table 6-3 demonstrates an overview of the most common file extensions for X.509 certificates and keys.

Table 6-3. *Common file extensions for X.509 certificates and keys*

Encoding		File extensions	Content	Comments
Base64 ASCII	PEM	.pem .cer .crt .key	Public keys (RSA or DSA) Private keys (RSA or DSA) X.509 certificates ASCII headers	May include the server certificate, intermediate certificate, and the private key in a single file Certificate enclosed between -----BEGIN CERTIFICATE---- And -----END CERTIFICATE-----
	PKCS#7	.p7a .p7b .p7c .spc	May have a private key Multiple certificates	No private keys can be enclosed in this format, but only certificates Certificate enclosed between -----BEGIN PKCS#7----- And -----END PKCS#7-----
Binary	DER	.der .cer .crt	Public keys (RSA or DSA) Private keys (RSA or DSA) X.509 certificates	Binary form and mainly used in Java-based web browsers
	PKCS#12	.pfx .p12	Public keys (RSA or DSA) Private keys (RSA or DSA) X.509 certificates	Can store server cert, intermediate cert, and private key in a single .pfx file with password protection Mainly used in Windows platform PKCS#12 became the default JDK keystore from Java 9 onward (JEP 229)[29]

Certificate Chains

One way to check the validity of a digital certificate is by checking its certificate chain.

What Is a Certificate Chain?

A certificate chain refers to your SSL certificate and how it is linked back to a trusted Certificate Authority. Simply put, it is a list of certificates (usually starting with an end-entity certificate like your server's certificate) followed by one or more CA certificates (with the last one being a self-signed certificate from a trusted CA) that helps an end user trace a certificate back to its trust root and decide whether it is trustworthy or not.

Note   A certificate chain is also referred to as *chain of trust*, *certification path*, or *chain of anchor*. We'll use these terms interchangeably.

From your browser's certificate to the CA, it is clear that a certificate chain comprises multiple intermediate certificates. That is, there are three types of actors in a certificate chain:

- Root certificate: A certificate that is issued and managed by the Certificate Authority. It comes predownloaded in most browsers and is automatically stored in a trust store.

- Intermediate certificate: This term refers to one or more intermediate certificates between the root certificate and the server certificate; that is, they act as the middleman between a CA and your machine by adding an extra layer of security.

- Server certificate: This is the certificate a user receives from a trusted Certificate Authority to install on their domain. The fact that is issued by a trusted CA deems the certificate trustworthy and valid.

Let's see how all that comes together in a browser by clicking the lock icon next to the URL and then clicking on certificate. For instance, here's how a Twitter certificate looks like:

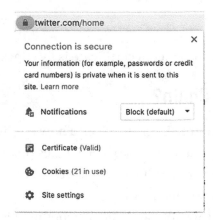

Let's now see how each certificate in the chain of trust looks like:

Root certificate

Intermediate certificate

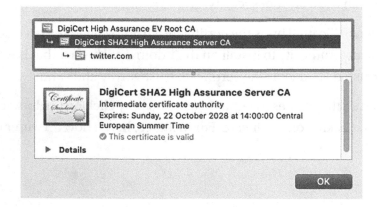

Server certificate

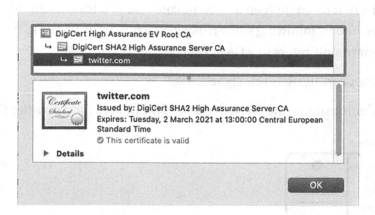

How It Works

When you visit a web page, your web browser tries to establish a secure connection with it. To do so, it tries to verify the identity of the web page at hand by following its certificate chain. Specifically, it starts tracing it backward until it reaches the associated certificate. If the certificate is verified and belongs to a trusted entity, the web page will be trusted. Otherwise, if the certificate cannot be chained back to a trusted entity, your browser will notify you with a warning about the certificate.

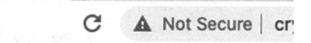

Properties

A certificate chain identifies the following properties:

- Each intermediate certificate's issuer matches the subject of the next certificate in the list.

- Each intermediate certificate is signed using the private key that corresponds to the next certificate in the chain.

- Each intermediate certificate's signature can be verified using the public key that corresponds to the next certificate in the chain.

- The last certificate in the list is also called a *trust anchor*, which means that it can be seen as a certificate that you trust given that it was issued by following some trustworthy procedure. That is, a trust anchor mainly refers to a CA certificate.

- The root certificate is self-signed.

Figure 6-4 demonstrates the aforementioned properties for a two-tier CA.

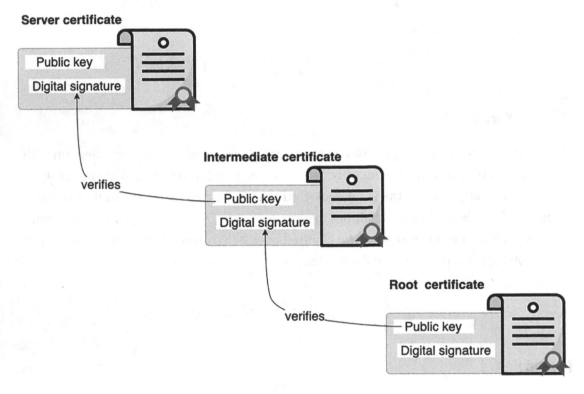

Figure 6-4. *Certificate chain for a two-tier CA*

Anatomy of an X.509 Certificate

An X.509 certificate specifies several fields related to its entity or the identity of its entity, for instance, **subject**, **issuing CA**, and other required information such as the certificate's **version** and **validity period.** Figure 6-5 demonstrates the anatomy of X.509 certificates.

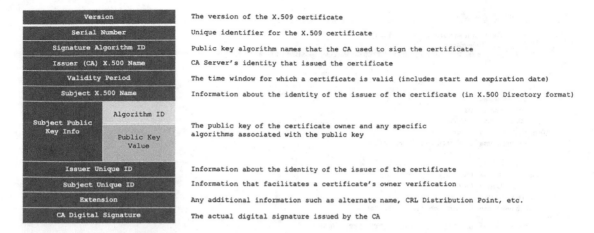

Version		The version of the X.509 certificate
Serial Number		Unique identifier for the X.509 certificate
Signature Algorithm ID		Public key algorithm names that the CA used to sign the certificate
Issuer (CA) X.500 Name		CA Server's identity that issued the certificate
Validity Period		The time window for which a certificate is valid (includes start and expiration date)
Subject X.500 Name		Information about the identity of the issuer of the certificate (in X.500 Directory format)
Subject Public Key Info	Algorithm ID	The public key of the certificate owner and any specific algorithms associated with the public key
	Public Key Value	
Issuer Unique ID		Information about the identity of the issuer of the certificate
Subject Unique ID		Information that facilitates a certificate's owner verification
Extension		Any additional information such as alternate name, CRL Distribution Point, etc.
CA Digital Signature		The actual digital signature issued by the CA

Figure 6-5. *Anatomy of X.509 certificates*

Sample Certificate

We earlier used the example of a Twitter certificate chain to showcase the *chain of trust* concept. We're sure you already noticed the "Details" drop-down at the bottom of each element of the certificate chain, which stands for the structure of the specified certificate. Let's unfold the "Details" of Twitter's Root certificate to see what its structure looks like:

Looks neat, doesn't it? Here comes the question, though: How could you generate your own public key certificate to ensure integrity in your communications?

How to Generate, Manage, and Sign X.509 Certificates

There are two ways to generate X.509 certificates: using a command line tool or programmatically.

Programmatically

Java used to support the creation of X.509 certificates within the *sun.security* package. However, this package is of course no longer supported in the latest versions, so you're better off using an external JCE provider (like Bouncy Castle) to help you generate self-signed X.509 certificates. A simple example can be found in *GenerateX509v3Certificate. java*. This example is pretty easy to digest, yet most of the demonstrated classes are nowadays deprecated; therefore, we included an additional example, *GenerateX509v3CertificateUp.java*, which utilizes the modern API classes of Bouncy Castle to generate a self-signed certificate. Unfortunately, there's a caveat here too with the main acting classes being difficult to remember.

That being said, the compromise between BC's API fluency and antiquity is somewhat irritating to the users as we'll see in the "JCE Providers" section. Again, things can get complicated, and that's only for self-signed certificates. To also involve CAs, you might even need to customize your BC implementation,[6] which is not handy at all; therefore, our recommendation is to use *keytool* for a standardized approach.

Keytool As a Certificate Life Cycle Management Tool

Every modern JDK version ships with a bunch of cool features, libraries, and tools, where, among others, *keytool* helps you generate and manage X.509v3 certificates.

Specifically, *keytool* offers the following features:

- Generate key pairs

- Create self-signed X.509v3 certificates

- Manage keystores

- Certificate life cycle management

- Keypair life cycle management

Tip   The keys and certificates generated using *keytool* may then be used to digitally sign your Java applications.

Note   Imagine a keystore as a database that stores certificates and keys. A keystore is protected with a password that is generated during the creation of the same. Moreover, private keys that reside in a keystore may also be protected by their own passwords.

In this section, we'll demonstrate how to generate key pairs and how to certify the public key from a certificate authority (CA) using *keytool*. Besides, we'll see how to implement a digital signature in Java SE.

Time for action. Let's start by opening a command line tool and running the following command to see the available options of *keytool*:

$ **keytool**
Key and Certificate Management Tool

Commands:

```
-certreq            Generates a certificate request
-changealias        Changes an entry's alias
-delete             Deletes an entry
-exportcert         Exports certificate
-genkeypair         Generates a key pair
-genseckey          Generates a secret key
-gencert            Generates certificate from a certificate request
-importcert         Imports a certificate or a certificate chain
-importpass         Imports a password
-importkeystore     Imports one or all entries from another keystore
-keypasswd          Changes the key password of an entry
-list               Lists entries in a keystore
-printcert          Prints the content of a certificate
-printcertreq       Prints the content of a certificate request
-printcrl           Prints the content of a CRL file
-storepasswd        Changes the store password of a keystore
-showinfo           Displays security-related information
```

As you can see, there are a few available options to work with keys, certificates, and key stores:

- Generate key pair

- Export certificate

- Import certificate

- List KeyStore entries

- Delete KeyStore entry

- Generate Certificate Request

In this example, we'll investigate the most important ones for the workflow of a digital signature (*genkeypair*, *importcert*, *certreq*, *exportcert*), but feel free to experiment with the rest at your own pace to further understand the mechanics of *keytool*.

Background for the Code Examples

As discussed, we'll here investigate a full example of a digital signature, from generating the key pairs to verifying the signature. Again, technically speaking, a digital signature is the encrypted hash of a message. In other words:

$$Digital\ signature = PrivateKeyEncryption(hashValueOf(message))$$

When a digital signature is sent over the Internet, all of its underlying individual ingredients are sent along (message, public key corresponding to the private key that was used to sign the document, encrypted hash, and algorithm used for the signing process).

A message recipient can verify the validity of the message in three steps:

- Generate new hash from the received message.

- Decrypt the received encrypted hash using the public key.

- Compare the two values.

If the two values match, the Digital Signature is considered to be verified. A signature's verification provides us with enough confidence that only the owner of the private key could be the trusted sender.

Warning   We only encrypt the message hash and not the message itself. In other words, digital signatures do not try to keep the message secret. Instead, they authenticate a message and prove that it was not tampered with.

Generating Key Pair

Generating a key pair is one of the most common tasks to use the Java *keytool* for. The generated key pair is inserted into a Java KeyStore file as a self-signed key pair.

Note   You need not memorize every single argument, as many of them are optional. Moreover, *keytool* will tell you if you are missing any required argument.

Example:

```
$ keytool -genkeypair -dname "CN=Teo Bais, o=Utrecht Java User Group,
c=NL" -alias senderKeyPair -keypass changeit -keystore senderkeystore.p12
-storepass changeit  -validity 730 -keyalg RSA -storetype PKCS12
```

The preceding command results in `Generating 2.048 bit RSA key pair and self-signed certificate (SHA256withRSA) with a validity of 730 days`

`    for: CN=Teo Bais, O=Utrecht Java User Group, C=NL`

That is, this command creates a private key and its corresponding public key for us. The public key is used to create an X.509 self-signed certificate and eventually a single-element certificate chain. We store the certificate chain and the private key in the keystore file *senderkeystore.p12,* which we can process using the KeyStore API.

Caution   Remember your keystore's password and alias, as it's needed in any other certificate operation that involves interaction with the keystore.

Tip   Why did we use a PKCS12 keystore instead of a JKS one? As we've seen in the preceding table, PKCS#12 can be used to store key pairs and certificates with pfx password protection, which is what makes it the most trustworthy keystore from Java 8 onward. Besides, JKS is considered insecure compared to PKCS12 nowadays as we can observe from the number of tools for brute-forcing these passwords of these keystore types. Hence, it became the default JDK keystore from Java 9 onward (JEP 229).[7]

Publishing Your Public Key

When you generate a certificate using *keytool*, it is stored on the keystore you specified during the generation of the same. However, it often happens that you want to share your certificate to prove your identity. This can happen with the *-exportcert* command, but you first need to decide whether you're going to use a self-signed certificate or one signed by a CA. For the former, you can simply use the *-exportcert* command:

```
keytool -exportcert -alias senderKeyPair -storetype PKCS12 -keystore
senderkeystore.p12 -storepass changeit -rfc  -file sender-certificate.cer
```

Otherwise, in case you're going to work with a CA, you first need to create a Certificate Signing Request (CSR), which is something every CA requests before creating a certificate for you. To do so, you can use *keytool*'s *-certreq* command:

```
keytool -certreq -alias senderKeyPair -storetype PKCS12    -keystore
senderkeystore.p12 -storepass changeit -rfc -file sender-certificate.csr
```

The *-rfc* flag notifies *keytool* to use a textual format rather than a binary format, for example, for export or import of certificates.

The CSR file, *sender_certificate.csr,* is then sent to a Certificate Authority for signing. CA processes your request, and when that's done, you receive a signed public key wrapped in an X.509 certificate, either in binary (DER) or text (PEM) format. Here, we've used the *rfc* option for a PEM format.

Importing Certificate

To install or verify a public key locally, you can use the *-importcert* command:

```
keytool -importcert -alias receiverKeyPair -storetype PKCS12   -keystore
receiverkeystore.p12 -storepass changeit -rfc -file sender-certificate.cer
```

For demonstration purposes, let's act as if we've already received a sender's certificate by using the certificate we earlier created. As you can see, a new keystore is automatically created if it doesn't exist.

So far, we've seen how the basic commands of *keytool* can help you create your public and private key and apply for a certificate request. Let's now see how we can verify a public key (e.g., coming from a CA or another sender) and, of course, how we can sign our messages with our private key in Java SE.

Digital Signature

Again, to create a digital signature of a message, we generate a hash from the message and encrypt it with our private key according to a chosen algorithm. So there are four elements involved:

- Private key

- Message

- Encryption algorithm of choice

- Hash of the message using the preferred encryption algorithm

Loading Private Key

Assuming we already have our message saved in a *message.txt* file, we first need to load our private key from the keystore using the Keystore API:

```
KeyStore keystore = KeyStore.getInstance("PKCS12");
keystore.load(getResourceAsStream(senderkeystore.p12), "changeit");
(PrivateKey) keystore.getKey("senderKeyPair", "changeit");
```

Initiating Signature

Encryption, hashing, and signature come out of the box in JCA's dedicated Signature API. That is, to initiate the process of signing, we first need to create an instance of the Signature class. To do so, we need to define the signing algorithm.

```
Signature signature = Signature.getInstance("SHA256withRSA");
```

Now that we've created a Signature instance, we can initialize it with a private key:

```
signature.initSign(privateKey);
```

Note   To facilitate our signing process, we here used SHA256withRSA algorithm, which offers both hashing and encryption capabilities.

Updating the Signature with the Message Bytes

All the magic happens in the Signature's objects, so now that we've instantiated an object with a signing algorithm, we need to tell it which particular message to encrypt and sign. First, we need to read the message:

```
byte[] messageBytes = Files.readAllbytes(Paths.get("message.txt"));
```

Then we update the signature and sign the message:

```
signature.update(messageBytes);
byte[] digitalSignature = signature.sign();
```

Saving the Signature into a File

Last, we save the signature into a file for later transmission:

```
Files.write(Paths.get("/digital-signature"), digitalSignature);
```

Verifying a Digital Signature

To verify the digital signature, the recipient first generates a new hash from the received message, and second, they decrypt the encrypted hash using the public key. Finally, they compared the two values, and if they match, the digital signature is considered to be verified.

So the same elements are needed here as well, with public key playing the main role this time and, of course, the encryption algorithm that needs to be known to the receiver. So let's play the entire scenario in reverse by first retrieving the public key using the Keystore API:

```
KeyStore keyStore = KeyStore.getInstance("PKCS12");
keyStore.load(new FileInputStream("receiverkeytore.p12"), "changeit");
Certificate certificate = keyStore.getCertificate("receiverKeyPair");
PublicKey publicKey = certificate.getPublicKey();
```

Now that we've retrieved the public key, we're all set for the signature verification process, so let's first instantiate a Signature class:

```
Signature signature = Signature.getInstance("SHA256withRSA");
```

Let's now initialize it by calling its *initVerify()* method, which takes a public key:

```
signature.initVerify(publicKey);
```

Our Signature instance has now been initialized with a public key, which may be used to decrypt a hashed message. Let's first obtain that message and then add it to our Signature instance (for verification) using *Signature#update()* method:

```
byte[] messageBytes = Files.readAllBytes(Paths.get("message.txt"));
signature.update(messageBytes);
```

Finally, we verify the signature using the Signature#*verify()* method, which returns a boolean value:

```
boolean isVerified = signature.verify(digitalSignature);
```

Under the digital-signatures module of our GitHub repository, you will find the examples for signature creation and verification under (*jca* package) as well as one more example (*custom* package) showcasing the traditional low-level APIs, which provide a way to customize the signing process. You might notice that the code examples are slightly different in terms of file manipulation. This is to make sure that you as a reader can focus on the topic being discussed (X.509 certificates). The Maven module uses a simple structure, which means that you should expect to find the generated signatures under */target/classes*.

In this section, we touched upon X.509 digital certificates, their structure, how to generate and manage them using *keytool*, and how to create and verify digital signatures using JCA's standard API. JCA is more powerful than you think though and let's see why.

JCE Providers

As Java developers who care about security, we can mainly use two core libraries that facilitate cryptography: the Java Cryptography Architecture (JCA) and the Java Cryptography Extension (JCE). The former is tightly integrated with the core Java API and delivers most of the basic cryptographic features, while the latter provides a variety of advanced cryptographic operations. JCE was originally a separate extension to JCA, but the difference between them is somewhat cosmetic these days, as JCE isn't an external extension since Java 1.4. JCE was initially a separate extension due to the US export restrictions on encrypting/decrypting technology. Back then, the cryptographic functionality would be bundled in JCE and downloaded separately. The JDK itself could therefore be freely exported. Since Java 1.4, these restrictions have been relaxed, and JCE is now part of the JDK itself.

Well-known Java SE security types such as *MessageDigest, KeyStore, SecureRandom, Certificate, Cipher,* and *Mac* are all part of JCA/JCE. You can run the *ListAvailableAlgorithms.java* demo to see which algorithms are supported on your machine or simply consult Appendix 2, which demonstrates a quick overview of the most important algorithms a bundled JCE provider (SunJCE for this appendix's case) may come with.

Note   Nowadays, JCE is a built-in part of JCA, and the term "JCE" slowly disappears from the Java ecosystem. In short, JCE is an archaic term. As Java developers of modern times, we can simply use JCA to access cryptography in Java and need not worry at all about JCE.

Note   Despite the relaxation of the US export restrictions, the cryptographic APIs are still organized into two distinct packages:

- The *java.security* and *java.security.** packages contain classes like *Signature* and *MessageDigest* (which earlier weren't subject to export controls).

- The *javax.crypto* package contains classes like *Cipher* and *KeyAgreement* (which earlier were subject to export controls).

In this section, we'll examine the need for JCE providers, the different types that exist out there, how to configure them, and what the role of Bouncy Castle is in all of it.

Note   The code snippets we will use throughout this section are part of the *chapter6-javase-underpinnings/jce-providers* module of our GitHub repository.

The Need for JCE Providers

Application security is often overlooked in software development. Fortunately, Java has recognized the importance of security with JCE by providing developers a powerful API that allows numerous types of encryption as well as several other security-related tasks.

Conceptually, developers need not be security experts to create secure applications. Ideally, an abstract API should be available for them to interact with and perform the necessary cryptographic operations. JCE offers such an abstraction in the form of *providers*.

In essence, we define as *provider* the underlying implementation of a particular security mechanism. That is, while JCA/JCE defines all the available cryptographic operations and objects, the actual implementations of the respective functionalities are located in separate classes, called *providers*. The providers implement the API defined in JCA/JCE and are responsible for providing the actual cryptographic algorithms.

Thanks to that, the whole cryptographic architecture is relatively flexible, as it separates the interfaces and generic classes from their implementations using the factory pattern. Hence, after the initialization, programmers need to only deal with abstract terms like "cipher," "secret key," etc.

Figure 6-6 demonstrates the role of JCE providers in a pluggable provider-based architecture.

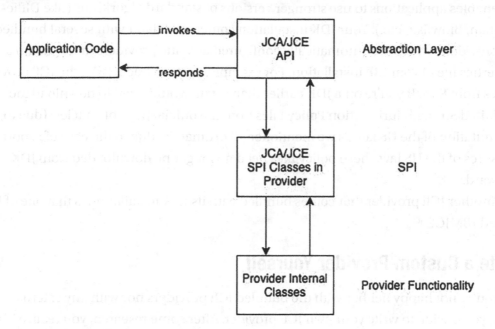

Figure 6-6. *JCE providers architecture*

Of course, users can plug in new, external, providers of their own. Let's see what the available options are.

Available JCE Providers

There are three types of JCE providers:

- The ones that ship with your JDK installation (for instance, SUN for the Oracle JVM, IBMJCE for the IBM one, etc.)

- The ones that are external to your JDK and can be plugged into it (like the IAIK and Bouncy Castle)

- Custom providers that you can write yourself

Let's take a quick look at each one of the aforementioned types.

Bundled with the JDK

JCE enables applications to use stronger versions of standard algorithms (like Diffie-Hellman, Blowfish, etc.). Your JDK installation comes by default with several bundled JCE providers, which are automatically configured as static providers in the *java.security* properties file of your JRE installation. For example, for the Oracle JVM, the JCE provider comes from Sun. If you're on a JDK earlier than 9, you would need to download the Unlimited Strength Jurisdiction Policy Files from the official page of Oracle[1] (due to the limitation of the US law as we mentioned). Fortunately, due to the ease of export measures of the US law, these policy files need no longer be downloaded from JDK 9 onward.

Another JCE provider that comes bundled with its JDK installation is that one of IBM named IBMJCE.[8]

Write a Custom Provider Yourself

Say you're not happy neither with the bundled JCE providers nor with any external ones. Thus, you decide to write your own JCE provider. After some research, you realize it's not that simple, as it requires a bunch of steps, research, and pain:[9]

1) Write Your Service Implementation Code

2) Give Your Provider a Name

3) Write Your Master Class, a Subclass of Provider

4) Create a Module Declaration for Your Provider

5) Compile Your Code

6) Place Your Provider in a JAR File

7) Sign Your JAR File, If Necessary

8) Prepare for Testing

9) Write and Compile Your Test Programs

10) Run Your Test Programs

11) Apply for US Government Export Approval If Required

12) Document Your Provider and Its Supported Services

13) Make Your Class Files and Documentation Available to Clients

That being said, you can implement and plug in your own providers too, but you should be careful with that. Implementing encryption correctly without security holes is not easy. Unless you know what you're doing, you're better off using the built-in Java provider, or a well-established external provider like Bouncy Castle.

External JCE Providers

Having come thus far, you might be wondering how external JCE providers differ from their bundled counterparts. Well, there are a few scenarios where external JCE providers might come in handy such as the following:

- Limitations of bundled JCE providers.

- You are running an older Java version.

- You want to implement certain or "unlimited" key sizes.

- You feel limited by the default JCE and wish to implement many more cipher suites and algorithms.

In the following, you can find a small inventory of popular external JCE providers.

IAIK-JCE

IAIK-JCE[10] is a Java-based Cryptographic Service Provider, which is being developed at the Institute for Applied Information Processing and Communications (IAIK) at the Graz University of Technology in Austria. It offers support for many common cryptographic operations, such as encryption (both symmetric and asymmetric), secure hash functions, and Mac, which we'll further investigate in the section "Key Generation and Key Agreement (Public Key Infrastructure (PKI)) and Message Authentication Code." IAIK-JCE was first released in 1996 and was, therefore, one of the first cryptography providers written entirely in Java. Last but not least, it is based on the same design principles as Oracle's JCA/JCE.

Key Features[11]

- Security aspects of the information society (in particular e-Commerce and e-Government)

- Cryptography and Crypto analysis

- Security and cryptography for the Java platform

- HW and SW implementations of cryptographic methods and protocols

- PKI and electronic signatures

- Network security

- Contributions to standardization processes in the specified fields

Less Popular JCE Providers

Other less popular JCE providers are the Fortanix JCE Provider, which is part of the Fortanix Self-Defending KMS,[12] and the Zulu Cryptography Extension Kit (CEK), which provides an upgrade to "unlimited" key sizes to any Zulu JDK.[13] Last but not least, Cryptix[14] was the first cryptographic library for Java when export controls were still in effect. Now that export controls are lifted, and with the rise of other libraries such as Bouncy Castle, there has been no active development since 2005.

Bouncy Castle

The Bouncy Castle provider[15] is a Java implementation of cryptographic algorithms that were developed by the Legion of the Bouncy Castle. It consists of two main components that support the base cryptographic capabilities: the "lightweight" API (suitable for use in any environment) and the Java Cryptography Extension (JCE) provider. We'll investigate what makes it special in the "How JCE Providers Work" section.

How to Install a JCE Provider

Depending on your JDK, different conditions may apply when it comes to setting up your JCE providers. In most cases, the latest JDK distributions come with a bundled JCE installation for which you need no further manual setup. However, there are scenarios where you might be required to set it up yourself (e.g., running an older JDK or a specific JDK that requires manual configuration).

In the latter cases, you normally can configure it by following these steps (but be sure to also consult your JDK provider's documentation):

1. Place the JAR containing the provider classes on your CLASSPATH (manual download or just using a build tool like Maven or Gradle).

2. Enable your provider class(es) by adding its name to the *java.security* file.

The java.security file is located on your JRE installation folder and contains entries like the following:

```
security.provider.1=SUN
security.provider.2=SunRsaSign
security.provider.3=SunEC
```

That is, for each provider, this file should have a statement of the following form:

```
security.provider.n=masterClassName
```

n declares the desired preference order for the specified provider (and is consulted when no specific provider is requested), while *masterClassName* specifies the fully qualified name of the provider's "master class". The provider vendor should provide you this name.

To list the currently installed JCE providers of your machine, run the *ListInstalledJceProviders.java* demo.

Alternatively, providers may be installed at runtime. The following snippet demonstrates how that could be done for the Bouncy Castle provider:

```
Security.addProvider(new BouncyCastleProvider());
```

Check out *RegisterBCProviderAtRuntime.java* example.

Caution   Installing an external JCE provider may often be troublesome when it comes to provider precedence at runtime. You can see that for yourself by running the *JceProviderPrecedentTest.java* example. As an application developer, you can specify which provider should be used by utilizing the preference order of the provider on your *java.security* file as we showed previously. Alternatively, you can do that programmatically by using the *insertProviderAt()* method like this:

```
Security.insertProviderAt(new BouncyCastleProvider(), 1)
```

RegisterBCProviderAtRuntimePosition.java example demonstrates how to govern provider precedence.

How JCE Providers Work

JCE providers are here to make our cryptographic operations easier. Regardless of the nature of your JCE provider (bundled or external), all JCE providers work the same way. The main class for any cryptographic operation is *Cipher*, which provides the functionality of a cryptographic cipher for encryption and decryption and forms the backbone of the JCE framework.

How to Encrypt with Cipher Class

- Instantiate a Cipher object using the *getInstance()* method.

- Initialize the Cipher using the *init()* method.

- Perform the cryptographic operation (encryption/decryption) using the *doFinal()* method.

Let's now zoom in on each one of the aforementioned steps.

Cipher Instantiation

Before using a Cipher instance, we need to create it. To do so, we can use the *Cipher#getInstance()* method by passing the desired transformation to it:

```
Cipher cipher = Cipher.getInstance("AES/CBC/PKCS5Padding")
```

Optionally, we may pass the provider name as a second argument (handy when using an external JCE provider):

```
Cipher.getInstance("AES/CBC/PKCS5Padding", "BC") // Bouncy Castle provider
```

A transformation is a compound string describing the set of cryptographic operations to be performed on the given input to produce some output. It includes the name of the cryptographic algorithm to be used (e.g., AES) and may optionally be followed by a feedback mode and padding scheme. Hence, a transformation may be of either of the following forms:

- *algorithm/mode/padding*

- *algorithm*

In the latter case, provider-specific default values are used for the mode and padding scheme. For example, SunJCE and SunPKCS11 providers use ECB as the default mode and PKCS5Padding as the default padding for many symmetric ciphers.

Sample transformations could be

- *AES/CBC/PKCS5Padding*

- *AES/CTR/NoPadding*

- *AES*

Tip   It is recommended to use transformations that fully specify the algorithm, mode, and padding instead of relying on the defaults.

Note   An encryption mode specifies details about how the algorithm should encrypt data. The vast majority of well-established JCE providers support the most prevalent cipher modes like *ECB*, *CBC*, *CFB*, *OFB*, and *CTR*. The same goes for paddings. To learn more about the default modes and paddings your JDK ships with, consult the official documentation.[16]

Cipher Initialization

Once you instantiated a Cipher object, you then need to initialize it by calling its *init()* method with a key or certificate and the operation mode of the cipher.

Note   Available operation modes for cipher are *ENCRYPT_MODE*, *DECRYPT_MODE*, *WRAP_MODE*, and *UNWRAP_MODE*.

Optionally, you can also pass

- A source of randomness, for example, by using the *SecureRandom* class

- A set of algorithm-specific parameters such as an initialization vector (IV)[17] (using *IvParameterSpec* class[18])

Here's how we could initialize a Cipher instance in encryption mode:

```
Key key = ... // get or generate your encryption key
cipher.init(Cipher.ENCRYPT_MODE, key)
```

Similarly, we could initialize a cipher on decryption mode like this:

```
Key key = ... // get or generate your encryption key
cipher.init(Cipher.DECRYPT_MODE, key)
```

Note   We'll cover key generation in depth in the section "Key Generation and Key Agreement (Public Key Infrastructure (PKI)) and Message Authentication Code."

Performing Encryption and Decryption

Having initialized your cipher with a key (or certificate) and any other necessary parameters (randomness, initialization, etc.) where applicable, you can encrypt and decrypt data using either one of these two methods:

- update(): Mostly used for cryptographic operations that involve more steps. Ideal for encrypting long files

- doFinal(): Ideal for cryptographic operations that can be implemented in one go

---

Note   There are several overridden versions of both methods with different parameters, but we'll here cover simple scenarios which we thought would be enough to get you started with cryptography in Java. Otherwise, we're out of scope for this book.

The *doFinal()* method returns an array of bytes containing the encrypted or decrypted message. Here's how a simple encryption operation could be performed:

```
byte[] plainText = "This is a secret message".getBytes();
byte[] cipherText = cipher.doFinal(plainText);
```

So what we've seen so far would look like this for an encryption operation:

```
byte[] plainText = "This is a secret message".getBytes();
byte[] keyBytes = "thisisa128bitkey".getBytes(); // 128-bit key for AES
SecretKey secretKey = new SecretKeySpec(keyBytes, "AES");

Cipher cipher = Cipher.getInstance("AES/ECB/PKCS5Padding");
cipher.init(Cipher.ENCRYPT_MODE, secretKey);

byte[] cipherText = cipher.doFinal(plainText);
```

You can find the full example at *SimpleECBEncryptionOnly.java*

For decryption, the first two steps of cipher instantiation and initialization would be the same. What only changes is the last part where we'd have to define decryption as operation mode:

```
// instantiate a Cipher object
// initialize the Cipher
...
cipher.init(Cipher.DECRYPT_MODE, secretKey);
byte[] decryptedMessageBytes = cipher.doFinal(cipherText);
```

You can find the full example at *SimpleECBExample.java*.

Tip   ECB mode is nowadays considered to be vulnerable and was here used just for demonstration purposes. For more secure options, consider using modes such as CTR or CBC. You can find examples covering these two modes and a few more examples on symmetric encryption and decryption (covering *IVParametercSpec*, nonce, byte array, etc.) under the *bundled/symmetric* package of the *jce-providers* module of our GitHub repository.

Asymmetric Encryption

We studied the bits and pieces of symmetric encryption, but what happens with asymmetric operations? Well, things do not differ that much there as well. Cipher class is still the main actor, yet there is a slight differentiation in the key generation process. Undoubtedly, for symmetric encryption, things can go easy with either hard-coding a key string or generating a key using the *SecretKey* class and wrapping it on the cipher to be securely transmitted with the message. On the other hand, setting up asymmetric encryption takes some more effort as we're not using the same key but key pairs. Again, we'll cover the key generation process both for symmetric and asymmetric encryption in the section "Key Generation and Key Agreement (Public Key Infrastructure (PKI)) and Message Authentication Code," but let's first get a grip on asymmetric encryption as a whole.

Asymmetric encryption with Cipher class (here, we're using RSA algorithm) is shown in the following *listing*.

Generate key pair using *KeyPairGenerator*:

```
KeyPairGenerator keyPairGenerator = KeyPairGenerator.getInstance("RSA");
keyPairGenerator.initialize(4096);
KeyPair keyPair = keyPairGenerator.generateKeyPair(); // keyPair object now
contains a public and a private key
```

Initialize a Cipher using the *init*() method:

```
Cipher cipher = Cipher.getInstance("RSA/ECB/OAEPWithSHA-256AndMGF1
Padding");
```

Sender encrypts the message with the public key:

```
cipher.init(Cipher.ENCRYPT_MODE, keyPair.getPublic());
byte[] cipherText = cipher.doFinal(originalMessageBytes);
```

Receiver decrypts the message with the private key:

```
cipher.init(Cipher.DECRYPT_MODE, keyPair.getPrivate());
byte[] decryptedMessageBytes = cipher.doFinal(cipherText);
```

You can find the complete example at *SimpleRSAExample.java* under *bundled/ asymmetric* as well as other examples on how to save randomly generated asymmetric keys in files and how to create and verify a digital signature.

Tip   When large messages are involved, RSA encryption and decryption can be slow as you are limited to encrypting messages that are the length of your RSA key. In such scenarios, a better solution is to use a "hybrid" approach that combines RSA with AES. You can find an example on how to do this at *RSAEncryptionWithAES.java* example.

Bouncy Castle

We've just seen how bundled JCE providers behave on symmetric and asymmetric encryption. Why such a fuss for an external JCE provider then? Well, bundled JCE providers may indeed not require to be downloaded as they come with your JDK and may also offer you a few options to choose from (as we've seen in ListInstalledJceProviders.java), but that doesn't mean they come with no price. One disadvantage they have is that different JDKs can have different providers, which might be troublesome when specifying a default provider that's not available in the active JDK. Another disadvantage of bundled JCE providers is that the number of supported algorithms is quite limited by covering only the most popular ones.

Nowadays, Bouncy Castle is the most prevalent external JCE provider. Here are the most important advantages it comes with:

- Defines more cipher suites and algorithms than the JCA/JCE implementation provided by Oracle (Sun).

- Provides a plethora of utilities to read arcane formats such as *PEM* and *ASN.1*; utilities which have otherwise would take us ages to build from scratch.

- Bouncy Castle has Australian roots, which means that you're running no US export policy risk if you're on an older JDK.

Note   Bouncy Castle has disadvantages as well. One of them is that you either have to download it and include it in your *classpath* as we showed earlier or add it to your Maven dependencies. Moreover, its steep learning curve makes it impossible to memorize the JCE corresponding classes, so you'll always need to be on the lookout for examples online, as the documentation alone is not sufficient.

Architecture of Bouncy Castle

To efficiently support the basic cryptographic capabilities, Bouncy Castle's architecture is organized into two main components: the "lightweight" API (suitable for use in any environment) and the Java Cryptography Extension (JCE) provider. Furthermore, it offers miscellaneous components that support additional functionality, such as S/MIME and PGP support are also built upon the JCE provider.

The lightweight API comprises a set of various APIs that implement the underlying cryptographic algorithms. Those APIs were designed in an easy-to-understand way, yet they offer the fundamental building blocks for the JCE provider with great success. The intent is to use the low-level API in mobile devices or other circumstances where memory may become an issue or when easy access to the JCE libraries is not possible. It consists of the following classes:[19]

- Clean room implementation of the JCE API

- Lightweight cryptographic API consisting of support for

    - BlockCipher

    - BufferedBlockCipher

    - AsymmetricBlockCipher

    - BufferedAsymmetricBlockCipher

    - StreamCipher

    - BufferedStreamCipher

    - KeyAgreement

    - IESCipher

    - Digest

    - Mac

    - PBE

    - Signers

- JCE-compatible framework for a Bouncy Castle provider "BC

- JCE-compatible framework for a Bouncy Castle postquantum provider "BCPQC"

Bouncy Castle's JCE provider is built upon the low-level APIs. Hence, the source code for the latter is exemplary to implementing many of the most frequent cryptographic problems using the low-level API. The JCE provider has been used for the development of many projects such as EJBCA,[20] the Open Source CA.

Consult Appendix 3 for a shortlisting of supported algorithms by Bouncy Castle. For a full listing, run the *ListAvailableAlgorithmsBC.java* demo.

Creating a Cipher

Again, *Cipher* is the main actor here as well. As we discussed, there are two approaches one can choose from when it comes to cryptography with Bouncy Castle: the lightweight API and the JCE-like one.

Using the JCE Like

This approach is not much different (for both symmetric and asymmetric operations) to what we showed earlier for the bundled JCE providers. You instantiate a Cipher object; you initialize it and finally perform the encryption/decryption operation you wish. The only point of attention is during the Cipher initialization, where you'd have to use the overloaded method of Cipher#getInstance() that takes two arguments, with the second argument being the provider. For example, here's how the Cipher initialization for our initial AES encryption example with CBC mode and PKCS5Padding would look like in this case:

```
Cipher.getInstance("AES/CBC/PKCS7Padding", new BouncyCastleProvider());
```

The rest of operations remain the same as you can see for yourself in *SimpleCBCExample.java* under *bouncycastle/symmetric/aes* package.

Using the Lightweight API

However, the lightweight API uses autonomous built-in classes for each one of the individual operations that comprise a cryptographic process, depending on the type of encryption (symmetric/asymmetric).

For example, the main interface for symmetric encryption is *BlockCipher*, which you initialize with the algorithm engine. Here's how you can initialize an AES:

```
BlockCipher aes = new AESEngine();
```

Second, depending on the mode you wish to use, you can wrap your engine around the corresponding mode interface. Here's how to wrap an AES engine around a CBC mode:

```
CBCBlockCipher aesCBC = new CBCBlockCipher(aes);
```

Finally, you apply the desired padding using the *PaddedBufferedBlockCipher* class. Here's how that looks like for PKCS7Padding on an AES engine with CBC mode:

```
PaddedBufferedBlockCipher cipher = new PaddedBufferedBlockCipher(aesCBC,
new PKCS7Padding());
```

So far, so good with our cipher's initialization. What about the encryption/decryption operations? *init()* and *doFinal()* methods are the main actors here as well (isn't it nice that BC chose for familiar method names after all?!), but with different signatures as you would expect (which belong to the *BufferedBlockCipher* class).

BlockCipher only contains the engine. The rest of operations better be implemented using *BufferedBlockCipher* (and *PaddedBlockCipher*, which extends it depending on the particular case you're investigating).

```
init(boolean forEncryption, CipherParameters cipherParams)
```

CipherParameters is an interface to help you specify any cipher initialization parameters. For example, you can use its *ParametersWithIV* implementation to specify an initialization vector.

```
byte[] iv = new byte[aes.getBlockSize()];
ParametersWithIV paramsWithIV = new ParametersWithIV(generateKey(), iv);
```

Once you've specified your initialization vector, you can call the *init()* method set for encryption:

```
cipher.init(true, paramsWithIV);
```

Finally, *BufferedBlockCipher#doFinal()* signature looks like the following:

```
doFinal(byte[] messageBytes, int outputBufferLength)
```

That is, if you wish to use the lightweight API of BC, you ought to perform your encryption operations using a temporary buffer for encryption or decryption.

Tip   The *BufferedBlockCipher* class offers a method to seamlessly process your temporary byte array as well (*BufferedBlockCipher#processBytes()*). You can *see* an example demonstrating such behavior at *SimpleCBCExampleWithBC.java*. Specifically, that example showcases an AES encryption in CBC mode with PKCS7Padding utilizing Bouncy Castle's lightweight API.

Note   Under *bouncycastle/symmetric* package, you can find other examples on AES, DES, and Twofish.

Asymmetric Encryption

So far, we've seen how to use Bouncy Castle's lightweight API to perform symmetric encryption, but as we've seen for bundled JCE providers, things slightly differ in asymmetric encryption, at least in regard to the operational side (e.g., key generation). Here, there's one more point you should pay attention to, which is the acting *Cipher* class. While you can perform symmetric encryption using *BlockCipher* as your main Cipher class, asymmetric encryption requires you to use *BlockCipher*'s counterpart for asymmetric encryption, which is the *AsymmetricBlockCipher*. But first, we cannot talk about asymmetric encryption without having our key pair in place, can we?! To do so, you can use the *RSAKeyPairGenerator* to initialize a key generator instance and then create the key pair using the *AsymmetricCipherKeyPair* class. Having come thus far, you already know the drill on asymmetric key pair generation, since it follows the same three steps as its symmetric counterpart for bundled JCE providers.

1. Instantiate a key pair generator:

```
RSAKeyPairGenerator rsaKeyPairGenerator = new RSAKeyPairGenerator();
```

2. Initialize the key pair generator with necessary parameters (e.g., type of the generator to be used, its strength, etc.):

```
rsaKeyPairGenerator.init(new RSAKeyGenerationParameters
    (
        new BigInteger("10001", 16), // public exponent
        SecureRandom.getInstance("SHA1PRNG"), // pseudo random
        generator
        1024, // strength
        80 // certainty
    ));
```

3. Generate the key pair with the specified input parameters:

```
AsymmetricCipherKeyPair keyPair = rsaKeyPairGenerator.generateKeyPair();
```

You can find the full example in *RSAKeyPairGeneratorWithBC.java*.

Caution   Beware of the *RSAKeyPairGenerator*'s initialization parameters you'll use or you're running a risk for your code to fail with a message "input too large for RSA cipher." In general, this is a risk you're taking the moment you decide to use BC's built-in *RSAKeyPairGenerator* to generate your asymmetric key pair; you have to be cautious with setting values for these parameters. Hence, our recommendation is to stick with the JCE provider-one (as we showed on the JCE bundled asymmetric encryption) for this operation, which takes care of the complex parts for you under the hood without giving you any headaches.

Now that we know how to generate an asymmetric key pair, let's see how to perform asymmetric encryption using BC's lightweight API. Again, we'll take the RSA algorithm as an example as we did for the preceding bundled JCE asymmetric example. The process is similar with different classes of course:

Firstly, instantiate your RSA engine with the help of *AsymmetricBlockCipher*:

```
AsymmetricBlockCipher cipher = new RSAEngine();
```

Then, add wrap mode and padding in your cipher. For example, here's how to specify OAEP encoding for your RSA engine:

```
cipher = new OAEPEncoding(cipher);
```

Initialize your cipher for encryption using the public key from the key pair you just generated:

```
cipher.init(true, keyPair.getPublic());
```

Note   *AsymmetricBlockCipher* has no *doFinal()* method, so you need to use the *processBlock()* method, which utilizes a temporary byte array to perform encryption and decryption, as we've seen previously.

Encrypt using the *AsymmetricBlockCipher#processBlock()* method:

```
byte[] cipherText = cipher.processBlock(plainTextBytes, 0, plainTextBytes.
length);
```

Decryption follows the same pattern. Initialize the cipher for decryption (so setting first parameter to false this time) using the private key from the generated key pair:

```
cipher.init(false, keyPair.getPrivate());
```

Decrypt using the *AsymmetricBlockCipher#processBlock()* method:

```
byte[] cipherText = cipher.processBlock(cipherText, 0, cipherText.length);
```

Find the full example in *SimpleRSAExampleWithBC.java* under *bouncycastle/asymmetric* package. Moreover, under the same package, you'll find its JCE-like counterpart example *SimpleRSAExample.java*, which uses JCE way with a key pair generated using BC provider. On the same vibe, you'll find other examples on El Gamal and Diffie-Hellman algorithms.

Bouncy Castle's lightweight API is somewhat peculiar to learn or memorize. Thus, we included a simplified UML diagram generated directly from IntelliJ to help you understand how different ciphers and other cryptographic classes are connected. You can find it under the */resources/bouncycastle-uml* directory of the *jce-providers* module.

We've seen BC examples using both JCE-like and lightweight API. For the more advanced people, we've also compiled a full cryptographic example under the *advanced* package, which contains encryption, decryption, signature creation, and verification.

Again, the lightweight API has been specifically developed for the circumstances where the rich API and integration requirements of the JCE are not required. As you can see for yourself from the *BouncyCastleCryptographyExample.java* or BC suffixed examples under the *bouncycastle/asymmetric* package, the lightweight API requires more effort from the developer to understand it, thereby making it not easy to initialize and utilize the algorithms. Moreover, the documentation is not always handy.[21] Our recommendation is thus to use a hybrid approach by combining JCE's functionalities (e.g., key pair generation) with a pinch of Bouncy Castle where JCE is not enough (e.g., specific algorithms JCE does not support).

Key Generation and Key Agreement (Public Key Infrastructure (PKI)) and Message Authentication Code

PKI is a framework that comprises a set of roles, policies, hardware, software, and procedures to address the seven key principles of secure communications. PKI utilizes two core elements: public key cryptography and CAs. PKI security is used in many different ways such as securing emails, web communications, digitally signing software, encrypting files, or smart card authentication.

PKI's operation is based on three main components: digital certificates, certificate authorities, and registration authorities.

At this point, we trust you're familiar with CAs and digital certificates, but what about Registration Authorities (RAs)?

A Registration Authority is the authority that performs all the necessary identification checks on behalf of the Certificate Authority so that the latter can issue a digital certificate to a requester. Specifically, a RA operates in three steps:

- Receives certificate signing request

- Verifies it

- Forwards certificate signing request to CA

Occasionally, a RA may also perform certificate life cycle management operations; for instance, it may handle certificate revocation requests.

It is important to mention that a RA is normally separated from the CA (mainly for security reasons). It is normally accessible via easy-to-consume APIs or user-friendly GUIs.

Note   You can find the code examples of this section under module *chapter6-javase-underpinnings/pki* of our GitHub repository.

How PKI Works

PKI merges the use of both symmetric and asymmetric encryption. It's a one-stop shop for the encryption of classified information and private identities.

It performs encryption by taking advantage of public key cryptography. Specifically, the two asymmetric keys it generates guarantee that sensitive information remains secure while being passed back and forth between the communicating parties.

Let's now examine other important items of public key cryptography such as key generation, key agreement, and Message Authentication Code (MAC).

Key Generation

In cryptography, the term *key generation* refers to the process of generating keys. A cryptographic key is used to encrypt/decrypt some data that needs to be encrypted/decrypted.

Depending on the kind of encryption algorithm at hand, there are two main types of keys:

- Symmetric keys

- Asymmetric keys

Symmetric keys are used for symmetric encryption algorithms. Symmetric encryption algorithms (such as DES and AES) use the same key for encryption and decryption; keeping data secret requires keeping the shared key secret.

Asymmetric keys are used for asymmetric encryption algorithms. Asymmetric encryption algorithms (such as RSA) use a public key and a private key and are often referenced as public key algorithms. The public key is made available to everyone (often using a digital certificate). A sender encrypts data with the receiver's public key, data that can be decrypted only by the holder of the private key corresponding to the public key.

To decrypt some piece of data, a party needs to know the key associated with that data. Moreover, when encryption and decryption are done by different parties, those parties need to agree on the key that will be used for their communication to be secure. This is referred to as *key exchange or key agreement*, which we'll examine in the next section.

Today, there are three popular mathematical properties used to generate private and public keys: RSA, ECC (Elliptic Curve Cryptography, which we'll dive into in the "Elliptic Curve Cryptography" section), and Diffie-Hellman. Each uses different algorithms to generate encryption keys, but they all rely on the same basic principles as far as the relationship between the public key and the private key is concerned.

You can find several examples on the aforementioned algorithms under the *keygen* package of the *pki* module of our GitHub repository, but the main concept of generating a key in Java remains the same.

Generating Symmetric Keys

To generate a symmetric key, you can use the *javax.crypto.KeyGenerator* class.

1. Creating a KeyGenerator instance

To create a *KeyGenerator* instance, you can call its *getInstance()* method passing the name of the encryption algorithm to create a key for as a parameter:

```
KeyGenerator keyGenerator = KeyGenerator.getInstance("AES");
```

This example creates a *KeyGenerator* instance that can generate keys for the AES encryption algorithm.

2. Initializing a KeyGenerator instance

After creating the *KeyGenerator* instance, you then need to initialize it, which is done by calling its *init()* method:

```
SecureRandom secureRandom = new SecureRandom();
int keyBitSize = 256;
keyGenerator.init(keyBitSize, secureRandom);
```

The *init()* method may be passed two arguments: the key size in bits and the *SecureRandom* instance to be used for the key generation process.

3. Generating a key

To generate a key, you can call the *KeyGenerator#generateKey()* method:

```
SecretKey secretKey = keyGenerator.generateKey();
```

You can find the full example in *SimpleKeyGenerator.java*.

Note   The resulting *SecretKey* instance can be passed to the *Cipher#init()* method, like the following:

```
cipher.init(Cipher.ENCRYPT_MODE, secretKey);
```

The default JCE provider (bundled with your JDK and named SunJCE) comes with a couple of PRNG generators.[22] For instance, we've included a couple of similar examples at *SimpleKeyGeneratorRNG.java* and *SimpleKeyGeneratorRNGLowCost.java*.

Tip   Deterministic random number generators have been the source of many software security breaches nowadays. For example, the fact that they use /dev/random on Linux may block waiting for sufficient entropy to build up. The best approach here is to use a nondefault PRNG and apply periodic seeding for increased entropy. You can find an example at *SecureRandomBestPracticeExample.java*.

Note   We generate keys to make sure our communications are secure. That is, encryption keys facilitate our cryptographic operations. You can find an example of how a symmetric key generated with *KeyGenerator* can help us with an AES encryption at *SimpleAESEncryptionWithKeyGenerator.java* example.

Generating Asymmetric Keys

Asymmetric encryption algorithms use asymmetric keys to encrypt and decrypt data. As we've seen in the section "Introduction to Cryptography," an asymmetric key pair consists of two keys: the public key and the private key.

To generate an asymmetric key pair, you can use the KeyPairGenerator class.

1. Creating a KeyPairGenerator instance

To create a *KeyPairGenerator* instance, you can call its *getInstance()* method passing the name of the encryption algorithm to generate the key pair for as a parameter:

```
KeyPairGenerator keyPairGenerator = KeyPairGenerator.getInstance("RSA");
```

2. Initializing a KeyPairGenerator instance

You can initialize a *KeyPairGenerator* instance by calling its *initialize()* method:

```
keyPairGenerator.initialize(2048); // key size of 2048 bits
```

3. Generating the key pair

In Java, a *KeyPair* object holds the public and private key objects associated with a key pair. To generate a *KeyPair*, you can call the *KeyPairGenerator#generateKeyPair()* method:

```
KeyPair keyPair = keyPairGenerator.generateKeyPair();
```

You may then need to retrieve the individual key objects (private and public keys) associated with the *KeyPair* instance:

```
PublicKey publicKey = keyPair.getPublic();
PrivateKey privateKey = keypair.getPrivate();
```

You can find the full example at SimpleKeyPairGeneratorExample.java.

Note   It is common to store key pairs in files. *RetrieveKeyPairObjectFromKeyFile. java* demonstrates how to retrieve a public and a private key object from key files with the help of *X509EncodedKeySpec* and *PKCS8EncodedKeySpec* classes, respectively.

Tip   Again, key generators facilitate a secure encryption process. That is, once we generate a key, we can directly pass it on to *Cipher* instance. Feel free to look back to *SimpleRSAExample.java* example to refresh your memory.

Elliptic Curve Cryptography

At this point, we felt Elliptic Curve Cryptography (ECC) is worth being devoted a reference, given that it nowadays is considered as an alternative to RSA.

What Is Elliptic Curve Cryptography?

ECC is a modern public key cryptography technique based on mathematical elliptic curves and is well known for creating smaller, faster, and more efficient cryptographic keys while maintaining high-security standards. Simply put, ECC focuses on asymmetric key pairs for encryption of web traffic.

What Is ECC Used For?

ECC is considered among the most commonly used implementation techniques for digital signatures in cryptocurrencies. For example, Bitcoin and Ethereum apply the Elliptic Curve Digital Signature Algorithm specifically in signing transactions.

Moreover, its shorter key length and efficiency in performance will enable it to be used by a plethora of web applications soon (e.g., encrypting data so that only authorized parties can decrypt it such as verification email that no one else but the recipient can read it).

Elliptic curves are also used in key agreement, digital signatures, and pseudorandom generators. Indirectly, they can be used for encryption by combining the key agreement with a symmetric encryption scheme, the so-called hybrid encryption with ECC. ECIES is an algorithm that implements that; under the hood, it is a key agreement followed by symmetric encryption. That being said, it's not possible to directly encrypt anything with ECIES; you should couple it to a symmetric cipher instead, which often is the best scheme for RSA encryption too. Feel free to check out the *SimpleECIESExample.java*, which demonstrates this use case.

Advantages

Public key cryptography is based on algorithms that are easy to process in one direction and difficult to process in the reverse direction. Look no further than RSA, which is cheap in multiplying prime numbers to get a larger number, yet factoring huge numbers back to the original primes makes it expensive. Moreover, RSA uses keys of a minimum size of 2048 bits, which slows it down.

ECC comes with a smaller key size, which is a great advantage, because it translates seamlessly to more power for smaller, mobile devices. The small key size makes ECC simple and thus cheaper in terms of energy cost. For example, for two keys of the same size, RSA's factoring encryption is more vulnerable.

Hence, ECC offers high security with faster, shorter keys compared to RSA.

How Secure Is It?

No doubt nothing comes without a cost so does ECC. ECDSA is a specific ECC algorithm and the most used one. However, it comes with a couple of flaws as well. To begin with, in ECDSA, every signature requires some random or unpredictable data as input, else an attacker can easily figure out the private key. An example here is the private key leakage of Sony's PlayStation 3 back in 2010 due to a flaw in the way random numbers were used in ECDSA.

The same happened with a few Android devices recently, which were found to be generating random values incorrectly, resulting in a massive theft of Bitcoins from devices running Bitcoin software. Esoteric attacks against specific implementations also apply here; for example, OpenSSL's implementation of ECDSA for curve secp256k1 (used by the Bitcoin protocol) was recently found to be vulnerable, which is maybe one of the reasons JDK 16 removed this particular curve from the SunEC provider.[23]

Tip   The danger of key leakage via poor random data or side-channel attacks is a concern but is manageable by ensuring that the system random number generator has enough entropy.

Other attacks like twist-security attacks are simply mitigated with careful parameter validation and curve choices. That is, ECC benefits seem to outweigh the risks in this case.

How Is ECC Different from RSA?

RSA uses prime numbers for one-way encryption operations like emails, data, and software signing. Specifically, its public key is a large number that is a product of two primes, plus a smaller number. The private key is a related number.

On the contrary, ECC's public key is both an equation for an elliptic curve and a point that lies on the same, whereas the private key is just a number. The use of elliptic curves enables ECC to use a smaller key size and therefore to maintain security. That is, ECC creates keys that are mathematically more difficult to crack; therefore, it is considered to be the next-generation implementation of public key cryptography and more secure than RSA.

The difference in the key size is notable if you have a look at Table 6-4.

Table 6-4. *Key length comparison between RSA and ECC*

RSA key length (bits)	ECC key length (bits)
1024	160
2048	224
3072	256
7680	384
15360	521

What Is an Elliptic Curve Digital Signature?

An Elliptic Curve Digital Signature (ECDSA) is a Digital Signature Algorithm (DSA) that uses keys derived from elliptic curve cryptography to ensure the uniqueness of each user and the security of each transaction. This type of DSA offers a functionally indistinguishable outcome compared to other DSAs, yet its smaller key size enables it to be more efficient and thus more preferable. *SignatureECDSAExample.java* demonstrates a signature creation and verification using ECDSA.

Feel free to experiment with the code examples we prepared under the *ecc* package of *pki* module to further understand how it all plays out in action.

Key Agreement

For two parties to communicate confidentially, they must first agree on a shared secret key that will be during their encrypted communication. This initial exchange of the encryption key is known as *key exchange.*

It is a common approach for key exchange systems to have one party generate the key and send it to the other party; the other party has no influence in the key generation process or whatsoever. Diffie–Hellman is a prevalent algorithm for key exchange that meets the preceding criteria. DH is a secure method to exchange cryptographic keys over a public communication channel.

Note   Exponential key exchange algorithms like Diffie–Hellman do not specify prior agreement or subsequent authentication of the parties; therefore, they are also called *anonymous key exchange* and are thus vulnerable to man-in-the-middle attacks.

To prevent man-in-the-middle (MITM) or similar attacks, there have been a wide variety of cryptographic authentication schemes and protocols that aim to provide authenticated key agreement. These methods generally mathematically bind the agreed key to other agreed-upon data, such as asymmetric keys, shared secret keys, and passwords. Let's start by examining DH's appliance to asymmetric keys.

Note   You can find the code examples of this section under *pki/keyagreement* module of our GitHub repository.

In Action

In order for two parties to establish a shared secret key, they first need to generate their own keys. Each party can do so by using either of the available key generators (*KeyPairGenerator* or *KeyGenerator*), a *KeyFactory*, or a result of an intermediate phase of the key agreement protocol:

```
KeyPairGenerator keygen = KeyPairGenerator.getInstance("DH");
```

Having chosen for a *KeyPairGenerator*, you need to initialize it with algorithm-specific parameters (in this case, DH parameters, which define a field prime p and a generator g):

```
keygen.initialize(new DHParameterSpec(p512, g512), new SecureRandom());
```

In Java, the *javax.crypto.KeyAgreement* class provides the functionality of a key agreement (or key exchange) protocol:

```
KeyAgreement keyAgreement = KeyAgreement.getInstance("DH");
```

The two sides can then generate their key pairs:

```
KeyPair aPair = keygen.generateKeyPair();
KeyPair bPair = keygen.generateKeyPair();
```

Each party's *KeyAgreement* instance needs to first be initialized with their private key:

```
aKeyAgreement.init(aPair.getPrivate());
bKeyAgreement.init(bPair.getPrivate());
```

For each of the correspondents in the key exchange, doPhase needs to be called with the public key of its counterpart and a lastPhase flag. For example, for a key exchange between two parties, doPhase needs to be called once, with the lastPhase flag set to true.

```
aKeyAgreement.doPhase(bPair.getPublic(), true);
bKeyAgreement.doPhase(aPair.getPublic(), true);
```

Find this example at *SimpleDHExample.java*.

Tip   For better results, we can always employ ECC; therefore, we included a DH example that uses ECC in *SimpleECDHExample.java*.

For a key exchange that involves more than two parties, say, three, for example, the *doPhase* method needs to be called twice: the first time we call it by setting the *lastPhase* flag to false and the second time by setting it to true. *ThreeWayDHExample.java* demonstrates a key agreement between three parties.

Every implementation of the Java platform is required to support Diffie-Hellman, the standard *KeyAgreement* algorithm. DH's key agreement aims to establish a symmetric key between two parties without requiring them to communicate that secret key. For example, it is common that two parties may negotiate a shared AES key or an HMAC over a potentially insecure communication channel. *AESEncryptionWithSharedSecret. java* example demonstrates this case. We'll cover its HMAC counterpart in the section "Message Authentication Codes."

Warning   This does not by itself provide authentication, however, so it is still vulnerable to MITM attacks without additional measures.

Caution   Key agreement vs. key generation. Key agreement starts with key generation. In other words, in order for two entities to agree on a shared key, they first need to generate their own keys.

Message Authentication Codes

In this section, we will examine another vital part of cryptography, Message Authentication Codes (MAC). A MAC is a short piece of information (sequence of bits) that can be attached to a message to verify where it originated and that it has not been tampered with.

Note   You can find the code examples of this section under *pki/mac* module of our GitHub repository.

MessageDigests and Hash Functions

Before diving into the basics of MAC, it is important to demystify how that's different to message digests and secure hash functions, looking at the confusion that prevails.

Hash function: An algorithm that can be applied to data like passwords or files to produce a value known as *digest*.

Message digest: A hash function that is created using a one-way formula. A message digest contains a string of digits.

Caution   A digest is the output of a hash function; for example, hash function SHA256 has a digest of 256 bits or in other words, it has a length of 32 bytes.

Common secure hash functions are MD5, SHA-256, SHA-512, and others. To see the available secure hash functions your JCE provider(s) supports, run *ListAvailableHashFunctions.java*.

How to Compute Secure Hash Functions

Java offers *MessageDigest* class to facilitate the process of calculating the cryptographic hash value of a text using a hash function.

You can instantiate a MessageDigest object by calling its *getInstance()* method passing the algorithm you wish to use for your cryptographic function:

```
MessageDigest md = MessageDigest.getInstance("SHA-256");
```

Calculate the message digest value by calling the *digest()* method, which takes a message's byte array as an argument:

```
byte[] hash = md.digest(message.getBytes());
```

Find the full example at *SimpleSHA256Hashing.java*.

Alternatively, you can use the *openssl*[24] command line tool. You can find examples under */resources/openssl* folder. In case of issues, *Get-FileHash*[25] for PowerShell would do on Windows.

The Need for MACs

While secure hash functions are used to guarantee the integrity of data, they lack authentication capabilities. Specifically, a hash code is blindly generated from a message without any kind of external input: what you obtain can be used to check if the message was altered during its travel. This is where MACs come to the rescue: they provide both integrity and authentication of a message by having an additional step in their hashing process; they use an additional key to encrypt the message digest.

This additional step not only assures the receiver that the message has not been modified but also that the sender is the one we are expecting. In other words, an intruder couldn't know the private key used to generate the code.

Caution   Secure hash function vs. MAC. While a secure hash function only needs a message as an input to produce a hash, a MAC needs both a message and a secret key.

To list the available MAC algorithms your JCE provider(s) comes with, run *ListAvailableMACs.java*.

How MAC Works

JCA delivers with a Mac engine that helps you generate Message Authentication Codes. As with other JCA engines that we've seen (*KeyGenerator, KeyAgreement, Signature*), to generate a MAC from a message, you need to follow three basic steps:

1. Create a MAC instance.

Creating a Mac instance is done using the *getInstance()* method, which takes the MAC algorithm name as a parameter:

```
Mac mac = Mac.getInstance("HmacSHA256");
```

2. Initialize the MAC instance.

You can initialize a Mac instance by calling its *init()* method passing as parameter the secret key to be used.

```
// first, generate a secret key
KeyGenerator keygen = KeyGenerator.getInstance("HmacSHA256");
Keygen.init(256);
SecretKey hmacKey = keygen.generateKey();
// initialize the MAC instance
mac.init(hmacKey);
```

3. Compute the MAC.

Once you've initialized your Mac, you can start calculating MAC values with it. Again, you can use either of the *update()* (multiple blocks of data) or *doFinal()* (single block of data) method to calculate a MAC:

```
byte[] hmac256 = mac.doFinal(message.getBytes());
```

You can find an example on *SimpleHmac256Example.java*. Moreover, *TwoSideHmac256Example.java* demonstrates a MAC generation and verification on the sides of sender and receiver (remember here the two sides need to share the same key).

Two Types of MAC

As we've seen previously, a MAC is generated based on a key that is shared between the sender and the receiver. Your key may originate from two sources:

- Block ciphers

- Hash functions

> **Note**   A MAC mechanism that is based on cryptographic hash functions is referred to as HMAC.

We've seen how it works for hash functions in the *SimpleHmac256Example.java*, but how about block ciphers? Well, that's not much different to the key generation we've shown in previous chapters. You just generate the key and then pass it to the MAC instance. You can find two examples utilizing AES and IDEA algorithms at *SimpleHmac256ExampleWithAESKey.java* and *SimpleHmac256ExampleWithIDEAKey.java*, respectively.

Moreover, you can use both types to generate a MAC that can be used for your encryption purposes. You can find examples on both at *AESEncryptionWithBlockCipherAsMac.java* and *AESEncryptionWithHashFunctionAsMac.java*.

Best Practices on MACs

- Make sure the symmetric key used on sender and receiver sides is kept secure.

- Use at least a key length of 128 bits.

- Use different keys for encryption and MACs.

- The strength of the secure hash function determines the security of your HMAC.

- Use secure hash functions that come from the SHA2 and SHA3 families.

- Try to avoid archaic algorithms from the 1990s such as HmacMD5 and HmacSHA1 from hash functions and CMAC from block ciphers.

PKI Conclusions

Undoubtedly, PKI is the most effective way to protect confidential information. Specifically, the process of backing a certificate involves numerous secure processes (such as timestamping, registration, validation) to ensure the privacy of both the identity and the underlying data affiliated with the certificate.

However, secure authentication alone is not enough; we should also focus on collaborating with trustworthy CAs and RAs. That is, top-performing CA and RA are considered to be a must nowadays, else we exclude ourselves from the "web of trust."

TLS in Java and TLS 1.3

Remember when in Chapter 2 we mentioned that SSL proved to be a vulnerable protocol for Internet communications somewhere in 2011? For the next seven years, security specialists would make great efforts to develop a more secure protocol when in 2018, TLS 1.3 comes to stay. TLS 1.3 is considered the most secure communication protocol nowadays, so if you're still using any of the predecessor (SSL, TLS 1.1, 1.2) protocols, please stop doing so, as they're vulnerable.

Note   You can find the code examples of this section under *chapter6-javase-underpinnings* /tls module of our GitHub repository.

What Is TLS

TLS is a cryptographic protocol that aims to secure end-to-end data communications over the Internet. All of us are familiar with the padlock that appears next to our browser's URL, which implies that a secure, powered-by-TLS-protocol session is established. However, TLS cannot guarantee secure data on end systems, but only the secure delivery of data over the Internet, thereby safeguarding it from eavesdroppers or intruders willing to forge the content at hand.

Why TLS Is Important

To understand the impact of TLS on the privacy and data integrity of everyday communications, imagine Internet transactions such as credit card details, logins, email, online chats, and teleconferencing being gleaned or monitored by others. Enriching a client-server interaction with TLS as the supported communication protocol ensures the transmitted data is encrypted by secure algorithms, leaving no potential leaks behind (e.g., data viewable by third parties).

Benefits of TLS 1.3

Let's now have a quick look at the major benefits of TLS 1.3.

Speed: Previous versions of TLS/SSL required a two round trip handshake. Luckily, it only takes one round trip for TLS 1.3 to establish a handshake.

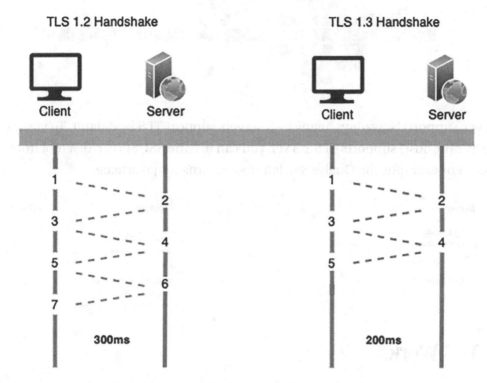

Figure 6-7. *Handshake comparison between TLS 1.2 and TLS 1.3. TLS 1.3 Handshake uses red color to indicate the handshake flow and purple to indicate the application data flow*

0-RTT (Zero Round Trip): Your browser now remembers which web pages it has already established a secure connection with, therefore requiring no round trip at all to establish a handshake with the same.

Improved Security: TLS 1.3 now removes obsolete and insecure features from TLS 1.2 (such as MD5 and SHA1).

Browser Support: A wide variety of browsers is supported:

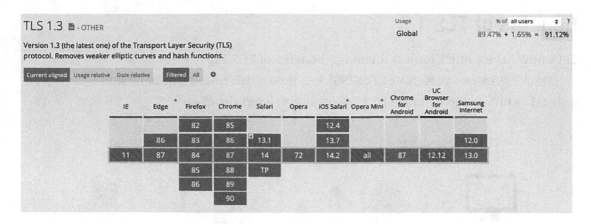

Server Support: Nowadays, many web servers support TLS by default. To verify that your server (or host) supports TLS 1.3 yet, you can use the SSL Server Test tool from Qualys.[26] For example, the Qualys SSL labs tool returns for jakarta.ee:

	Server	Test time	Grade
1	**52.203.36.44** ec2-52-203-36-44.compute-1.amazonaws.com Ready	Sat, 27 Mar 2021 11:20:53 UTC Duration: 58.424 sec	A+
2	**167.172.136.193** Ready	Sat, 27 Mar 2021 11:21:52 UTC Duration: 57.985 sec	A+

How TLS Works

To ensure secure data transmission, TLS uses a hybrid approach that combines symmetric and asymmetric cryptography and guarantees a good compromise between performance and security.

On the one hand, it uses symmetric cryptography to securely generate a session key that is used for encrypting data on the sender's side and decrypting the same data on the receiver's side; the session key is discarded when the session is over.

On the other hand, public key cryptography ensures a verified identity for the communicating parties; authentication can be made optional, but it is generally required for at least one of the parties (typically the server).

Tools and Algorithms That Can Be Used

Again, TLS uses both symmetric and asymmetric key algorithms to compromise a good balance between performance and security. To do so, it requires that one party receives the other's public key and encrypts a small chunk of data either by using a symmetric key or some data used to generate it. The rest of the communication remains encrypted with the use of a symmetric key algorithm, which is typically faster.

Different key generation and key agreement algorithms can be used including RSA and Diffie-Hellman (DH). Moreover, DH offers a couple of suitable variations, like Ephemeral Diffie-Hellman (DHE), Elliptic Curve Diffie-Hellman (ECDH), and Ephemeral Elliptic Curve Diffie-Hellman (ECDHE).

Note   DHE and ECDHE are preferred nowadays as they offer *Perfect Forward Secrecy*, which is a modern method to ensure that all transactions sent over the Internet are secure by creating a unique session key for each transaction. Hence, past sessions are protected against future compromises. Again, DH is somewhat vulnerable for specific implementations, so be sure to use the best practices for secure random generation and large key size as we discussed in the previous section.

TLS Protocol Details

TLS consists of two subprotocols:

- Record Protocol: It defines the rules for breaking down the data into blocks and encrypt/decrypt them.

- Handshake: It defines the process to establish common cryptographic parameters between two parties.

The Record Protocol

TLS splits large amounts of data to be exchanged into smaller chunks, which are also known as *records*. Each record may be encrypted or compressed, appended, or padded with a MAC, depending on the connection's state. Let's now have a look at the key elements of a record by providing a short description for each one of them.

Table 6-5. *TLS record structure*

Byte	+0	+1	+2	+3
0	Content type			
1-4	Version		Length	
5-n	Payload			
n-m	MAC			
m-p	Padding (applicable to ciphers only)			

- Content type: Designates the type of data encapsulated.

- Length: The length of the record; maximum record size is 16KB.

- Version: The TLS version that is used; for example, *TLSv1.3*.

- Payload: The encapsulated data, which may either be control or procedural messages of the TLS itself, or the application data TLS needs to transfer.

Looking at the diverse role the payload field has, it goes without saying that TLS defines not only the procedure to establish and monitor the transfer of data but also the structure of payloads to be transferred.

The following is a step-by-step overview of TLS operation on the sender's and receiver's side:

- Read messages for transmission.

- Split messages into smaller chunks of data.

- Compress the data should compression be required and enabled.

- Calculate a MAC.

- Encrypt the data.

- Transmit the resulting data to the peer.

Upon successful transmission, the encrypted data is handed over to the TCP layer for transport. The reverse order of steps applies to the receiving end:

- Read data received from the sender.

- Decrypt the data.

- Verify the MAC.

- Decompress the data should compression be required and enabled.

- Reassemble the message fragments.

- Deliver the message to upper protocol layers.

Handshake

The specifications (cipher suite, keys, etc.) required to exchange application data by TLS are agreed upon in the "TLS handshake" between the client and the server. Figure 6-8 demonstrates a basic TLS Handshake with DH where only the server (but not the client) is authenticated.

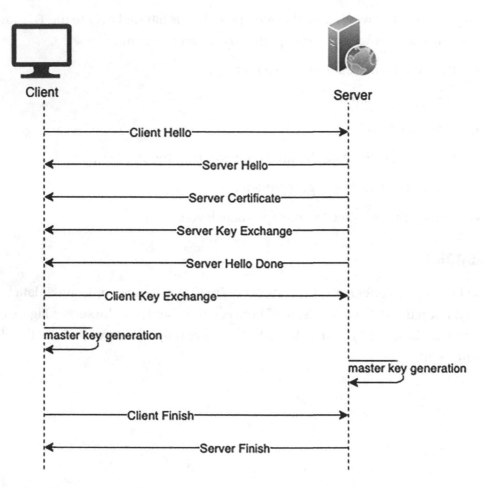

Figure 6-8. *TLS Handshake*

- Client Hello: Client notifies the server of the supported protocol and ciphers.

- Server Hello: Server chooses the protocol and the cipher to be used based on the client's input. Remember, protocol and cipher are suggested by the client but chosen by the server.

- Server Certificate: Server sends its certificate to the client. Moreover, if the server wishes the client to be authenticated, it could also ask for the client's certificate.

- Server Key Exchange: Server sends the public DH parameters and a hash of its digital signature to the client to prove its identity.

- **Server Hello Done:** Server notifies the client of a successful message delivery. At this point, they've reached an agreement on the TLS version and cipher.

- **ClientKeyExchange:** The client uses the server's public key to transmit its encrypted DH parameters.

- **Key Generation:** Not a message but a process that indicates that client and server have successfully generated the session (or master) key separately.

- **Finish Messages:** First check that everything went OK; contains the hash of the previous messages that were exchanged and is encrypted with the session key. If either of the server or client is not able to decrypt this message, something went wrong.

TLS in Java

In 2011, JDK 7 shipped with support for TLSv1.2. However, for compatibility reasons, it was enabled by default only on server sockets and disabled on clients. A few years later, in 2018, Java SE 11 was released and included support for TLS1.3; backward compatibility was not provided though.

Java 11 didn't introduce any new classes or methods for TLS 1.3. It just added a couple of new constants for the new protocol name (*TLSv1.3*), cipher suites (e.g., *TLS_AES_128_GCM_SHA256*), etc., which is a great advantage, as it makes switching to the latest TLS version quite easy.

Specifically, all you need to do is use JSSE[27] to set up the desired protocol and ciphers with the rest of your code remaining intact. Here are a couple of examples to get you started with setting up TLS 1.3 protocol at the client endpoint:

- Specify the supported protocols of an existing connection with the `SSLSocket.setEnabledProtocols` method:

```
sslSocket.setEnabledProtocols(new String[] { "TLSv1.3",
"TLSv1.2"});
```

- Create a TLS 1.3-based *SSLContext*:

```
SSLContext ctx = SSLContext.getInstance("TLSv1.3");
```

- Specify the supported protocols for connections obtained through *HttpsURLConnection* or the method *URL#openStream()* with the *https.protocols* system property:

```
java -Dhttps.protocols="TLSv1.3,TLSv1.2" MyApplication
```

As you can see, specific networking classes like SSLContext need to be used here, which come from the JSSE API (Java Secure Socket Extension). Let's double-click on it.

JSSE API

The JSSE API enables secure Internet communications by providing a Java framework for the standard SSL and TLS protocols. It aims to supplement the core cryptographic and network services defined by the *java.net* and *java.security* and packages. To do so, it provides support for networking socket classes, trust managers, key managers, and a socket factory framework to simplify socket creation. As Figure 6-9 demonstrates, the most important classes are SSLSocket SSLSocketFactory, KeyManagerFactory, and TrustManagerFactory.

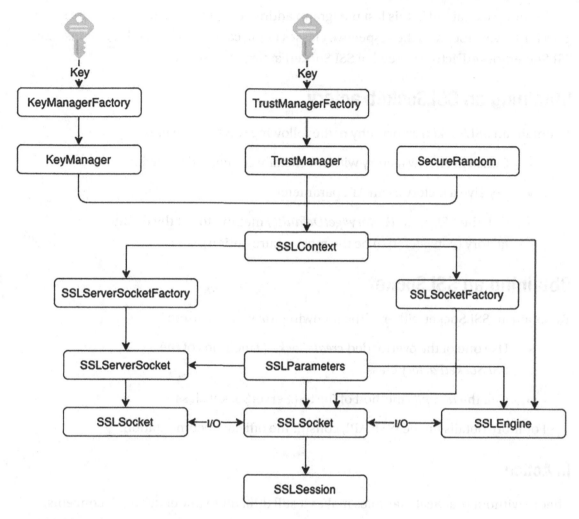

Figure 6-9. *JSSE API overview*

That is, JSSE API offers factories for creating a variety of client and server sockets for SSL and TLS. Moreover, it offers key and trust manager interfaces and factories, including our beloved X.509-specific key and trust managers that we've investigated in the section "X.509 Digital Certificates."

You can create an SSLSocket using an SSLSocketFactory or an SSLServerSocket that accepts an inbound connection. Subsequently, instances of SSLSocketFactory are created using an SSLContext, which, under the hood, creates an SSLEngine to handle any I/O operations. The SSLEngine part is taken care of by the framework, though, so no need to worry about that.

403

What we explained in this last paragraph addresses client operations, but the same goes for servers too, with the respective classes being called where needed, for instance, SSLServerSocketFactory instead of SSLSocketFactory, and so on.

Obtaining an SSLSocketFactory

To obtain an SSLSocketFactory, any of the following ways can be used:

- Construct a new factory with specifically configured behavior.

- Receive a factory as an API parameter.

- Call the *SSLSocketFactory#getDefault()* method to get the default factory (considered to be the most secure option).

Obtaining an SSLSocket

To obtain an SSLSocket, either of the following ways can be used:

- Use one of the overloaded *createSocket()* methods of the *SSLSocketFactory* class.

- Call the *accept()* method of the SSLServerSocket class.

For more details on the JSSE API, consult the official documentation.[28]

In Action

Theory without practical examples makes it still difficult to understand the concepts, so let's now see how all that plays out in practice. To initiate a transaction using TLS1.3 protocol, you first need to instantiate an *SSLSocket* using *SSLSocketFactory*:

```
SSLSocketFactory sslSocketFactory = (SSLSocketFactory) SSLSocketFactory.
getDefault();
SSLSocket sslSocket = (SSLSocket) sslSocketFactory.createSocket("google.
com", 443);
```

Second, specify your TLS 1.3 parameters (protocol and cipher suite):

```
sslSocket.setEnabledProtocols(new String[] {"TLSv1.3"});
sslSocket.setEnabledCipherSuites(new String[] {"TLS_AES_128_GCM_SHA256"});
```

Your protocol settings have been configured, so you may now start the handshake:

```
sslSocket.startHandshake();
```

Then the input/output stream follows as in any other network protocol development. Find the full example at *SimpleTLS13Example.java*.

At some point, you might want to use client authentication for you cannot use the default factory from *SSLSocketFactory*. Hence, you need to create an *SSLSocket* using its factory, which is fed with an *SSLContext* object that holds your keystore (where your certificate resides). The following are the steps:

Load the keystore using *KeyManagerFactory*:

```
// get an instance of KeyManagerFactory
KeyManagerFactory keyManagerFactory = KeyManagerFactory.
getInstance("SunX509");

// load the keystore as you're used to
KeyStore keystore = KeyStore.getInstance("PKCS12");
keystore.load(new FileInputStream(KEYSTORE_PATH), KEYSTORE_PASSWORD);
// initiate your KeyManagerFactory instance with your KeyStore instance
keyManagerFactory.init(keystore, KEYSTORE_PASSWORD);
// instantiate a TLS SSLContext
SSLContext sslContext = SSLContext.getInstance("TLS");
// initialize your SSL context with the keystore managers that are set
sslContext.init(keyManagerFactory.getKeyManagers(), null, null);
// get a socket factory from the ssl context you just configured
SSLSocketFactory sslSocketFactory = sslContext.getSocketFactory();
// create a socket, set everything up for TLS and start handshake
sslSocket = (SSLSocket) sslSocketFactory.createSocket("google.com", 443);
sslSocket.setEnabledProtocols(PROTOCOLS);
sslSocket.setEnabledCipherSuites(CIPHER_SUITES);
sslSocket.startHandshake();
```

Find the full example at SimpleTLS13ExampleClientAuth.java.

Also, in the examples, you can find a client-server interaction demonstrating the feedback loops between SSLSocketFactory and SSLServerSocketFactory: *TLS13ClientAndServer.java*.

Takeaways on TLS

Here are the key takeaways from this section:

- Use TLS v1.3.

- Beware who you trust.

- No published attack for TLS since 2006 doesn't necessarily mean that there isn't one. Mind your security mechanisms.

- When in doubt, use your toolbox (openssl, curl, nmap, ssldump, Portecle).

Java SE Underpinnings Outro

This chapter tried to describe in detail the most important security aspects Java SE comes with to remind you of the strength of Java SE and help you build secure applications. Hence, here's our main takeaway.

Sidebar: Nowadays, intruders are smarter and so are their techniques to take control of your system. Three main things can ensure application security when in place: public key cryptography, signed certificates, and certificate authorities. Treat your application with respect by making sure the right security measures are in place.

References

[1] https://docs.oracle.com/en/java/javase/15/security/
java-authentication-and-authorization-service-
jaas-reference-guide.html#GUID-164692CF-6790-488C-
BF86-39F7C5CF0F5A

[2] https://docs.oracle.com/en/java/javase/15/docs/
api/jdk.security.auth/com/sun/security/auth/login/
ConfigFile.html

[3] https://cve.mitre.org/cgi-bin/cvename.
cgi?name=CVE-2021-45105

[4] https://openjdk.java.net/jeps/411

[5] https://docs.oracle.com/en/java/javase/15/security/
java-authentication-and-authorization-service-jaas-
reference-guide.html#GUID-2A935F5E-0803-411D-B6BC-
F8C64D01A25C

[6] www.mayrhofer.eu.org/post/create-x509-certs-in-java/

[7] https://openjdk.java.net/jeps/229

[8] www.ibm.com/docs/en/sdk-java-
technology/8?topic=guide-jce-provider

[9] https://docs.oracle.com/en/java/javase/15/security/
howtoimplaprovider.html#GUID-1D2FDA77-743C-47CB-9C
CB-2585FEC0607A

[10] https://jce.iaik.tugraz.at/

[11] https://jce.iaik.tugraz.at/about-us/

[12] https://support.fortanix.com/hc/en-us/article
s/360018362951-JCE

[13] www.azul.com/products/zulu-and-zulu-enterprise/zulu-
cryptography-extension-kit/

[14] www.cryptix.org/

[15] www.bouncycastle.org/

[16] https://docs.oracle.com/en/java/javase/15/
docs/specs/security/standard-names.html#cipher-
algorithm-names

[17] https://en.wikipedia.org/wiki/Initialization_vector

[18] https://docs.oracle.com/en/java/javase/15/docs/api/
java.base/javax/crypto/spec/IvParameterSpec.html

[19] www.bouncycastle.org/specifications.html

[20] www.ejbca.org/

[21] https://docs.oracle.com/en/java/javase/15/docs/specs/security/standard-names.html#securerandom-number-generation-algorithms

[22] https://jdk.java.net/16/release-notes

[23] https://github.com/openssl/openssl

[24] https://docs.microsoft.com/en-us/powershell/module/microsoft.powershell.utility/get-filehash?view=powershell-7.1

[25] www.ssllabs.com/ssltest/

[26] https://docs.oracle.com/en/java/javase/15/security/java-secure-socket-extension-jsse-reference-guide.html#GUID-93DEEE16-0B70-40E5-BBE7-55C3FD432345

Appendix 1. Commonly Used AuthPermissions in JAAS

Permission	Description	Sample
getSubject	Allows for the retrieval of the Subject(s) associated with the current Thread	Permission javax.security.auth. AuthPermission "getSubject";
modifyPrincipals	Allows the caller to modify the set of Principals associated with a Subject	Permission javax.security. auth.AuthPermission "modifyPrincipals"
modifyPublicCredentials	Allows the caller to modify the set of public credentials associated with a Subject	Permission javax.security. auth.AuthPermission "modifyPublicCredentials";
modifyPrivateCredentials	Allows the caller to modify the set of private credentials associated with a Subject	Permission javax.security. auth.AuthPermission "modifyPrivateCredentials";

(continued)

Permission	Description	Sample
doAs	Allows the caller to invoke the Subject.doAs methods	Permission javax.security.auth.AuthPermission "doAs";
doAsPrivileged	Allows the caller to invoke the Subject.doAsPrivileged methods	Permission javax.security.auth.AuthPermission "doAsPrivileged";
createLoginContext.<name>	Allows code to instantiate a LoginContext with the specified name. name is used as the index into the installed login Configuration (returned by Configuration.getConfiguration()). name can be wildcarded (set to '*') to allow for any name	Permission javax.security.auth.AuthPermission "createLoginContext.SimpleJAASApp";

Appendix 2. Supported Algorithms Provided by SunJCE (Bundled JCE Provider)

Symmetric Encryption Algorithms provided by SunJCE

1. DES: Default key length of 56 bits

2. AES

3. RC2, RC4, and RC5

4. IDEA

5. Triple DES: Default key length of 112 bits

6. Blowfish: Default key length of 56 bits

7. PBEWithMD5AndDES

8. PBEWithHmacSHA1AndDESede

9. DES ede

Modes of encryption

1. ECB

2. CBC

3. CFB

4. OFB

5. PCBC

Asymmetric Encryption Algorithms implemented by SunJCE

1. RSA

2. Diffie-Hellman: Default key length of 1024 bits

Hashing/Message Digest Algorithms implemented by SunJCE

1. MD5: Default size of 64 bytes

2. SHA1: Default size of 64 bytes

Appendix 3. Supported Algorithms by Bouncy Castle

Symmetric Encryption Algorithms provided by SunJCE

1. AES

2. Blowfish

3. DES

4. 3DES

5. IDEA

6. Serpent

7. Twofish

8. RC6

Modes of encryption

1. ECB

2. CBC

3. CFB

4. OFB

5. OCB

6. CCM

7. GCM

8. EAX

Asymmetric Encryption Algorithms implemented by SunJCE

1. RSA

2. Diffie-Hellman

3. El Gamal

4. Elliptic Curve Cryptography

Hashing/Message Digest Algorithms implemented by SunJCE

1. SHA-2

2. MD5

411

CHAPTER 7

Jakarta EE Implementations

Overview

In the previous chapter, we had a look at several security features and mechanisms that Java SE supports under the hood.

Having done the necessary introductions, this chapter discusses and demonstrates the most prevalent implementations for Jakarta EE.

We start off with a close look at the findings of the 2021 Jakarta EE Developer Survey, and then we showcase prevailing open source implementations like GlassFish, WildFly, Open Liberty, and Tomcat/TomEE alongside their features.

Specification Usage

A 2021 survey by Arjan Tijms showed that Jakarta EE 8 has already gained quite some usage with around 40% using it either exclusively or alongside other versions of Jakarta EE and Java EE.

© Arjan Tijms, Teo Bais, and Werner Keil 2022
A. Tijms et al., *The Definitive Guide to Security in Jakarta EE*, https://doi.org/10.1007/978-1-4842-7945-8_7

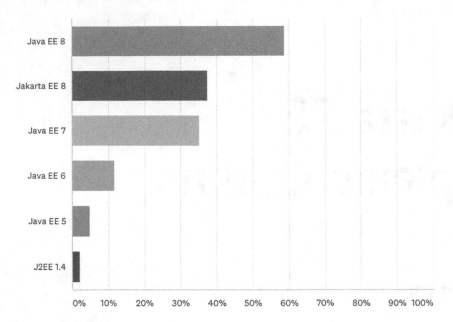

Figure 7-1. *Usage of Java EE/Jakarta EE versions*

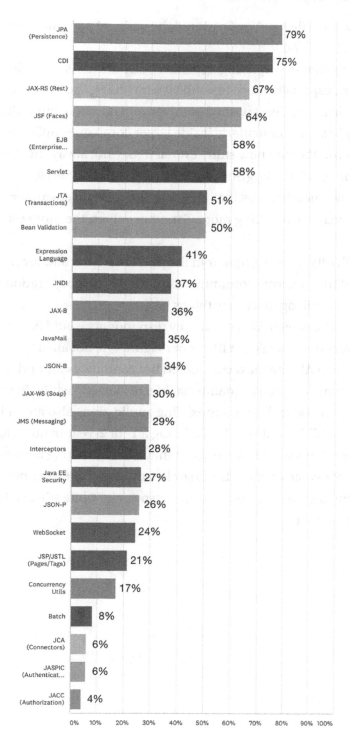

Figure 7-2. *Usage of Java EE/Jakarta EE APIs*

Another question in that survey answered the usage of particular Java EE or Jakarta EE APIs as seen in Figure 7-2.

The top three are not so surprising, especially CDI, which is used alongside many other specs. Others, especially those beyond 50% including Faces, JTA, or EJB were often proclaimed dead or at least wished archived and optional, but it shows in real life Enterprise applications particularly inside larger companies unlike marketing and PR that try to focus on the "hot new stuff" even if it may not always be that mature, traditional technologies including Servlets, EJB, or SOAP Web Services are still widely used and trusted over new features that may be offered to end customers, but in business-critical areas like handling money or other values, the more established APIs are still dominant.

So while REST APIs are very popular in the public Internet and for B2C communication, B2B or internal communication inside one cooperation is often a lot less adventurous and willing to try new things fast.

However, looking at which APIs the survey respondents would like to see updated most in the next version(s) of Jakarta EE, as per Figure 7-3, not all of the top ten most widely used specs and APIs are also considered hot candidates for updates and improvement. So some are seen as mature, stable, or "legacy" while they are still widely used across the enterprise and for many existing applications also aren't likely to go away even in Jakarta EE 15 or above. Considering a 1- or 2-year major release cycle most of the survey respondents would like to see, it may not be too long before Jakarta EE 15. And while some APIs could become frozen or legacy, possibly even optional for the Full Jakarta EE Platform, they are unlikely to vanish especially while still used by over a third of all applications or more.

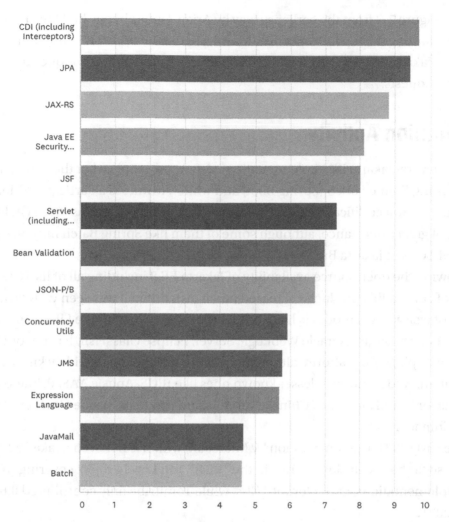

Figure 7-3. *APIs most liked to be updated in the next version(s) of Jakarta EE*

The 2021 Jakarta EE Developer Survey included feedback about the specifications that received the most feature requests (most popular specifications identified by respondents).

Figure 7-4. *Top four specifications with most feature requests from 2021 Jakarta EE Developer Survey*

While Figure 7-3 from the earlier survey by Arjan Tijms already had Java EE Security at the time among the top four specifications desired to be updated in upcoming versions of Jakarta EE, the 2021 Jakarta EE Developer Survey saw it conquer the top spot by feature requests.

Contribution Activity

There are several Jakarta EE implementations. A few only apply what they find suitable like the Spring Framework or Spring Boot, and while VMware is a Participant Member of Jakarta EE, a full certification of any frameworks or products against the TCK has not been of great importance, although some of them like Spring Batch may well pass individual TCKs of Jakarta Batch.

Following the open source availability of Jakarta EE 8 including all of its TCKs, the number of compatible products increased much faster than it was seen with Java EE 6–8. A bunch of well-known products like Red Hat JBoss, IBM WebSphere Liberty including the Open Liberty project, Oracle WebLogic Server, Eclipse GlassFish, Payara, or FUJITSU Enterprise Application Platform, although the latter may not be so widely known outside Asia or Japan. And some even lesser known ones like JEUS, Apusic AAS, Primeton AppServer, or Thunisoft AS, all Chinese vendors and products maybe almost unknown outside China.

Since early 2021, the contribution by Microsoft, which is not even a Jakarta EE WG member, so far has been close to 10% in the "EE4J" Top Level Project covering API, many implementations, and relevant TCKs, while Tomitribe only contributed 0.6% in January 2021.

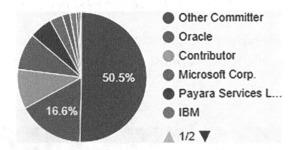

Figure 7-5. *Eclipse EE4J Organization Contribution Activity, January 2021 (1/2)*

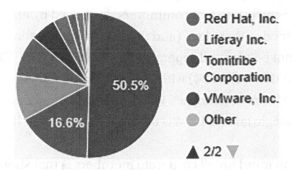

Figure 7-6. *Eclipse EE4J Organization Contribution Activity, January 2021 (2/2)*

Toward the end of 2021 in late December, this changed with relatively new Jakarta EE participant member ManageCat LLC holding the last place behind Microsoft at 0.4%, so it contributed less than that, while Tomitribe even fell out of the list and got subsumed as "Others," which means it contributed less than 0.1%.

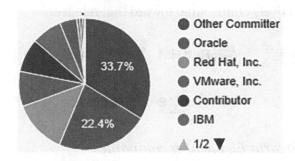

Figure 7-7. *Eclipse EE4J Organization Contribution Activity, December 2021 (1/2)*

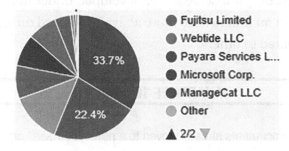

Figure 7-8. *Eclipse EE4J Organization Contribution Activity, December 2021 (2/2)*

While contributions by individual committers decreased by around 15% within the year 2021, it still remained at first place (and the "Contributor" slice is somewhat fuzzy and probably should not be counted separately, but together with "Other Committer," which, combined, would be over 40%) with Oracle second, followed by Red Hat. Others led by Spring maker VMware at nearly 9% with only single-digit percentages, making Tomitribe the only strategic Jakarta EE WG member contributing less than 0.1% in the course of Q4/2021.

One thing to keep in mind for all corporate members is that should their employees contribute using a personal or free mail account like Google Mail, Hotmail/Outlook, etc., then they may not always be properly associated to their company but instead fall under "Other Committer" or "Contributor."

Figure 7-9 shows the active Jakarta EE member companies in late 2021. Also, a noteworthy time because Jakarta EE 9.1 was in the pipeline toward a release candidate and eventual finalization, so while only a snapshot, it shows which committers and member companies actively contributed toward that release.

Figure 7-9. *Active Jakarta EE member companies*

Of course, implementations maintained elsewhere are not counted here, but it applies to almost every of these companies, Red Hat, Oracle, IBM, Payara, or VMware, because GlassFish is the only full-scale server developed under the "EE4J" umbrella, so it provides a feeling which members were more actively involved during the development of Jakarta EE 9.1 compared to others.

JAKARTA EE 10 LOOKOUT

After the specification documents already moved to a new "jakartaee" organization in GitHub, the specification projects themselves also relocate from "EE4J" on the path toward a Jakarta EE 10 finalization. Although there is just one Eclipse TLD (`https://projects.eclipse.org/projects/ee4j`) so far, contributions to both GitHub organizations are counted and allocated to the member companies as long as committers use their corporate accounts.

Implementation Usage

The 2021 Jakarta EE Developer Survey showed Spring Framework in most cases via Spring Boot is the predominant Java Enterprise/Web Application framework, used by 60% of the respondents, up 16% compared to 2020. Jakarta EE also gained 12% coming second at 47%, so nearly half of all who took the survey use Jakarta EE. MicroProfile also went up 5% now at 34% usage, leaving Micronaut and Dropwizard in the single-digit region.

Of course, one must not forget that while Spring, Dropwizard, and Micronaut offer a sometimes more intuitive and convenient approach for developers at the cost of more vendor lock-in compared to using the Jakarta EE specs directly or via a "microservice layer" like MicroProfile, all of the mentioned frameworks are at least partly based on Jakarta EE or Java EE. From version 6 onward, the Spring stack will be based on Jakarta EE 9.1, and VMware's contribution activity shows it contributed to Jakarta EE almost as much as other vendors like Oracle and Red Hat in the course of 2021.

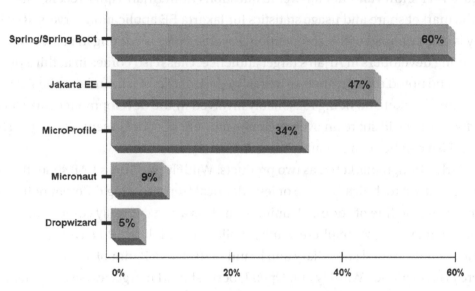

Figure 7-10. *Java frameworks according to the Jakarta EE 2021 Developer Survey*

Following a comparison of the ten most relevant Java EE servers Arjan Tijms had published in May 2014, he repeated this analysis again about a year ago for Jakarta EE.

A few things have changed over the years. Of the initial top ten implementations:

- JBoss/WildFly

- Eclipse GlassFish

- Oracle WebLogic

- Apache Geronimo

- Apache/Tomitribe TomEE

- IBM WebSphere

- IBM WebSphere Liberty

- TmaxSoft JEUS

- Caucho Resin

- OW2 JOnAS

several vanished or play almost no role when it comes to market share or Jakarta EE certification nowadays.

Figure 7-11 shows another answer to questions from Arjan Tijms' recent survey about the market share and usage statistics for Jakarta EE application servers. Red Hat's WildFly is clearly ahead of the competition. Payara Server is coming in at the second place among developers in Arjan's target audience. GlassFish comes in at third place.

It must be noted that Payara is essentially a fork of GlassFish, and despite Payara gaining more market and being reasonably involved in the development of Jakarta EE (see before), they still share an overwhelming amount of code. Essentially, Payara Server and GlassFish can be seen as part of the same family.

Similarly, though marketed as two products, WildFly and JBoss EAP share the same code base and are technically more or less identical (representing different points in time on the overall line of code). Meaning TomEE as a server family comes third, in a tie with the Open Liberty/WebSphere family, similar to WildFly/EAP. Leaving aside that Red Hat is now a fully owned subsidiary and brand of IBM, like Rational and others, but so far, there is no evidence WildFly and Open Liberty should merge, at least not medium to short term.

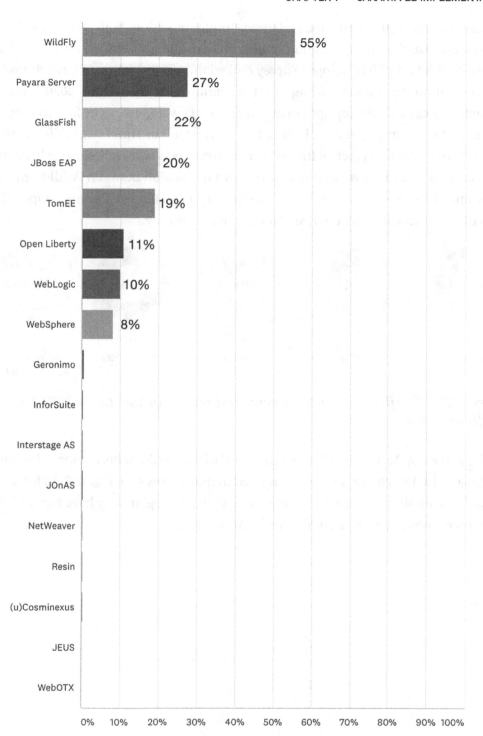

Figure 7-11. *Usage of Java EE/Jakarta EE application servers in 2020*

Besides GlassFish, the previous reference implementation, both WildFly and Open Liberty were also the first application servers that are already certified for Jakarta EE 9.

The 2021 Jakarta EE Developer Survey ranked the top five Jakarta EE runtimes/ implementations by usage. Showing a partial overlap with Arjan Tijms' 2020 survey, although Tomcat took the top spot in the Jakarta EE Developer Survey followed by WildFly and newcomer Quarkus. Eclipse Jetty also wasn't in Tijms' list, while the usage of JBoss EAP in the fifth place of the Jakarta EE survey was relatively close to his earlier one. As the Jakarta EE Developer Survey makes a distinction between WildFly and EAP, it clearly must have counted TomEE separate from Tomcat, but like Payara or OpenLiberty, it also did not make it to the top five of the Jakarta EE survey.

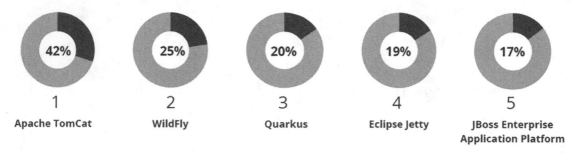

Figure 7-12. *Top five runtimes/implementations according to the 2021 Jakarta EE Developer Survey*

The survey by Arjan Tijms had about a third of the participants compared to the 2021 Jakarta EE Developer Survey. Compared to that survey (see Figure 7-13 for a regional distribution), participants from the Asia Pacific region may have been a little underrepresented in the one conducted by Arjan Tijms.

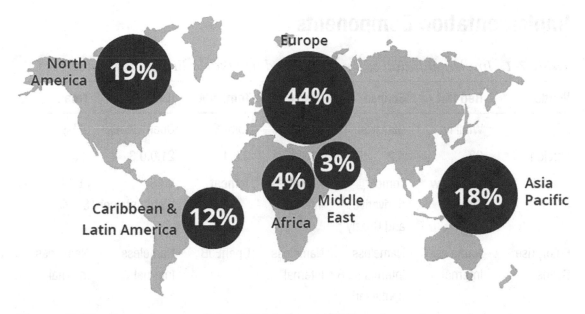

Figure 7-13. *Participants of the 2021 Jakarta EE Developer Survey by region*

Also, the developer audience often tends to be more open source affine, and all Jakarta EE–certified application servers from Asian countries like China, South Korea, and Japan are proprietary closed source products.

Therefore, based on the two summaries by Arjan Tijms, we also continued to include Tmax JEUS in a list of six Jakarta EE application servers or server families in Table 7-1, because both the exact market share and underlying components are very little known for proprietary products by FUJITSU, TmaxSoft, Apusic, BES, InforSuite, Primeton, TongWeb, or Thunisoft.

TomEE in Spring 2021 certified against the Jakarta EE 9.1 Web Profile, the first time since a TomEE version did against Java EE 6. Resin also remained at Java EE 6 with seemingly no plans to update these. JOnAS has disappeared off the face of the earth, and so has Geronimo as a server, although a few implementations, primarily under the hood of TomEE, still exist.

Implementation Components

Table 7-1. *Implementation components used by Jakarta EE application servers*

Vendor	Red Hat	Eclipse	Oracle	Tomitribe	IBM	Tmax
AS	WildFly	GlassFish	WebLogic	TomEE	Open Liberty	JEUS
Version	23	6.2	14.1.1	8.0.1	21.0.0.3	8.5
Servlet	Undertow Servlet	Tomcat derivative and Grizzly *	Nameless Internal	Tomcat	WAS WebContainer	JEUS Servlet
Enterprise Beans	Nameless Internal	Nameless Internal (EJB container)	Nameless Internal	OpenEJB	Nameless Internal	Nameless Internal
Connectors	IronJacamar	Nameless Internal (Connectors-runtime)	Nameless Internal	Geronimo Connector	Nameless Internal	Nameless Internal
Authentication	Part of Elytron	Jaspic provider (part of GlassFish)	Part of WebLogic Security	Part of Tomcat	Nameless Internal	Nameless Internal
Authorization	Part of Elytron	Exousia inside GlassFish	Part of WebLogic Security	Part of Tomcat	Nameless Internal	Nameless Internal
Transactions	Narayana	Nameless Internal	Nameless Internal	Geronimo Transaction	Nameless Internal	JEUS Transaction Manager
Messaging	ActiveMQ Artemis	OpenMQ	WebLogic JMS	ActiveMQ Classic	Liberty messaging	JEUS JMS

(Continued)

Table 7-1. (*Continued*)

Vendor	Red Hat	Eclipse	Oracle	Tomitribe	IBM	Tmax
Concurrency	Concurrency CI	Concurrency CI	Nameless Internal (WebLogic concurrent)	Nameless Internal (part of OpenEJB-Core)	Nameless Internal	JEUS Concurrent (part of JEUS)
WebSocket	Undertow WebSocket	Tyrus	Tyrus	Tomcat WebSocket (part of Tomcat)	Liberty WebSocket	JEUS WebSocket (part of JEUS)
CDI	Weld	Weld*	Weld	Open WebBeans	Weld	Weld
Validation	Hibernate Validator	Hibernate Validator	Hibernate Validator	BVal	Hibernate Validator	Hibernate Validator
REST	RESTEasy	Jersey	Jersey	RESTEasy	RESTEasy	Jersey
Persistence	Hibernate	EclipseLink	EclipseLink	OpenJPA	EclipseLink	EclipseLink
Faces	Mojarra	Mojarra	Mojarra	MyFaces	MyFaces	Mojarra
JSON Processing	Part of GlassFish *	Part of GlassFish	Part of GlassFish *	Johnzon	Part of GlassFish *	Part of GlassFish *
JSON Binding	Yasson	Yasson	Yasson	Johnzon	Yasson	Yasson
Expression Language	EL CI jbossorg-2	EL CI	EL CI	Jasper EL (part of Tomcat)	Jasper EL	EL CI
Mail	Jakarta Mail Impl	Jakarta Mail Impl	Jakarta Mail Impl	Geronimo JavaMail	Jakarta Mail Impl	Jakarta Mail Impl
Security	Soteria jbossorg-1	Soteria	Soteria	TomEE Security	Nameless Internal	Soteria (modified)
Batch	JBeret	JBatch FRI	JBatch FRI	Geronimo BatchEE	JBatch FRI (internal copy)	JBatch FRI

Asterisk (*) behind a component name and version means the given vendor uses an implementation by another vendor.

The versions are the most recent stable/final version of each component used.

GlassFish

Eclipse Glassfish is the compatible implementation of Jakarta EE maintained by the community. The most recent implementation of Jakarta EE 9.1 is GlassFish 6.2.x

Authentication

GlassFish implements all required profiles of Jakarta Authentication including the Servlet Container Profile. GlassFish uses the Authorization SPI in specific contexts.

Passwords

Passwords are your first line of defense against unauthorized access to applications and data of Eclipse GlassFish.

Master Password and Keystores

The master password is independent from a user account and not used for authentication. Eclipse GlassFish only uses the master password to encrypt the keystore and truststore for the domain administration server (DAS) and instances.

When you create a new GlassFish domain, a new self-signed certificate is generated and stored in the domain keystore and truststore. The DAS needs the master password to open these at startup. Associated server instances also need the master password to open their copy of these stores during startup.

If you use a utility like keytool to modify the keystore or truststore, you must provide the master password there too. The master password is a shared password and must be the same for the DAS and all instances in the domain in order to manage the instances from the DAS. However, because Eclipse GlassFish never transmits the master password over the network, it is up to you to keep the master password in sync between the DAS and instances.

Understanding Master Password Synchronization

The master password is used to encrypt the keystore and truststore for the DAS and instances. The DAS needs the master password to open these stores at startup. Similarly, the associated server instances need the master password to open their copy of these stores at startup.

Eclipse GlassFish keeps the keystore and truststore for the DAS and instances in sync, which guarantees that all copies of the stores are encrypted with the same master password at a given time.

However, GlassFish does not synchronize the master password itself, and it is possible that the DAS and instances might attempt to use different master passwords.

If you do use a master password file, you assume the responsibility for using the change-master-password subcommand on the DAS and instances to keep the master password file in sync.

Default Master Password

Eclipse GlassFish uses the known phrase "changeit" as the default master password. This master password is not stored in a file. The default password is a convenience feature and provides no additional security because it is assumed to be widely known.

All Eclipse GlassFish subcommands work as expected with the default master password, and there are no synchronization issues.

Warning   While you find the default password as a convenience feature for development and research, nobody in their sane minds would use those kinds of things in a production environment.

Rudimentary, manual master password synchronization is also something that makes running Eclipse GlassFish in the Cloud, especially distributed around the globe, cumbersome, but that's not what GlassFish was intended for.

There are several vendors offering distributions of GlassFish itself or products based on it like ManageFish or Payara, which are production ready and provide improved master password synchronization among other things.

Saving the Master Password to a File

The `change-master-password --savemasterpassword` option indicates whether the master password should be written to the file system in the master-password file for the DAS or a node. The default is `false`.

For a domain, the master password is kept in `domain-dir/master-password`.

On a node, the master password file is kept in `nodes/node-name/agent/master-password`. You can set a master password at the node level, and all instances created on that node will use that `master-password` file. To do this, use the `--nodedir` option and provide a node name.

You might want to save the master password to the file so that the `start-domain` subcommand can start the server without having to prompt for the password. There are additional options for using a master password with the `start-instance` and `start-cluster` subcommands.

The `master-password` file is encoded, not encrypted. You must use file system encryption to protect it.

Using the Master Password Creating a Domain

The `create-domain --usemasterpassword` option specifies whether the keystore is encrypted with a master password that is built into the system, or by a user-defined master password.

If `false` (default), the keystore is encrypted with the default master password of Eclipse GlassFish.

If `true`, the subcommand obtains the master password from the `AS_ADMIN_MASTERPASSWORD` entry in the password file you specified in the `--passwordfile` option of the `asadmin` command. Or if none is defined, `--usemasterpassword` prompts the user for the master password.

Administration Password

An administration password, also known as the admin password, is used to invoke the administration console and the `asadmin` command. As with the default admin username, the default admin password is usually set during installation, but it can be changed later.

Encoded Passwords

Files that contain encoded passwords need to be protected using file system permissions. These include the following:

- `domain-dir/master-password`

  This file contains the encoded master password and should be protected with file system permission 600 (Linux).

- Any password file created to pass as an argument by using the `--passwordfile` argument of the `asadmin` command should be protected with file system permissions. Also, any password file being used for a temporary purpose, like as setting up SSH for nodes, should be deleted after usage.

Web Browsers and Password Storage

Most web browsers can save login credentials entered through HTML forms. This function can be customized. If the function is enabled, then credentials entered by a user are stored on their local system and retrieved by the browser on future visits to the same web application.

This function is convenient for users but can also be a security risk. The stored credentials can be captured by an attacker who gains access to the computer, either locally or through some remote malware. A malicious website can retrieve such stored credentials for other applications by exploiting browser vulnerabilities or through application-level cross-domain attacks. To prevent your web browser from saving login credentials for the Eclipse GlassFish admin console, choose "No" or "Never for this page" when prompted by the browser during login.

Authentication Realms

An authentication realm, also called security policy domain or security domain, is a scope by which Eclipse GlassFish defines a common security policy. "Realm," just like with other containers like Tomcat, is essentially an "Identity Store" by another name, coined before Jakarta Security was incepted. GlassFish is preconfigured with the file, certificate, and administration realms.

Including those, the following authentication realms can be used:

- File realm

- Administration realm

- Certificate realm

- LDAP realm

- JDBC realm

- Oracle Solaris realm

- PAM realm

- Custom realm

Create an Authentication Realm

To create an authentication realm, use the `create-auth-realm` subcommand in remote mode.

1. Ensure the server is running; remote subcommands only work with a running server.

2. Create a realm via `create-auth-realm` subcommand.

See the following example for creating a realm named "db":

```
asadmin> create-auth-realm --classname com.iplanet.ias.security.
auth.realm.DB.Database --property defaultuser=admin:Password=admin db
Command create-auth-realm executed successfully.
```

You find the full syntax and options of the subcommand by typing `asadmin help create-auth-realm` in the command line.

List Authentication Realms

Use the `list-auth-realms` subcommand in remote mode to list the existing authentication realms.

1. Ensure the server is running; remote subcommands only work with a running server.

2. List available realms with the `list-auth-realms` subcommand.

Example of listing all authentication realms on "localhost":

```
asadmin> list-auth-realms
db
certificate
file
admin-realm
Command list-auth-realms executed successfully.
```

Update an Authentication Realm

Use the set subcommand to modify an existing authentication realm.

1. List realms using the list-auth-realms subcommand.

2. Modify values for the specified thread pool by using the set subcommand.

3. To apply changes, restart GlassFish.

Delete an Authentication Realm

Use the delete-auth-realm subcommand in remote mode to delete an existing authentication realm.

1. Ensure the server is running; remote subcommands only work with a running server.

2. List realms with the list-auth-realms subcommand.

3. If necessary, notify users about the realm being deleted.

4. Delete the realm using the delete-auth-realm subcommand.

5. To apply your changes, restart Eclipse GlassFish.

Here's an example to delete the previously created realm "db":

```
asadmin> delete-auth-realm db
Command delete-auth-realm executed successfully.
```

This example shows how the user `Calvin` can be assigned the role of `Architect`

```
<glassfish-web-app>
    <security-role-mapping>
        <role-name>Architect</role-name>
        <principal-name>Calvin</principal-name>
    </security-role-mapping>
</glassfish-web-app>
```

Exousia

Eclipse Exousia 1.0 implements Jakarta Authorization version 2.0. It provides default implementations of these authorization modules and algorithms, as defined and mandated by the Jakarta Authorization specification. It provides a low-level SPI for authorization modules, which are repositories of permissions facilitating subject-based security by determining whether a given subject has a matching permission, and algorithms to transform security constraints for specific containers (like Jakarta Servlet, REST, or Enterprise Beans) into these permissions.

From GlassFish 6.2.1 onward, Exousia is the GlassFish Authorization subsystem, but Exousia can also serve the same purpose for other containers, for example, Piranha Cloud, which has special provisions for Tomcat too.

Configuring Exousia in GlassFish

By default, Eclipse GlassFish provides a simple, in-memory authorization engine that implements the Jakarta Authorization specification.

Eclipse GlassFish includes both administration console support and CRUD-like CLI commands to maintain Jakarta Authorization providers:

- create: `create-jacc-provider`

- delete: `delete-jacc-provider`

- list: `list-jacc-providers`

JACC (Java Authorization Contract for Containers) was an older term for what's now Jakarta Authorization. Eclipse GlassFish by default includes two Jakarta Authorization providers named "default" and "simple." You should not delete those default providers.

You can add new authorization providers using the `create-jacc-provider` subcommand. Each authorization provider is stored as a `jacc-provider` element under `security-service` of the domain's `domain.xml` file.

Manage Authorization Providers from the Admin Console

To use the GlassFish admin console to manage authorization providers, perform the following steps:

1. Select "Configurations" and expand the entry.

2. Select the server configuration for which you want to administer authorization providers and expand the selection.

3. Select "Security" and expand the entry.

4. Select "JACC Providers"; the JACC providers (authorization providers) page is displayed, showing existing authorization providers.

5. To create a new provider, click "New."

6. Enter name, policy configuration, and provider for the new provider as well as optional properties.

7. To delete an existing authorization provider, select that provider and click "Delete."

JACC Providers

Manage Java Authorization Contract for Containers (JACC) providers.

Configuration Name: server-config

JACC Providers (2)		
Select	Name	Policy Provider
☐	default	org.glassfish.exousia.modules.locked.SimplePolicyProvider
☐	simple	org.glassfish.exousia.modules.locked.SimplePolicyProvider

Figure 7-14. *Manage Jakarta Authorization (JACC) providers in admin console*

Manage Authorization Providers from the Command Line

To use the CLI to manage Jakarta Authorization providers, perform the following steps:

1. To create an authorization provider, use the `create-jacc-provider` subcommand of `asadmin`; see the following example:

```
asadmin> create-jacc-provider
        --policyproviderclass org.glassfish.exousia.modules.locked.
        SimplePolicyProvider
        --policyconfigfactoryclass com.sun.enterprise.security.
        provider.PolicyConfigurationFactoryImpl
testAuthorization
```

2. To delete an authorization provider, use the `delete-jacc-provider` subcommand; see this example:

```
asadmin> delete-jacc-provider testAuthorization
```

3. To list available providers, use the `list-jacc-providers` subcommand; see the following example:

```
asadmin> list-jacc-providers
default
simple
Command list-jacc-providers executed successfully.
```

Using Exousia with Tomcat

Exousia recently added integration support specifically for Tomcat so that all you need to do is add it as a dependency. To use Exousia and Jakarta Security in Tomcat, create a Maven project with the following dependencies:

```
<dependency>
    <groupId>jakarta.platform</groupId>
    <artifactId>jakarta.jakartaee-api</artifactId>
    <version>9.1.0</version>
    <scope>provided</scope>
</dependency>
```

```xml
<dependency>
    <groupId>org.glassfish.soteria</groupId>
    <artifactId>jakarta.security.enterprise</artifactId>
    <version>2.0.1</version>
</dependency>

<dependency>
    <groupId>org.glassfish.exousia</groupId>
    <artifactId>exousia</artifactId>
    <version>1.0.0</version>
</dependency>

<dependency>
    <groupId>org.jboss.weld.servlet</groupId>
    <artifactId>weld-servlet-shaded</artifactId>
    <version>4.0.0.Final</version>
</dependency>
```

Since Tomcat has a read-only JNDI, a file in [war root]/META-INF/context.xml is required with the following content to make the BeanManager available:

```xml
<?xml version='1.0' encoding='utf-8'?>
<Context>
    <Resource
        name="BeanManager"
        auth="Container"
        type="jakarta.enterprise.inject.spi.BeanManager"
        factory="org.jboss.weld.resources.ManagerObjectFactory"
    />
</Context>
```

Then you have to add the following classes:

```java
@BasicAuthenticationMechanismDefinition(realmName = "realm")
@ServletSecurity(value = @HttpConstraint(rolesAllowed = "g1"))
@WebServlet(urlPatterns = "/SecureServlet")
public class SecureServlet extends HttpServlet {

    private static final long serialVersionUID = 1L;
```

```java
    @Inject
    SecurityContext securityContext;

    @Override
    protected void doGet(HttpServletRequest request, HttpServletResponse
    response)
    throws ServletException, IOException {
        response.getWriter().println(
            "Has access to /foo/bar " +
            securityContext.hasAccessToWebResource("/foo/bar", "GET"));
        response.getWriter().println(
            "Has access to /foox/bar " +
            securityContext.hasAccessToWebResource("/foox/bar", "GET"));
    }
}
```

and

```java
@ApplicationScoped
public class MyIdentityStore implements IdentityStore {
    public CredentialValidationResult validate(UsernamePasswordCredential
    usernamePasswordCredential) {
        if (usernamePasswordCredential.compareTo("u1", "p1")) {
            return new CredentialValidationResult("u1", new
            HashSet<>(asList("g1")));
        }

        return INVALID_RESULT;
    }
}
```

Call your web app "security-test" and deploy it to Tomcat 10, call "http://
localhost:8080/security-test/SecureServlet" in a web browser, and you'll get a
basic authentication dialog. Enter username "u1" and password "p1" to see the following
response:

```
Has access to /foo/bar true
Has access to /foox/bar false
```

Behind the scenes, Jakarta Security installed a `ServerAuthModule` into Tomcat using Weld to look up a CDI bean with the `@BasicAuthenticationMechanismDefinition` annotation. This bean then calls our `IdentityStore` implementation `MyIdentityStore` to validate the provided credentials. Besides that, Exousia copied the security constraints collected by Tomcat to a Jakarta Authorization module, which is a Permission Store, queried by Jakarta Authorization.

```
package org.glassfish.exousia.spi.tomcat;

import static jakarta.servlet.annotation.ServletSecurity.
TransportGuarantee.CONFIDENTIAL;
import static jakarta.servlet.annotation.ServletSecurity.
TransportGuarantee.NONE;
import static java.util.Arrays.asList;
import static java.util.Collections.emptyMap;
import static org.apache.catalina.authenticator.Constants.REQ_JASPIC_
SUBJECT_NOTE;

import java.lang.reflect.Field;
import java.util.ArrayList;
import java.util.HashSet;
import java.util.List;

import javax.security.auth.Subject;

import org.apache.catalina.Context;
import org.apache.catalina.connector.Request;
import org.apache.catalina.connector.RequestFacade;
import org.apache.catalina.webresources.StandardRoot;
import org.apache.tomcat.util.descriptor.web.SecurityCollection;
import org.apache.tomcat.util.descriptor.web.SecurityConstraint;
import org.glassfish.exousia.AuthorizationService;
import org.glassfish.exousia.constraints.WebResourceCollection;

import jakarta.servlet.ServletContext;
import jakarta.servlet.ServletException;
```

```
import jakarta.servlet.ServletRequest;
import jakarta.servlet.ServletRequestEvent;
import jakarta.servlet.ServletRequestListener;
import jakarta.servlet.ServletRequestWrapper;
import jakarta.servlet.http.HttpFilter;
import jakarta.servlet.http.HttpServletRequest;

/**
 *
 * @author Arjan Tijms
 *
 */
public class TomcatAuthorizationFilter extends HttpFilter implements
ServletRequestListener {

    private static final long serialVersionUID = 1L;

    public static ThreadLocal<HttpServletRequest> localServletRequest = new
    ThreadLocal<>();

    @Override
    public void init() throws ServletException {
        ServletContext servletContext = getFilterConfig().
        getServletContext();

        StandardRoot root = (StandardRoot) servletContext.
        getAttribute("org.apache.catalina.resources");
        Context context = root.getContext();

        // Get all the security constraints from Tomcat
        SecurityConstraint[] constraints = context.findConstraints();
        List<String> declaredRoles = asList(context.findSecurityRoles());
        boolean isDenyUncoveredHttpMethods = root.getContext().
        getDenyUncoveredHttpMethods();

        AuthorizationService.setThreadContextId(servletContext);
```

```
// Initialize the AuthorizationService, which is a front-end for
Jakarta Authorization.
// It specifically tells Jakarta Authorization how to get the
current request, and the current subject
AuthorizationService authorizationService = new
AuthorizationService(
    servletContext,
    () -> getSubject(localServletRequest.get())));

authorizationService.setRequestSupplier(() ->
localServletRequest.get());

// Copy all the security constraints that Tomcat has collected to
the Jakarta Authorization
// repository as well. That way Jakarta Authorization can work with
the same data as Tomcat
// internally does.
authorizationService.addConstraintsToPolicy(
    convertTomcatConstraintsToExousia(constraints),
    new HashSet<>(declaredRoles), isDenyUncoveredHttpMethods,
    emptyMap());

}

@Override
public void requestInitialized(ServletRequestEvent sre) {
    // Sets the initial request.
    // Note that we should actually have the request used before every
    filter and Servlet that will be executed.
    localServletRequest.set((HttpServletRequest)
    sre.getServletRequest());

    // Sets the context ID in the current thread. The context ID is a
    unique name for the current web application and
    // is used by Jakarta Authorization and Exousia.
    AuthorizationService.setThreadContextId(sre.getServletContext());
}
```

441

```java
@Override
public void requestDestroyed(ServletRequestEvent sre) {
    localServletRequest.remove();
}

/**
 * Transforms the security constraints (web.xml, annotations, and
   programmatic) from the Tomcat types to Exousia types.
 *
 * @param tomcatConstraints
 * @return
 */
private List<org.glassfish.exousia.constraints.SecurityConstraint>
convertTomcatConstraintsToExousia(org.apache.tomcat.util.descriptor.
web.SecurityConstraint[] tomcatConstraints) {
    if (tomcatConstraints == null || tomcatConstraints.length == 0) {
        return null;
    }

    List<org.glassfish.exousia.constraints.SecurityConstraint>
    exousiaConstraints = new ArrayList<>();

    for (SecurityConstraint tomcatConstraint : tomcatConstraints) {

        List<WebResourceCollection> exousiaWebResourceCollections = new
        ArrayList<>();
        for (SecurityCollection tomcatSecurityCollection :
        tomcatConstraint.findCollections()) {
            exousiaWebResourceCollections.add(new
            WebResourceCollection(
                    tomcatSecurityCollection.findPatterns(),
                    tomcatSecurityCollection.findMethods(),
                    tomcatSecurityCollection.findOmittedMethods()));
        }

        exousiaConstraints.add(new org.glassfish.exousia.constraints.
        SecurityConstraint(
                exousiaWebResourceCollections,
```

```
                   new HashSet<>(asList(tomcatConstraint.
                   findAuthRoles())),
                   "confidential".equalsIgnoreCase(tomcatConstraint.
                   getUserConstraint()
                   ? CONFIDENTIAL : NONE));

    }

    return exousiaConstraints;
}

/**
 * Gets the authenticated Subject (if any) from the Tomcat specific
   location inside the HttpServletRequest instance.
 *
 * @param httpServletRequest the instance to get the Subject from
 * @return the Subject if the caller authenticated via Jakarta
   Authentication (JASPIC), otherwise null
 */
private static Subject getSubject(HttpServletRequest
httpServletRequest) {
    return (Subject) getRequest(unwrapFully(httpServletRequest)).
    getNote(REQ_JASPIC_SUBJECT_NOTE);
}


@SuppressWarnings("unchecked")
private static <T extends ServletRequest> T unwrapFully(ServletRequest
request) {
    ServletRequest currentRequest = request;
    while (currentRequest instanceof ServletRequestWrapper) {
        ServletRequestWrapper wrapper = (ServletRequestWrapper)
        currentRequest;
        currentRequest = wrapper.getRequest();
    }
    return (T) currentRequest;
}
```

```
private static Request getRequest(RequestFacade facade) {
    try {
        Field requestField = RequestFacade.class.
        getDeclaredField("request");
        requestField.setAccessible(true);

        return (Request) requestField.get(facade);
    } catch (NoSuchFieldException | SecurityException |
    IllegalArgumentException | IllegalAccessException e) {
        throw new IllegalStateException(e);
    }

}

}
```

Note   Exousia copied the security constraints from Tomcat, but Tomcat keeps its own internal repository for authorization. The assumption is that both Tomcat and Exousia perform the exact same algorithm, but there can be minor differences. A possible improvement would be to integrate Exousia further in Tomcat by wrapping the Realm and delegating methods like hasUserDataPermission, hasResourcePermission, and hasRole.

Soteria

Eclipse Soteria is the compatible implementation of Jakarta Security.

A Very Brief History

The word "Soteria" is Greek and means "rescue," "wellbeing," or "salvation."

The term was picked in a survey conducted by Werner Keil among EG members while Soteria was the RI of JSR 375. Especially in Europe, it is also used in a healthcare context, often related to clinics for psychological problems, but that was a pure coincidence. Especially after the transition to Eclipse Foundation, the legal team checked all trademarks for the term that might exist and had no concerns, while other projects, especially "Ozark" (the MVC-compatible implementation), had to be renamed to "Krazo."

Authentication Mechanisms

The foundation of the authentication mechanism implementation is `HttpAuthenticationMechanism`, which makes the respective mechanism available as a CDI bean. The implemented method `validateRequest()` returns an `AuthenticationStatus` object containing the status of that authentication. The specification provides out-of-the-box mechanisms for basic authentication and form-based authentication.

Eclipse GlassFish supports the following authentication mechanisms for deployment descriptors as mandated by the Servlet spec:

- Basic

  Uses the standard Basic Authentication Scheme described in RFC 2617. There is no encryption of credentials unless you use SSL. This type is not a secure method unless used with SSL.

- Form

  The application provides its own custom login and error pages. The communication protocol is HTTP with optional SSL. There is no encryption of user credentials unless SSL is used.

- Client-Cert

  The server authenticates the client using a public key certificate. The communication protocol is HTTPS.

- Digest

  The server authenticates a user based on a username and a password. Unlike Basic authentication, the plain text password is never sent over the network, although a hash of the password.

Jakarta Security has versions of Basic and Form that MUST match the Servlet spec, but GlassFish doesn't use them in web applications when defined in the `web.xml`, only when defined via annotations.

Here's an example for the BasicAuthenticationMechanism in Soteria:

```
package org.glassfish.soteria.mechanisms;

import static java.lang.String.format;
import static jakarta.security.enterprise.identitystore.
CredentialValidationResult.Status.VALID;
import static jakarta.xml.bind.DatatypeConverter.parseBase64Binary;
import static org.glassfish.soteria.Utils.isEmpty;

import jakarta.security.enterprise.AuthenticationException;
import jakarta.security.enterprise.AuthenticationStatus;
import jakarta.security.enterprise.authentication.mechanism.http.
BasicAuthenticationMechanismDefinition;
import jakarta.security.enterprise.authentication.mechanism.http.
HttpAuthenticationMechanism;
import jakarta.security.enterprise.authentication.mechanism.http.
HttpMessageContext;
import jakarta.security.enterprise.credential.Password;
import jakarta.security.enterprise.credential.UsernamePasswordCredential;
import jakarta.security.enterprise.identitystore.CredentialValidationResult;
import jakarta.security.enterprise.identitystore.IdentityStoreHandler;
import jakarta.servlet.http.HttpServletRequest;
import jakarta.servlet.http.HttpServletResponse;

import org.glassfish.soteria.cdi.CdiUtils;

/**
 * Authentication mechanism that authenticates using basic authentication
 *
 * @author Arjan Tijms
 *
 */
public class BasicAuthenticationMechanism implements
HttpAuthenticationMechanism {

    private final BasicAuthenticationMechanismDefinition
    basicAuthenticationMechanismDefinition;
```

```
// CDI requires a no-arg constructor to be portable
// It's only used to create the proxy
protected BasicAuthenticationMechanism() {
    basicAuthenticationMechanismDefinition = null;
}

public BasicAuthenticationMechanism(BasicAuthenticationMechanismDefinition
basicAuthenticationMechanismDefinition) {
    this.basicAuthenticationMechanismDefinition =
    basicAuthenticationMechanismDefinition;
}

    @Override
    public AuthenticationStatus validateRequest(HttpServletRequest
    request, HttpServletResponse response, HttpMessageContext
    httpMsgContext) throws AuthenticationException {

            String[] credentials = getCredentials(request);
            if (!isEmpty(credentials)) {

                IdentityStoreHandler identityStoreHandler = CdiUtils.
                getBeanReference(IdentityStoreHandler.class);

                CredentialValidationResult result =
                identityStoreHandler.validate(
                new UsernamePasswordCredential(credentials[0], new
                Password(credentials[1])));

                if (result.getStatus() == VALID) {
                    return httpMsgContext.notifyContainerAboutLogin(
                        result.getCallerPrincipal(),
                        result.getCallerGroups());
                            }
                }

                    if (httpMsgContext.isProtected()) {
                            response.setHeader("WWW-Authenticate",
                            format("Basic realm=\"%s\"", basic
                            AuthenticationMechanismDefinition.
                            realmName()));
```

```
                            return httpMsgContext.responseUnauthorized();
            }

            return httpMsgContext.doNothing();
        }

        private String[] getCredentials(HttpServletRequest request) {

            String authorizationHeader = request.
            getHeader("Authorization");
            if (!isEmpty(authorizationHeader) && authorizationHeader.
            startsWith("Basic ") ) {
                    return new String(parseBase64Binary(
                    authorizationHeader.substring(6))).split(":");
            }
            return null;

        }

}
```

Supported Runtimes

Soteria runs on the following Jakarta EE CI runtimes:

- GlassFish

- Payara

- WildFly

- Open Liberty

In addition, all implementations that use Soteria under "Implementation Components" run or contain it.

With some adjustments, it also runs on TomEE, but since TomEE 9+ and Open Liberty come with their own implementations of Jakarta Security (not based on Soteria), those can be a little more complicated.

Example Configuration

Here's an example configuration of Eclipse GlassFish in the `security-service` section of the `domain.xml` configuration file:

```
<security-service>

    <!-- Identity Stores -->
    <auth-realm classname="com.sun.enterprise.security.auth.realm.file.
    FileRealm" name="admin-realm">
        <property name="file" value="${com.sun.aas.instanceRoot}/config/
        admin-keyfile"></property>
        <property name="jaas-context" value="fileRealm"></property>
    </auth-realm>
    <auth-realm classname="com.sun.enterprise.security.auth.realm.file.
    FileRealm" name="file">
        <property name="file" value="${com.sun.aas.instanceRoot}/config/
        keyfile"></property>
        <property name="jaas-context" value="fileRealm"></property>
    </auth-realm>
    <auth-realm classname="com.sun.enterprise.security.auth.realm.
    certificate.CertificateRealm" name="certificate">
    </auth-realm>

    <!-- Authorization modules -->
    <jacc-provider policy-provider="org.glassfish.exousia.modules.
    locked.SimplePolicyProvider" name="default" policy-configuration-
    factory-provider="org.glassfish.exousia.modules.locked.
    SimplePolicyConfigurationFactory">
<property name="repository" value="${com.sun.aas.instanceRoot}/generated/
policy" />
    </jacc-provider>
    <jacc-provider policy-provider="org.glassfish.exousia.modules.
    locked.SimplePolicyProvider" name="simple" policy-configuration-
    factory-provider="org.glassfish.exousia.modules.locked.
    SimplePolicyConfigurationFactory" />
```

```
<audit-module classname="com.sun.enterprise.security.ee.Audit"
name="default">
    <property name="auditOn" value="false"></property>
  </audit-module>

  <!-- Authentication Mechanisms -->
  <message-security-config auth-layer="SOAP">
    <provider-config provider-type="client" provider-id="XWS_
    ClientProvider" class-name="com.sun.xml.wss.provider.
    ClientSecurityAuthModule">
      <request-policy auth-source="content"></request-policy>
      <response-policy auth-source="content"></response-policy>
      <property name="encryption.key.alias" value="s1as"></property>
      <property name="signature.key.alias" value="s1as"></property>
      <property name="dynamic.username.password" value="false">
      </property>
      <property name="debug" value="false"></property>
    </provider-config>
    <provider-config provider-type="client" provider-id=
    "ClientProvider" class-name="com.sun.xml.wss.provider.
    ClientSecurityAuthModule">
      <request-policy auth-source="content"></request-policy>
      <response-policy auth-source="content"></response-policy>
      <property name="encryption.key.alias" value="s1as"></property>
      <property name="signature.key.alias" value="s1as"></property>
      <property name="dynamic.username.password" value="false">
      </property>
      <property name="debug" value="false"></property>
      <property name="security.config" value="${com.sun.aas.
      instanceRoot}/config/wss-server-config-1.0.xml"></property>
    </provider-config>
    <provider-config provider-type="server" provider-id="XWS_
    ServerProvider" class-name="com.sun.xml.wss.provider.
    ServerSecurityAuthModule">
      <request-policy auth-source="content"></request-policy>
      <response-policy auth-source="content"></response-policy>
```

```
            <property name="encryption.key.alias" value="s1as"></property>
            <property name="signature.key.alias" value="s1as"></property>
            <property name="debug" value="false"></property>
        </provider-config>
        <provider-config provider-type="server" provider-id=
        "ServerProvider" class-name="com.sun.xml.wss.provider.
        ServerSecurityAuthModule">
            <request-policy auth-source="content"></request-policy>
            <response-policy auth-source="content"></response-policy>
            <property name="encryption.key.alias" value="s1as"></property>
            <property name="signature.key.alias" value="s1as"></property>
            <property name="debug" value="false"></property>
            <property name="security.config" value="${com.sun.aas.
            instanceRoot}/config/wss-server-config-1.0.xml"></property>
        </provider-config>
    </message-security-config>
    <message-security-config auth-layer="HttpServlet">
        <provider-config provider-type="server" provider-id=
        "GFConsoleAuthModule" class-name="org.glassfish.admingui.common.
        security.AdminConsoleAuthModule">
            <request-policy auth-source="sender"></request-policy>
            <response-policy></response-policy>
            <property name="loginPage" value="/login.jsf"></property>
            <property name="loginErrorPage" value="/loginError.jsf">
            </property>
        </provider-config>
    </message-security-config>
    <property name="default-digest-algorithm" value="SHA-256">
    </property>
</security-service>
```

WildFly

Authentication

Starting with WildFly 18, Elytron implements the Servlet profile of Jakarta Authentication. For the Jakarta Authentication implementation to be enabled for a web application, the web application needs to be associated with either an Elytron http-authentication-factory or a security-domain.

This enables Elytron security handlers for the deployed applications and activates the Elytron security framework.

When the Elytron security framework is activated for a deployed application, the globally registered AuthConfigFactory is called when requests are handled. It checks if an AuthConfigProvider implementation has been registered for the particular deployment. If an AuthConfigProvider is found, then Jakarta Authentication will be used; if no AuthConfigProvider is found, then the authentication configuration for the deployment will be used instead. This could result in one of these options:

- Using authentication mechanisms by authentication-factory.

- Using mechanisms defined in web.xml.

- The application does not use any authentication.

To authenticate a Jakarta Authentication provider, add an <authentication-jaspi> element to your security domain as seen in the following example:

```
<authentication-jaspi>
    <login-module-stack name="...">
      <login-module code="..." flag="...">
        <module-option name="..." value="..."/>
      </login-module>
    </login-module-stack>
    <auth-module code="..." login-module-stack-ref="...">
      <module-option name="..." value="..."/>
    </auth-module>
</authentication-jaspi>
```

The login module is also configured that way as a standard authentication module. So far, the web-based administration console does not allow to configure JASPI authentication modules; therefore, you have to stop WildFly and manually add the configuration to the WILDFLY_HOME /domain/configuration/domain.xml or WILDFLY_HOME/standalone/configuration/standalone.xml files.

Updates to AuthConfigFactory are immediately available without having to redeploy your applications.

All web applications deployed to WildFly/JBoss EAP contain a security domain resolved in the following order:

1. From deployment descriptors or annotations in the deployed applications

2. A value defined in the default-security-domain in the Elytron subsystem

3. Default to other

To make an AuthConfigProvider available for your deployed application, register a jaspi-configuration in the Elytron subsystem.

ServerAuthModule

The following example contains two ServerAuthModule definitions:

```
/subsystem=elytron/jaspi-configuration=simple-configuration:add(layer=Http
Servlet, application-context="default-host /webctx", description="Elytron
Test Configuration", server-auth-modules=[{class-name=org.wildfly.security.
examples.jaspi.SimpleServerAuthModule, module=org.wildfly.security.
examples.jaspi, flag=OPTIONAL, options={a=b, c=d}}, {class-name=org.
wildfly.security.examples.jaspi.SecondServerAuthModule, module=org.wildfly.
security.examples.jaspi}])
```

This results in the following configuration:

```
<jaspi>
    <jaspi-configuration name="simple-configuration" layer="HttpServlet"
    application-context="default-host /webctx" description="Elytron Test
    Configuration">
        <server-auth-modules>
```

```
            <server-auth-module class-name="org.wildfly.security.examples.
            jaspi.SimpleServerAuthModule" module="org.wildfly.security.
            examples.jaspi" flag="OPTIONAL">
                    <options>
                            <property name="a" value="b"/>
                            <property name="c" value="d"/>
                    </options>
            </server-auth-module>
            <server-auth-module class-name="org.wildfly.security.examples.
            jaspi.SecondServerAuthModule" module="org.wildfly.security.
            examples.jaspi"/>
        </server-auth-modules>
    </jaspi-configuration>
</jaspi>
```

Within that configuration, one or more `server-auth-module` sections can be defined with the following attributes:

`class-name`: The fully qualified class name of the `ServerAuthModule`

`module`: The module to load the `ServerAuthModule` from

flag: The control flag to indicate how this module operates in relation to the other modules

`options`: Configuration options to be passed into the `ServerAuthModule` on initialization

A configuration defined that way is immediately registered with the `AuthConfigFactory`. Any existing deployments using Elytron, matching the layer and `application-context`, will immediately start making use of this configuration, without the need to restart the server.

Programmatic Configuration

Jakarta Authentication allows applications to dynamically register custom `AuthConfigProvider` implementations, but the specification does not provide the actual implementations to be used or a standard way to create instances of these implementations. Elytron contains a simple utility that deployments can use.

The following example demonstrates how to use this API to register a configuration:

```
String registrationId = org.wildfly.security.auth.jaspi.
JaspiConfigurationBuilder.builder("HttpServlet", servletContext.
getVirtualServerName() + " " + servletContext.getContextPath())
    .addAuthModuleFactory(SimpleServerAuthModule::new, Flag.OPTIONAL,
    Collections.singletonMap("a", "b"))
    .addAuthModuleFactory(SecondServerAuthModule::new)
.register();
```

The code could be executed in the init() method of a Servlet to register the AuthConfigProvider specific to that deployment. The application context has also been assembled by referring to the ServletContext.

The register() method returns the resulting registration ID that can be used to remove this registration directly from the AuthConfigFactory.

Authorization

WildFly and JBoss EAP based on it implement Jakarta Authorization within the Elytron security subsystem.

To configure Jakarta Authorization for your WildFly security domain, modify your jboss-web.xml to include the required parameters. Add the Jakarta authorization policy to the authorization stack of the security domain, with the required flag.

See the following example:

```
<security-domain name="jacc" cache-type="default">
    <authentication>
        <login-module code="UsersRoles" flag="required">
        </login-module>
    </authentication>
    <authorization>
        <policy-module code="JACC" flag="required"/>
    </authorization>
</security-domain>
```

The `jboss-web.xml` file is located in the `WEB-INF` directory of your web application and contains JBoss-specific configuration for the web container. To Jakarta Authorization-enable your security domain, you need to include the `<security-domain>` element and set the `<use-jboss-authorization>` element to true. See the following XML:

```
<jboss-web>
    <security-domain>jacc</security-domain>
    <use-jboss-authorization>true</use-jboss-authorization>
</jboss-web>
```

Configuring Jakarta Enterprise Beans to use a security domain and to use Jakarta Authorization differs from web applications. For Jakarta Enterprise Beans, you can declare method permissions on a method or group of methods, in the `ejb-jar.xml` descriptor. Within the `<ejb-jar>` element, child `<method-permission>` elements contain information about Jakarta Authorization roles.

See this example configuration:

```
<ejb-jar>
  <assembly-descriptor>
    <method-permission>
      <description>The employee and temp-employee roles can access any
      method of the EmployeeService bean </description>
      <role-name>employee</role-name>
      <role-name>temp-employee</role-name>
      <method>
        <ejb-name>EmployeeService</ejb-name>
        <method-name>*</method-name>
      </method>
    </method-permission>
  </assembly-descriptor>
</ejb-jar>
```

You can also apply authentication and authorization mechanisms for a Jakarta Enterprise Beans by using a security domain, just as you can do for a web application. Security domains are declared in `jboss-ejb3.xml` descriptor under the `<security>` child element. In addition to the security domain, you can also specify `<run-as-principal>`, which changes the principal, Jakarta Enterprise Beans run as.

Example:

```
<ejb-jar>
   <assembly-descriptor>
       <security>
       <ejb-name>*</ejb-name>
       <security-domain>myDomain</security-domain>
       <run-as-principal>myPrincipal</run-as-principal>
       </security>
   </assembly-descriptor>
</ejb-jar>
```

Creating a Custom Policy Provider

A custom policy provider is used when you need a custom `java.security.Policy`, for example, if you want to integrate with an external authorization or identity service to check permissions. To create a custom policy provider, you will need to implement the `Policy`, create a custom module with the implementation, and use the implementation from the module in Elytron:

```
/subsystem=elytron/policy=policy-provider-a:add(custom-policy={class-name=MyPolicyProvide
```

Security

WildFly uses a slightly modified version of Eclipse Soteria to implement Jakarta Security.

Open Liberty/WebSphere Liberty

Open Liberty 21 implements the Jakarta EE 9.1 security specifications.

To enable its Application Security 3.0 feature, add the following element to your `server.xml` file, inside the `featureManager` element:

```
<feature>appSecurity-3.0</feature>
```

User Registry

You can configure Open Liberty to authenticate and authorize users by using a basic user registry. Like the "Realm" or "Login Module" of other containers, this is essentially an "Identity Store" by another name. The basic user registry contains user credentials that applications need for security-related tasks. To configure a basic user registry, the Application Security feature must be enabled in the server.xml file. The following example shows the configuration of a basic user registry in the server.xml file:

```
<basicRegistry id="basic" realm="BasicRealm">
    <user name="Bob" password="bobpwd" />
    <user name="John" password="johnpwd" />
</basicRegistry>
```

To configure a basic user registry with multiple users, you can create groups for users with unique group names as shown in the following example:

```
<basicRegistry id="basic" realm="BasicRealm">
  <user name="Bob" password="bobpwd" />
  <user name="John" password="johnpwd" />
  <user name="user1" password="user1pwd"/>
  <user name="user2" password="user2pwd" />

  <group name="myAdmins">
    <member name="Bob" />
    <member name="user1" />
  </group>

  <group name="users">
    <member name="user1" />
    <member name="user2" />
  </group>
</basicRegistry>
```

Configure a basic user registry with QuickStart security.

When you want to configure a basic user registry, you can use the quickStartSecurity element to automatically configure a registry that grants the administrator role to a user. The administrator role gives the user the authority to manage applications. To configure a basic user registry with the quickStartSecurity element, the Application Security feature must be enabled in the `server.xml` file. The following example shows the `server.xml` file configuration to define the username and password for a user that is granted the administrator role with the quickStartSecurity element:

```
<quickStartSecurity userName="Bob" userPassword="bobpwd" />
```

QuickStart security configuration is intended for test purposes and not for production use.

LTPA keys

When the Application Security feature is enabled, Lightweight Third-Party Authentication (LTPA) is enabled by default. The following example shows the configuration of the `ltpa` element in the `server.xml` file:

```
<ltpa keysFileName="yourLTPAKeysFileName.keys" keysPassword="keysPassword"
expiration="120" />
```

LTPA configuration can provide Single Sign-on (SSO) to secure applications.

Disable LTPA Cookies for TAI

LTPA cookies contain secure tokens that are used to verify user credentials and enable SSO. When you don't want to rely on LTPA tokens for SSO, you can use other methods, such as a Trust Association Interceptor (TAI), for authentication. A TAI is used to validate HTTP requests between a third-party security server and an Open Liberty server to complete authentication. The following example shows how to disable LTPA cookies for TAI by specifying `disableLtpaCookie` with a value of true in the `server.xml` file:

```
<trustAssociation id="sample" disableLtpaCookie="true" />
```

REST API Access Roles

You can configure roles for your Open Liberty server to grant users and groups that are defined in a user registry access to select administrative REST APIs. The administrator role (`administrator-role`) provides read and write access to administrative REST APIs. The reader role (`reader-role`) provides read-only access to administrative REST APIs. Users with the reader role can monitor the server but do not have permission to modify it.

In the following example, a user named "Bob" and an "employees" group are granted the reader role. A user who is named Wanda and a group that is named managers are granted the administrator role:

```
<reader-role>
    <user>Bob</user>
    <group>employees</group>
</reader-role>

<administrator-role>
    <user>Wanda</user>
    <group>managers</group>
</administrator-role>
```

If you prefer to use access IDs to identify users or groups, you can use the user-access-id or group-access-id elements, as shown in the following example:

```
<reader-role>
    <user-access-id>user:BasicRealm/Bob</user-access-id>
    <group-access-id>group:BasicRealm/employees</group-access-id>
</reader-role>

<administrator-role>
    <user-access-id>user:BasicRealm/Wanda</user-access-id>
    <group-access-id>group:BasicRealm/managers</group-access-id>
</administrator-role>
```

Jakarta EE Security Packages Used

The following Jakarta EE Security APIs are used by this feature:

- jakarta.security.auth.message
- jakarta.security.auth.message.callback
- jakarta.security.auth.message.config
- jakarta.security.auth.message.module
- jakarta.security.enterprise
- jakarta.security.enterprise.authentication.mechanism.http

- jakarta.security.enterprise.credential

- jakarta.security.enterprise.identitystore

Develop Dependent Features

If you develop a feature depending on this feature, include the following declaration in the Subsystem-Content header of your feature manifest:

```
com.ibm.websphere.appserver.appSecurity-3.0; type="osgi.subsystem.feature"
```

Example Application

The following example application shows how to use form authentication for a simple web front end in Open Liberty. It specified security constraints for a servlet and uses the SecurityContext to determine the role of a logged-in user.

The servlet class:

```
package io.openliberty.guides.ui;

import java.io.IOException;
import jakarta.inject.Inject;
import jakarta.security.enterprise.SecurityContext;
import jakarta.security.enterprise.authentication.mechanism.http.
FormAuthenticationMechanismDefinition;
import jakarta.security.enterprise.authentication.mechanism.http.
LoginToContinue;
import jakarta.servlet.ServletException;
import jakarta.servlet.annotation.HttpConstraint;
import jakarta.servlet.annotation.ServletSecurity;
import jakarta.servlet.annotation.WebServlet;
import jakarta.servlet.http.HttpServlet;
import jakarta.servlet.http.HttpServletRequest;
import jakarta.servlet.http.HttpServletResponse;
```

```
@WebServlet(urlPatterns = "/home")
@FormAuthenticationMechanismDefinition(
    loginToContinue = @LoginToContinue(errorPage = "/error.html",
                                       loginPage = "/welcome.html"))
@ServletSecurity(value = @HttpConstraint(rolesAllowed = { "user", "admin" },
  transportGuarantee = ServletSecurity.TransportGuarantee.CONFIDENTIAL))
public class HomeServlet extends HttpServlet {

    private static final long serialVersionUID = 1L;

    @Inject
    private SecurityContext securityContext;

    protected void doGet(HttpServletRequest request, HttpServletResponse
    response)
        throws ServletException, IOException {
        if (securityContext.isCallerInRole(Utils.ADMIN)) {
            response.sendRedirect("/admin.jsf");
        } else if  (securityContext.isCallerInRole(Utils.USER)) {
            response.sendRedirect("/user.jsf");
        }
    }

    protected void doPost(HttpServletRequest request, HttpServletResponse
    response)
        throws ServletException, IOException {
        doGet(request, response);
    }
}
```

Example web.xml:

```
<?xml version="1.0" encoding="UTF-8"?>
<web-app xmlns="http://xmlns.jcp.org/xml/ns/javaee"
    xmlns:xsi="http://www.w3.org/2001/XMLSchema-instance"
    xsi:schemaLocation="http://xmlns.jcp.org/xml/ns/javaee http://xmlns.
    jcp.org/xml/ns/javaee/web-app_3_1.xsd"
    version="3.1">
    <display-name>Liberty Project</display-name>
```

```
<!-- WebAppJSF: Faces Servlet -->
<servlet>
  <servlet-name>Faces Servlet</servlet-name>
  <servlet-class>jakarta.faces.webapp.FacesServlet</servlet-class>
  <load-on-startup>1</load-on-startup>
</servlet>

<!-- WebAppJSF: Faces Servlet Mapping -->
<servlet-mapping>
  <servlet-name>Faces Servlet</servlet-name>
  <url-pattern>*.jsf</url-pattern>
</servlet-mapping>

<welcome-file-list>
  <welcome-file>/index.html</welcome-file>
</welcome-file-list>

<!-- SECURITY ROLES -->
<security-role>
  <role-name>admin</role-name>
</security-role>

<security-role>
  <role-name>user</role-name>
</security-role>

<!-- SECURITY CONSTRAINTS -->
<security-constraint>
  <web-resource-collection>
    <web-resource-name>AdminViewProperties</web-resource-name>
    <url-pattern>/admin.jsf</url-pattern>
    <http-method>GET</http-method>
  </web-resource-collection>
  <auth-constraint>
    <role-name>admin</role-name>
  </auth-constraint>
</security-constraint>
```

```xml
    <security-constraint>
      <web-resource-collection>
        <web-resource-name>UserViewProperties</web-resource-name>
        <url-pattern>/user.jsf</url-pattern>
        <http-method>GET</http-method>
      </web-resource-collection>
      <auth-constraint>
        <role-name>user</role-name>
      </auth-constraint>
    </security-constraint>
    <deny-uncovered-http-methods/>

    <!-- Handle 403 Error -->
    <error-page>
      <error-code>403</error-code>
      <location>/error403.html</location>
    </error-page>
</web-app>
```

Example userRegistry.xml:

```xml
<server description="Sample Liberty server">
  <basicRegistry id="basic" realm="WebRealm">
    <user name="bob"
      password="{xor}PTA9Lyg7" /> <!-- bobpwd -->
    <user name="alice"
      password="{xor}PjM2PDovKDs=" />  <!-- alicepwd -->
    <user name="carl"
      password="{xor}PD4tMy8oOw==" />  <!-- carlpwd -->
    <user name="dave"
      password="{xor}Oz4pOi8oOw==" />  <!-- davepwd -->

    <group name="Manager">
      <member name="bob" />
    </group>

    <group name="TeamLead">
      <member name="carl" />
```

```
    </group>

    <group name="Employee">
      <member name="alice" />
      <member name="bob" />
      <member name="carl" />
    </group>

    <group name="PartTime">
      <member name="dave" />
    </group>
  </basicRegistry>
</server>
```

And server.xml:

```
<server description="Sample Liberty server">

  <featureManager>
    <feature>appSecurity-3.0</feature>
    <feature>jsf-2.3</feature>
    <feature>servlet-4.0</feature>
  </featureManager>
  <variable name="default.http.port" defaultValue="9080"/>
  <variable name="default.https.port" defaultValue="9443"/>

  <httpEndpoint id="defaultHttpEndpoint"
    httpPort="${default.http.port}"
    httpsPort="${default.https.port}" />

  <include location="userRegistry.xml"/>

  <application location="guide-security-intro.war" type="war"
               id="guide-security-intro.war"
               name="guide-security-intro.war" context-root="/">
    <application-bnd>
      <security-role name="admin">
        <group name="Manager" />
        <group name="TeamLead" />
```

```
        </security-role>
        <security-role name="user">
          <group name="Employee" />
        </security-role>
      </application-bnd>
    </application>
</server>
```

Tomcat/TomEE

Authentication

Tomcat 10 implements the Servlet Container Profile of Jakarta Authentication 2.0.

As TomEE is based on Tomcat, it also builds on the same foundations.

Jakarta Authentication in Tomcat can be configured in two ways:

- At container level in a static configuration file $CATALINA_BASE/conf/
  jaspic-providers.xml

- At web application level dynamically through the Jakarta
  Authentication API

The static Jakarta Authentication configuration overrides any <login-config> in deployed web application's WEB-INF/web.xml files.

Static Configuration

AuthConfigProvider

To use implementations of AuthConfigProvider in Tomcat, it can be configured inside a <jaspic-providers> element of the $CATALINA_BASE/conf/jaspic-providers.xml file. Here's an example:

```
<provider name="any"
          className="fully.qualified.implementation.class.Name"
          layer="HttpServlet"
          appContext="Catalina/localhost /contextPath"
          description="any">
  <property name="see-provider-documentation"
```

```
        value="see-provider-documentation" />
</provider>
```

The name and description attributes are for documentation purposes only and currently not used by Tomcat. className must be the fully qualified name of an AuthConfigProvider implementation. The layer attribute only supports HttpServlet. The appContext must consist of

- Engine name

- A forward slash (/)

- Host name

- A single blank space

- The context path

If the particular AuthConfigProvider implementation supports configuration properties, these may be provided as <property> elements inside the <provider> element.

ServerAuthModule

To use an implementation of ServerAuthModule in Tomcat, you need some supporting classes. Either a custom-specific implementation or a simple wrapper class Tomcat provides for SAMs. This wrapper can be configured inside the <jaspic-providers> element of the $CATALINA_BASE/conf/jaspic-providers.xml:

```
<provider name="any"          className="org.apache.catalina.authenticator.
jaspic.SimpleAuthConfigProvider"
        layer="HttpServlet"
        appContext="Catalina/localhost /contextPath"
        description="any">
  <property name="org.apache.catalina.authenticator.jaspic.ServerAuthModule.1"
          value="fully.qualified.implementation.class.Name" />
  <property name="see-provider-documentation"
          value="see-provider-documentation" />
</provider>
```

The configuration is similar to the `AuthConfigProvider` with a few differences.

The `className` attribute must be `org.apache.catalina.authenticator.jaspic.SimpleAuthConfigProvider`. `ServerAuthModule`(s) are specified via properties. The property name must be `org.apache.catalina.authenticator.jaspic.ServerAuthModule.n` where n is the index of the module. The index must start at 1 an increment in steps of 1 until all modules are defined. The value of the property must be the fully qualified class name of the module.

This is the `SimpleServerAuthModule` class:

```
package org.apache.catalina.authenticator.jaspic;

import java.util.Map;

import jakarta.security.auth.callback.CallbackHandler;

import jakarta.security.auth.message.AuthException;
import jakarta.security.auth.message.config.AuthConfigFactory;
import jakarta.security.auth.message.config.AuthConfigProvider;
import jakarta.security.auth.message.config.ClientAuthConfig;
import jakarta.security.auth.message.config.ServerAuthConfig;

/**
 * Basic implementation primarily intended for use when using third-party
 * {@link jakarta.security.auth.message.module.ServerAuthModule}
   implementations
 * that only provide the module.
 */
public class SimpleAuthConfigProvider implements AuthConfigProvider {

    private final Map<String,String> properties;

    private volatile ServerAuthConfig serverAuthConfig;

    public SimpleAuthConfigProvider(Map<String,String> properties,
    AuthConfigFactory factory) {
        this.properties = properties;
        if (factory != null) {
            factory.registerConfigProvider(this, null, null, "Automatic
            registration");
```

```
    }
}

/**
 * {@inheritDoc}
 * <p>
 * This implementation does not support client-side authentication and
 * therefore always returns {@code null}.
 */
@Override
public ClientAuthConfig getClientAuthConfig(String layer, String
appContext, CallbackHandler handler) throws AuthException {
    return null;
}

@Override
public ServerAuthConfig getServerAuthConfig(String layer, String
appContext, CallbackHandler handler) throws AuthException {
    ServerAuthConfig serverAuthConfig = this.serverAuthConfig;
    if (serverAuthConfig == null) {
        synchronized (this) {
            if (this.serverAuthConfig == null) {
                this.serverAuthConfig = createServerAuthConfig(layer,
                appContext, handler, properties);
            }
            serverAuthConfig = this.serverAuthConfig;
        }
    }
    return serverAuthConfig;
}

protected ServerAuthConfig createServerAuthConfig(String layer, String
appContext, CallbackHandler handler, Map<String,String> properties) {
    return new SimpleServerAuthConfig(layer, appContext, handler,
    properties);
    }
```

```
@Override
public void refresh() {
    ServerAuthConfig serverAuthConfig = this.serverAuthConfig;
    if (serverAuthConfig != null) {
        serverAuthConfig.refresh();
    }
}
}
```

Dynamic Configuration

Jakarta Authentication modules and configuration can be packaged within a WAR file with the web application. The web application can then register the required authentication configuration when it starts using the standard Jakarta Authentication SPIs.

If parallel deployment is being used, then dynamic configuration should not be used. The Jakarta Authentication API assumes that a context path is unique for any given host, which is not the case when deploying in parallel. When you need parallel deployment, you should use static authentication configuration instead. Also, all versions of the application should use the same authentication configuration.

Authorization

What Is a Realm?

As you remember from Chapter 3, a "Realm" is an "Identity Store" in Tomcat storing users, passwords, and other attributes of valid users plus a list of roles associated with each user.

Tomcat defines a Java interface `org.apache.catalina.Realm` to be implemented by extensions called plug-in.

Tomcat includes the following default implementations of the `Realm`:

- `DataSourceRealm`: Accesses authentication data stored in a relational database, via a JDBC `DataSource`

- `JNDIRealm`: Accesses authentication information from an LDAP server, accessed via JNDI

- UserDatabaseRealm: Authentication data stored in a user database, typically backed by an XML file conf/tomcat-users.xml

- MemoryRealm: Authentication information stored in an in-memory object, initialized from an XML file conf/tomcat-users.xml

- JAASRealm: Accesses authentication information through the Java Authentication and Authorization Service (JAAS) API

Using tomcat-users.xml

Here's a Tomitribe example on how to authorize a TomEE/Tomcat application using the built-in tomcat-users.xml file.

First, we define users and roles in tomcat-users.xml:

```
<tomcat-users>
 <user name="tomcat" password="tomcat" roles="tomcat"/>
 <user name="user" password="user" roles="user"/>

 <user name="tom" password="secret1" roles="admin,manager"/>
 <user name="emma" password="secret2" roles="admin,employee"/>
 <user name="bob" password="secret3" roles="admin"/>
</tomcat-users>
```

Then we define security constraints to protect a Jakarta REST resource:

```
<web-app
 xmlns="http://xmlns.jcp.org/xml/ns/javaee"
 xmlns:xsi="http://www.w3.org/2001/XMLSchema-instance"
 xsi:schemaLocation="http://xmlns.jcp.org/xml/ns/javaee http://xmlns.jcp.
 org/xml/ns/javaee/web-app_3_1.xsd"
 version="3.1"
>
 <!-- Security constraints -->
 <security-constraint>
   <web-resource-collection>
     <web-resource-name>Protected admin resource/url</web-resource-name>
     <url-pattern>/api/movies/*</url-pattern>
     <http-method-omission>GET</http-method-omission>
   </web-resource-collection>
```

```
  <auth-constraint>
    <role-name>admin</role-name>
  </auth-constraint>
 </security-constraint>
</web-app>
```

and, finally, a simple Jakarta REST API class:

```
@Path("/movies")
@Produces(MediaType.APPLICATION_JSON)
@Consumes(MediaType.APPLICATION_JSON)
@TomcatUserIdentityStoreDefinition
@BasicAuthenticationMechanismDefinition
@ApplicationScoped
public class MovieAdminResource {
    private static final Logger LOGGER = Logger.
    getLogger(MovieAdminResource.class.getName());
    @Inject
    private MovieStore store;
    // Jakarta REST security context wired with Jakarta Security
    @Context
    private jakarta.ws.rs.core.SecurityContext securityContext;
    @POST
    public Movie addMovie(final Movie newMovie) {
        LOGGER.info(getUserName() + " adding new movie " + newMovie);
        return store.addMovie(newMovie);
    }
    // See source file for full content
    private String getUserName() {
        if (securityContext.getUserPrincipal() != null) {
            return String.format("%s[admin=%s]",
                                securityContext.getUserPrincipal().getName(),
                                securityContext.isUserInRole("admin"));
        }
        return null;
    }
}
```

Security

While using Exousia with Tomcat or Supported Runtimes by Soteria earlier in this chapter showed how Tomcat or TomEE can be used together with Soteria and Exousia, TomEE also comes with its own implementation of Jakarta Security.

It includes LDAP or JDBC identity stores out of the box, but let's have a look at how to create a very simple custom IdentityStore for TomEE. The only thing you need to do is to implement jakarta.security.enterprise.identitystore.IdentityStore. All relevant methods in the interface have default implementations, making it easier to just implement what you need. By default, an identity store is used for both validating user credentials and providing groups/roles of the authenticated user. Depending on what validationTypes() returns, you have to implement validate() and/or getCallerGroups(), which also receives the result of validate().

Let's look at a very simple example:

```
@ApplicationScoped
public class TestIdentityStore implements IdentityStore {

    public CredentialValidationResult validate(Credential credential) {

        if (!(credential instanceof UsernamePasswordCredential)) {
            return INVALID_RESULT;
        }

        final UsernamePasswordCredential usernamePasswordCredential =
        (UsernamePasswordCredential) credential;
        if (usernamePasswordCredential.compareTo("jon", "doe")) {
            return new CredentialValidationResult("jon", new
            HashSet<>(asList("foo", "bar")));
        }

        if (usernamePasswordCredential.compareTo("iron", "man")) {
            return new CredentialValidationResult("iron", new
            HashSet<>(Collections.singletonList("avengers")));
        }

        return INVALID_RESULT;
    }
}
```

This simple example shows a hard-coded `IdentityStore`, knowing just two users, each of them with different roles.

Note   Your IdentityStore implementation must be a CDI bean for TomEE to recognize it.

CHAPTER 8

MicroProfile JWT

What Is JWT?

JSON Web Token (JWT) is an open standard filed under RFC 7519 to securely transmit information between different applications or services via JSON strings.

JWT is compact, human readable, and digitally signed using a private or public key pair Identity Provider (IdP). So the integrity and authenticity of the token can be verified by other involved parties.

The main purpose of JWT is not to hide data but to ensure its authenticity. JWT is mainly used to sign and encode but not encrypt data, although the tokens may also be encrypted based on another set of standards including JSON Web Signature (JWS) and JSON Web Encryption (JWE).

JWT is a token-based stateless authentication mechanism. Since it is based on a client-side stateless session, servers don't need a persistence mechanism like a database to save information about the session. JWT tokens follow a well-defined and known standard that is becoming the most common token format to protect services.

Use Cases

Two of the main use cases for JSON Web Token are

- Authorization
- Information Exchange

Authorization is probably the most common use case for JWT. Once the user has logged into a system, each subsequent request will include the JWT, allowing the user to access pages, services, and resources that are permitted by that token. Single Sign-On is

© Arjan Tijms, Teo Bais, and Werner Keil 2022
A. Tijms et al., *The Definitive Guide to Security in Jakarta EE*, https://doi.org/10.1007/978-1-4842-7945-8_8

a feature that widely uses JWT nowadays, especially in public APIs, because of its small overhead and ability to be easily used across different domains.

Information Exchange: JSON Web Tokens are a good way of securely transmitting information between parties. Because JWTs can be signed – for example, using public/ private key pairs – you can be sure the senders are who they say they are. Additionally, as the signature is calculated using the header and the payload, you can also verify that the content has not been tampered with.

Why Do We Need JWT?

The HTTP protocol is stateless; therefore, a new request such as GET /order/42 doesn't know anything about the previous ones like PUT /order with the same id, and a user would have to authenticate again for every new request.

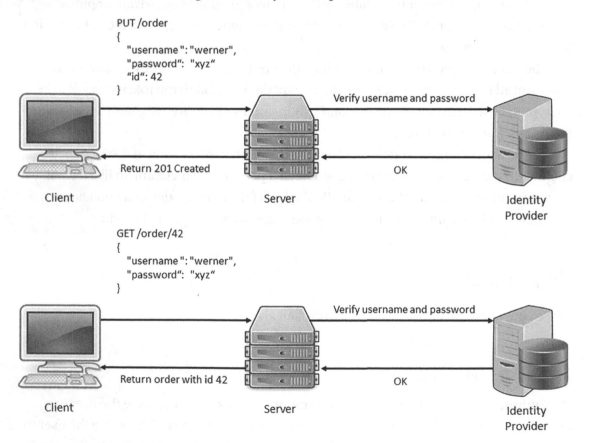

Figure 8-1. *Repeating authentication for every new HTTP API request*

This is often dealt with by using Server-Side Sessions (SSS). First, the login credentials like username and password are checked; if they are correct, the server will create a session id, store it, and return it to the client. In Jakarta EE applications based on Servlets, this cookie sent to the client is usually called JSESSIONID.

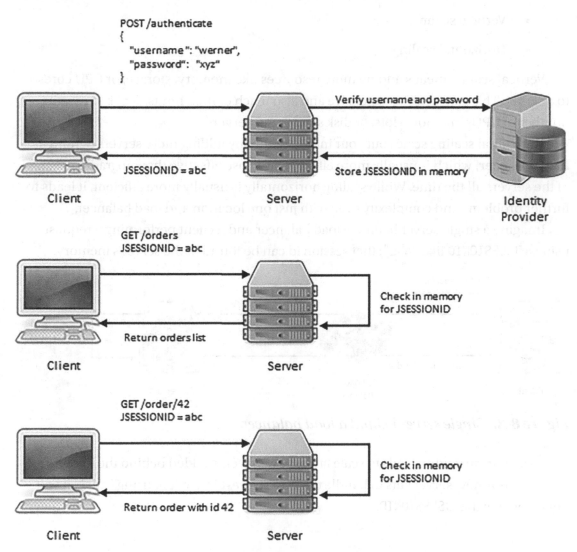

Figure 8-2. *Using SSS, reducing the number of authentications against the Identity Provider*

This approach can fix one problem but may create others like scalability issues. While Server-Side Sessions may work well for most web sites and even a few ecommerce shops, in an API-driven era, some endpoints can face a massive number of requests forcing the provider to scale. There are two ways to scale:

- Vertical scaling

- Horizontal scaling

Vertical scaling means adding more resources like memory, storage, or CPU cores to a server. This can be quite expensive and also reach certain limits, for example, the number of CPUs, memory slots, or disk storage per server.

Horizontal scaling scales out your infrastructure by adding more servers behind a **load balancer**, which is usually more efficient and cost-effective than upgrading each of the servers all the time. While scaling horizontally is usually more efficient, it leads to further problems and complexity even with just one location and load balancer.

Imagine a single server behind a load balancer and a client performing a request using a JSESSIONID like "abc"; that session id can be found in the server's memory.

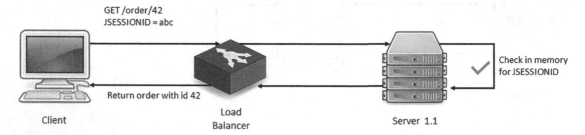

Figure 8-3. *Single server behind a load balancer*

If the infrastructure needs to scale and a new server is added behind the load balancer, this new server gets to handle the next request by a client using "abc"; it will not recognize that JSESSIONID.

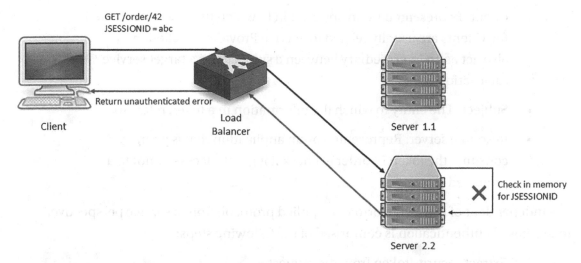

Figure 8-4. *New server behind LB, user not recognized*

The authentication fails because the new server has no "abc" sessions in its memory yet. There are three main workarounds to address this.

Synchronize the sessions between servers, which can be tricky and error-prone, especially in a globally distributed architecture.

Use an external database or session caching mechanism. This can be helpful but adds more components to the infrastructure, and especially in a distributed environment, this cache or DB will need its own replication.

Or accept the stateless nature of HTTP and try to find a solution that works for it.

That's where JSON Web Token comes to the rescue, because each token is compact and self-contained, so it contains all the necessary information to allow or deny an API request without having to perform any replication or costly lookups first.

How Does It Work?

Token-based authentication mechanisms allow systems to authenticate, authorize, and verify identities based on a security token. Usually, the following entities are involved:

- Issuer: Responsible for issuing security tokens as a result of successfully asserting an identity (authentication). Issuers are usually related with Identity Providers.

- Client: Represented by an application to which the token was issued for. Clients are usually related to Service Providers. A client may also act as an intermediary between a subject and a target service (delegation).

- Subject: The entity to which the information in a token refers to.

- Resource server: Represented by an application that is going to consume the token in order to check if it grants access or not to a protected resource.

Independent of the token format or applied protocol, from a service perspective, token-based authentication is comprised of the following steps:

1. Extract security token from the request

   For RESTful services, this is usually achieved by obtaining the token from the Authorization header.

2. Perform validation checks against the token

   This step usually depends on the token format and security protocol in use. The objective is to make sure the token is valid and can be consumed by the application. It may involve signature, encryption, and expiration checks.

3. Introspect the token and extract information about the subject

   This step usually depends on the token format and security protocol in use. The objective is to obtain all the necessary information about the subject from the token.

4. Create a security context for the subject

Based on the information extracted from the token, the application creates a security context for the subject in order to use the information wherever necessary when serving protected resources.

JWT Structure

A JSON Web Token has three parts:

- Header
- Payload
- Signature

Each of these parts is separated by a "." character.
Therefore, every JWT looks like

`Header.Payload.Signature`

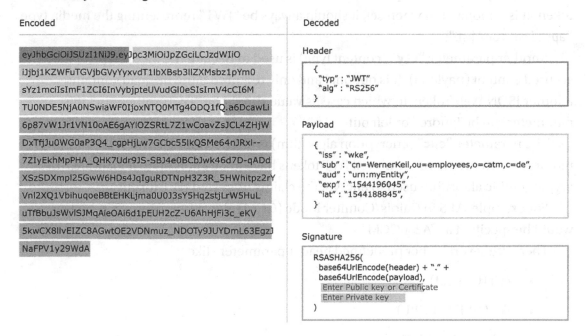

Figure 8-5. *JWT structure*

Header

The header describes the JSON Web Token itself. It contains the information about the type of the token and the algorithm used to generate the signature.

The algorithm parameter **"alg"** must be present in every JWT header. The most common algorithms are HMAC with a SHA-256 hash ("HS256") or RSA with the same ("RS256") and more recently ECDSA P-256 with SHA-256 ("ES256"). The allowed values are specified by the JSON Web Encryption (JWE) standard RFC 7516.

In our example, the header contains the algorithm and type parameters:

```
{
    "typ" : "JWT",
    "alg" : "RS256"
}
```

The type parameter **"typ"** is used to declare the IANA media type (RFC 6838) of the token. It is optional, but when set, it should always be "JWT", representing the media type `"application/jwt"`.

Another parameter **"cty"** (content type) is used to declare the media type of the secured content (payload). It is optional and only required if the payload contains another JSON Web Token, in which case its value should be "JWT"; otherwise, this parameter can be ignored or left out.

The parameter **"enc"** (encryption algorithm) is defined for use with JWE. It is only required when the claims or nested JWT tokens have to be encrypted. It identifies the cryptographic algorithm used to encrypt the claims or nested JWT tokens.

For example, AES in Galois/Counter Mode (GCM) algorithm using a 256-bit key would be specified as "A256GCM".

There are several other predefined header parameters like

- crit (Critical)

- jku (JWK Set URL)

- jwk (JSON Web Key)

- kid (Key ID)

- x5u (X.509 URL)

- x5t (X.509 Certificate SHA-1 Thumbprint)

- x5t#S256 (X.509 Certificate SHA-256 Thumbprint)

Payload

The payload or body is the essential part of the JWT containing security statements like the identity of the user and granted permissions. JWT calls them claims.

There are three types of JWT claim names:

1. Registered claim

2. Public claim

3. Private claim

Registered claims are the predefined claims. Public claims can be any user-defined information, and private claims are those which the producer and consumer of JWT agreed to use in a specific application.

In order to validate a JWT, we should check some registered claims as well. Some important registered claims are defined in Table 8-1.

Table 8-1. *Registered JWT claims*

Claim name	Description	Reference
iss	The token issuer	RFC7519, Section 4.1.1
sub	The principal that is the subject of the JWT	RFC7519, Section 4.1.2
aud	The recipients of the JWT	RFC7519, Section 4.1.3
exp	The expiration time on or after which the JWT must not be accepted for processing	RFC7519, Section 4.1.4
nbf	Time before which the JWT must not be accepted for processing	RFC7519, Section 4.1.5
iat	Time at which the issuer generated the JWT	RFC7519, Section 4.1.6
jti	Unique identifier for the JWT	RFC7519, Section 4.1.7

"iss" (Issuer) Claim

The "iss" (issuer) claim identifies the principal that issued the JWT. The processing of this claim is generally application specific. The "iss" value is a case-sensitive string containing a URI value. The use of this claim is optional. We should validate that the issuer is a valid URL or the JWT was sent by an expected issuer.

"sub" (Subject) Claim

The "sub" (subject) claim identifies the principal that is the subject of the token. Claims in a JWT are statements about the subject. The "sub" value is a case-sensitive string containing a URI value. The use of this claim is optional.

"aud" (Audience) Claim

The "aud" (audience) claim identifies the recipients of the token. Each principal intended to process the JWT must identify itself with a value in the audience claim. If the principal processing the claim does not identify itself with a value in the "aud" claim when this claim is present, then the JWT must be rejected. In general, the "aud" value is an array of case-sensitive strings, each containing a URI value. The use of this claim is optional.

"exp" (Expiration Time) Claim

The "exp" (expiration time) claim identifies the expiration time on or after which the token will not be accepted for processing. The processing of the "exp" claim requires that the current date/time must be before the expiration date/time listed in the "exp" claim. Its value must be a numeric timestamp. The use of this claim is optional.

"nbf" (Not Before) Claim

The "nbf" (not before) claim identifies the time before which the JWT must not be accepted for processing. The processing of the "nbf" claim requires that the current date/time must be after or equal to the not-before date/time listed in the "nbf" claim. Its value must be a number containing a numeric date value. This claim is optional.

"iat" (Issued At) Claim

The "iat" (issued at) claim identifies the time at which the token was issued. This claim can be used to determine the age of the JWT. Its value must be a number containing a numeric date value. This claim is optional.

"jti" (JWT ID) Claim

The "jti" (JWT ID) claim provides a case-sensitive unique identifier for the JWT. The identifier value must be assigned in a manner that ensures that there is a negligible probability that the same value will be accidentally assigned to a different data object; if the application uses multiple issuers, collisions must be prevented among values produced by different issuers as well. The "jti" claim can be used to prevent the JWT from being reused. The use of this claim is optional.

Signature

The third part of the JSON Web Token is the signature. It is the most important part of a JWT to validate it and ensure it was not modified or tampered with and can be trusted. The signature is generated using the payload and a secret key; therefore, anyone in possession of this key can generate new tokens with valid signatures.

The most commonly used cryptographic algorithms to generate a signature are

- HS256, which is short for HMAC-SHA256

- RS256, short for RSA-SHA256

- ES256, short for ECDSA P-256 SHA-256

HS256 is a symmetric key encryption and involves a secret key being shared between two parties. This secret key is used to encrypt the data, and on the receiver side, the same key is used to decrypt the data. HS256 signatures are generated using a secret key that is validated at the receiving end (resource server). On the receiver side, using the payload and secret key, the signature has to be generated again and compared to the signature part of the incoming JWT. Since only the authentication server and resource server are in possession of the secret key, it is not possible to tamper with the JWT, and we can ensure its validity.

The Trouble with HS256

A major disadvantage of the HS256 algorithm is that the secret key needs to be accessible both when generating and validating tokens.

For a monolithic application, this is usually not a big problem, but if you have a distributed system built out of multiple services running independently of each other or same cloud environment having multiple endpoints, you have to choose between two evils:

- You can set up a dedicated service for token generation and verification. Any service that receives a token from a client needs to make a call to the authentication service to verify the token. For busy systems under a heavy load, this may create a performance bottleneck.

- You can configure the secret key into every service that receives tokens from clients, allowing them to validate a token without having to make a call to the authentication service. However, having the secret key in multiple locations across the cloud increases the risk of it being compromised or stolen, and once that happens, an attacker could generate valid tokens and impersonate any user in the system. Being forced to replace a compromised secret key or even just updating it regularly for safety reasons adds a maintenance burden to your microservice architecture that is very similar to the problem of synchronizing Server-Side Sessions we discussed earlier.

RS256 (asymmetric key encryption or public key encryption) involves two keys: a public key and a private key. The private key is used to generate the signature, while the public key is used to validate the signature. In this case, the private key is only in possession of the authentication server generating the JWT, and we do not need to distribute the private key. On the resource server, we can validate the token using the public key. Both keys are non-interchangeable; one can only be used to generate, while the other can only be used to validate a token.

ES256 is also a public key encryption mechanism based on the Elliptic Curve Digital Signature Algorithm (ECDSA). It provides equivalent security to RSA cryptography but uses shorter key sizes with greater processing speed for many operations. This means ECDSA digital signatures will be substantially smaller in terms of length than equivalently strong RSA digital signatures, which is an advantage especially in distributed systems with often many services and calls where smaller and faster is also cheaper in most cases.

Obtaining the Public Key

In practice, public keys are often obtained manually from the JWT issuer and stored in or passed to the binary of a microservice. If your public keys do not change too frequently, storing them in the binary image or on disk is a feasible option for most environments. For example, SSL/TLS certificates for HTTPS, also public key based, are usually configured in the JVM itself and last for up to two years.

As an alternative, public keys may be obtained by the microservice at runtime, from the JWT issuer via HTTPS request.

JSON Web Key Set (JWKS) is a set of keys that contains the public keys used to verify any JWT issued by the authorization server. Most authorization servers expose a discovery endpoint like `https://<your-domain>/.well-known/jwks.json`.

You can use this endpoint to configure your application or API to automatically locate the JSON Web Key Set endpoint (`jwks_uri`), which contains the public key used to sign the token.

MicroProfile in Relation to Jakarta EE

Several members of the Java Enterprise Edition platform expert group in the Java Community Process (JCP), where Java EE had been standardized back then, have been in favor of other, smaller profiles than the "Web Profile" for some time, a simplified Java EE variant for web development that was first introduced with Java EE 6. Most of these members were individuals in the JCP and the relevant expert groups, while representatives of large providers and companies such as Oracle, Sun, and IBM feared a higher level of complexity for their products and users through additional profiles. So it stayed with the web profile. But it wasn't as lightweight as microframeworks.

Microframeworks are a kind of "slimmed-down" web framework that is limited to API calls without supporting more complex business logic. Microframeworks exist for a wide variety of programming languages including some that are more common on the Web such as PHP, Ruby, Python, and JavaScript/Node.js.

Some microframeworks were also developed for Java but are based only partially or not at all on Java standards, which makes joint use with enterprise systems more difficult and also increases the learning curve for developers. One reason why many of the individuals and manufacturers in the JCP wanted to break new ground in order not to miss the train to microservices or to only drive second class in it. Microservices are an architecture pattern in which complex applications are composed of small independent services. An important aspect of this is being able to update individual services without having to change others and redeliver others, as is the case with traditional "monolithic" systems. This makes it much easier to develop even larger systems in an agile and iterative manner and to deliver them step by step and to offer users partial areas for testing and use.

A certain agility in the process and the development of Java EE was felt by many members of the community. In mid-2015, Oracle announced a postponement of Java EE 8 to 2017, similar to Java SE 9. When a year later in the course of 2016 there was no recognizable activity by Oracle in many Java EE 8 components and the reference implementation "Glassfish" practically came to a standstill, Java EE Evangelist Reza Rahman left the company and was a driving force behind the Java EE Guardians (now Jakarta EE Ambassadors) for the independent promotion of Java in the Enterprise area. The list is now very long and started with James Gosling, the creator of Java; it also includes all three authors of this book: Arjan Tijms, Teo Bais, and Werner Keil. Teo and Werner serve on the Leadership Council of the Jakarta EE Ambassadors.

Around the same time, software manufacturers, Java user groups, and individuals represented in the JCP, almost all of them also Java EE Guardians, started the MicroProfile Initiative to create a standard-compliant microframework for the Java platform. It soon became clear that being part of an established open source community would be more effective than setting up a "MicroProfile Foundation" yourself. And contact was made with communities such as Apache, Linux, and the Eclipse Foundation about possible participation.

Shortly before Christmas 2016, after the decision for Eclipse, MicroProfile was recognized as a project by the Eclipse Foundation. While MicroProfile 1.0 was announced in September, preparations for an official 1.0 release have been underway since the beginning of 2017. Even if some manufacturers have already built preversions into their products, this is a release candidate or prerelease version, as is the case with the annual Eclipse "Release Train." Until the official version was published, the target was the first quarter of 2017.

Since its inception, the Eclipse Foundation has expanded significantly in the tool and die sector and has established itself as a manufacturer-neutral platform from development tools to technologies for the IoT (Internet of Things) to industry-specific projects for the automotive industry or science and healthcare. In this respect, the Eclipse Foundation acts like a good partner on the way to a manufacturer-independent solution for microservices. There are many different members and manufacturers working together on projects such as Microsoft, IBM, Oracle, Red Hat, SAP, and Pivotal, whose Spring Cloud may be seen as a middle thing of inspiration and essential competition for MicroProfile and the committers involved. With projects such as Eclipse Gemini, the company was still trying to establish "Spring Dynamic Modules" OSGi components for the enterprise area as a project from several providers under the name SpringSource, which partially succeeded.

For example, Oracle representative Mike Keith, then lead of what is now Jakarta Persistence (JPA), was among the Gemini developers, but Gemini has not really been active in recent years. JPA was a good example of a Jakarta EE standard that always had its reference implementation (RI) at Eclipse in the EclipseLink project. Something MicroProfile believed would also be possible in certain areas, but standardization was and still is not the primary goal of MicroProfile, although it may change a bit with its recent adoption of the Eclipse Foundation Specification Process (EFSP), which is also used by Jakarta EE in a more specialized form, and creation of a MicroProfile Working Group. Anil Gaur, Oracle Vice President of Engineering for "Enterprise and Cloud" at the time, said at JavaOne, "That MicroProfile efforts were complementary to what the Java Community Process did with Java EE" and they were looking forward to making contributions to both. By implementing several MicroProfile specs in Project Helidon, Oracle still does nowadays.

While the hopes behind Eclipse MicroProfile were to be faster paced and more "agile" until release 3.3, it was still based on Java EE 8 and has not adopted Jakarta EE 8 until MicroProfile 4.0, while Jakarta EE 8 had been available almost one and a half years earlier and was already used by several other competing microframeworks like Spring Boot.

So it's almost like the rabbit racing against the turtle which stayed behind thinking it would be way faster but then ended up falling asleep. A main reason for this is the exact same people and contributors involved in Jakarta EE that some also contribute to MicroProfile and they cannot spend the same amount of time on multiple projects simultaneously, which is why there will always be a certain gap between Jakarta EE and MicroProfile catching up, unless there are enough dedicated feature owners for both of them.

Although MicroProfile 4.0 had adopted Jakarta EE 8 as a dependency and the change to a proper Working Group similar to Jakarta EE itself took some time, plus applying the EFSP may sound like an excuse, one or the other specification, in particular MicroProfile

JWT 1.2, seemed quite rushed and failed to properly update any reference to Java EE and the old Java EE 8 JSRs in the latest specification. While some issues marked for 2.0 were not yet closed either, most of these look like they were addressed by the 2.0 version of MP-JWT about a year later. Another worrisome event, not the first time, that MicroProfile had to roll back or fix a major problem after the final release of a new version was that 4.0 immediately had to be superseded by a 4.0.1 emergency fix due to circular dependencies between some of its components. Adding to the impression, the release may have been a bit rushed "under the Christmas Tree," and quality expectations Jakarta EE has met for over two decades now may not always be met by MicroProfile or some of its components.

While Jakarta EE has countless compatible implementations often days after its release, there have only been two compatible implementations (by the same company) of MicroProfile 5.0 according to the Eclipse Wiki: `https://wiki.eclipse.org/MicroProfile/Implementation`, almost two months after MP 5 had been released, also the same two that were 4.1 compatible.

The MicroProfile front page still mentions lots of members like KumuluzEE, Hammock, or Launcher, but they all vanished into oblivion years ago and stopped producing a compatible implementation after MP 3.5. Some like Hammock even collapsed after MicroProfile 1.1. Since MicroProfile 4.0, only three runtimes by two vendors (IBM and Red Hat are under the same roof now) – Open Liberty/WebSphere Liberty, WildFly, and Payara – cared to publish the compatibility with MicroProfile specifications. Maybe there are a few more, but if they even pass the TCKs, they don't bother sharing that. Almost as if the "revolution" MicroProfile once had hoped to start has eaten most of its children by now. And there isn't so much left of the promise to have a big choice compared to a single-vendor solution like Spring Boot because at the end of the day, you may only have two or three vendors, with two of them even belonging to the same corporation.

MP-JWT As an Authentication Mechanism for Jakarta EE

Why Do We Need MicroProfile JWT?

A frustrating aspect of many standards is that some aim to be a jack of all trades offering a massive number of choices. This is definitely the case with JWT, which allows multiple types of digital signatures and many possible claims. While the possibilities are infinite, so many options mean infinite opportunities for interoperability issues.

A critical goal of MicroProfile JWT is to take just enough of these options that the basic interoperability across enterprises can be achieved in a way that favors microservices in particular.

The focus of the MicroProfile JWT specification is the definition of the required format of JWT usable for interoperable authentication and authorization. MP-JWT also maps JWT claims to various Jakarta EE container APIs and makes the set of claims available through getter methods.

The sources for the specification, API, and TCK are available from the Eclipse microprofile-jwt-auth GitHub repository.

The purpose of MP-JWT as a token format depends on the agreement between identity providers and service providers. This means identity providers – responsible for issuing tokens – should be able to issue interoperable tokens using the MP-JWT format in a way that service providers can understand in order to validate the token and gather information about a subject. With that respect, requirements for the MicroProfile JWT are the following:

1. Be usable as an authentication token

2. Be usable as an authorization token that contains Jakarta EE application level roles indirectly granted via a groups claim

3. Able to support additional standard claims described in IANA JWT specification as well as nonstandard claims

To meet those requirements, MP-JWT introduced two new claims:

-   "upn": A human-readable claim that uniquely identifies the subject or user principal of the token, across MicroProfile services accessing the token

-   "groups": The token subject's group memberships that will be mapped to Java EE style application level roles in the MicroProfile service container

The specification (as of 2.0) is based on the following Jakarta EE API dependencies:

-   Jakarta RESTful Web Services 3.0

-   Jakarta JSON Processing 2.0

- Jakarta JSON Binding 2.0

- CDI 3.0

- Jakarta Annotations 2.0

The MicroProfile JWT specification is focused on the ability of microservices to verify JWTs and does not define the following:

- JWT creation: Tokens will typically be created by a dedicated service in the enterprise like an API Gateway or an Identity Provider.

- RSA public key distribution: Distributing the public key of the gateway or identity provider is out of scope for MP-JWT. Like TLS/SSL certificates, they may not change often, and distributing them manually or installing them, for example, docker images, is a common practice.

- Automatic JWT propagation: Microservices using MP-JWT have a guaranteed and standard way to obtain the JWT on incoming calls. However, propagation must be done by the microservice itself in the application code by placing the JWT in the Authorization header of outgoing HTTP calls.

It is a critical goal of MicroProfile JWT that the token can be both verified and propagated by each microservice. For reasons discussed in the "The Trouble with HS256" section, MicroProfile JWT chooses RSA-based digital signatures only.

The RSA public key of the Authorization Server, which creates the JWTs, can be installed on all the microservices in advance of any actual HTTP requests. When calls come into a microservice, it will use this RSA public key to verify the JWT and determine if the caller's identity is valid. If any HTTP calls are made by the microservice, it should pass the JWT in those calls, propagating the caller's identity forward to other microservices.

As defined by the JWT standard, the **"alg"** header parameter must be present. If claims or nested JWT tokens are encrypted, **"enc"** is also a mandatory header parameter.

The use of the header parameters **"typ"** and **"kid"** is recommended.

While the JWT specification declares pretty much every registered claim as optional, MicroProfile JWT requires the following claims to be present:

- iss

- iat

- exp

The use of these JWT claims is recommended by MP-JWT:

- sub

- jti

- aud

In addition to the registered JWT claims listed in Table 8-1, MicroProfile JWT defines the following public claims of its own.

Table 8-2. *MP-JWT public claims*

Claim name	Description	Reference
upn	Provides the user principal name in the `java.security.` `Principal` interface This claim is required	MP-JWT 2.0 specification
groups	Provides the list of group names that have been assigned to the principal of the MP-JWT. This typically will require a mapping at the application container level to application deployment roles, but a one-to-one between group names and application role names is required to be performed in addition to any other mapping. This claim is optional	MP-JWT 2.0 specification

It is recommended that JWT tokens have a **"groups"** claim if the endpoint requires authorization, but MP-JWT implementations can map the groups from other claims if the tokens have been issued by OpenID Connect and other providers that currently do not support MP-JWT.

If no groups information can be extracted directly from the **"groups"** claim or via custom mappers from other claims in a given token, then this token can be accepted if the endpoint requires authentication only.

Numeric date values used by **"exp"**, **"iat"**, and other date-related claims are a JSON numeric value representing the number of **seconds** from 1970-01-01T00:00:00Z UTC until the specified UTC date/time, ignoring leap seconds.

MicroProfile JWT implementations may enforce that JWT tokens contain all the recommended headers and claims. The recommended headers and claims may become required in the future versions of the MP-JWT specification.

An example minimal MP-JWT in JSON would be

```json
{
    "typ": "JWT",
    "alg": "RS256",
    "kid": "abc-1234567890"
}
{
    "iss": "https://server.example.com",
    "jti": "a-123",
    "exp": 1311281970,
    "iat": 1311280970,
    "sub": "24400320",
    "upn": "jdoe@server.example.com",
    "groups": ["red-group", "green-group", "admin-group"],
}
```

The MicroProfile JWT specification defines a **JsonWebToken** java.security. Principal interface extension that makes this set of required claims available via get methods. The JsonWebToken interface definition is

```java
package org.eclipse.microprofile.jwt;
public interface JsonWebToken extends Principal {{

/**
 * Returns the unique name of this principal. This either
 * comes from the upn claim, or if that is missing,
 * the preferred_username claim. Note that for
 * guaranteed interoperability a upn claim should be used.
```

```
 *
 * @return the unique name of this principal.
 */
@Override
String getName();

/**
 * Get the raw bearer token string originally passed in the
 * authentication header
 * @return raw bear token string
 */
default String getRawToken() {
  return getClaim(Claims.raw_token.name());
}

/**
 * The iss(Issuer) claim identifies the principal that issued
 * the JWT
 * @return the iss claim.
 */
default String getIssuer() {
    return getClaim(Claims.iss.name());
}

/**
 * The aud(Audience) claim identifies the recipients that the
 * JWT is intended for.
 * @return the aud claim.
 */
default Set<String> getAudience() {
    return getClaim(Claims.aud.name());
}

/**
 * The sub(Subject) claim identifies the principal that is
 * the subject of the JWT. This is the token issuing
 * IDP subject, not the
```

```
 *
 * @return the sub claim.
 */
default String getSubject() {
    return getClaim(Claims.sub.name());
}

/**
 * The jti(JWT ID) claim provides a unique identifier for the JWT. The
identifier value MUST be assigned in a manner that ensures that there is a
negligible probability that the same value will be accidentally assigned
to a different data object; if the application uses multiple issuers,
collisions MUST be prevented among values produced by different issuers as
well. The "jti" claim can be used to prevent the JWT from being replayed.
 * @return the jti claim.
 */
default String getTokenID() {
    return getClaim(Claims.jti.name());
}

/**
 * The exp (Expiration time) claim identifies the expiration
 * time on or after which the JWT MUST NOT be accepted
 * for processing in seconds since 1970-01-01T00:00:00Z UTC
 * @return the exp claim.
 */
default long getExpirationTime() {
    return getClaim(Claims.exp.name());
}
/**
 * The iat(Issued at time) claim identifies the time at which
 * the JWT was issued in seconds since
 * 1970-01-01T00:00:00Z UTC
 * @return the iat claim
 */
```

```java
default long getIssuedAtTime() {
    return getClaim(Claims.iat.name());
}

/**
 * The groups claim provides the group names the JWT principal
 * has been granted.
 *
 * This is a MicroProfile specific claim.
 * @return a possibly empty set of group names.
 */
default Set<String> getGroups() {
    return getClaim(Claims.groups.name());
}

/**
 * Access the names of all claims are associated with this token.
 * @return non-standard claim names in the token
 */
Set<String> getClaimNames();

/**
 * Verify is a given claim exists
 * @param claimName - the name of the claim
 * @return true if the JsonWebToken contains the claim,
 * false otherwise
 */
default boolean containsClaim(String claimName) {
    return claim(claimName).isPresent();
}

/**
 * Access the value of the indicated claim.
 * @param claimName - the name of the claim
 * @return the value of the indicated claim if it exists,
 * null otherwise.
 */
<T> T getClaim(String claimName);
```

```
/**
 * A utility method to access a claim value in an
 * {@linkplain Optional} wrapper
 * @param claimName - the name of the claim
 * @param <T> - the type of the claim value to return
 * @return an Optional wrapper of the claim value
 */
default <T> Optional<T> claim(String claimName) {
    return Optional.ofNullable(getClaim(claimName));
}

/**
 * A utility method to access a claim value in an
 * {@linkplain Optional} wrapper
 * @param claim - the claim
 * @param <T> - the type of the claim value to return
 * @return an Optional wrapper of the claim value
 */
default <T> Optional<T> claim(Claims claim) {
    return claim(claim.name());
}
```

The token may contain any number of other custom and standard claims. An example MP-JWT that contains additional "auth_time", "preferred_username", "acr", and "nbf" claims and a custom "roles" claim is

```
{
    "typ": "JWT",
    "alg": "RS256",
    "kid": "abc-1234567890"
}
{
    "iss": "https://server.example.com",
    "aud": ["s6BhdRkqt3"],
    "exp": 1311281970,
    "iat": 1311280970,
    "sub": "24400320",
```

```
    "upn": "jdoe@server.example.com",
    "groups": ["red-group", "green-group", "admin-group"],
    "roles": ["auditor", "administrator"],
    "jti": "a-123",
    "auth_time": 1311280969,
    "preferred_username": "jdoe",
    "acr": "phr",
    "nbf": 1311288970
}
```

The Claims enum encapsulates an enumeration of all the standard JWT-related claims along with a description and the required Java type for the claim as returned from the JsonWebToken#getClaim(String) method:

```
package org.eclipse.microprofile.jwt;
public enum Claims {
// The base set of required claims that MUST have non-null values in the
JsonWebToken
iss("Issuer", String.class),
sub("Subject", String.class),
exp("Expiration Time", Long.class),
iat("Issued At Time", Long.class),
jti("JWT ID", String.class),
upn("MP-JWT specific unique principal name", String.class),
groups("MP-JWT specific groups permission grant", Set.class),
raw_token("MP-JWT specific original bearer token", String.class),
// The IANA registered, but MP-JWT optional claims
aud("Audience", Set.class),
nbf("Not Before", Long.class),
auth_time("Time when the authentication occurred", Long.class),
updated_at("Time the information was last updated", Long.class),
azp("Authorized party - the party to which the ID Token was issued",
String.class
),
nonce("Value used to associate a Client session with an ID Token",
String.class),
```

```
at_hash("Access Token hash value", Long.class),
c_hash("Code hash value", Long.class),
full_name("Full name", String.class),
family_name("Surname(s) or last name(s)", String.class),
middle_name("Middle name(s)", String.class),
nickname("Casual name", String.class),
given_name("Given name(s) or first name(s)", String.class),
preferred_username("Shorthand name by which the End-User wishes to be
referred to
", String.class),
email("Preferred e-mail address", String.class),
email_verified("True if the e-mail address has been verified;
otherwise false",
Boolean.class),
gender("Gender", String.class),
birthdate("Birthday", String.class),
zoneinfo("Time zone", String.class),
locale("Locale", String.class),
phone_number("Preferred telephone number", String.class),
phone_number_verified("True if the phone number has been verified; otherwise
false", Boolean.class),
address("Preferred postal address", JsonObject.class),
acr("Authentication Context Class Reference", String.class),
amr("Authentication Methods References", String.class),
sub_jwk("Public key used to check the signature of an ID Token",
JsonObject.class
),
cnf("Confirmation", String.class),
sip_from_tag("SIP From tag header field parameter value", String.class),
sip_date("SIP Date header field value", String.class),
sip_callid("SIP Call-Id header field value", String.class),
sip_cseq_num("SIP CSeq numeric header field parameter value", String.class),
sip_via_branch("SIP Via branch header field parameter value", String.class),
orig("Originating Identity String", String.class),
dest("Destination Identity String", String.class),
```

```
mky("Media Key Fingerprint String", String.class),
jwk("JSON Web Key Representing Public Key", JsonObject.class),
jwe("Encrypted JSON Web Key", String.class),
kid("Key identifier", String.class),
jku("JWK Set URL", String.class),
UNKNOWN("A catch all for any unknown claim", Object.class)
;
...
/**
 * @return A desccription for the claim
 */
public String getDescription() {
    return description;
}
```

Note that the "groups" and "aud" claims should only be injected into a Set of String, not as a comma-delimited string.

The current complete set of valid claim types is therefore (excluding the invalid Claims.UNKNOWN Void type)

- java.lang.String

- java.lang.Long and long

- java.lang.Boolean and boolean

- java.util.Set<java.lang.String>

- jakarta.json.JsonValue.TRUE/FALSE

- jakarta.json.JsonString

- jakarta.json.JsonNumber

- jakarta.json.JsonArray

- jakarta.json.JsonObject

Custom claims not handled by the Claims enum must be any of the types defined in the valid claim types list.

Using JWT Bearer Tokens to Protect Services

For the current MP-JWT specification, use cases are based on a scenario where services belong to the same security domain. This avoids dealing with the complexities associated with federation of security domains. With that in mind, we assume that any information carried along with a token could be understood and processed (without any security breaches) by the different services involved.

The scenario can be described as follows:

```
A client sends a HTTP request to Service A including the JWT as a
bearer token:
GET /resource/1 HTTP/1.1
Host: example.com
Authorization: Bearer mF_9.B5f-4.1JqM
```

On the server, a token-based authentication mechanism in front of *Service A* performs all steps described in the "How Does It Work?" section. As part of the security context creation, the server establishes role and group mappings for the subject based on the JWT claims. The role to group mapping is fully configurable by the server along the lines of the Jakarta EE RBAC security model.

On the server side, it becomes trivial to pass the security context (the JWT) as a header. After a user or caller has logged into the API gateway or identity provider and obtained a JWT, enforcing the JWT on future calls by the user involves three main steps:

- Authenticate the caller: Identify the caller by reading a standard claim (e.g., username) in the JWT and validate the signature of the JWT.

- Authorize the caller: By using the roles of the group listed in the claim, enforce access control in the application.

- Propagate caller context: Pass the JWT token in subsequent calls so other microservices involved can also service the request.

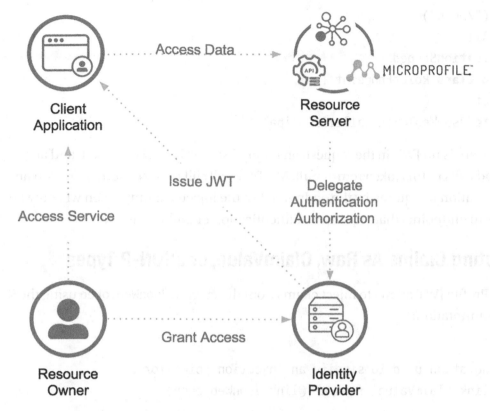

Figure 8-6. *Accessing a service protected by MP-JWT*

Mapping MP-JWT Tokens to Jakarta EE Container APIs

These are the requirements to expose a JWT via Jakarta EE container APIs. For the 2.0 release of MP-JWT, the only mandatory container integration is Jakarta REST and dependency injection of the MP-JWT types.

CDI Injection Requirements

Injecting JsonWebToken

An MP-JWT implementation must support injection of the currently authenticated caller as a JsonWebToken being @RequestScoped, even if an outer bean may be @ApplicationScoped:

```
@Path("/endp")
@DenyAll
@ApplicationScoped
public class RolesEndpoint {
@Inject
private JsonWebToken callerPrincipal;
```

If there is no JWT in the request, an empty `JsonWebToken` is injected, and all method calls to this token return null. MP-JWT will still perform authentication and authorization if required by the endpoint, but the injected empty token will only be visible to endpoints that require no authentication or authorization.

Injecting Claims As Raw, ClaimValue, or JSON-P Types

MicroProfile JWT allows to inject claims from the current `JsonWebToken` using the @ Claim annotation:

```
/**
 * Annotation used to signify an injection point for a
 * {@link ClaimValue} from a {@link JsonWebToken}
 */
@Qualifier
@Retention(RetentionPolicy.RUNTIME)
@Target({ElementType.FIELD, ElementType.METHOD, ElementType.PARAMETER,
ElementType
.TYPE})
public @interface Claim {
/**
 * The value specifies the id name the claim to inject
 * @return the claim name
 * @see JsonWebToken#getClaim(String)
 */
@Nonbinding
String value() default "";

/**
 * An alternate way of specifying a claim name using the
```

```
 * {@linkplain Claims} enum
 * @return the claim enum
 */
@Nonbinding
Claims standard() default Claims.UNKNOWN;
}
```

Where they use @Dependent scoping MP-JWT implementations are required to support injection of the claim values using any of the following:

- The raw type associated with the JsonWebToken claim value as defined in the Claims enum

- The org.eclipse.microprofile.jwt.ClaimValue wrapper

- jakarta.json.JsonValue JSON-P subtypes

The org.eclipse.microprofile.jwt.ClaimValue interface wraps around Principal:

```
/**
 * A representation of a claim in a {@link JsonWebToken}
 * @param <T> the expected type of the claim
 */
public interface ClaimValue<T> extends Principal {
/**
 * Access the name of the claim.
 * @return The name of the claim as seen in the
 * JsonWebToken content
 */
@Override
public String getName();

/**
 * Access the value of the claim.
 * @return the value of the claim.
 */
public T getValue();
}
```

The following example code shows how to inject different types of claims using each of the forms ClaimValue and JsonValue as well as the raw claim types:

```java
import org.eclipse.microprofile.jwt.Claim;
import org.eclipse.microprofile.jwt.ClaimValue;
import org.eclipse.microprofile.jwt.Claims;

@Path("/endp")
@DenyAll
@RequestScoped
public class RolesEndpoint {
...

// Raw types
@Inject
@Claim(standard = Claims.raw_token)
private String rawToken;
@Inject // 1.
@Claim(standard=Claims.iat)
private Long issuedAt;

// ClaimValue wrappers
@Inject // 2.
@Claim(standard = Claims.raw_token)
private ClaimValue<String> rawTokenCV;
@Inject
@Claim(standard = Claims.iss)
private ClaimValue<String> issuer;
@Inject
@Claim(standard = Claims.jti)
private ClaimValue<String> jti;

@Inject // 3.
@Claim("jti")
private ClaimValue<Optional<String>> optJTI;
@Inject
@Claim("jti")
private ClaimValue objJTI;
```

```
@Inject // 4.
@Claim("aud")
private ClaimValue<Set<String>> aud;
@Inject
@Claim("groups")
private ClaimValue<Set<String>> groups;
   @Inject // 5.
   @Claim(standard=Claims.iat)
   private ClaimValue<Long> issuedAtCV;
   @Inject
   @Claim("iat")
   private ClaimValue<Long> dupIssuedAt;
   @Inject
   @Claim("sub")
   private ClaimValue<Optional<String>> optSubject;
   @Inject
   @Claim("auth_time")
   private ClaimValue<Optional<Long>> authTime;

   @Inject // 6.
   @Claim("custom-missing")
   private ClaimValue<Optional<Long>> custom;
   //
   @Inject
   @Claim(standard = Claims.jti)
   private Instance<String> providerJTI;

   @Inject // 7.
   @Claim(standard = Claims.iat)
   private Instance<Long> providerIAT;
   @Inject
   @Claim("groups")
   private Instance<Set<String>> providerGroups;
   //
   @Inject
   @Claim(standard = Claims.jti)
```

```
private JsonString jsonJTI;
@Inject
@Claim(standard = Claims.iat)
private JsonNumber jsonIAT;

@Inject // 8.
@Claim("roles")
private JsonArray jsonRoles;
@Inject
@Claim("customObject")
private JsonObject jsonCustomObject
```

1. Injection of a nonproxyable raw type like java.lang.Long must happen in a RequestScoped bean as the producer will have dependent scope.

2. Injection of the raw MP-JWT token string.

3. Injection of the "jti" token id as an Optional<String> wapper.

4. Injection of the "aud" audience claim as a Set<String>. This is the required type as seen by looking at the Claims.aud enum value's Java type member.

5. Injection of the issued at time claim using an @Claim that references the claim name using the Claims.iat enum value.

6. Injection of a custom claim that does exist will result in an Optional<Long> value for which isPresent() will return false.

7. Another injection of a nonproxyable raw type like java.lang. Long, but the use of the jakarta.enterprise.inject.Instance interface allows the injection into non-RequestScoped contexts.

8. Injection of a JsonArray of role names via a custom "roles" claim.

The example shows different ways to specify the name of a claim using either a string or a Claims enum value. The string form allows the use of nonstandard claims, while the Claims enum helps prevent misspellings or typos.

Jakarta REST Container API Integration

The behavior of the following Jakarta REST security-related methods is required for MP-JWT implementations.

jakarta.ws.rs.core.SecurityContext.getUserPrincipal()

The java.security.Principal returned from these methods must be an instance of org.eclipse.microprofile.jwt.JsonWebToken.

jakarta.ws.rs.core.SecurityContext#isUserInRole(String)

This method must return true for any name that is included in the MP-JWT "groups" claim, as well as for any role name that has been mapped to a group name in the MP-JWT "groups" claim.

Using Jakarta Annotations

The expectation for use of security annotations declared by Jakarta Annotations

- @RolesAllowed
- @PermitAll
- @DenyAll

is that MP-JWT containers support the behavior as described in the respective sections of Jakarta Annotations (Sections 3.9–3.12 of Jakarta Annotations 2.0). In particular, the interaction between the annotations should be as described in Section 3.12 of Jakarta Annotations 2.0.

In terms of mapping the MP-JWT claims and role names used in @RolesAllowed, the role names mapped to group names in the MP-JWT "groups" claim must result in a positive authorization decision wherever the security constraint is applied.

Other Jakarta EE Integration

This section describes the expected behavior of other Jakarta EE container APIs.

Jakarta Security

The method jakarta.security.enterprise.identitystore. IdentityStore.getCal
lerGroups(CredentialValidationResult) should return the set of names found in the
"groups" claim in the JWT if it exists, otherwise an empty set.

JAKARTA EE 10 LOOKOUT

Jakarta Security in Jakarta EE 10 or a later version will support a new authentication
mechanism for OpenID Connect, but it will not be possible to have an application where
OpenID and MicroProfile JWT are active at the same time due to a restriction of the spec that
you can't have two mechanisms active in the same deployable application. This restriction
may be dropped in future versions of Jakarta EE after 10. So far, it means you need to
separate your applications or services to ensure MicroProfile JWT and OpenID Connect run
in two separate containers. Given the Microservice nature of most modern applications,
especially using Eclipse MicroProfile, it should not be hard to separate them.

Jakarta Authentication

The jakarta.security.auth.Subject returned by the jakarta.security.jacc.
PolicyContext.getContext(String key) method with the standard "jakarta.
security.auth.Subject.container" key must return a Subject that has a java.
security.Principal of type org.eclipse.microprofile.jwt.JsonWebToken among its
set of Principal values returned by getPrincipals(). Similarly, Subject#getPrincipa
ls(JsonWebToken.class) must return a set with at least one value. This means that the
following code snippet must pass the assertion:

```
Subject subject = (Subject) PolicyContext.getContext(
"javax.security.auth.Subject.container");
Set<? extends Principal> principalSet = subject.
getPrincipals(JsonWebToken.class);
assert principalSet.size() > 0;
```

Jakarta Enterprise Beans

The java.security.Principal returned from the jakarta.ejb.SessionContext.getCallerPrincipal() method must be an instance of org.eclipse.microprofile.jwt.JsonWebToken.

The method jakarta.ejb.SessionContext#isCallerInRole(String) must return true for any name included in the MP-JWT "groups" claim, as well as for any role name that has been mapped to a group name in that claim.

Jakarta Servlet

Overriding @LoginConfig from web.xml login-config

If a deployment with a web.xml descriptor contains a login-config element, an MP-JWT implementation should view the web.xml metadata as an override to the deployment annotation.

jakarta.servlet.http.HttpServletRequest.getUserPrincipal()

The java.security.Principal returned from this method MUST be an instance of org.eclipse.microprofile.jwt.JsonWebToken.

jakarta.servlet.http.HttpServletRequest#isUserInRole(String)

This method must return true for any name that is included in the MP-JWT "groups" claim, as well as for any role name that has been mapped to a group name in the MP-JWT "groups" claim.

Example Application

Let's take a concrete example. The source code is available at https://github.com/Apress/definitive-guide-jakarta-ee-security/tree/main/chapter8-microprofile-jwt

To run the example:

1. git clone https://github.com/Apress/definitive-guide-jakarta-ee-security

2.   cd chapter8-microprofile-jwt/mp-jwt-wallet

3.   Run `mvn test` in the `mp-jwt-wallet` folder to build and run the example tests

The project files are

- MyRestApp.java: The Jakarta REST application class

- MySecureWallet.java: A REST resource endpoint

- MySecureWalletTest.java: An Arquillian/TestNG unit test to deploy and exercise the `MySecureWallet` endpoint

- resources: Test resources directory

- web.xml: Servlet metadata descriptor to define security constraints

- jwt-roles.properties: A properties file used to define token group to application role mappings

- privateKey.pem: The test private key used to sign the token

- project-defaults.yml: A WildFly-Swarm configuration file that sets up the security domain

- publicKey.pem: The test public key used to verify the token signature

- Token1.json: The JSON content for test token 1

- Token1-50000-limit.json: The json content for test token 1 with an alternate warningLimit claim

- Token2.json: The JSON content for test token 2

- Token3.json: The JSON content for test token 3

- Token-noaccess.json: The JSON content for a test token that should not map to any valid access roles

Listing 8-1 provides the Jakarta REST Application class. In addition to the standard REST/CDI annotations that define the application root path and scope, there is the MP-JWT `@LoginConfig`, which declares the "MP-JWT" authentication method, and a `"jwt-jaspi"` realmName. The MP-JWT runtime will use this information to set up the authentication mechanism to be based on MicroProfile JWT bearer tokens.

Listing 8-1. MyRestApp.java

```
package org.eclipse.microprofile.test.jwt;

import jakarta.enterprise.context.ApplicationScoped;
import jakarta.ws.rs.ApplicationPath;
import jakarta.ws.rs.Path;
import jakarta.ws.rs.core.Application;

import org.eclipse.microprofile.auth.LoginConfig;

// We set the authentication method to the MP-JWT for the MicroProfile
JWT method
// the realmName maps the security-domains setting in the project-
defaults.yml
@LoginConfig(authMethod = "MP-JWT", realmName = "jwt-jaspi")
@ApplicationScoped
@ApplicationPath("/wallet")
public class MyRestApp extends Application {
}
```

The REST endpoint resource is defined in MySecureWallet.java. This is a simplified hypothetical cryptocurrency online wallet allowing to view the balance, credit, or debit money to and from the wallet.

The wallet endpoint uses Jakarta REST, CDI, and Jakarta Security annotations to define the behavior. A notable MP-JWT feature is the injection of JsonWebToken and a warningLimit claim instance:

```
@Inject
private JsonWebToken jwt;
@Inject
@Claim("warningLimit")
private Instance<Optional<JsonNumber>> warningLimitInstance;
```

The JsonWebToken holds the MP-JWT bearer token of the currently authenticated caller. The warningLimitInstance is a view to a custom token claim called "warningLimit". We use the CDI Instance interface to access the claim because MySecureWallet is @ApplicationScoped while claim values are produced with a

513

@Dependent scope, which is associated with the @RequestScoped token. Without using Instance, the CDI container would bind the "warningLimit" claim value to the first value found when the resource was created.

We use Optional<JsonNumber> for the "warningLimit" claim because not every caller's token may contain the custom claim, avoiding null values or exceptions. The injected JsonWebToken is used in the debit endpoint:

```
if (dAmount > whaleLimit) {
  if (securityContext.isUserInRole("Whale")) {
    // Validate the spending limit from the token claim
    JsonNumber spendingLimit = jwt.getClaim("spendingLimit");
    if (spendingLimit == null || spendingLimit.doubleValue() < dAmount) {
        return Response.status(Response.Status.BAD_REQUEST).build();
    }
  } else {
    return Response.status(Response.Status.FORBIDDEN).build();
  }
}
```

We check if the debit amount is above a whaleLimit value, and if, assuming the caller has the role "Whale", the debit amount is below the "spendingLimit" claim value in the token. The warningLimitInstance is used in the generateBalanceInfo method:

```
Optional<JsonNumber> warningLimit = warningLimitInstance.get();
if (warningLimit.isPresent()) {
  if (warningLimit.get().doubleValue() > usdBalance.doubleValue()) {
      String warningMsg = String.format("balance is below warning
      limit: %s",
warningLimit.get());
      result.add("warning", warningMsg);
  }
}
```

If the caller's JsonWebToken has a "warningLimit" claim value, that value is compared to the current balance, and if the balance is below the warningLimit, a warning message is added to the balance info JsonObject.

Role Handling

To understand how the MP-JWT token is used for authorization based on Jakarta Security annotations in the `MySecureWallet` endpoint, let's first have a look at the `Token1.json` payload:

Listing 8-2. Token1.json

```json
{
 "iss": "https://server.example.com",
 "jti": "a-123",
 "sub": "24400320",
 "upn": "jdoe@example.com",
 "preferred_username": "jdoe",
 "aud": "wallet",
 "exp": 1311281970,
 "iat": 1311280970,
 "auth_time": 1311280969,
 "groups": [
   "ViewBalance", "Debtor", "Creditor"
 ],
 "spendingLimit": 2500,
 "warningLimit": 90000
}
```

Here, the "groups" claim contains the base RBAC information providing the names of the groups (collections of role names) that a caller bearing this token is granted. The various @RolesAllowed uses define role names allowed to access a protected endpoint. We heard earlier that an MP-JWT implementation is required to provide a group to role mapping. Therefore, this token bearer will have at least the "ViewBalance", "Debtor", and "Creditor" roles. MP-JWT containers are free to provide additional group to role mapping configurations. How this is done depends on the container implementation, as this is a feature of Jakarta Security defined as an implementation detail.

In Red Hat containers like Thorntail or WildFly, this can be done by configuring a JAAS. The `resources/project-defaults.yml` file contains the following `security.security-domains.jwt-jaspi.jaspi-authentication` subtree:

```
login-module-stacks:
 roles-lm-stack:
  login-modules:
    # This stack performs the token verification and group to role mapping
    - login-module: rm
      code: org.wildfly.swarm.mpjwtauth.deploy.auth.jaas.JWTLoginModule
      flag: required
      module-options:
        rolesProperties: jwt-roles.properties
```

This defines a JWTLoginModule, a JAAS login module authenticating the MP-JWT token by verifying issuer, signer, and expiration. It also performs the one-to-one group to role mapping of the token "groups" claim and will augment the roles with any additional group name to role name mapping that is specified in the jwt-roles.properties file found in the deployment classpath. The resources/jwt-roles.properties file contains this entry:

```
Debtor=Whale
```

The "Debtor" group will be assigned the role name "Whale" in addition to the role name "Debtor." If you look through all the various *.json files for the test token contents, there is no "groups" claim with the "Whale" name. That role name, we saw being used in the debit endpoint logic, is assigned to tokens with the "Debitor" group through this secondary mapping.

The test code is based on TestNG and Arquillian providing a deployment archive that contains the application code and resources being tested. This is the deployment creation method for MySecureWalletTest:

```
/**
* Create a CDI aware Jakarta REST application archive with our
* endpoints and
* @return the Jakarta REST application archive
* @throws IOException - on resource failure
*/
@Deployment(testable=true)
public static WebArchive createDeployment() throws IOException {
```

```
// Get the public key of the token signer
URL publicKey = MySecureWalletTest.class.getResource("/publicKey.pem");
WebArchive webArchive = ShrinkWrap
        .create(WebArchive.class, "MySecureEndpoint.war")
        // Place the public key in the war as /MP-JWT-SIGNER - Wildfly/
        Thorntail specific
        .addAsManifestResource(publicKey, "/MP-JWT-SIGNER")
        .addClass(MySecureWallet.class)
        .addClass(MyJaxrsApp.class)
        .addAsWebInfResource(EmptyAsset.INSTANCE, "beans.xml")
        // Add Wildfly-Swarm specific configuration of the
        security domain
        .addAsResource("project-defaults.yml", "/project-defaults.yml")
        .addAsWebInfResource("jwt-roles.properties", "classes/jwt-roles.
        properties")
        .setWebXML("WEB-INF/web.xml")
        ;
    System.out.printf("WebArchive: %s\n", webArchive.toString(true));
    return webArchive;
}
```

The purpose of the createDeployment method is the creation of the webArchive. This is a web application archive abstraction to contain

- The public key of the signer.

- The MySecureWallet and MyRestApp classes.

- The WildFly/Thorntail-specific project-defaults.yml file we partially saw before.

- The jwt-roles.properties file used to augment the group to role name mapping we saw earlier.

- A standard web.xml descriptor specifying that the entire deployment should be secured. This is a current requirement for the WildFly/ Thorntail MP-JWT implementation that will be removed in future releases.

Running the Tests

You can run the tests by cloning the project into your favorite IDE and making use of its TestNG integration, or by calling the Maven test goal from a command line. To run all tests, execute mvn `test`.

See the README.md file in the example project for more detailed instructions.

Future Improvements

Further improvements of this example include upgrades to newer MicroProfile versions where available and required.

We also consider using the Java Money and Currency API (`http://javamoney. github.io/`) as soon as Jakarta JSON supports its monetary types the same way as Jakarta Bean Validation already does, because current JSON bindings of the JavaMoney API rely on Jackson Data Binding, which is likely incompatible with the JSON data types used by MP-JWT.

Conclusion

There are several reasons why JWT is becoming so widely adopted:

- JWT is an open standard that can be used for authentication and authorization once users have authenticated.

- JWT tokens cannot be forged or modified (without detection), unless you know or get hold of the secret key.

- Token validation doesn't require an additional trip and can be validated locally by each service.

- JWT is easy to use, and there are many great frameworks for implementing it in your applications.

- Given the JSON format, it is solely based on claims or attributes to carry authentication and authorization information about a subject.

- Makes it easier to support different types of access control mechanisms such as ABAC, DAC, RBAC, and Context-Based Access Control.

- Message-level security using signature and encryption as defined by both JWS and JWE standards.

- Widely adopted by multiple Single Sign-On solutions and well-known standards like OpenID Connect given its small overhead and ability to be used across different security domains (federation).

- Given the JSON format, processing JWT tokens becomes easy and lightweight, especially considering Jakarta EE standards like JSON-P or different third-party libraries like Nimbus and Jackson.

- Parties can easily agree on a specific set of claims in order to exchange both authentication and authorization information. Defining this along with the Java API and mapping to Jakarta REST APIs are the primary tasks of the MicroProfile JWT specification.

- However, as MicroProfile grows and produces more and more specs, fewer vendors can afford to create compatible implementations, and the choice among them for some specs can be almost as limited as with single-vendor solutions like Spring Boot or Spring Security.

APPENDIX A

Spring Security

What Is Spring Security?

Spring Security is a security framework that works especially well with the Spring Framework or Spring Web MVC and more recently Reactive applications using Spring Flux as well, Spring Security is a continuation of Acegi Security, a powerful security framework. But the problem was it required a lot of cumbersome XML configuration to realize it. Spring embraced it into the family from version 2.0 and, since then, refined it to its present state. Although the XML configuration is still possible, Spring's new spirit of convention over configuration also influenced it the same way we also see in Jakarta EE. It is possible to perform all security configurations with annotation rather than XML, although the provision is still there for backward compatibility and to leverage certain flexibility. Its primary goal is to handle authentication and authorization for web requests and method invocations.

Brief History

Spring Security began in late 2003 as "The Acegi Security System for Spring," initially created by Ben Alex; remember the first chapter; based on questions asked on the Spring Developers' mailing list whether there had been any Spring-based security implementation. Back then, the Spring community was relatively small, and Spring itself had only existed as a SourceForge project from early 2003. The answer to the question was that it was worthwhile, although a lack of time and resources prevented its exploration back then.

With that in mind, a simple security implementation was built but remained unreleased. A few weeks later, another member of the Spring community asked about security, and this code was offered to them.

© Arjan Tijms, Teo Bais, and Werner Keil 2022
A. Tijms et al., *The Definitive Guide to Security in Jakarta EE*, https://doi.org/10.1007/978-1-4842-7945-8

Other similar questions followed, and by January 2004, around 20 people were using the code. These initial users were joined by others who suggested a SourceForge project of its own, which was created in March 2004.

Back then, the project didn't have its own authentication modules. J2EE Container Managed Security was used for the authentication process, with the first version of Acegi Security instead focusing on authorization. This was suitable at first, but as more users requested support for additional containers, the limitation of container-specific authentication realm interfaces became evident. Adding new JARs to the container's classpath also caused issues, which was a common source of admin confusion and misconfiguration. Acegi Security authentication services were introduced. And around a year later, Acegi Security became an official Spring Framework subproject. The 1.0.0 final release was published in May 2006 – after more than two and a half years of production use by numerous projects and hundreds of improvement requests and community contributions. Acegi Security became an official Spring project toward the end of 2007 and was rebranded to "Spring Security."

Overview

Concepts

Spring Security is based on three main concepts:

- Authentication

- Authorization

- Servlet Filters

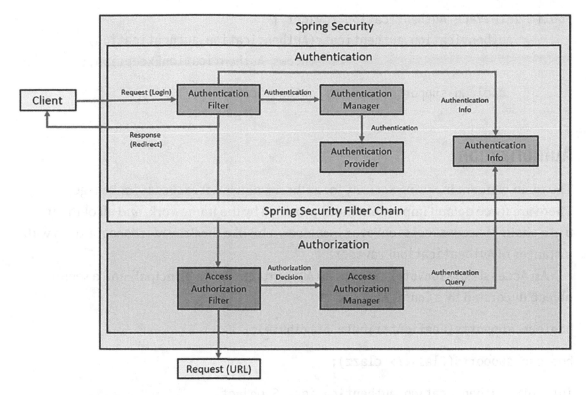

Figure A-1. *Spring Security authentication/authorization flow*

Authentication

The main interface for authentication in Spring Security is `AuthenticationManager`, which has just one method, `authenticate()`.

```
public interface AuthenticationManager {
  Authentication authenticate(Authentication authentication)
    throws AuthenticationException;
}
```

The most common implementation of `AuthenticationManager` is `ProviderManager`, which delegates to a chain of `AuthenticationProvider` instances. An `AuthenticationProvider` is similar to an `AuthenticationManager`, but it has another method allowing a caller to check whether it supports a particular authentication type.

```
public interface AuthenticationProvider {
        Authentication authenticate(Authentication authentication)
                                    throws AuthenticationException;

        boolean supports(Class<?> authentication);
}
```

Authorization

The main element in Spring Security for authorization is `AccessDecisionManager`. There are three default implementations provided by the framework, and all of them use a chain of `AccessDecisionVoter` instances, a bit like the `ProviderManager` does with instances of `AuthenticationProvider`.

An `AccessDecisionVoter<S>` uses an `Authentication` (a principal) and a secure object, decorated by a `ConfigAttribute`:

```
boolean supports(ConfigAttribute attribute);
```

```
boolean supports(Class<?> clazz);
```

```
int vote(Authentication authentication, S object,
        Collection<ConfigAttribute> attributes);
```

The interface `ConfigAttribute` encapsulates access information metadata in a secured resource. Figure A-2 shows the hierarchy of configuration attributes.

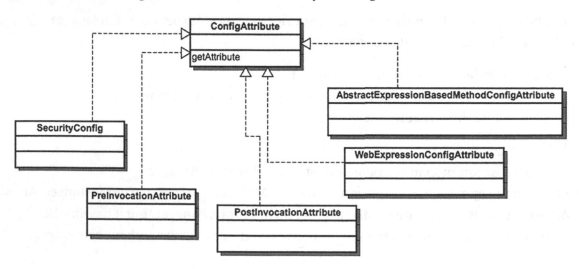

Figure A-2. *Config Attribute hierarchy*

Servlet Filters

The web tier of Spring Security is based on standard Jakarta EE Servlet Filters, although as of Spring Security and Framework 5, that is at most Jakarta EE 8. The Spring Security filter chain builds on several filters to cover different security constraints of a web application. Figure A-3 shows the typical chain of these filters for a single HTTP request.

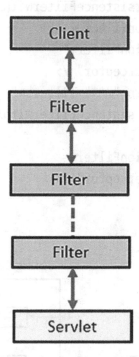

Figure A-3. *Filter chain for a single HTTP request*

For the container, Spring Security is just a single filter, composed of multiple filters for different purposes. Spring Security is installed as a single filter in the chain. This filter, named FilterChainProxy, contains all the details about the different security filters available through the security filter chain. Using the Proxy Pattern, it determines which SecurityFilterChain will be invoked for an incoming request.

Here's an example:

```
<bean id="filterChainProxy" class="org.springframework.security.web.
FilterChainProxy">
  <sec:filter-chain-map path-type="ant">
    <sec:filter-chain pattern="/webServices/**" filters="
          securityContextPersistenceFilterWithASCFalse,
          basicAuthenticationFilter,
          exceptionTranslationFilter,
          filterSecurityInterceptor" />
    <sec:filter-chain pattern="/**" filters="
          securityContextPersistenceFilterWithASCTrue,
          formLoginFilter,
          exceptionTranslationFilter,
          filterSecurityInterceptor" />
  </sec:filter-chain-map>
</bean>
```

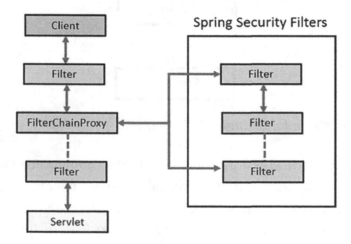

Figure A-4. *Filter chain proxy*

However, FilterChainProxy is not called directly but via the
DelegatingFilterProxy filter. Using it, you will see something like this in the web.xml
file of your web application:

```
<filter>
    <filter-name>myFilter</filter-name>
    <filter-class>org.springframework.web.filter.DelegatingFilterProxy
    </filter-class>
</filter>

<filter-mapping>
    <filter-name>myFilter</filter-name>
    <url-pattern>/*</url-pattern>
</filter-mapping>
```

Components

Major components and features of Spring Security are

- ACL

- CSRF Protection

- Security Interceptor

- Tag Library

- User Details and Service

- XML Namespace

ACL

Access control lists (ACLs) are part of the authorization process in Spring Security, but ACLs work at a finer-grained level of an application. Essentially, ACLs map resources, users, and permissions. They allow you to define rules like "User Werner has administrative permission on the web app X," while "User John has read access to the web app X."

CSRF Protection

Using Cross-Site Request Forgery (CSRF), a hacker can modify the state of HTTP methods like PUT, GET, or POST, redirecting the client, for example, by clicking a modified link to an unsecure web page, allowing to steal sensitive user information. Common CSRF attacks include the following:

- HTTP GET method: Making a victim click a fake GET link to intercept sensitive information like username/password, etc.

- HTTP POST method: Same as GET but uses the POST method

In Spring Security 5, CSRF Protection is enabled by default in Java applications. If you really need to disable it, you can add `.csrf().disable()` to the configuration.

To enable the CSRF Protection on the server side, you need to include the CSRF token in your requests from clients by adding

```
<input type="hidden" name="${_csrf.parameterName}" value="${_csrf.token}"/>
```

Security Interceptor

One of the most important components of Spring Security is the Security Interceptor.

With an abstract default implementation `AbstractSecurityInterceptor` and two concrete subclasses, `FilterSecurityInterceptor` and `MethodSecurityInterceptor`, it decides if a particular call to a secured resource should be allowed or not.

Tag Library

The Spring Security Taglibs provide support for security information and constraints in JSP web applications. You can use the following tags:

- Authorize

- Authentication

- Accesscontrollist

- Csrfinput

- CsrfMetaTags

All you need to do is add the `spring-security-taglibs` dependency to the `pom.xml` file of your application:

```
<dependency>
<groupId>org.springframework.security</groupId>
<artifactId>spring-security-taglibs</artifactId>
<version>5.6.0.RELEASE</version>
</dependency>
```

User Details and Service

`UserDetailsService` is a core interface in Spring Security; it has just one method named `loadUserByUsername()` which we can implement to retrieve the user's authentication and authorization information, called `UserDetails`.

```
UserDetails loadUserByUsername(java.lang.String username) throws
UsernameNotFoundException
```

This is an example for an implementation:

```
@Service
public class CustomUserDetailService implements UserDetailsService {

    @Autowired
    private CustomerRepository customerRepository;

    @Override
    public UserDetails loadUserByUsername(String username) throws
    UsernameNotFoundException {
        final CustomerEntity customer = customerRepository.
        findByEmail(username);
        if (customer == null) {
            throw new UsernameNotFoundException(username);
        }
        UserDetails user = User.withUsername(customer.getEmail()).
        password(customer.getPassword()).authorities("USER").build();
        return user;
    }
}
```

and how you can use it via InMemoryUserDetailsManager:

```
@Bean
@Override
public UserDetailsService userDetailsService() {
        UserDetails user =
                        User.builder()
                                    .passwordEncoder(s -> encode(s))
                                    .username("user")
                                    .password("password")
                                    .roles("USER")
                                    .build();

        return new InMemoryUserDetailsManager(user);
}
```

InMemoryUserDetailsManager indirectly implements the UserDetailsService interface. It reads an in-memory HashMap and loads the UserDetails by calling the loadUserByUsername() method.

XML Namespace

The XML namespace is an important part of the framework, although it is actually not mandatory. Knowing the Spring Framework's namespaces, you may understand what happens when you define your security-specific XML configuration in your application context.

If you don't know how they work, maybe you think Spring is somehow made aware of how to treat these specific elements and how to load them in the general Spring application context. Either way, here, we will explain in some detail the process behind the definition of a custom namespace in Spring and, particularly, the elements in the Spring Security namespace.

Originally, Spring did not support custom XML. All that Spring understood was its own classes defined in the standard Spring Core namespace, where you can define <bean>s on a case-by-case basis and can't really define anything conceptually more complex without adding that complexity yourself to the configuration. This <bean>-based configuration was, and still is, very good for configuring general-purpose bean instances, but it can get messy really fast for defining more domain-specific utilities. And beyond being messy, it is also very poor at expressing the business domain of the beans you want to define.

Instead of

```xml
<bean id="myPolicyAdmin" class="org.springframework.security.oauth2.client.
OAuth2RestTemplate">
        <constructor-arg>
            <bean class="org.springframework.security.oauth2.client.token.
            grant.password.ResourceOwnerPasswordResourceDetails">
                <property name="accessTokenUri" value="${accessToken
                EndpointUrl}" />
                <property name="clientId" value="${clientId}" />
                <property name="clientSecret" value="${clientSecret}" />
                <property name="username" value="${policyAdminUserName}" />
                <property name="password" value="${policyAdminUserPassword}" />
            </bean>
        </constructor-arg>
    </bean>
```

you can use annotations:

```java
@Bean
public ResourceOwnerPasswordResourceDetails resourceDetails(@Value(
"${accessTokenEndpointUrl}") String accessTokenUri,
@Value("${clientId}") String clientId,
@Value("${clientSecret}") String clientSecret,
@Value("${policyAdminUserName}") String username,
@Value("${policyAdminUserPassword}") String password) {
ResourceOwnerPasswordResourceDetails rd = new
ResourceOwnerPasswordResourceDetails ();
rd.setAccessTokenUri(accessTokenUri);
rd.setClientId(clientId);
rd.setUsername(username);
rd.setPassword(password);
return rd;
}
```

```
@Bean
public OAuth2RestTemplate restTemplate(ResourceOwnerPasswordResourceDetails
resourceDetails) {
return new OAuth2RestTemplate(resourceDetails);
}
```

Spring Security Reactive

Spring Boot 2.0	
Reactor	
Reactive Stack	Servlet Stack
Netty, Servlet 3.1+ Containers	Servlet Containers
Reactive Streams Adapters	Servlet API
Spring Security Reactive	Spring Security
Spring WebFlux	Spring MVC
Spring Data Reactive Repositories (Mongo, Cassandra, Redis, Couchbase)	Spring Data Repositories (JDBC, JPA, NoSQL)

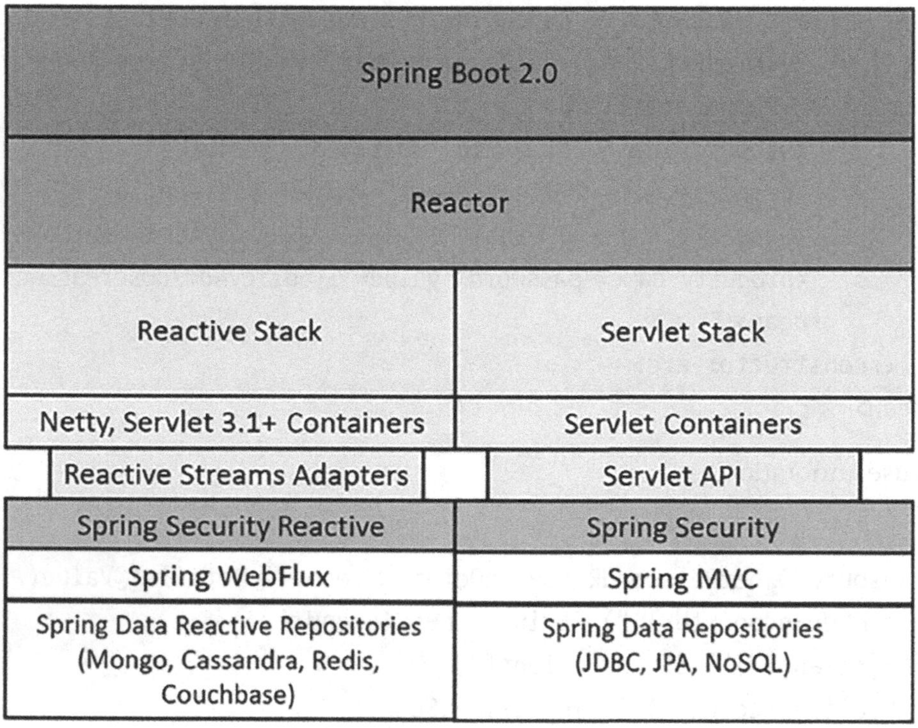

Figure A-5. *Spring Security 5 stacks*

With Spring Security 5, Spring Framework 5, and Spring Boot 2, there are two major stacks:

1. Servlet Stack

2. Reactive Stack

The Servlet Stack is based on Spring MVC, while the Reactive Stack is based on Spring WebFlux, which is fully nonblocking, supports Reactive Streams back pressure, and runs on servers like Netty and other Servlet 3.1+ containers.

Here's an example for a traditional REST Controller using Spring MVC:

```
@RestController
public class ProductController {
    @Autowired
    ProductService ps;

    @RequestMapping("/products")
    public List<Product> productListing() {
        return ps.findAll();
    }
}
```

And here the same with Reactive Spring using WebFlux:

```
@Bean
public RouterFunction<ServerResponse> productListing(ProductService ps) {
    return route().GET("/products", req -> ok().body(ps.findAll()))
      .build();
}
```

A minimal implementation of UserDetailsService we just learned about looks as follows using Reactive Spring Security:

```
@Bean
@EnableWebFluxSecurity
public class HelloWebFluxSecurityConfig {
    @Bean
    public MapReactiveUserDetailsService userDetailsService() {
        UserDetails user = User.withDefaultPasswordEncoder()
            .username("user")
            .password("password")
            .roles("USER")
            .build();
        return new MapReactiveUserDetailsService(user);
    }
}
```

Example Application

Here's a simple Basic Auth example application using Spring Security for the Servlet Stack and Reactive Spring Security. You can find it under https://github.com/Apress/definitive-guide-jakarta-ee-security/tree/main/appendixa-spring-security.

Servlet

The Servlet example application consists of a HelloController class:

```
@RestController
public class HelloController {

        @GetMapping("/")
        public String hello() {

                Authentication authentication = SecurityContextHolder.
                getContext().getAuthentication();
                String currentPrincipalName = authentication.getName();

                return "Hello " + currentPrincipalName;
        }

}
```

A Security Configuration:

```
@Configuration
@EnableWebSecurity
public class WebSecurityConfig extends WebSecurityConfigurerAdapter {

        @Override
        protected void configure(HttpSecurity http) throws Exception {
                http.authorizeRequests()
                        .anyRequest().authenticated()
                        .and()
                        .httpBasic();
        }
```

```java
    @Bean
    @Override
    public UserDetailsService userDetailsService() {
            UserDetails user =
                        User.builder()
                                    .passwordEncoder(s -> encode(s))
                                    .username("user")
                                    .password("password")
                                    .roles("USER")
                                    .build();

            return new InMemoryUserDetailsManager(user);
    }

    private String encode(String s) {
            return passwordEncoder().encode(s);
    }

    @Bean
    public PasswordEncoder passwordEncoder() {
            return new BCryptPasswordEncoder();
    }
}
```

And the Spring Boot application class:

```java
@SpringBootApplication
public class SpringSecurityBasicAuthExample {

        public static void main(String[] args) {
                SpringApplication.run(SpringSecurityBasicAuthExample.
                class, args);
        }

}
```

Reactive

Similarly, the WebFlux Reactive example application consists of a
HelloController class:

```java
@RestController
public class HelloController {

    @GetMapping("/public")
    public Mono<String> publicHello(Principal principal) {
        return Mono.just("Hello " + getPrincipalName(principal) + ", from a
        public page");
    }

    @GetMapping("/private")
    public Mono<String> privateHello(Principal principal) {
        return Mono.just("Hello " + getPrincipalName(principal) + ", from a
        private page");
    }

    private String getPrincipalName(Principal principal) {
        return principal == null ? "anonymous" : principal.getName();
    }
}
```

A Security Configuration:

```java
@Configuration
@EnableWebFluxSecurity
public class ReactiveSecurityConfig {

    @Bean
    public SecurityWebFilterChain securityWebFilterChain(ServerHttpSecurity
    http) {
        return http.authorizeExchange()
                .pathMatchers("/private").hasRole("USER")
                .matchers(EndpointRequest.toAnyEndpoint()).hasRole("ADMIN")
                .anyExchange().permitAll()
                .and().httpBasic()
```

```java
            .and().build();
    }

    /**
     * Sample in-memory user details service.
     */
    @Bean
    public MapReactiveUserDetailsService userDetailsService() {
        return new MapReactiveUserDetailsService(
                    User.builder()
                                    .passwordEncoder(s -> encode(s))
                                    .username("user")
                                    .password("password")
                                    .roles("USER")
                            .build(),
                        User.builder()
                                    .passwordEncoder(s -> encode(s))
                        .username("admin")
                        .password("password")
                        .roles("USER,ADMIN")
                                    .build());
    }

        private String encode(String s) {
                return passwordEncoder().encode(s);
        }

        @Bean
        public PasswordEncoder passwordEncoder() {
                return new BCryptPasswordEncoder();
        }
}
```

And again the Spring Boot application class:

```
@SpringBootApplication
public class ReactiveSecureApplication {

    public static void main(String[] args) {
        SpringApplication.run(ReactiveSecureApplication.class, args);
    }
}
```

The only minor difference is that the Reactive application knows two roles, USER and ADMIN, with two respective usernames, while the Servlet-based application uses just one role and user for the entire web application.

Comparison to Jakarta EE Security

First of all, the Spring Framework and with it Spring Security, Spring Boot, and most other parts of the Spring stack have always used Java EE. As of Spring 5, they are compatible with Jakarta EE 8, while Spring Framework 6 plans to build on top of Jakarta EE 9.1.

Spring Security uses the Jakarta EE Servlet Filter, while the authentication mechanism of Jakarta Security and the underlying spec Jakarta Authentication does more or less the same thing. The Jakarta Security IdentityStore is very close to the UserDetailService of Spring Security; both offer different implementations like in-memory, LDAP, file, or database storage. Other key concepts, especially SecurityContext, exist under even exactly the same name, so it'll be interesting to see how Spring Security 6 or above might use it when embracing Jakarta EE 9.1 or higher.

While over 15 years ago, when Spring Security and Apache Shiro, which we'll see in the next appendix, were created out of lacking simplicity or even entire concepts in JASPIC or JAAS, much has improved with Jakarta Security. Fine-grained ACLs are probably among the functionalities and components that Spring Security offers a little more domain oriented, while the same can be found in Jakarta Security or Jakarta REST (currently still quite redundant as of Jakarta EE 9.1 or 10) in a more technical sense, but especially for web applications or RESTful web APIs, those web resources often match business needs like add a user or similar CRUD operations. Encryption support similar to Apache Shiro is more convenient in Spring Security, while under Jakarta EE and Java SE, using the Java Cryptographic Extension (JCE) on its own, without, for example, Bouncy Castle or similar encryption frameworks, can be extremely cumbersome.

Spring Security and the Spring stack have a long history and broad community support, but it comes with a certain vendor lock-in, often making it harder to combine Spring and non-Spring libraries.

APPENDIX B

Apache Shiro

What Is Shiro?

Apache Shiro is an open source security framework that provides application developers intuitive, simple ways of supporting

- Authentication
- Authorization
- Cryptography
- Session Management

The word "shiro" means castle in Japanese.

Brief History

Shiro was created out of developer's needs not met by standards around that time. Les Hazlewood and Jeremy Haile created a security framework named JSecurity at SourceForge between 2004 and 2008 because they could not find an existing Java security framework suitable for their needs and JAAS (we already learned about in Chapter 1) did not work well for them. Their effort started roughly around the same time as Acegi Security in 2004, also at SourceForge, which was then the largest independent open source hosting community, a lot like GitHub is now. JSecurity attracted more committers including Peter Ledbrook, Alan Ditzel, and Tim Veil.

In 2008, JSecurity was submitted to the Apache Software Foundation and accepted into its Incubator program mentored toward becoming a top-level Apache Project. Under the ASF Incubator, JSecurity was first renamed Ki (pronounced "Key"), only to be soon renamed Shiro due to trademark concerns. The project grew in the Apache

© Arjan Tijms, Teo Bais, and Werner Keil 2022
A. Tijms et al., *The Definitive Guide to Security in Jakarta EE*, https://doi.org/10.1007/978-1-4842-7945-8

Incubator, adding Kalle Korhonen as committer. In July 2010, the Shiro team released its official version 1.0. Following the release of the first version, the Shiro project created a Project Management Committee (PMC) and elected Les Hazlewood as its chair. On September 22, 2010, Shiro became a top-level Apache project.

Overview

Shiro is based on three core concepts:

- Subject

- SecurityManager

- Realm

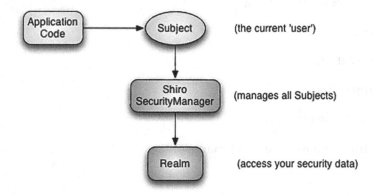

Figure B-1. *Shiro concepts*

Subject

The Subject is basically a "view" of the current user. While "User" suggests a human person, a "Subject" can also be a service or a corporate entity.

SecurityManager

The SecurityManager, not to be mistaken for the API type soon to be removed from the JDK, is the central element of Shiro's architecture.

Realm

A realm manages a set of users, roles, and permissions. A user belongs to and logs into a realm. Realms are isolated from one another and can only manage and authenticate users they control. Realms usually have a direct correlation with a data source, for example, a database, LDAP directory, file system, or a similar resource.

Features

Figure B-2 shows the main concerns of Shiro as well as other supporting features.

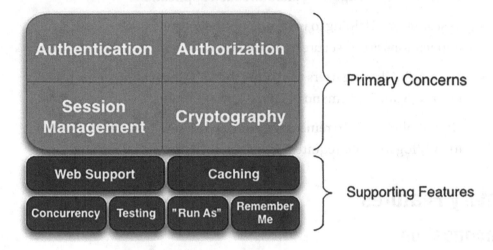

Figure B-2. *Shiro features*

- Authentication across multiple pluggable data sources including

  - LDAP/Active Directory

  - JDBC

  - JNDI

- Authorization based on roles or fine-grained permissions:

  - Know if a user is assigned a certain role or not.

  - Know if a user is allowed to do something or not.

- Session Management: Use in both web and "serverless," or any environment where Single Sign-On, clustered, or distributed sessions are required.

- Cryptography: Secure data with cryptographic algorithms beyond the standard Java ciphers and hashes, yet easy to use.

Other supporting Shiro features are the following:

- Web support: Helps secure web applications

- Caching: To ensure applications run fast and efficient

- Concurrency: Supporting multithreaded applications

- Test support: Helping to write unit or integration tests to check if your applications are as secure as expected

- "Run As": Allowing users to assume the identity of another user, a bit like the "sudo" command of Linux

- "Remember Me": To remember users across sessions, allowing them to only log in when required, for example, if the session expired

Primary Features

Authentication

Shiro aims to make authentication intuitive and easy to use despite a variety of features, these are the highlights:

- Subject Based

- Single Method Call

- Detailed Exception Hierarchy

- Built-in "Remember Me"

- Pluggable Data Sources

- Using Multiple Realms

Steps to Authenticate a Subject

Authenticating a Subject can be broken down into three steps:

1. Collect the Subject's submitted principals and credentials.

2. Submit the principals and credentials for authentication.

3. If the submission was successful, grant access; otherwise, retry authentication or block access.

Here's how to use Shiro's API for these steps:

Collect the Subject's submitted principals and credentials

```
//Most common scenario of username/password pair:
UsernamePasswordToken token = new UsernamePasswordToken(username, password);

//"Remember Me" built-in:
token.setRememberMe(true);
```

In this case, we used the UsernamePasswordToken, supporting the most common username/password authentication approach. This is an implementation of Shiro's org.apache.shiro.authc.AuthenticationToken interface, which is the base interface of Shiro's authentication system to represent submitted principals and credentials.

Shiro does not care how you acquire this information: perhaps the data was entered via HTML form, or maybe retrieved from an HTTP header, or maybe through command line arguments. The process of an application collecting information from users is completely decoupled from Shiro's AuthenticationToken concept.

You may construct and represent AuthenticationToken instances any way you like; it is protocol agnostic.

This example also shows that we have indicated that we wish Shiro to perform "Remember Me" services for authentication.

Authorization

Authorization has three main elements:

- Permission

- Role

- User (Subject)

Permissions

Permissions are an essential aspect of security policies. They allow what can be done in an application. Common permissions for data elements are Create, Read, Update, and Delete, commonly known as *CRUD*.

Granularity

Shiro allows very fine-grained permissions where required, in any granularity, for example:

- Resource level: The broadest definition, for example, allowing a user to edit customer records or finances

- Instance level: Permissions that are specific to a particular instance of a resource, not just the general type. Such as allowing a user to access the customer records of IBM, but not Red Hat

- Attribute level: Allowing to specify permissions for an attribute of an instance or resource, for example, the home address or work address of an IBM employee

Here's a permission example. We check if users have permission to print using a "Colour Printer" and those who do will see a "print" button; the others don't. This is an example of an instance-level permission.

```
Subject currentUser = SecurityUtils.getSubject();

Permission printPermission = new PrinterPermission("ColourPrinter","print");

If (currentUser.isPermitted(printPermission)) {
    // show the print button?)
} else {
    // don't show the button?
}
```

Users

A user or "Subject" (because as mentioned, it can also be a service or corporate entity) can be any actor in your application. In most cases, you'd obtain the current Subject by using org.apache.shiro.SecurityUtils:

```
Subject currentUser = SecurityUtils.getSubject();
```

Roles

Remember the RBAC from Chapter 2, roles are a set of permissions, allowing to assign permissions to a role instead of each individual user.

Shiro provides two types of roles:

- Implicit roles

- Explicit roles

Application role checks are usually the assignment of an **implicit** role. A user with the role "administrator" can view customer data. The names of the roles are not necessarily related to a business requirement or scenario, while an **explicit** role already comes with permissions it needs. For example, a user with the role "editor" has the "publish chapters" permission assigned to it.

```
Realm realm = new MyPublishingRealm();
SecurityManager securityManager = new DefaultSecurityManager(realm);

SecurityUtils.setSecurityManager(securityManager);
Subject currentUser = SecurityUtils.getSubject();

if (!currentUser.isAuthenticated()) {
  UsernamePasswordToken token
    = new UsernamePasswordToken("user", "password");
  token.setRememberMe(true);
  try {
      currentUser.login(token);
  } catch (UnknownAccountException uae) {
      log.error("Username Not Found!", uae);
  } catch (IncorrectCredentialsException ice) {
      log.error("Invalid Credentials!", ice);
  } catch (LockedAccountException lae) {
      log.error("Your Account is Locked!", lae);
  } catch (AuthenticationException ae) {
      log.error("Unexpected Error!", ae);
  }
}
```

```
log.info("User [" + currentUser.getPrincipal() + "] logged in
successfully.");
if (currentUser.hasRole("admin")) {
    log.info("Welcome Admin");
} else if(currentUser.hasRole("editor")) {
    log.info("Welcome, Editor!");
} else if(currentUser.hasRole("author")) {
    log.info("Welcome, Author");
} else {
    log.info("Welcome, Guest");
}

if(currentUser.isPermitted("chapters:write")) {
    log.info("You can write a chapter");
} else {
    log.info("You are not permitted to write a chapter!");
}

if(currentUser.isPermitted("chapters:save")) {
    log.info("You can save chapters");
} else {
    log.info("You can not save chapters");
}

if(currentUser.isPermitted("chapters:publish")) {
    log.info("You can publish chapters");
} else {
    log.info("You can not publish chapters");
}

Session session = currentUser.getSession();
session.setAttribute("key", "value");
String value = (String) session.getAttribute("key");
if (value.equals("value")) {
    log.info("Retrieved the correct value! [" + value + "]");
}

currentUser.logout();
```

Session Management

Once we got the current user, we can retrieve their session:

```
Session session = currentUser.getSession();
session.setAttribute( "key", "value" );
```

The Session is a Shiro-specific instance containing most of what you'd know from the Jakarta Servlet HttpSession with a few extras, and it is independent of an HTTP environment.

Inside a web application, the Session will be HttpSession based. But in a non-web environment, Shiro will automatically use its own Session Management by default. This means you get to use the same API in your applications, regardless of the deployment environment. This opens new possibilities especially for "serverless" applications, as the application requiring sessions does not need to use HttpSession or EJB Stateful Session Beans.

Cryptography

The main cryptography aspects of Shiro are

- Simplicity
- Cipher features
- Hash features

Simplicity

Shiro offers a simplicity layer on top of JCE or the JDK Cipher Hash classes (there called Message Digest) classes.

Cipher Features

Unlike the JCE factory methods using String token arguments, the Shiro Ciphers are easier to use by instantiating a class and configure it with JavaBeans methods. For example, a new AesCipherService():

```
String key = Hex.encodeToString(new AesCipherService().generateNewKey().
getEncoded());
System.out.println("0x" + key);
```

Hash Features

Shiro provides hash implementations of MD5, SHA1, SHA-256, and other popular algorithms:

```
user.setPassword(new Sha256Hash(user.getPassword()).toHex());
service.create(user);
    // ...
```

Comparison to JAAS

For many applications, container-managed security is insufficient for more than just a public website or intranet with an "admin console." JAAS and EJB security models required static definitions only developers could change, adding the need to often redeploy an application long before DevOps and the concept of continuous delivery or deployment were as common as they are now.

- No built-in "Remember Me" functionality, although Servlet 3.0 made this easier to add.

- No straightforward way to redisplay login page with login errors in case you've specified the same page as both login page and error page. There are some tricks, however.

- No remembering of POST request data when a form is submitted while the session is expired. There is no way to retain this data for resubmission other than homebrewing an authentication filter or going for a third-party one.

- No permission-based restriction. A "permission" basically checks a specific task/action depending on the currently logged-in user which may be shared across multiple roles. Role-based restriction is sometimes too rough, requiring you to create ridiculous meta-roles like "SUPER_USER", "POWER_USER", "SUPER_ADMIN", "ALMOST_ADMIN", "HR", "HR_ASSISTANT", and so on.

- No container-independent way of configuring the data source containing users/roles. Not all containers offer the same granularity of configuring the data source, making the data source or even the data model potentially unportable across containers. JASPIC is intended to solve that, but it has as of now still container-specific problems.

Using Shiro with Jakarta EE Servlets

To use Shiro with Jakarta Servlets, we need a servlet context listener so that Shiro can perform its global initialization and a Servlet filter for the authentication/authorization works where Shiro wraps the request/response around Shiro-controlled ones (so that, e.g., #{request.remoteUser} and so on still keep its functionality). Add those to /WEB-INF/web.xml as follows:

```
<listener>
    <listener-class>org.apache.shiro.web.env.EnvironmentLoaderListener
    </listener-class>
</listener>
<filter>
    <filter-name>shiroFilter</filter-name>
    <filter-class>org.apache.shiro.web.servlet.ShiroFilter
    </filter-class>
</filter>
<filter-mapping>
    <filter-name>shiroFilter</filter-name>
    <url-pattern>/*</url-pattern>
    <dispatcher>REQUEST</dispatcher>
    <dispatcher>FORWARD</dispatcher>
    <dispatcher>INCLUDE</dispatcher>
    <dispatcher>ERROR</dispatcher>
</filter-mapping>
```

Note, FORWARD and INCLUDE dispatchers are never internally used by Jakarta Faces on Facelets, but they are kept here in web.xml for the sake of completeness (perhaps you want to use Jakarta Server Pages in the same web app). If you intend to navigate to a JSF resource that possibly requires rechecking authentication, then you'd better make it a GET request by either a GET link/button or a POST-Redirect-GET action. That's when you should use <h:outputLink> instead of <h:commandLink>.

Use an INI file to configure Shiro. There are several default filters available. If you need BASIC authentication, use the authcBasic filter. If you need FORM authentication, use authc filter.

Let's start with the simplest configuration, a BASIC authentication on everything inside the /app/ subfolder of the web app and a single admin user. Create a /WEB-INF/shiro.ini file with the following content:

```
[users]
admin = password

[urls]
/app/** = authcBasic
```

Form-Based Authentication

Turning it into form-based authentication is just a matter of changing authBasic to authc (again, see the list of default filters for the filter name). Only, the login page path defaults to /login.jsp. As JSP is a deprecated view technology since JSF 2.0 at December 2009, we obviously don't want to keep this setting as such. We want to change it to Facelets as /login.xhtml. This can be done by setting the authc.loginUrl entry. Note that you also need to include it in the [urls] list. Also note that I of course assume that you've mapped the FacesServlet on a URL pattern of *.xhtml. If you're using a different URL pattern, then you should also change it as such in the INI file.

```
[main]
authc.loginUrl = /login.xhtml

[users]
admin = password

[urls]
/login.xhtml = authc
/app/** = authc
```

The shiro.ini file syntax follows a JavaBean/Jakarta EL-like configuration of properties. If you look closer at FormAuthenticationFilter, you'll see that loginUrl is actually a property of FormAuthenticationFilter! The shiro.ini basically interprets the entry key as a setter operation and uses the entry value as the set value. This configuration style, however, requires Apache Commons BeanUtils in the web app. So drop its JAR in /WEB-INF/lib as well.

The HTML form syntax of /login.xhtml as shown in the following is also rather straightforward. Remember, you can without problems use "plain HTML" in a JSF/Facelets page. Note that Shiro sets the login failure error message as a request attribute with the default name shiroLoginFailure. This was nowhere mentioned in the Shiro web documentation! I figured it by looking at the JavaDoc of FormAuthenticationFilter.

```
<h2>Login</h2>
<form method="post">
    <label for="username">Username:</label>
    <input type="text" id="username" name="username" />
    <br/>
    <label for="password">Password:</label>
    <input type="password" id="password" name="password" />
    <br/>
    <label for="rememberMe">Remember me:</label>
    <input type="checkbox" id="rememberMe" name="rememberMe"
    value="true" />
    <br/>
    <input type="submit" value="Login" />
    <span class="error">#{shiroLoginFailure}</span>
</form>
```

Note that the failure message just represents the fully qualified class name of the thrown exception, for example, org.apache.shiro.authc.UnknownAccountException. This is intended to be further used as key of some i18n resource bundle like so #{bundle[shiroLoginFailure]} or perhaps a Map property.

Remember Me

The form-based authentication example as shown in the previous chapter has also a "Remember Me" checkbox. It indeed sets a rememberMe cookie on the response with some long and encrypted value. However, after I deleted the JSESSIONID cookie in the browser, it still brought me back to the login page as if the "Remember Me" was never ticked.

We have to use UserFilter instead of the FormAuthenticationFilter. As per the default filters listing, it has the name user. Let's fix the shiro.ini accordingly:

```
[main]
authc.loginUrl = /login.xhtml
user.loginUrl = /login.xhtml

[users]
admin = password

[urls]
/login.xhtml = authc
/app/** = user
```

to make it work.

Note that I had to duplicate authc.loginUrl and user.loginUrl to prevent authentication failures on authc from being still redirected to the default login URL /index.jsp. It would make more sense if the UserFilter basically extends from FormAuthenticationFilter so that both cases are covered. Maybe Shiro has its own reasons for this separation of both filters, but I don't see it for now.

By the way, the cookie value turns out to be a Base64 encoded representation of an AES encrypted representation of a serialized representation of a collection of principals. Basically, it contains the necessary username information that is decryptable with the right key (which a hacker can, in case of a default key, easily figure by just looking at Shiro's source code). Not my favorite approach, but the AES encryption is really strong, and you can (must) specify a custom AES cipher key or even a complete custom manager that can deal with the cookie value format you need. The custom AES cipher key can, if necessary, be specified as follows in shiro.ini according to this example in the Shiro INI documentation:

```
securityManager.rememberMeManager.cipherKey = 0x3707344A4093822299F31D008
```

The value is obviously fully to your choice. You can generate your own as follows using Shiro's own cryptographic API:

```
String key = Hex.encodeToString(new AesCipherService().generateNewKey().
getEncoded());
System.out.println("0x" + key);
```

Behavior on Session Expiration

The behavior on session expiration is rather straightforward on GET requests. When not remembered, it shows the login page, and on successful login, it redirects you to the initially requested page, complete with the original query string. Exactly as expected.

The behavior is, however, not consistent for POST requests.

Synchronous POST Without Remember Me

This discarded all the POST data, and the user was after the login redirected to the application root instead of the initial page. You'd have to navigate to the initial page and reenter all the POST data yourself. As to the wrong redirect to the root, this turns out to be the default fallback URL for the case there's no saved request. However, there's definitely a saved request, so I peeked around in the source code and it turns out that the saved request is only valid on a GET request, and thus, for POST, the fallback URL is used instead.

Well, this makes perhaps sense in some cases, but this should really have been better documented. In case of JSF, it doesn't harm if you use the POST URL for a GET request as JSF by default submits the <h:form> to exactly the same URL as the page being requested by GET (also known as "postback"). A concrete solution to the problem of being redirected to the wrong URL is discussed later in the "Programmatic Login" section.

Further, it would have been nice if Shiro remembered the POST request body as well and, upon a successful login via POST, replaced the current request body with it and performed a 307 redirect. Or, perhaps, at least offer a way to obtain the saved POST request parameters by programmatic means so that the developer can choose for setting the initial POST request URL as login form URL and all POST request parameters as hidden input fields of the login form. When the login is successful, then Shiro should not perform a redirect, but just let the request continue to the application. Theoretically, this is possible with a custom Shiro filter.

Synchronous POST with Remember Me

On a default JSF setup, this failed with a ViewExpiredException. This is not Shiro's fault. The actual login was successfully performed. However, as the session is expired, the JSF view state is also expired. You can solve this by either setting the javax.faces. STATE_SAVING_METHOD to client or by using OmniFaces <o:enableRestorableView>. Once fixed that, the login went smoothly. All the POST data was successfully submitted. Of course, the login happens within the very same request already, and effectively no redirect has taken place.

Asynchronous POST Without Remember Me

This failed without any feedback. Shiro forced a synchronous redirect to the login URL, which resulted in an Ajax response that is effectively empty, leaving the end user with no form of feedback. The end user is facing the same page as if the form submits nothing. In JSF Ajax, redirects are not instructed by an HTTP 302 response, but by a special XML response.

It'd be nice if Shiro performed an if ("partial/ajax".equals(request.getHeader("Faces-Request"))) check and returned the appropriate XML response. Fortunately, it's possible to extend Shiro's authentication filter to take this into account. A concrete solution is discussed later in the "Make Shiro JSF Ajax Aware" section.

Asynchronous POST with Remember Me

This behaved exactly the same as the synchronous one described at point 2. The principle is also not much different though. You're, however, dependent on having a decent Ajax exception handler if you would get feedback about the ViewExpiredException or not.

Using a JSF Form

Instead of a plain HTML form, you can of course also use a JSF form so that you can benefit from JSF built-in required="true" validation or get a look and feel matching the rest of the site (e.g., via PrimeFaces). As a Jakarta Faces developer, you should probably know that JSF prepends the ID of the parent form to the ID (and also name) attribute of the input components. However, Shiro checks by default the request parameters with the exact username, password, and "Remember Me" only. Fortunately, this can be configured in shiro.ini. Look in the JavaDoc of FormAuthenticationFilter; there are setters for the properties usernameParam, passwordParam, and rememberMeParam.

Given a JSF form in /login.xhtml:

```
<h2>Login</h2>
<h:form id="login">
    <h:panelGrid columns="3">
        <h:outputLabel for="username" value="Username:" />
        <h:inputText id="username" required="true" />
        <h:message for="username" />

        <h:outputLabel for="password" value="Password" />
        <h:inputSecret id="password" required="true" />
        <h:message for="password" />

        <h:outputLabel for="rememberMe" value="Remember Me" />
        <h:selectBooleanCheckbox id="rememberMe" />
        <h:panelGroup />

        <h:panelGroup />
        <h:commandButton value="Login" />
        <h:panelGroup styleClass="error" rendered="#{not facesContext.
        validationFailed}">
            #{shiroLoginFailure}
        </h:panelGroup>
    </h:panelGrid>
</h:form>
```

and the following shiro.ini:

```
[main]
authc.loginUrl = /login.xhtml
authc.usernameParam = login:username
authc.passwordParam = login:password
authc.rememberMeParam = login:rememberMe
user.loginUrl = /login.xhtml
```

```
[users]
admin = password

[urls]
/login.xhtml = authc
/app/** = user
```

you're good to go. Note that there's no backing bean. That's not necessary given that Shiro is performing the business logic by itself based on the request parameters.

It's not possible to login via Ajax this way. The submit itself would work fine and you would be logged in, but the navigation does not work. You won't be navigated to the initially requested page at all. So if you're using JSF component libraries with built-in Ajax facilities like PrimeFaces, then you'd need to set ajax="false" on the command button. Also, input validation should not be done via Ajax. It will work, but those requests will trigger Shiro's "remember the last accessed restricted page" mechanism and cause Shiro to redirect to the wrong URL after successful login, namely, the one on which the Ajax validation request is fired.

If you really need to login or validate with Ajax, you may consider programmatic login.

Programmatic Login

Shiro also offers a programmatic login possibility. This is more useful if you want to be able to utilize, for example, Ajax-based validation on the required input fields and/or want to be able to perform the login by Ajax. The programmatic login API is documented:

```
SecurityUtils.getSubject().login(new UsernamePasswordToken(username,
password, remember));
```

by the Shiro web documentation.

```
WebUtils.redirectToSavedRequest(request, response, fallbackURL);
```

obtains the saved request URL to perform a redirect to that URL.

This would, however, not work when the current request concerns a JSF Ajax request. As explained before, it has to return a special XML response instructing the JSF Ajax engine to perform a redirect by itself. This functionality is provided by JSF's own

ExternalContext#redirect() method that transparently distinguishes between Ajax and non-Ajax requests. So we really need to have just the saved request URL so that we could perform the redirect ourselves. A look into the Shiro sources reveals how it deals with the saved request URL:

```
String savedRequestURL = WebUtils.getAndClearSavedRequest(request).
getRequestUrl();
```

Okay, let's put the pieces together. First, create a backing bean (for practical reasons, we're using CDI-managed bean annotations instead of JSF managed bean annotations; further annotation-based restriction will be discussed and that works only in managed beans when using CDI; feel, however, free to use JSF managed bean annotations instead for programmatic login):

```java
package com.example.controller;

import java.io.IOException;

import javax.enterprise.context.RequestScoped;
import javax.inject.Named;

import org.apache.shiro.SecurityUtils;
import org.apache.shiro.authc.AuthenticationException;
import org.apache.shiro.authc.UsernamePasswordToken;
import org.apache.shiro.web.util.SavedRequest;
import org.apache.shiro.web.util.WebUtils;
import org.omnifaces.util.Faces;
import org.omnifaces.util.Messages;

@Named
@RequestScoped
public class Login {

    public static final String HOME_URL = "app/index.xhtml";

    private String username;
    private String password;
    private boolean remember;
```

```java
public void submit() throws IOException {
    try {
        SecurityUtils.getSubject().login(new Username
        PasswordToken(username, password, remember));
        SavedRequest savedRequest = WebUtils.getAndClear
        SavedRequest(Faces.getRequest());
        Faces.redirect(savedRequest != null ? savedRequest.
        getRequestUrl() : HOME_URL);
    }
    catch (AuthenticationException e) {
        Messages.addGlobalError("Unknown user, please try again");
        e.printStackTrace(); // TODO: logger.
    }
}

// Add/generate getters+setters.
}
```

Note that as you're reading this chapter, I'll for simplicity also assume that you're familiar with OmniFaces that minimizes some FacesContext boilerplate. The Faces and Messages utility classes are from OmniFaces.

Now change the login form in /login.xhtml accordingly to submit that and perform the necessary Ajax "magic":

```html
<h2>Login</h2>
<h:form id="login">
    <h:panelGrid columns="3">
        <h:outputLabel for="username" value="Username:" />
        <h:inputText id="username" value="#{login.username}"
        required="true">
            <f:ajax event="blur" render="m_username" />
        </h:inputText>
        <h:message id="m_username" for="username" />
```

```
<h:outputLabel for="password" value="Password:" />
<h:inputSecret id="password" value="#{login.password}"
required="true">
    <f:ajax event="blur" render="m_password" />
</h:inputSecret>
<h:message id="m_password" for="password" />

<h:outputLabel for="rememberMe" value="Remember Me:" />
<h:selectBooleanCheckbox id="rememberMe" value="#{login.
remember}" />
<h:panelGroup />

<h:panelGroup />
<h:commandButton value="Login" action="#{login.submit}" >
    <f:ajax execute="@form" render="@form" />
</h:commandButton>
<h:messages globalOnly="true" layout="table" />
    </h:panelGrid>
</h:form>
```

Now edit the shiro.ini accordingly to get rid of authc filter:

```
[main]
user.loginUrl = /login.xhtml

[users]
admin = password

[urls]
/login.xhtml = user
/app/** = user
```

This approach also fixes the problem that Shiro by default redirects to a fallback URL when the saved request concerns a POST request.

Noted should be that when the page with the POST form is been requested by GET with a request parameter like so /customers/edit.xhtml?id=42 in order to set the Customer via <f:viewParam> and so on, then you would after successful login be redirected to /customers/edit.xhtml. This is not exactly Shiro's fault; it's JSF itself who is by default submitting to a URL without the query string in the <h:form>. If you have those parameters defined as <f:viewParam>, then you can just replace the form by the OmniFaces <o:form> as follows to include the view parameters in the form action URL:

```
<o:form includeViewParams="true">
    ...
</o:form>
```

This way, Jakarta Faces will submit to the URL with the view parameters in the query string and thus give you the opportunity to redirect to exactly that URL after successful login. See also this stackoverflow.com question and answer.

Programmatic Logout

The programmatic logout API is also simple, but it is nowhere mentioned in the Shiro web documentation. It was, however, easily found with common sense and IDE autocomplete on the Subject instance. So here is the one-liner:

```
SecurityUtils.getSubject().logout();
```

You can invalidate the HTTP session, but that doesn't remove the "Remember Me" cookie in case you're using it and the user would be auto-logged in again on the subsequent request when "Remember Me" was ticked. So invalidating the session should merely be done to clean up any user-related state in the session, not to perform the actual logout.

Here's how the logout backing bean could look like:

```
package com.example.controller;

import java.io.IOException;

import javax.enterprise.context.RequestScoped;
import javax.inject.Named;

import org.apache.shiro.SecurityUtils;
import org.omnifaces.util.Faces;

@Named
@RequestScoped
```

```
public class Logout {

    public static final String HOME_URL = "login.xhtml";

    public void submit() throws IOException {
        SecurityUtils.getSubject().logout();
        Faces.invalidateSession();
        Faces.redirect(HOME_URL);
    }
}
```

Note that the redirect is really mandatory as the invalidated session is still available in the response of the current request. It's only not available anymore in the subsequent request. Also note that this issue is not specific to Shiro/JSF, just to HTTP in general.

In the view, provide a command that invokes #{logout.submit}.

```
<h:form>
    <h:commandButton value="logout" action="#{logout.submit}" />
</h:form>
```

Make Shiro JSF Ajax Aware

A redirect to login page once the session expired wasn't properly dealt with in case of JSF Ajax requests; users end up with no feedback.

Fortunately, the Shiro API is designed in such a way that this is fairly easily overridable with the following filter:

```
package com.example.filter;

import java.io.IOException;

import javax.servlet.ServletRequest;
import javax.servlet.ServletResponse;
import javax.servlet.http.HttpServletRequest;

import org.apache.shiro.web.filter.authc.UserFilter;

public class FacesAjaxAwareUserFilter extends UserFilter {
```

```
private static final String FACES_REDIRECT_XML = "<?xml version=\"1.0\"
encoding=\"UTF-8\"?>"
        + "<partial-response><redirect url=\"%s\"></redirect></partial-
        response>";

@Override
protected void redirectToLogin(ServletRequest req, ServletResponse res)
throws IOException {
    HttpServletRequest request = (HttpServletRequest) req;

    if ("partial/ajax".equals(request.getHeader("Faces-Request"))) {
        res.setContentType("text/xml");
        res.setCharacterEncoding("UTF-8");
        res.getWriter().printf(FACES_REDIRECT_XML, request.
        getContextPath() + getLoginUrl());
    }
    else {
        super.redirectToLogin(req, res);
    }
}

}
```

To run it, set it as user filter in shiro.ini (not the @WebFilter annotation or web.xml!):

```
[main]
user = com.example.filter.FacesAjaxAwareUserFilter
user.loginUrl = /login.xhtml

[users]
admin = password

[urls]
/login.xhtml = user
/app/** = user
```

Session expiration on Ajax requests is now properly handled.

Configuring JDBC Realm

In a bit sane Java EE web application wherein the container managed authentication is insufficient, the users are more than often not stored in some text file, but instead in a SQL database, along with their roles. In Shiro, you can use a Realm to configure it to obtain the users and roles (and permissions) from a SQL database. One of the ready-to-use realms is the JdbcRealm, which is relatively easy to set up via shiro.ini. Note also that this way the Realm is fully portable across different containers, which is definitely a big plus.

In this step, we'll set up a test database with the help of the embedded database engine H2 (formerly known as Hypersonic) and create a JPA model and an EJB service. Note that the H2/JPA/EJB part is not necessary for the functionality of Shiro. You're free to choose any database vendor and how you model your data or interact with it. In any way, the JPA/EJB examples are concretely used in the Register user and Hashing the password cases later on.

For documentation purposes only (you don't need to create them yourself), the (Hibernate-generated) DDLs of the tables look like this:

```
create table User (
    id bigint generated by default as identity (start with 1),
    password varchar(255) not null,
    username varchar(255) not null,
    primary key (id),
    unique (username)
)

create table UserRoles (
    userId bigint not null,
    role varchar(255)
)
```

The role column could better have been an enumerated type (enum, set, etc.) depending on DB make/version. This is, however, beyond the scope of this appendix.

First, download the H2 JAR file (the JAR file from Maven or SourceForge is enough) and drop it in /WEB-INF/lib. Then edit shiro.ini accordingly to get rid of the [users] entry and utilize the users database via a JdbcRealm:

```
[main]
# Create and setup user filter.
user = com.example.filter.FacesAjaxAwareUserFilter
user.loginUrl = /login.xhtml

# Create JDBC realm.
jdbcRealm = org.apache.shiro.realm.jdbc.JdbcRealm

# Configure JDBC realm datasource.
dataSource = org.h2.jdbcx.JdbcDataSource
dataSource.URL = jdbc:h2:~/test
dataSource.user = sa
dataSource.password = sa
jdbcRealm.dataSource = $dataSource

# Configure JDBC realm SQL queries.
jdbcRealm.authenticationQuery = SELECT password FROM User WHERE username = ?
jdbcRealm.userRolesQuery = SELECT role FROM UserRoles WHERE userId =
(SELECT id FROM User WHERE username = ?)

[urls]
/login.xhtml = user
/app/** = user
```

Note that the JavaBeans/Jakarta EL-style properties of the data source in shiro.ini should actually match the properties of the real data source instance.

Here, it's not yet possible to test the login as the database is empty. Continue to the next steps to create the model and the service so that we can create users.

JPA Model and EJB Service

Now the model and service. First, create the user role enum, com.example.model.Role:

```
package com.example.model;

public enum Role {

    EMPLOYEE, MANAGER, ADMIN;

}
```

Then create the user entity com.example.model.User:

```
package com.example.model;

import java.util.List;

import javax.persistence.CollectionTable;
import javax.persistence.Column;
import javax.persistence.ElementCollection;
import javax.persistence.Entity;
import javax.persistence.EnumType;
import javax.persistence.Enumerated;
import javax.persistence.FetchType;
import javax.persistence.GeneratedValue;
import javax.persistence.GenerationType;
import javax.persistence.Id;
import javax.persistence.JoinColumn;
import javax.validation.constraints.NotNull;

@Entity
@NamedQueries({
    @NamedQuery(
        name = "User.find",
        query = "SELECT u FROM User u WHERE u.username = :username AND
        u.password = :password"),
    @NamedQuery(
        name = "User.list",
        query = "SELECT u FROM User u")
})
```

```java
public class User {

    @Id
    @GeneratedValue(strategy = GenerationType.IDENTITY)
    private Long id;

    @NotNull
    @Column(unique = true)
    private String username;

    @NotNull
    private String password;

    @ElementCollection(targetClass = Role.class, fetch = FetchType.EAGER)
    @Enumerated(EnumType.STRING)
    @CollectionTable(name = "UserRoles", joinColumns = { @JoinColumn
    (name = "userId") })
    @Column(name = "role")
    private List<Role> roles;

    // Add/generate getters+setters and hashCode+equals.
}
```

Then create the following service class, com.example.service.UserService:

```java
package com.example.service;

import java.util.List;

import javax.ejb.Stateless;
import javax.enterprise.context.RequestScoped;
import javax.enterprise.inject.Produces;
import javax.inject.Named;
import javax.persistence.EntityManager;
import javax.persistence.PersistenceContext;

import org.omnifaces.cdi.ViewScoped;

import com.example.model.User;

@Stateless
```

```java
public class UserService {

    @PersistenceContext
    private EntityManager em;

    public User find(Long id) {
        return em.find(User.class, id);
    }

    public User find(String username, String password) {
        List<User> found = em.createNamedQuery("User.find", User.class)
            .setParameter("username", username)
            .setParameter("password", password)
            .getResultList();
        return found.isEmpty() ? null : found.get(0);
    }

    @Produces
    @Named("users")
    @RequestScoped
    public List<User> list() {
        return em.createNamedQuery("User.list", User.class).getResultList();
    }

    public Long create(User user) {
        em.persist(user);
        return user.getId();
    }

    public void update(User user) {
        em.merge(user);
    }

    public void delete(User user) {
        em.remove(em.contains(user) ? user : em.merge(user));
    }

}
```

Then create the persistence unit in /META-INF/persistence.xml (note that this configuration drops all DB tables on every server restart; it's just for demo purposes):

```
<persistence-unit name="test-jsf-shiro">
    <jta-data-source>java:app/H2/test</jta-data-source>
    <class>com.example.model.User</class>

    <properties>
        <!-- Hibernate specific properties. -->
        <property name="hibernate.dialect" value="org.hibernate.
        dialect.HSQLDialect" />
        <property name="hibernate.hbm2ddl.auto" value="create-drop" />
        <property name="hibernate.show_sql" value="true" />

        <!-- EclipseLink specific properties. -->
        <property name="eclipselink.ddl-generation" value="create-
        tables" />
        <property name="eclipselink.ddl-generation.output-mode"
        value="database" />
    </properties>
</persistence-unit>
```

Note, that all preceding boilerplate code is not mandatory for the functions of Shiro. It's merely to create and find users as demonstrated in the following chapter.

Register User

In order to create users via JSF, we need the following backing bean:

```
package com.example.controller;

import javax.annotation.PostConstruct;
import javax.ejb.EJB;
import javax.enterprise.context.RequestScoped;
import javax.inject.Named;

import org.omnifaces.util.Messages;
```

```java
import com.example.model.User;
import com.example.service.UserService;

@Named
@RequestScoped
public class Register {

    private User user;

    @EJB
    private UserService service;

    @PostConstruct
    public void init() {
        user = new User();
    }

    public void submit() {
        try {
            service.create(user);
            Messages.addGlobalInfo("Registration succeed, new user ID
            is: {0}", user.getId());
        }
        catch (RuntimeException e) {
            Messages.addGlobalError("Registration failed: {0}",
            e.getMessage());
            e.printStackTrace(); // TODO: logger.
        }
    }

    public User getUser() {
        return user;
    }

}
```

and this view, /register.xhtml, using among others OmniFaces <o:importConstants>
to ease importing enums into <f:selectItems> and OmniFaces omnifaces.
GenericEnumConverter in order to convert the selected roles to a proper List<Role>
instead of a List<String>:

```
<o:importConstants type="com.example.model.Role" />

<h2>Register</h2>
<h:form id="register">
    <h:panelGrid columns="3">
        <h:outputLabel for="username" value="Username:" />
        <h:inputText id="username" value="#{register.user.username}"
        required="true">
            <f:ajax event="blur" render="m_username" />
        </h:inputText>
        <h:message id="m_username" for="username" />

        <h:outputLabel for="password" value="Password:" />
        <h:inputSecret id="password" value="#{register.user.password}"
        required="true">
            <f:ajax event="blur" render="m_password" />
        </h:inputSecret>
        <h:message id="m_password" for="password" />

        <h:outputLabel for="roles" value="Roles:" />
        <h:selectManyCheckbox id="roles" value="#{register.user.roles}"
        required="true"
            layout="pageDirection" converter="omnifaces.GenericEnum
            Converter">
            <f:selectItems value="#{Role}" />
        </h:selectManyCheckbox>
        <h:message id="m_roles" for="roles" />
```

```
    <h:panelGroup />
    <h:commandButton value="Register" action="#{register.submit}" >
        <f:ajax execute="@form" render="@form" />
    </h:commandButton>
    <h:messages globalOnly="true" layout="table" />
</h:panelGrid>
</h:form>
```

Finally, at this point, we should be able to create users via database queries and log them in programmatically via a JDBC realm!

If you want to have an overview of all users, just start off with this table (note that this effectively retrieves the list via @Produces annotation of UserService#list()):

```
<h2>Users</h2>
<h:dataTable value="#{users}" var="user">
    <h:column>#{user.id}</h:column>
    <h:column>#{user.username}</h:column>
    <h:column>#{user.password}</h:column>
    <h:column>#{user.roles}</h:column>
</h:dataTable>
```

Don't forget to Ajax-update it on registration, if necessary.

Hashing the Password

Storing password plain text in the DB is not secure, so we'd like to hash them, if necessary, with a salt. Shiro offers multiple helper classes for hashing, allowing you to do the job with minimal effort. Let's pick SHA256.

First, edit the Register#submit() method accordingly to hash the password as follows. (Note: Don't use redisplay="true" in the JSF password field! Otherwise, the hashed value would be reflected in the UI.)

```
user.setPassword(new Sha256Hash(user.getPassword()).toHex());
service.create(user);
// ...
```

Then tell Shiro's JDBC realm to hash like that as well. Add the following lines to the end of the [main] section of shiro.ini:

```
# Configure JDBC realm password hashing.
credentialsMatcher = org.apache.shiro.authc.credential.
HashedCredentialsMatcher
credentialsMatcher.hashAlgorithmName = SHA-256
jdbcRealm.credentialsMatcher = $credentialsMatcher
```

Using Shiro with Spring

Spring Security

While Spring Security and Shiro overlap in most areas, they can be combined. Storing password plain text in the DB is not secure, so we'd like to hash them, if necessary. Shiro has a couple of helper classes in packages org.apache.shiro.spring.config.web. autoconfigure as well as org.apache.shiro.spring.boot.autoconfigure.

See the following example:

```
import org.apache.shiro.spring.boot.autoconfigure.
ShiroAnnotationProcessorAutoConfiguration;
import org.apache.shiro.spring.boot.autoconfigure.ShiroAutoConfiguration;
import org.apache.shiro.spring.config.web.autoconfigure.
ShiroWebAutoConfiguration;
import org.apache.shiro.spring.config.web.autoconfigure.
ShiroWebFilterConfiguration;
import org.springframework.boot.SpringApplication;
import org.springframework.boot.autoconfigure.SpringBootApplication;

@SpringBootApplication(exclude = {ShiroAutoConfiguration.class,
        ShiroAnnotationProcessorAutoConfiguration.class,
        ShiroWebAutoConfiguration.class,
        ShiroWebFilterConfiguration.class})
public class Application {
```

```
    public static void main(String[] args) {
        SpringApplication.run(Application.class, args);
    }
}
```

while in this example, the password encoding is done via Spring Security:

```
import org.springframework.context.annotation.Bean;
import org.springframework.security.config.annotation.authentication.
builders.AuthenticationManagerBuilder;
import org.springframework.security.config.annotation.web.builders.
HttpSecurity;
import org.springframework.security.config.annotation.web.configuration.
EnableWebSecurity;
import org.springframework.security.config.annotation.web.configuration.
WebSecurityConfigurerAdapter;
import org.springframework.security.crypto.bcrypt.BCryptPasswordEncoder;
import org.springframework.security.crypto.password.PasswordEncoder;

@EnableWebSecurity
public class SecurityConfig extends WebSecurityConfigurerAdapter {

    @Override
    protected void configure(HttpSecurity http) throws Exception {
        http.csrf().disable().authorizeRequests(authorize -> authorize.
        antMatchers("/index", "/login")
            .permitAll()
            .antMatchers("/home", "/logout")
            .authenticated()
            .antMatchers("/admin/**")
            .hasRole("ADMIN"))
            .formLogin(formLogin -> formLogin.loginPage("/login")
                .failureUrl("/login-error"));
    }
```

```
    @Override
    protected void configure(AuthenticationManagerBuilder auth) throws
    Exception {
        auth.inMemoryAuthentication()
            .withUser("Werner")
            .password(passwordEncoder().encode("werner"))
            .authorities("READ", "WRITE")
            .roles("ADMIN")
            .and()
            .withUser("Arjan")
            .password(passwordEncoder().encode("arjan"))
            .authorities("READ")
            .roles("USER");
    }

    @Bean
    public PasswordEncoder passwordEncoder() {
        return new BCryptPasswordEncoder();
    }

}
```

It could also use the cryptographic library of Shiro where it fits the needs of an application better or provides functionality not found the same way in Spring Security.

Outlook

In this appendix, we learned about Apache Shiro. Now it's time to look at Identity Management solutions in the last one.

APPENDIX C

Identity Management

In this appendix, we'll be looking at Identity Management solutions for Java and the JVM. Except the Java Identity API that started as a JCP standard but Oracle as a Spec Lead eventually withdrew it, most of them are proprietary yet open source, and some build on top of Jakarta EE or Java EE specs, while others like Shibboleth are maintained by an Industry Consortium not so different from Apache Foundation or Eclipse Foundation and based on the OASIS Open standard SAML.

Java Identity API

A Very Brief History

The Java Identity API JSR 351 passed its approval ballot in October 2011, followed by expert group formation in November 2011. The expert group consisted of representatives from Oracle, IBM, Red Hat, SAP, and Goldman Sachs as well as individuals including Werner Keil.

The JSR was led by Ron Monzillo whom we already heard about in the first chapter and who had worked for Sun and later Oracle on a number of security-related Java standards. The reference implementation was called "Nobis," the Latin word for "us." The goals of the Identity standard were the following:

- Define a representation for an Identity in Java

- Secure usage (creation, exchange, governance) of these "'identities" via a standard API

- A uniform, high-level programming model for application to interact with identity attribute repositories in heterogeneous domain models

© Arjan Tijms, Teo Bais, and Werner Keil 2022
A. Tijms et al., *The Definitive Guide to Security in Jakarta EE*, https://doi.org/10.1007/978-1-4842-7945-8

Why Was It Needed?

Until that point, the Java Platform did not provide first class standard interfaces to manage identities. With increased use of web services in modern applications, adoption of SSO, and federated identity, there was a desire to standardize these identities. Existing Java elements like X509Certificate and Kerberos provided some encapsulation of identity attributes, but only in a limited form.

Instead of having a fractured nonstandard model, there was a desire to define a set of standards, which could be leveraged by application or identity framework developers, offering solid support for propagation and consumption of distributed identities. Similar examples would be JDBC or JNDI. Both APIs help developers communicate with underlying data sources or naming services in a loosely coupled way through standard interfaces in a pluggable architecture where different implementations can be used to connect various databases (Oracle, MySQL, Sybase DB2, nowadays also NoSQL) or LDAP servers (Active Directory, OID, Sun, Apache, Red Hat, IBM Tivoli, Admin4, etc.).

Overview of Java Identity API

The Java Identity API aimed to

- Let applications interact with heterogeneous identity repositories in a portable standard-based manner

- Allow vendors to implement it using an attribute service framework to seamlessly interact with identity attributes in multiple repositories, for example, Microsoft, Google, Facebook, Twitter, LinkedIn, etc., via protocols/APIs like OAuth or OpenID Connect, SAML, etc.

- Allow applications to become attribute providers via an attribute service framework and developers to build upon those services

- Prevent vendor lock-in by proprietary nonstandard frameworks and applications

Existing elements of the Java Security object model like Policy, Principal, or Subject were meant to be integrated with the new Identity API. Support of programmatic and annotation-driven access to the API using CDI was desired.

A new specification often plans to introduce terms that may sound abstract outside its context or even have a different meaning in other specifications and APIs in a few cases. Table C-1 provides a list of terms and key concepts of the Java Identity API.

Table C-1. *Java identity terminology*

Term	Description
Entity	A collection of "attributes," for example, a person can have multiple attributes like "first name," "last name," "social security number," "Twitter handle," etc.
Attribute	A name (username, email, etc.), value ("foo@bar.com", etc.), and metadata like issuer, expiry, etc., somewhat similar to JWT
Entity Reference	A secure handle to an entity
Attribute Reference	A secure handle to the attribute itself
Attribute Repository	A set of contracts to integrate with an identity store
Repository Agent	Allows to access a specific Attribute Repository and query its content
Repository Descriptor	Describes the relationship between a Repository Agent and the Attribute Repository bound to that agent
Attribute Provider	Interacting with a Repository Agent to perform client requests against it
Attribute Service	A service component exposing high-level interfaces to handle identities to client applications

The Java Identity API was meant to be compact and lightweight, consisting of the API packages given in Table C-2 under the "`javax.security.identity`" namespace intended to fit with other Java security standards under "`javax.security`".

Table C-2. *Java identity API packages*

Package	Description
javax.security.identity	Top-level package containing the identity attribute and reference types
javax.security.identity.annotations	Annotations providing a portable identity programming model
javax.security.identity.auth	Identity attribute and reference types to use with Java `Subject` or `AccessControlContext`
javax.security.identity.client	High-level programming interfaces to the identity attribute services
javax.security.identity.client. expression	Provider-independent expressions used for attribute queries
javax.security.identity.client. qualifiers	CDI annotations to be used as qualifiers to inject identity attributes
javax.security.identity.permission	Permissions and actions to protect the interfaces of the attribute service
javax.security.identity.provider	Interfaces to be implemented by attribute providers and repository agents (the SPI of the Identity JSR)

The annotations, interfaces, or classes shown in Tables C-3 and C-4 were defined by the Java Identity API.

Table C-3. *Java identity annotations*

Term	Annotation
Entity	javax.security.identity.annotations.IDEntity
Attribute	javax.security.identity.annotations.IdentityAttribute
Entity Reference	javax.security.identity.annotations.EntityReference

Table C-4. *Java identity interfaces and classes*

Term	API type
Attribute	javax.security.identity.IDAttribute
Entity Reference	javax.security.identity.IDEntityReference
Attribute Reference	javax.security.identity.IDAttributeReference
Attribute Repository	javax.security.identity.provider. AttributeRepository
Attribute Provider	javax.security.identity.provider.AttributeProvider
Repository Agent	javax.security.identity.provider.RepositoryAgent
Repository Descriptor	javax.security.identity.client.RepositoryDescriptor

Usage of the Identity API

An application that wanted to use the Identity API to facilitate repository integrations of third parties. The following example outlines a sequence of steps in which an application could leverage the API, obtaining handles to the underlying identities and attributes:

1. Concrete implementation of the `LookupService` interface. Encapsulating the `ProviderLookupService` and `AttributeLookupService`.

2. An instance of `ProviderLookupContext` is obtained as result of binding the `LookupService` with an implementation of `RepositoryAgent`.

3. `ProviderLookupContext` is used to get a reference to `AttributeProvider` that is bound to the range of entities contained in the repository identified by the `ProviderLookupContext`.

4. The `AttributeProvider` is a gateway to access to the identity repository and exposes CRUD like features via `RepositoryLookupService` and `RepositoryUpdateService`.

The reference implementation provided specific integrations including contributors to open source projects and common social networks. Facebook, Twitter, and LinkedIn were among the identity repositories integrated within the RI "Nobis" as well as programming interfaces and protocols, including Facebook Connect, Google-ID, and OAuth 2.0.

Here is how Facebook was accessed via an implementation of RepositoryAgent

```
@Named("Facebook")
public class FacebookRepositoryAgent implements RepositoryAgent {
    public AttributeRepository getAttributeRepository(String
    repositoryName) {
      TableIdentifier tID = null;
      AttributeRepository rvalue = null;
      try {
          tID = FacebookTableID.valueOf(repositoryName);
          rvalue = repositoryTable.get(tID);
      } catch (IllegalArgumentException iae) {
      }
      if (rvalue == null) {
          rvalue = new FacebookAttributeRepository(new
          RepositoryDescriptor(FacebookRepositoryAgent.class,tID.
          name()));
          repositoryTable.put(tID,rvalue);
      }
      return rvalue;
    }
A Facebook AttributeRepository
public class FacebookAttributeRepository implements AttributeRepository {
   private RepositoryDescriptor _repositoryDescriptor;
   private ProviderLookupContext _context; FacebookLookupService _
   lookupService;

   public FacebookAttributeRepository(RepositoryDescriptor descriptor) {
       _repositoryDescriptor = descriptor;
       _context = new ProviderLookupContext(descriptor);
       _lookupService = new FacebookLookupService(this);
   }
```

```
     public RepositoryDescriptor getRepositoryDescriptor() {
       return _repositoryDescriptor;
  }
[...]
     public IDPredicate and(IDPredicate ... predicates) {
       return new FacebookPredicate(_context, IDBooleanOperator.and,
       predicates);
  }
```

Exploring elements in a Facebook Social Graph

```
JsonObject graphValues = getResponseValues(graphResponse);
     user = (String) graphValues.get(userPropertyName);
     Iterator<String> it = graphValues.keys();
     while (it.hasNext()) {
           String key = it.next();
           final URI id = new URI(userInfoEndpoint + "/" + key);
           final Collection<String> names = new ArrayList<String>();
           final Object value = graphValues.get(key);
           final IDAttributeValue attributeValue = new
           IDAttributeValue() {
                public Serializable getValue() {
                     return (Serializable) value;
                }
                public Collection getValues() {
                     return Collections.EMPTY_LIST;
                }
           };
}
```

The elements in the social graph would be returned via other Jakarta EE (then Java EE) standards like JSON Processing.

Lessons Learned from the Identity API

While the Java Identity JSR 3251 was eventually withdrawn, it offered sometimes merely inspiration, sometimes even a bit more to multiple other security specs in Jakarta EE, particularly Jakarta Security.

Concepts of

- Identity

- Identity Store

- Attribute/Authentication Repository

- Attribute/Identity Provider

and several others are found across Jakarta EE security standards or different security frameworks like Spring Security, Shiro, and Keycloak, which we are going to learn about next.

Keycloak

What Is Keycloak?

Keycloak is an open source identity, access management, and Single Sign-On solution for applications and services. Users can authenticate against Keycloak rather than each individual application. Reliving the application from dealing with login forms, authentication, or storing user's identities. Keycloak also offers social logins, support for desktop or mobile apps, and integration into other solutions including LDAP, Active Directory, OAuth, OpenID Connect, or SAML.

Brief History

The first release of Keycloak was published in September 2014 after development had started about a year before. In 2016, Red Hat switched the Red Hat SSO product from being based on the PicketLink framework to the Keycloak upstream project after it had already merged the PicketLink codebase into Keycloak.

Since then, Keycloak saw almost manic release cycles and version number changes. At the end of June 2016 around the time Red Hat made Keycloak the basis for its SSO product, version 2.0.0 was released. About a year later, 3.0.0 came out, followed by Keycloak 4.0.0 in June 2018.

There probably was a bit of an influence by the Java and OpenJDK release cadence pushing out a new major version of the JDK every six months and a Long-Term Service version every 2 years as of 2021, but not only Keycloak but also other projects by Red Hat like WildFly seemed version-crazy after 2019 because Keycloak 5.0.0 was released in March 2019 with 6.0.0 only a month later. And in November 2019, the version number had jumped to 8. As of August 2021, the most recent Keycloak version is 15.0.2. While the pace at least on the first digit sometimes looks like it slowed down a bit, the versions 13–15 were all released in 2021 alone, which makes it look like Red Hat follows a major release nearly every 3–4 months at the very least. Sometimes faster with only minor slowdown in the second half of 2021. The release notes are sometimes just one-liners, which makes one wonder how the giant leap of version numbers was justified, but it looks like marketing drives it and the underlying WildFly numbers also increase even more than Keycloak at 25, with WildFly 22–25 all realized in 2021 as well.

Overview of Keycloak

Concepts

Keycloak is based on the following concepts:

- Authentication

- Authorization

- Credentials

- Realm

Authentication

This is a provider example determining, if the request meets the authenticator's requirements:

```
package org.keycloak.authentication;

public interface Authenticator extends Provider {

    /**
     * Initial call for the authenticator.  This method should check the
       current HTTP request to determine if the request
     * satifies the Authenticator's requirements.  If it doesn't, it should
       send back a challenge response by calling
     * the AuthenticationFlowContext.challenge(Response).  If this
       challenge is a authentication, the action URL
     * of the form must point to
     *
     * /realms/{realm}/login-actions/authenticate?code={session-
       code}&execution={executionId}
     *
     * or
     *
     * /realms/{realm}/login-actions/registration?code={session-
       code}&execution={executionId}
     *
     * {session-code} pertains to the code generated from
       AuthenticationFlowContext.generateAccessCode().  The {executionId}
     * pertains to the AuthenticationExecutionModel.getId() value obtained
       from AuthenticationFlowContext.getExecution().
     *
     * The action URL will invoke the action() method described below.
     *
     * @param context
     */
    void authenticate(AuthenticationFlowContext context);
```

```
/**
 * Called from a form action invocation.
 *
 * @param context
 */
void action(AuthenticationFlowContext context);

/**
 * Does this authenticator require that the user has already been
   identified?  That AuthenticatorContext.getUser() is not null?
 *
 * @return
 */
boolean requiresUser();

/**
 * Is this authenticator configured for this user.
 *
 * @param session
 * @param realm
 * @param user
 * @return
 */
boolean configuredFor(KeycloakSession session, RealmModel realm,
UserModel user);

/**
 * Set actions to configure authenticator
 *
 */
void setRequiredActions(KeycloakSession session, RealmModel realm,
UserModel user);

/**
 * Overwrite this if the authenticator is associated with
 * @return
 */
```

```java
    default List<RequiredActionFactory> getRequiredActions(KeycloakSession
    session) {
        return Collections.emptyList();
    }

    /**
     * Checks if all required actions are configured in the realm and
       are enabled
     * @return
     */
    default boolean areRequiredActionsEnabled(KeycloakSession session,
    RealmModel realm) {
        for (RequiredActionFactory raf : getRequiredActions(session)) {
            RequiredActionProviderModel rafpm = realm.getRequiredAction
            ProviderByAlias(raf.getId());
            if (rafpm == null) {
                return false;
            }
            if (!rafpm.isEnabled()) {
                return false;
            }
        }
        return true;
    }
}
```

Password Policies

Many organizations have special password policies. Keycloak has a rich set of password policies to choose via the Admin Console, for example, hashing the password, the hash algorithm used for it; combinations of digits, upper- and lowercase characters, special characters, or a regular expression the password should match; as well as common security measures like number to contain the username, not using the same password multiple times, or the expiry date, after which the password must be changed.

Authentication Flow

The sequence of actions by a user or service to authenticate in Keycloak is called authentication flow:

```
package org.keycloak.authentication;

public interface AuthenticationFlow {
    String BASIC_FLOW = "basic-flow";
    String FORM_FLOW = "form-flow";
    String CLIENT_FLOW = "client-flow";

    Response processAction(String actionExecution);
    Response processFlow();
    boolean isSuccessful();
    default List<AuthenticationFlowException> getFlowExceptions(){
        return Collections.emptyList();
    }
}
```

Keycloak includes various authentication flows out of the box. Those can be configured as required, and where your application may need something different, you can always create your own authentication flow from scratch or start by copying an existing one.

Figure C-1 shows the available authentication flows in a browser:

- Cookie

- Identity Provider Redirector

- Forms

  - Username/Password

  - OTP

- Kerberos

At least one of them has to be enabled for successful authentication.

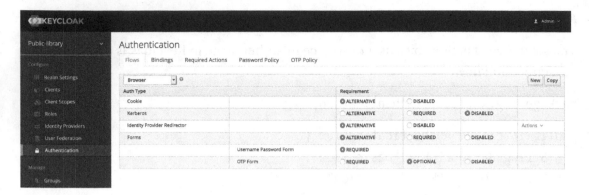

Figure C-1. *Browser authentication flows*

For Single Sign-On, Keycloak supports two major protocols:

- OpenID Connect (OICD)

- SAML

OIDC is the preferred method and more commonly used with RESTful APIs, while SAML (which we are going to learn more about in the next section on Shibboleth) gained more popularity with SOAP Web Services, especially in the academic world.

SAML relies on XML messages and documents, while OIDC with REST being format agnostic most often uses JWT for identity and access tokens.

For OIDC, Keycloak defines three main authentication flows:

- Authorization code flow: For browser-based or server-side applications.

- Implicit flow: For browser-based applications, this flow is not as secure as Authorization Code Flow and deprecated as of OAuth 2.1, so it can be used for backward compatibility, but it's not recommended anymore.

- Client credentials grant: For consumers of RESTful web services, involves storing a secret, so the clients should trust the services they consume.

Authorization

Keycloak supports multiple authorization policies and allows to combine different access control mechanisms like

- Attribute-based access control (ABAC)

- Role-based access control (RBAC)

- User-based access control (UBAC)

- Context-based access control (CBAC)

- Rule-based access control

- Time-based access control

- Custom access control mechanisms via a Policy Provider SPI

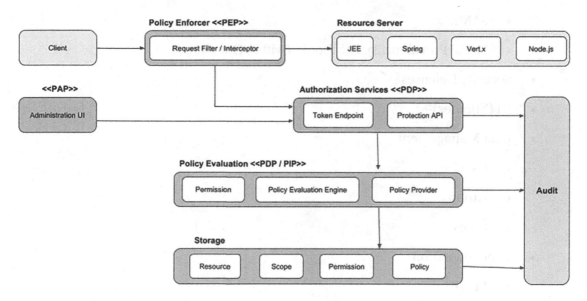

Figure C-2. *Keycloak authorization architecture*

Credentials

Credentials are pieces of data that Keycloak uses to verify the identity of a user. Some examples are passwords, one-time passwords, digital certificates, iris scans, or fingerprints.

Realm

A realm allows to manage a set of users, credentials, roles, and groups. A user belongs to and logs into a realm. Realms are isolated from one another and can only manage and authenticate users they control.

Features

The main features of Keycloak are

- Clients (per application)
- Events
- Identity Providers
  - OpenID Connect
  - SAML
  - Social Providers like Facebook, Twitter, Google, etc.
- Security Defenses
- UI (Themes)
- User Management
  - Users
  - Groups
  - Roles
- User Federation
  - LDAP
  - Active Directory
  - Custom Providers

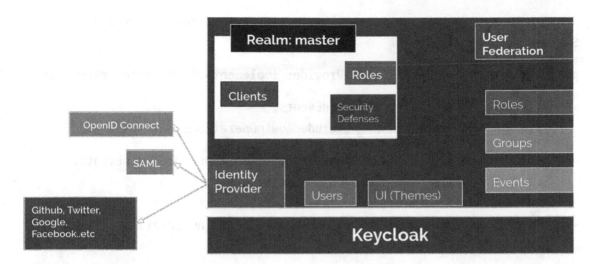

Figure C-3. *Keycloak features*

Clients

Clients in Keycloak are entities (applications or services) that wish to authenticate a user within a realm. They can also request identity information or an access token so that they can securely invoke other services across the network secured by Keycloak. During the authentication process, the client needs to send its ID and secret. These credentials are obtained by registering the client in the authentication server.

With many applications to secure and maintain in an organization, it can become tedious to configure protocol mappers and scope for all these clients. Keycloak lets you define shared client configurations in a client template.

Events

Keycloak provides extensive auditing functionalities. Every interaction can be recorded and reviewed. There are two kinds of events:

- Login events

- Admin events

Login events occur every time a user-related action around authentication takes place, for example, login, logout, login attempts that were unsuccessful, or when a user account gets updated. Admin events are triggered by every change via the Admin API, either via Admin Console, REST API, or Command Line Interface. A Listener SPI allows you to create plug-ins and listen for these events.

Here is an example `EventListenerProvider` implementation writing events to `System.out`:

```
public class SysoutEventListenerProvider implements EventListenerProvider {

    private Set<EventType> excludedEvents;
    private Set<OperationType> excludedAdminOperations;

    public SysoutEventListenerProvider(Set<EventType> excludedEvents,
    Set<OperationType> excludedAdminOpearations) {
        this.excludedEvents = excludedEvents;
        this.excludedAdminOperations = excludedAdminOpearations;
    }

    @Override
    public void onEvent(Event event) {
        // Ignore excluded events
        if (excludedEvents != null && excludedEvents.contains
        (event.getType())) {
            return;
        } else {
            System.out.println("EVENT: " + toString(event));
        }
    }

    @Override
    public void onEvent(AdminEvent event, boolean includeRepresentation) {
        // Ignore excluded operations
        if (excludedAdminOperations != null && excludedAdminOperations.
        contains(event.getOperationType())) {
            return;
        } else {
            System.out.println("EVENT: " + toString(event));
        }
    }
}
```

```java
private String toString(Event event) {
    StringBuilder sb = new StringBuilder();

    sb.append("type=");
    sb.append(event.getType());
    sb.append(", realmId=");
    sb.append(event.getRealmId());
    sb.append(", clientId=");
    sb.append(event.getClientId());
    sb.append(", userId=");
    sb.append(event.getUserId());
    sb.append(", ipAddress=");
    sb.append(event.getIpAddress());

    if (event.getError() != null) {
        sb.append(", error=");
        sb.append(event.getError());
    }

    if (event.getDetails() != null) {
        for (Map.Entry<String, String> e : event.getDetails().
        entrySet()) {
            sb.append(", ");
            sb.append(e.getKey());
            if (e.getValue() == null || e.getValue().indexOf(' ')
            == -1) {
                sb.append("=");
                sb.append(e.getValue());
            } else {
                sb.append("='");
                sb.append(e.getValue());
                sb.append("'");
            }
        }
    }

    return sb.toString();
}
```

```java
    private String toString(AdminEvent adminEvent) {
        StringBuilder sb = new StringBuilder();

        sb.append("operationType=");
        sb.append(adminEvent.getOperationType());
        sb.append(", realmId=");
        sb.append(adminEvent.getAuthDetails().getRealmId());
        sb.append(", clientId=");
        sb.append(adminEvent.getAuthDetails().getClientId());
        sb.append(", userId=");
        sb.append(adminEvent.getAuthDetails().getUserId());
        sb.append(", ipAddress=");
        sb.append(adminEvent.getAuthDetails().getIpAddress());
        sb.append(", resourcePath=");
        sb.append(adminEvent.getResourcePath());

        if (adminEvent.getError() != null) {
            sb.append(", error=");
            sb.append(adminEvent.getError());
        }

        return sb.toString();
    }

    @Override
    public void close() {
    }

}
```

and its factory:

```java
public class SysoutEventListenerProviderFactory implements
EventListenerProviderFactory {

    private Set<EventType> excludedEvents;
    private Set<OperationType> excludedAdminOperations;

    @Override
    public EventListenerProvider create(KeycloakSession session) {
```

```java
        return new SysoutEventListenerProvider(excludedEvents,
        excludedAdminOperations);
    }

    @Override
    public void init(Config.Scope config) {
        String[] excludes = config.getArray("exclude-events");
        if (excludes != null) {
            excludedEvents = new HashSet<>();
            for (String e : excludes) {
                excludedEvents.add(EventType.valueOf(e));
            }
        }

        String[] excludesOperations = config.getArray("excludes
        Operations");
        if (excludesOperations != null) {
            excludedAdminOperations = new HashSet<>();
            for (String e : excludesOperations) {
                excludedAdminOperations.add(OperationType.valueOf(e));
            }
        }
    }

    @Override
    public void postInit(KeycloakSessionFactory factory) {

    }
    @Override
    public void close() {
    }

    @Override
    public String getId() {
        return "sysout";
    }

}
```

User Federation

When your organization has a user database, Keycloak allows us to synchronize with it. By default, it supports LDAP and Active Directory, but you can create custom extensions for any identity store using the Keycloak User storage API.

Keycloak can also act as a proxy between your users and external identity providers.

Using Keycloak with Jakarta EE

Keycloak more than most other Security frameworks we already learned about is based on Jakarta EE. While a version of Keycloak running on the more lightweight "Cloud Native" Quarkus instead of WildFly is in the making, both use Jakarta EE, directly or indirectly.

JSP

To use Keycloak from a Jakarta Server Pages application, a Controller simplifies access to the Servlet environment from the JSP:

```
public class Controller

    private static final ObjectMapper mapper = new ObjectMapper();

    static {
        mapper.enable(SerializationFeature.INDENT_OUTPUT);
        mapper.setSerializationInclusion(Include.NON_NULL);
    }

    public void handleLogout(HttpServletRequest req) throws
    ServletException {
        if (req.getParameter("logout") != null) {
            req.logout();
        }
    }

    public boolean isLoggedIn(HttpServletRequest req) {
        return getSession(req) != null;
    }
```

```java
public boolean showToken(HttpServletRequest req) {
    return req.getParameter("showToken") != null;
}

public AccessToken getIDToken(HttpServletRequest req) {
    return getSession(req).getToken();
}

public AccessToken getToken(HttpServletRequest req) {
    return getSession(req).getToken();
}

public String getAccountUri(HttpServletRequest req) {
    KeycloakSecurityContext session = getSession(req);
    String baseUrl = getAuthServerBaseUrl(req);
    String realm = session.getRealm();
    return KeycloakUriBuilder.fromUri(baseUrl).
    path(ServiceUrlConstants.ACCOUNT_SERVICE_PATH)
            .queryParam("referrer", "app-profile-jsp")
            .queryParam("referrer_uri", getReferrerUri(req)).
            build(realm).toString();
}

private String getReferrerUri(HttpServletRequest req) {
    StringBuffer uri = req.getRequestURL();
    String q = req.getQueryString();
    if (q != null) {
        uri.append("?").append(q);
    }
    return uri.toString();
}
```

```java
    private String getAuthServerBaseUrl(HttpServletRequest req) {
        AdapterDeploymentContext deploymentContext = (AdapterDeployment
        Context) req.getServletContext().getAttribute(AdapterDeployment
        Context.class.getName());
        KeycloakDeployment deployment = deploymentContext.resolve
        Deployment(null);
        return deployment.getAuthServerBaseUrl();
    }

    public String getTokenString(HttpServletRequest req) throws
    IOException {
        return mapper.writeValueAsString(getToken(req));
    }

    private KeycloakSecurityContext getSession(HttpServletRequest req) {
        return (KeycloakSecurityContext) req.getAttribute(KeycloakSecurityC
        ontext.class.getName());
    }
}
```

The web app consists of the following JSPs index.jsp:

```html
<html>
<head>
    <meta http-equiv="Content-Type" content="text/html;
    charset=windows-1252">
    <title>Keycloak Example App</title>

    <link rel="stylesheet" type="text/css" href="styles.css"/>
</head>
<body>
<jsp:useBean id="controller" class="org.keycloak.quickstart.profilejee.
Controller" scope="request"/>
<% controller.handleLogout(request); %>

<c:set var="isLoggedIn" value="<%=controller.isLoggedIn(request)%>"/>
<c:if test="${isLoggedIn}">
    <c:redirect url="profile.jsp"/>
</c:if>
```

600

```
<div class="wrapper" id="welcome">
    <div class="menu">
        <button name="loginBtn" onclick="location.href = 'profile.jsp'"
        type="button">Login</button>
    </div>

    <div class="content">
        <div class="message">Please login</div>
    </div>
</div>
</body>
</html>
```

And profile.jsp:

```
<html>
<head>
    <meta http-equiv="Content-Type" content="text/html;
    charset=windows-1252">
    <title>Keycloak Example App</title>
    <link rel="stylesheet" type="text/css" href="styles.css"/>
</head>
<body>
<jsp:useBean id="controller" class="org.keycloak.quickstart.profilejee.
Controller" scope="request"/>
<c:set var="idToken" value="<%=controller.getIDToken(request)%>"/>
<c:set var="tokenString" value="<%=controller.getTokenString(request)%>"/>
<c:set var="accountUri" value="<%=controller.getAccountUri(request)%>"/>
<c:set var="showToken" value="<%=controller.showToken(request)%>"/>

<div class="wrapper" id="profile">
    <div class="menu">
        <button name="profileBtn" onclick="location.href = 'profile.
        jsp'">Profile</button>
        <button name="tokenBtn" onclick="location.href = 'profile.jsp?
        showToken=true'">Token</button>
```

```
        <button name="logoutBtn" onclick="location.href = 'index.
        jsp?logout=true'" type="button">Logout</button>
        <button name="accountBtn" onclick="location.href = '${accountUri}'"
        type="button">Account</button>
    </div>

    <c:if test="${showToken}">
        <div class="content">
            <div id="token-content" class="message">${tokenString}</div>
        </div>
    </c:if>

    <c:if test="${!showToken}">
        <div class="content">
            <div id="profile-content" class="message">
                <table cellpadding="0" cellspacing="0">
                    <tr>
                        <td class="label">First name</td>
                        <td><span id="firstName">${idToken.givenName}
                        </span></td>
                    </tr>
                    <tr class="even">
                        <td class="label">Last name</td>
                        <td><span id="lastName">${idToken.familyName}
                        </span></td>
                    </tr>
                    <tr>
                        <td class="label">Username</td>
                        <td><span id="username">${idToken.preferred
                        Username}</span></td>
                    </tr>
                    <tr class="even">
                        <td class="label">Email</td>
                        <td><span id="email">${idToken.email}</span></td>
                    </tr>
                </table>
```

```
            </div>
        </div>
    </c:if>
</div>
</body>
</html>
```

Registered in /WEB-INF/web.xml:

```xml
<web-app xmlns="https://jakarta.ee/xml/ns/jakartaee"
        xmlns:xsi="http://www.w3.org/2001/XMLSchema-instance"
        xsi:schemaLocation="https://jakarta.ee/xml/ns/jakartaee
        https://jakarta.ee/xml/ns/jakartaee/web-app_5_0.xsd"
        version="5.0">
  <security-constraint>
        <web-resource-collection>
            <web-resource-name>app</web-resource-name>
            <url-pattern>/profile.jsp</url-pattern>
        </web-resource-collection>
        <auth-constraint>
            <role-name>*</role-name>
        </auth-constraint>
    </security-constraint>

    <login-config>
        <auth-method>KEYCLOAK</auth-method>
    </login-config>

    <security-role>
        <role-name>*</role-name>
    </security-role>
</web-app>
```

Jakarta REST

This example shows how to use Keycloak with Jakarta REST and Persistence:

```
import java.security.Principal;
import java.util.HashMap;
import java.util.HashSet;
import java.util.List;
import java.util.Map;
import java.util.UUID;

import jakarta.inject.Inject;
import jakarta.persistence.EntityManager;
import jakarta.persistence.Query;
import jakarta.servlet.http.HttpServletRequest;
import jakarta.ws.rs.Consumes;
import jakarta.ws.rs.DELETE;
import jakarta.ws.rs.GET;
import jakarta.ws.rs.POST;
import jakarta.ws.rs.Path;
import jakarta.ws.rs.PathParam;
import jakarta.ws.rs.Produces;
import jakarta.ws.rs.core.Context;
import jakarta.ws.rs.core.Response;
import jakarta.ws.rs.core.Response.Status;

import org.keycloak.KeycloakSecurityContext;
import org.keycloak.authorization.client.AuthzClient;
import org.keycloak.authorization.client.ClientAuthorizationContext;
import org.keycloak.authorization.client.resource.ProtectionResource;
import org.keycloak.example.photoz.ErrorResponse;
import org.keycloak.example.photoz.entity.Album;
import org.keycloak.example.photoz.util.Transaction;
import org.keycloak.representations.idm.authorization.
PermissionTicketRepresentation;
import org.keycloak.representations.idm.authorization.
ResourceRepresentation;
import org.keycloak.representations.idm.authorization.ScopeRepresentation;
```

```java
@Path("/album")
@Transaction
public class AlbumService {

    public static final String SCOPE_ALBUM_VIEW = "album:view";
    public static final String SCOPE_ALBUM_DELETE = "album:delete";

    @Inject
    private EntityManager entityManager;

    @Context
    private HttpServletRequest request;

    @POST
    @Consumes("application/json")
    public Response create(Album newAlbum) {
        Principal userPrincipal = request.getUserPrincipal();

        newAlbum.setId(UUID.randomUUID().toString());
        newAlbum.setUserId(userPrincipal.getName());

        Query queryDuplicatedAlbum = this.entityManager.createQuery("from
        Album where name = :name and userId = :userId");

        queryDuplicatedAlbum.setParameter("name", newAlbum.getName());
        queryDuplicatedAlbum.setParameter("userId", userPrincipal.
        getName());

        if (!queryDuplicatedAlbum.getResultList().isEmpty()) {
            throw new ErrorResponse("Name [" + newAlbum.getName() + "]
            already taken. Choose another one.", Status.CONFLICT);
        }

        try {
            this.entityManager.persist(newAlbum);
            createProtectedResource(newAlbum);
        } catch (Exception e) {
            getAuthzClient().protection().resource().delete(newAlbum.
            getExternalId());
        }
```

```java
        return Response.ok(newAlbum).build();
    }

    @Path("{id}")
    @DELETE
    public Response delete(@PathParam("id") String id) {
        Album album = this.entityManager.find(Album.class, id);

        try {
            deleteProtectedResource(album);
            this.entityManager.remove(album);
        } catch (Exception e) {
            throw new RuntimeException("Could not delete album.", e);
        }

        return Response.ok().build();
    }

    @GET
    @Produces("application/json")
    public Response findAll() {
        return Response.ok(this.entityManager.createQuery("from Album where
        userId = :id").setParameter("id", request.getUserPrincipal().
        getName()).getResultList()).build();
    }

    @GET
    @Path("/shares")
    @Produces("application/json")
    public Response findShares() {
        List<PermissionTicketRepresentation> permissions = getAuthz
        Client().protection().permission().find(null, null, null,
        getKeycloakSecurityContext().getToken().getSubject(), true, true,
        null, null);
        Map<String, SharedAlbum> shares = new HashMap<String,
        SharedAlbum>();
```

```
    for (PermissionTicketRepresentation permission : permissions) {
        SharedAlbum share = shares.get(permission.getResource());

        if (share == null) {
            share = new SharedAlbum(Album.class.cast(entityManager.
            createQuery("from Album where externalId = :externalId").
            setParameter("externalId", permission.getResource()).
            getSingleResult()));
            shares.put(permission.getResource(), share);
        }

        if (permission.getScope() != null) {
            share.addScope(permission.getScopeName());
        }
    }

    return Response.ok(shares.values()).build();
}

@GET
@Path("{id}")
@Produces("application/json")
public Response findById(@PathParam("id") String id) {
    List result = this.entityManager.createQuery("from Album where
    id = :id").setParameter("id", id).getResultList();

    if (result.isEmpty()) {
        return Response.status(Status.NOT_FOUND).build();
    }

    return Response.ok(result.get(0)).build();
}

private void createProtectedResource(Album album) {
    try {
        HashSet<ScopeRepresentation> scopes = new HashSet<ScopeRepresen
        tation>();

        scopes.add(new ScopeRepresentation(SCOPE_ALBUM_VIEW));
        scopes.add(new ScopeRepresentation(SCOPE_ALBUM_DELETE));
```

```java
        ResourceRepresentation albumResource = new Resource
        Representation(album.getName(), scopes, "/album/" + album.
        getId(), "http://photoz.com/album");

        albumResource.setOwner(album.getUserId());
        albumResource.setOwnerManagedAccess(true);

        ResourceRepresentation response = getAuthzClient().
        protection().resource().create(albumResource);

        album.setExternalId(response.getId());
    } catch (Exception e) {
        throw new RuntimeException("Could not register protected
        resource.", e);
    }
}

private void deleteProtectedResource(Album album) {
    String uri = "/album/" + album.getId();

    try {
        ProtectionResource protection = getAuthzClient().protection();
        List<ResourceRepresentation> search = protection.resource().
        findByUri(uri);

        if (search.isEmpty()) {
            throw new RuntimeException("Could not find protected
            resource with URI [" + uri + "]");
        }

        protection.resource().delete(search.get(0).getId());
    } catch (Exception e) {
        throw new RuntimeException("Could not search protected
        resource.", e);
    }
}
```

```
    private AuthzClient getAuthzClient() {
        return getAuthorizationContext().getClient();
    }

    private ClientAuthorizationContext getAuthorizationContext() {
        return ClientAuthorizationContext.class.cast(getKeycloakSecurity
        Context().getAuthorizationContext());
    }

    private KeycloakSecurityContext getKeycloakSecurityContext() {
        return KeycloakSecurityContext.class.cast(request.getAttribute
        (KeycloakSecurityContext.class.getName()));
    }
}
```

Using Keycloak with Spring
Spring Security

Keycloak can be Identity manager to a Spring Security application as in this example.
ApplicationController:

```
import javax.servlet.ServletException;
import javax.servlet.http.HttpServletRequest;

import org.keycloak.KeycloakSecurityContext;
import org.springframework.beans.factory.annotation.Autowired;
import org.springframework.stereotype.Controller;
import org.springframework.ui.Model;
import org.springframework.web.bind.annotation.RequestMapping;
import org.springframework.web.bind.annotation.RequestMethod;

/**
 * @author <a href="mailto:psilva@redhat.com">Pedro Igor</a>
 */
@Controller
public class ApplicationController {
```

```
@Autowired
private HttpServletRequest request;

@RequestMapping(value = "/protected", method = RequestMethod.GET)
public String handleProtected(Model model) {
    configCommonAttributes(model);
    return "protected";
}

@RequestMapping(value = "/protected/premium",
method = RequestMethod.GET)
public String handlePremium(Model model) {
    configCommonAttributes(model);
    return "premium";
}

@RequestMapping(value = "/protected/arjan", method = RequestMethod.GET)
public String handleAliceResources(Model model) {
    configCommonAttributes(model);
    return "arjan";
}

@RequestMapping(value = "/logout", method = RequestMethod.GET)
public String handleLogoutt() throws ServletException {
    request.logout();
    return "redirect:/";
}

@RequestMapping(value = "/", method = RequestMethod.GET)
public String handleHome(Model model) throws ServletException {
    configCommonAttributes(model);
    return "home";
}

@RequestMapping(value = "/accessDenied", method = RequestMethod.GET)
public String handleAccessDenied() throws ServletException {
    return "access-denied";
}
```

```
    private void configCommonAttributes(Model model) {
        model.addAttribute("identity", new Identity(getKeycloakSecurity
        Context()));
    }

    private KeycloakSecurityContext getKeycloakSecurityContext() {
        return (KeycloakSecurityContext) request.getAttribute(Keycloak
        SecurityContext.class.getName());
    }
}
```

Identity:

```
import java.util.List;

import org.keycloak.AuthorizationContext;
import org.keycloak.KeycloakSecurityContext;
import org.keycloak.representations.idm.authorization.Permission;

/**
 * <p>This is a simple facade to obtain information from authenticated
   users. You should see usages of instances of this class when
 * rendering the home page (@code home.ftl).
 *
 * <p>Instances of this class are are added to models as attributes in
   order to make them available to templates.
 *
 * @author <a href="mailto:psilva@redhat.com">Pedro Igor</a>
 * @see org.keycloak.quickstart.springboot.web.ApplicationController
 */
public class Identity {

    private final KeycloakSecurityContext securityContext;

    public Identity(KeycloakSecurityContext securityContext) {
        this.securityContext = securityContext;
    }

    /**
```

```
 * An example on how you can use the {@link AuthorizationContext} to
   check for permissions granted by Keycloak for a particular user.
 *
 * @param name the name of the resource
 * @return true if user has was granted with a permission for the given
   resource. Otherwise, false.
 */
public boolean hasResourcePermission(String name) {
    return getAuthorizationContext().hasResourcePermission(name);
}

/**
 * An example on how you can use {@link KeycloakSecurityContext} to
   obtain information about user's identity.
 *
 * @return the user name
 */
public String getName() {
    return securityContext.getIdToken().getPreferredUsername();
}

/**
 * An example on how you can use the {@link AuthorizationContext} to
   obtain all permissions granted for a particular user.
 *
 * @return
 */
public List<Permission> getPermissions() {
    return getAuthorizationContext().getPermissions();
}

/**
 * Returns a {@link AuthorizationContext} instance holding all
   permissions granted for an user. The instance is build based on
 * the permissions returned by Keycloak. For this particular
   application, we use the Entitlement API to obtain permissions for
   every single
```

```
    * resource on the server.
    *
    * @return
    */
   private AuthorizationContext getAuthorizationContext() {
       return securityContext.getAuthorizationContext();
   }
}
```

SecurityConfig:

```
import java.io.InputStream;

import org.keycloak.adapters.KeycloakConfigResolver;
import org.keycloak.adapters.KeycloakDeployment;
import org.keycloak.adapters.KeycloakDeploymentBuilder;
import org.keycloak.adapters.spi.HttpFacade;
import org.keycloak.adapters.springsecurity.KeycloakConfiguration;
import org.keycloak.adapters.springsecurity.config.
KeycloakWebSecurityConfigurerAdapter;
import org.springframework.beans.factory.annotation.Autowired;
import org.springframework.context.annotation.Bean;
import org.springframework.security.config.annotation.authentication.
builders.AuthenticationManagerBuilder;
import org.springframework.security.config.annotation.web.builders.
HttpSecurity;
import org.springframework.security.core.session.SessionRegistryImpl;
import org.springframework.security.web.authentication.session.
RegisterSessionAuthenticationStrategy;
import org.springframework.security.web.authentication.session.
SessionAuthenticationStrategy;

/**
 * @author <a href="mailto:psilva@redhat.com">Pedro Igor</a>
 */
@KeycloakConfiguration
public class SecurityConfig extends KeycloakWebSecurityConfigurerAdapter {
```

```java
/**
 * Registers the KeycloakAuthenticationProvider with the authentication
   manager.
 */
@Autowired
public void configureGlobal(AuthenticationManagerBuilder auth) {
    auth.authenticationProvider(keycloakAuthenticationProvider());
}

/**
 * Defines the session authentication strategy.
 */
@Bean
@Override
protected SessionAuthenticationStrategy sessionAuthentication
Strategy() {
    return new RegisterSessionAuthenticationStrategy(new Session
    RegistryImpl());
}

@Override
protected void configure(HttpSecurity http) throws Exception {
    super.configure(http);
    http.logout().logoutSuccessUrl("/home")
            .and()
            .authorizeRequests()
            .antMatchers("/**").hasAuthority("user");
}

/**
 * Overrides default keycloak config resolver behaviour (/WEB-INF/
   keycloak.json) by a simple mechanism.
 * <p>
 * This example loads other-keycloak.json when the parameter use.other
   is set to true, e.g.:
 * {@code ./gradlew bootRun -Duse.other=true}
 *
```

```
 * @return keycloak config resolver
 */
@Bean
public KeycloakConfigResolver keycloakConfigResolver() {
    return new KeycloakConfigResolver() {

        private KeycloakDeployment keycloakDeployment;

        @Override
        public KeycloakDeployment resolve(HttpFacade.Request facade) {
            if (keycloakDeployment != null) {
                return keycloakDeployment;
            }

            String path = "/keycloak.json";
            InputStream configInputStream = getClass().
            getResourceAsStream(path);

            if (configInputStream == null) {
                throw new RuntimeException("Could not load Keycloak
                deployment info: " + path);
            } else {
                keycloakDeployment = KeycloakDeploymentBuilder.
                build(configInputStream);
            }

            return keycloakDeployment;
        }
    };
}
}
```

Shibboleth

What Is Shibboleth?

Shibboleth is a web-based software that supports Single Sign-On (SSO) between different organizations or applications. It is open source and mainly used for Single Sign-On via the Security Assertion Markup Language (SAML) protocol. It currently does not integrate with other protocols and standards like OAuth or OpenID Connect.

It helps sites make informed authorization decisions for accessing protected resources and provides federated identity for authentication and authorization, allowing cross-domain Single Sign-On.

Origin of the Term

A shibboleth is a kind of linguistic password. A way of speaking or pronouncing used by a group of people to identify another person as a member or a nonmember of a particular group. A bit like slang or special dialects. The group making the identification has some social power to set the standards for membership in their group. Who is "in" and who is "out."

The story behind the word is recorded in the biblical Book of Judges. The word shibboleth in ancient Hebrew dialects meant "ear of grain" (or "stream"). Some groups pronounced it with a "sh" sound, but speakers of related dialects pronounced it with "s." In the biblical story, two Semitic tribes, the Ephraimites and the Gileadites, fight each other. The Gileadites defeat the Ephraimites and set up a blockade across the Jordan River to catch the escaping Ephraimites who were trying to get back to their territory. The guards asked each person who wanted to cross the river to say the word shibboleth. The Ephraimites, who had no "sh" sound in their language, pronounced the word with "s" and were thus recognized as the enemy and killed.

Brief History

The Shibboleth project started as part of Internet2 efforts. It is now managed by the Shibboleth Consortium. Shibboleth started in 2000 to support collaboration between organizations with different or incompatibly authentication and authorization systems. After design, development, and testing, Shibboleth Identity Provider (IdP) 1.0 was released in July 2003, followed by Shibboleth IdP 1.3 in August 2005. Version 2.0 of the Shibboleth software was a major upgrade in March 2008. Including IdP and Service Provider (SP) components as well as an upgrade to SAML 2.0. Version 3.0 of Shibboleth was released on February 25, 2015.

In April 2013, Jisc, Internet2, and SWITCH became the first Principal Members by establishing the Shibboleth Consortium as a formal means of financially supporting the Shibboleth project. Between 2014 and 2020, the membership of the Shibboleth Consortium grew from 9 to 53. It is used especially in the academic sector by members like the MIT, University of California, Cornell University, and Oxford, just to name a few of the most prominent members.

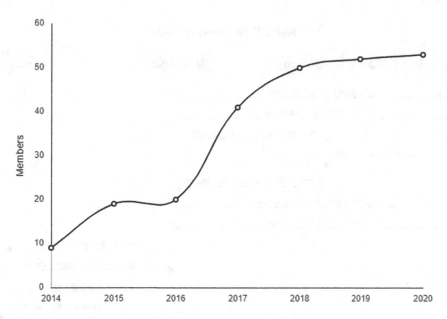

Figure C-4. *Shibboleth Consortium membership growth (Source: The Shibboleth Consortium, 2020)*

Overview of Shibboleth

Shibboleth is a web-based Single Sign-On system made up of three components:

- The Identity Provider (IdP), responsible for user authentication and providing user information to the Service Provider (SP). It is located at the home organization maintaining the user's account.

617

- The Service Provider (SP), responsible for protecting an online resource and consuming information from the IdP. It is located at the resource organization.

- The Discovery Service (DS) helps the SP discover the user's IdP. It may be located anywhere on the Web and optional in some cases.

Interactions

Figure C-5 shows the interactions between the user, located at their web browser (User Agent); the IdP, located at their organization; and the SP, located at the resource organization.

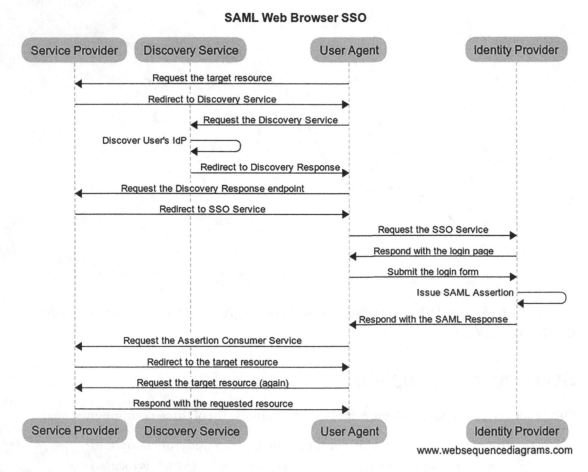

Figure C-5. *SAML Web Browser interactions*

1. The user (agent) requests at target resource at the SP.

2. The request gets redirected to the Discovery Service (where applicable).

3. The user agent requests the Discovery Service.

4. The request is redirected to the Discovery response endpoint at the SP.

5. Requesting the Discovery response endpoint at the SP.

6. Redirect to SSO Service at the IdP.

7. Requesting SSO Service at the IdP.

8. Response with login page.

9. The user submits the login form, getting a SAML assertion issued for him.

10. IdP responds with the SAML Response page.

11. Requesting Assertion Consumer Service at the SP.

12. Redirect to target resource.

13. Requesting target resource at SP again.

14. SP responds with the target resource.

Using Shibboleth with Jakarta EE

If you would like to use a Shibboleth SP together with a Jakarta EE Application Server, you need to propagate the user identity from the SP to the AS through a caller `Principal`.

To do this, you can either implement a container-specific JAAS `LoginModule` or the `ServerAuthModule` (SAM) of Jakarta Authentication.

Here's an example of a very simple SAM:

```
package org.my.sam;

import java.io.IOException;
import java.security.Principal;
import java.util.Map;
```

```
import jakarta.security.auth.Subject;
import jakarta.security.auth.callback.Callback;
import jakarta.security.auth.callback.CallbackHandler;
import jakarta.security.auth.callback.UnsupportedCallbackException;
import jakarta.security.auth.message.AuthException;
import jakarta.security.auth.message.AuthStatus;
import jakarta.security.auth.message.MessageInfo;
import jakarta.security.auth.message.MessagePolicy;
import jakarta.security.auth.message.callback.CallerPrincipalCallback;
import jakarta.security.auth.message.callback.GroupPrincipalCallback;
import jakarta.security.auth.message.module.ServerAuthModule;
import jakarta.servlet.ServletException;
import jakarta.servlet.http.HttpServletRequest;
import jakarta.servlet.http.HttpServletResponse;
import jakarta.servlet.http.HttpSession;

public class SpAsBridgeSam implements ServerAuthModule {

    public static class MyOrgPrincipal implements Principal {

        public MyOrgPrincipal(String name) {
            this.name = name;
        }
        private final String name;
        @Override
        public String getName() {
            return name;
        }

    }

    private static final Class<?>[] SUPPORTED_MESSAGE_TYPES = new
    Class<?>[] { HttpServletRequest.class, HttpServletResponse.class };
    private static final String LOGIN_URL = "http://my.org/Shibboleth.
    sso/Login";
    private static final String LOGOUT_URL = "http://my.org/Shibboleth.sso/
    Logout";
    private boolean isProtectedResource;
```

```java
private CallbackHandler ch;

// Post-construct initialization goes here
@Override
public void initialize(MessagePolicy requestPolicy, MessagePolicy
responsePolicy, CallbackHandler ch, Map options) throws AuthException {
    this.ch = ch;
    isProtectedResource = requestPolicy.isMandatory();
}

// Authentication logic and optional request pre-processing goes here
@Override
public AuthStatus validateRequest(MessageInfo mi, Subject client,
Subject service) throws AuthException {
    HttpServletRequest hreq = (HttpServletRequest)
    mi.getRequestMessage();
    HttpServletResponse hres = (HttpServletResponse)
    mi.getResponseMessage();
    String username = getUsername(hreq);
    String[] groups = getUsergroups(hreq);
    if ((username != null) && (!username.trim().isEmpty()) &&
    (groups != null)) {
        try {
            ch.handle(new Callback[] {
                    new CallerPrincipalCallback(client, new
                    MyOrgPrincipal(username)),
                    new GroupPrincipalCallback(client, groups) });
        }
        catch (UnsupportedCallbackException | IOException e) {
            e.printStackTrace();
            throw new AuthException("Could not authenticate user.");
        }
        return AuthStatus.SUCCESS;
    }
```

```java
    else if (!isProtectedResource) {
        return AuthStatus.SUCCESS;
    }
    else {
        try {
            hres.sendRedirect(LOGIN_URL);
        }
        catch (IOException ioe) {
            ioe.printStackTrace();
            throw new AuthException("Could not authenticate user.");
        }
        return AuthStatus.SEND_CONTINUE;
    }
}

// Validation of response and optional post-processing goes here
// Not typically used, as --unless it had initially been wrapped-- the
   response is already committed
// by the time this method is called
@Override
public AuthStatus secureResponse(MessageInfo messageInfo, Subject
service) throws AuthException {
    return AuthStatus.SEND_SUCCESS;
}

// Logout logic goes here
// The spec is a bit unclear regarding this method, thus I'm unsure
   whether it's best to directly modify the Subject
// or use container facilities
@Override
public void cleanSubject(MessageInfo mi, Subject client) throws
AuthException {
    HttpServletRequest hreq = (HttpServletRequest)
    mi.getRequestMessage();
    HttpServletResponse hres = (HttpServletResponse)
    mi.getResponseMessage();
```

```java
            HttpSession hs = hreq.getSession(false);
            if (hs != null) {
                try {
                    hs.invalidate();
                }
                catch (IllegalStateException ise) {
                    ise.printStackTrace();
                    throw new AuthException("Could not invalidate user
                    session.");
                }
            }
            try {
                hreq.logout();
                hres.sendRedirect(LOGOUT_URL);
            }
            catch (ServletException | IOException e) {
                e.printStackTrace();
                throw new AuthException("Could not complete user logout.");
            }
        }

        @Override
        public Class<?>[] getSupportedMessageTypes() {
            return SUPPORTED_MESSAGE_TYPES;
        }

        private String getUsername(HttpServletRequest hreq) {
            return (String) hreq.getAttribute("eduPersonPrincipalName");
        }

        private String[] getUsergroups(HttpServletRequest hreq) {
            String groupsAttribute = (String) hreq.getAttribute("eduPerson
            Affiliation");
            String[] groups = null;
            if (groupsAttribute != null) {
                groups = groupsAttribute.split(";");
                for (int i = 0; i < groups.length; i++) {
```

```
            groups[i] = groups[i].trim();
        }
    }
    return groups;
    }

}
```

To deploy the SAM in GlassFish, you need a `domain.xml` configuration like this:

```xml
<?xml version="1.0" encoding="UTF-8"?>
<domain log-root="${com.sun.aas.instanceRoot}/logs" application-
root="${com.sun.aas.instanceRoot}/applications" version="13">
...
    <configs>
    ...
        <config name="server-config">
            ...
            <security-service>
                ...
                <message-security-config auth-layer="HttpServlet">
                    ...
                    <!-- "provider-type" attribute is typically
                    "server" -->
                    <provider-config provider-type="server" provider-
                    id="SpAsBridgeSam" class-name="org.my.sam.
                    SpAsBridgeSam">
                        <!-- Options that will be passed to your SAM via
                        the "options" Map argument of its initialize
                        method -->
                        <property name="org.my.sam.SpAsBridgeSam.FOO"
                        value="BAR"/>
                        ...
                        <request-policy/>
                        <response-policy/>
                    </provider-config>
                    ...
```

```
        </message-security-config>
        ...
      </security-service>
      ...
    </config>
    ...
  </configs>
  ...
</domain>
```

Now you have to declare the roles for your application, either using annotations or a deployment descriptor like web.xml:

```xml
<?xml version="1.0" encoding="UTF-8"?>
<web-app
    xmlns:xsi="http://www.w3.org/2001/XMLSchema-instance"
    xmlns="http://xmlns.jcp.org/xml/ns/javaee"
    xsi:schemaLocation="http://xmlns.jcp.org/xml/ns/javaee http://xmlns.
    jcp.org/xml/ns/javaee/web-app_3_1.xsd"
    id="WebApp_ID"
    version="3.1"
    metadata-complete="false">
    ...
    <security-constraint>
        <web-resource-collection>
            <web-resource-name>myOrgProtectedResources</web-resource-name>
            <url-pattern>/protected/*</url-pattern>
        </web-resource-collection>
        <auth-constraint>
            <role-name>staff</role-name>
            <role-name>student</role-name>
        </auth-constraint>
    </security-constraint>
```

```
    <security-role>
        <role-name>staff</role-name>
        <role-name>student</role-name>
    </security-role>
</web-app>
```

Finally map the groups to roles in a `glassfish-web.xml` file like the following:

```
<?xml version="1.0" encoding="UTF-8"?>
<!DOCTYPE glassfish-web-app  PUBLIC "-//GlassFish.org//DTD GlassFish
Application Server 3.1 Servlet 3.0//EN" "http://glassfish.org/dtds/
glassfish-web-app_3_0-1.dtd">
<glassfish-web-app httpservlet-security-provider="SpAsBridgeSam">
    <context-root>/myApp</context-root>
    <security-role-mapping>
        <role-name>staff</role-name>
        <group-name>staff</group-name>
    </security-role-mapping>
    <security-role-mapping>
        <role-name>student</role-name>
        <group-name>student</group-name>
    </security-role-mapping>
</glassfish-web-app>
```

All you need to do is restart the AS like GlassFish and deploy your Jakarta EE application.

Summary

In this final appendix, we learned about Identity Management. How the idea of standardization through the JCP would have led to a Java EE specification, but despite its failure to complete, inspired many of the Jakarta EE Security specs and technologies you read about in this book: Keycloak, which, thanks to the IBM/Red Hat ecosystem, is widely used as Identity Management in many cloud and API solutions, and Shibboleth, which is the oldest solution, over two decades, but still actively used with a growing community, especially in research and the academic sector.

Index

A

abort() method, 330

Access control context, 333–336

Access control list (ACL), 59, 60, 527

Access control models, 60–63

Acegi, 15, 17, 521

Administration password, 430

Apache Shiro

    authentication, 544, 545

    authorization

        permissions, 546

        roles, 547

        user, 546

    cryptography, 549

    features, 543, 544

    history, 541, 542

    JAAS, 550

    with Jakarta EE

        asynchronous POST without
            remember me, 556

        asynchronous POST with
            remember me, 556

        behavior on session expiration, 555

        hashing password, 573

        JDBC realm configuration, 565, 566

        JPA model and EJB service, 567–570

        JSF Form, 556, 558

        programmatic login, 558, 560–562

        programmatic logout API, 562, 563

        register user, 570, 572, 573

        remember me, 554

        servlets, 551–553

        Shiro JSF Ajax aware, 563, 564

        synchronous POST without
            remember me, 555

        synchronous POST with
            remember me, 556

    open source security
        framework, 541

    realm, 543

    SecurityManager, 542

    subject, 542

    session management, 549

    with Spring security, 574–576

appContext identifier, 32

Applets, 1, 180, 184

Application security, 44

    authorization results mapping, 53

    Bean business methods, 52

    fulfilling, original request, 51

    initial authentication, 50

    initial request, 49

    URL authorization, 51

AsymmetricBlockCipher, 377, 378

AsymmetricCipherKeyPair class, 377

Asymmetric encryption
    algorithms, 342, 343, 411

Asymmetric keys, 381, 383

AuthConfigProvider, 23, 31, 141–147,
    454, 466

authenticate() method, 28, 106, 276

authenticateUser(), 167, 168, 174

627

Printed in the United States
by Baker & Taylor Publisher Services